The
Economist
Guide

JAPAN

The
Economist
Guide

JAPAN

Hutchinson

Published in Great Britain by
Hutchinson Business Books Limited
An imprint of Century Hutchinson
Limited
20 Vauxhall Bridge Road, London
SW1V 2SA

The publishers welcome corrections
and suggestions from business
travellers; please write to
The Editor,
The Economist Guides,
Axe and Bottle Court,
70 Newcomen Street,
LONDON SE1 1YT

Series Editor Stephen Brough
Assistant Series Editor Brigid Avison
Editors Rick Morris (*first edition*);
Jane Carroll (*second edition overview*),
Isla MacLean (*second edition travel*)
Designer Alistair Plumb (*first edition*)
Alison Donovan (*second edition*)
Editorial Assistants Karen Eves
Mary Pickles, Bettina Whilems
Production Controller Shona Burns
Indexer Fiona Barr

Contributors *Overview* Martin
Bloom, Ray Granger, Michael
Houser, John Breen, Paul Maidment,
Alan Pinnell, Dick Wilson; *travel*
Lesley Downer

First edition published in Great
Britain 1987
Second edition published in Great
Britain 1990

**British Library Cataloguing in
Publication Data**

Japan. - (The Economist guides)
1. Japan - Visitors' guides
915.2'0448

ISBN 0-09-174396-6

Maps and diagrams (first edition) by
Eugene Fleury; adapted (second
edition) by Lovell Johns, Oxford,
England
Typeset by Tradespools, Frome,
England
Printed in Italy by Arnoldo
Mondadori, Verona

Contents

Glossary

ASEAN Association of Southeast Asian Nations. An economic and trade association

Article 65 A legal provision which maintains a strict separation between banks and securities dealers

Diet The Japanese parliament

gaijin Literally "outside person." The Japanese word for a foreigner

GATT General Agreement on Tariffs and Trade. Over 100 countries are signatories

GDP Gross Domestic Product. The best measure of a country's economic performance, *GDP* is the total value of a country's annual output of goods and services. Normally valued at market prices, it can be calculated at factor cost, by subtracting indirect taxes and adding subsidies

GNP Gross National Product

G5 Abbreviation for Group of Five. Its members are: Britain, France, Japan, the USA and West Germany

IMF International Monetary Fund

Invisible trade Exports and imports of services, such as banking, insurance and foreign travel

JETRO Japan External Trade Organization. A Japanese government agency whose main function now is to help foreign firms wising to export to Japan

JNTO Japan National Tourist Organization

JR Japan Railways

JTB Japan Travel Bureau

KDD Kokusai Denshin Denwa. Japan's international telecommunications authority

Keidanren Japan's leading business organization, equivalent to Britain's CBI

keiretsu gaisha A large industrial group whose many companies are generally based around a trading company and a major bank

LDP Liberal Democratic Party. Japan's leading political party

meishi A business card

MITI Ministry of International Trade and Industry. One of the legendary powers behind Japan's postwar economic renaissance and still a force to be reckoned with

M2 One of the definitions of money supply used by governments when determining monetary policy

nemawashi Literally "to dig around the root of a tree to prepare it for transplanting." *Nemawashi* is a process of consultation designed to produce a consensus, and is frequently used in both Japanese companies and society at large

NTT Nippon Telegraph and Telephone Corporation. Japan's major domestic telecommunications authority

OECD Organisation for Economic Cooperation and Development

Plaza Agreement An agreement reached in Japan, in September 1985, by finance ministers of the Group of Five countries. It has had the effect of revaluing the Japanese yen against major world currencies

ringi-sho An intra-office memorandum to obtain the approval of all concerned for a proposed course of action

samurai The Japanese warrior caste that formed the aristocracy from the 11th to the 19th centuries

senmon shosha A trading company specializing in a particular product area

shogun A military commander. The shoguns became military dictators who effectively ruled until 1867

shunto The annual "spring wages offensive" when representatives of management and unions agree pay rises for the year

sogo shosha The 13 largest Japanese general trading companies

tatami A straw floor-mat. It is also used as a unit of square measurement: 1 tatami = 1.62 sq metre

TIC Tourist Information Centre

TSE Tokyo Stock Exchange

zaibatsu Prewar industrial groups which were disbanded during the US Occupation but have re-emerged in somewhat different form

zaikai A collective term for Japan's powerful top businessmen

Using the guide

The Economist Guide to Japan is an encyclopedia of business and travel information. If in doubt about where to look for specific information, consult either the Contents list or the Index.

City guides

Each city guide follows a standard format: information and advice on arriving, getting around, city areas, hotels, restaurants, bars, entertainment, shopping, sightseeing, sports and fitness, and a directory of local business and other facilities such as secretarial and translation agencies, couriers, hospitals with 24hr accident and emergency departments, and telephone-order florists. There is also a map of the city centre locating recommended hotels, restaurants and other important addresses.

For easy reference, all main entries for hotels, restaurants and sights are listed alphabetically.

Abbreviations

Credit and charge cards AE American Express; CB Carte Blanche; DC Diners Club; MC Mastercard (Access); V Visa.
Figures Millions are abbreviated to m; billions (meaning one thousand million) to bn. Trillions are used to mean one thousand billion.

Publisher's note

Although *The Economist Guide to Japan* is intended first and foremost to provide practical information for business people travelling *in* Japan, the general information will also be helpful to anyone doing business with Japan, wherever and however that business may be conducted.

Price bands (yen)

Price bands are denoted by symbols (see below). These correspond approximately to the following actual prices at the time of going to press. (Although the actual prices will inevitably go up, the relative price category is likely to remain the same.)

Hotels
(one person occupying a single room)

¥/	up to Y10,000
¥//	Y10,000–15,000
¥///	Y15,000–20,000
¥////	Y20,000–Y25,000
¥/////	Y25,000–30,000
¥//////	over Y30,000

Restaurants
(a typical meal including wine)

¥/	up to Y5,000
¥//	Y5,000 to Y10,000
¥///	Y10,000 to Y15,000
¥////	Y15,000 to Y20,000
¥/////	over Y20,000

INTRODUCTION

For all the reams of articles, stacks of books and reels of film produced about it, Japan remains one of the world's least understood and, surprisingly, most unloved countries. It is common knowledge that Japan has experienced a man-made miracle, growing out of the rubble of 1945 to become the second strongest economy in the non-communist world. In 1986 Japan's national per capita income overtook that of its postwar occupier, the United States. Yet conventional answers to such questions as how Japan achieved its present strength, what makes it tick, what, if any, are its aims, and even how sophisticated are its society and economy are laden with myth and misunderstanding.

For their part, the Japanese themselves remain inward-looking and clannish, despite the fact that every year Japan's influence on the world increases. Its exports are everywhere, its multinationals are building factories overseas and employing thousands of Westerners. In the 1980s it took over from the Arab countries as the nation investing the most money overseas each year. It is home to the world's biggest banks, securities houses, shipbuilders, steelmakers and consumer electronics firms. Even its politicians are, reluctantly, making more confident and prominent appearances on the world stage.

Rags to riches

Japan's path to modernity is usually dated from 1945. This is misleading. The foundations of modern Japan were laid from 1868, after the American navy and European traders had forced Japan to re-open itself to the world for the first time in over two centuries. It was Japan's victory over Russia in 1905 that first shocked the West into taking this Asian country seriously as a military and industrial force.

In the years up to World War II, Japan absorbed modern capitalism and technology rapidly in the belief that industrial strength was the best means to guarantee survival. Big industrial groups became established, including such now-familiar names as Mitsubishi, Mitsui and Sumitomo. However, amid the depressed world economy of the 1930s, Japan's pursuit of industrial growth was mixed with domestic poverty and insecurity to yield militarism and colonial ambition.

Defeat in the Pacific War (1941–45), combined with postwar land reform, eradicated the country's feudal aristocracy and much of its class system, as well as any military or colonial ambitions. This left Japan free to concentrate on domestic economic growth and enabled a new generation of entrepreneurs – Akio Morita of Sony and Soichiro Honda among them – to rise alongside the restructured industrial groups.

The Japan that grew so rapidly in the next two decades was run by many of the same politicians and industrialists as before the war. There was continuity as well as change. The labour force was highly literate, thanks to the spread of mass education in the 1930s, and cheap because so many of the population were still peasant farmers. Factors such as these gave a potential for growth, although fresh ingredients were needed to ensure that it was achieved.

Among these ingredients, two stand out. One was the achievement of industrial peace after a turbulent patch in the 1950s. Big firms traded the offer of job security ("lifetime employment") in return for moderate, productivity-linked wage claims.

The other ingredient is governmental guidance and control. Leadership by the celebrated Ministry of International Trade and Industry (MITI) and the Ministry of Finance amounted to less than the "Japan Inc" that Westerners like to imagine, but was important, nevertheless. The ministries, however, have never been able to countermand opposition from business. Industries were protected against foreign competition in the 1950s and 1960s, but fierce competition was the rule at home. The ministries' most important roles have been as an intermediary between firms and as a think tank. In the 1970s and 1980s, as trade protection and control of import licences disappeared, so did many of the ministries' powers.

More open than it looks

"Japan Inc" is a powerful myth, but a myth nevertheless. Concerted thinking was, indeed, responsible for arguably Japan's greatest success in the past three decades: the speed with which its economy and industry adjusted to the two oil-price hikes. But it certainly no longer means that the country is a closed shop to foreign business.

Japan is a hard place for foreigners to do business but, as one of the world's largest and most lucrative consumer markets, it is worth the effort. Painstaking research is the watchword – exactly the Japanese technique when exporting to foreign markets. The firms that have fared best in Japan have been those that adapted their methods to local needs and have built a Japanese work force on Japanese lines: with job security, a family atmosphere and the sense that the firm is there for the employees, as well as for the shareholders. The likelihood is that Japan will gradually become an easier place in which to do business. Since the country's current account surplus promises to be durable, the strong yen is likely to stay, making imports more competitive. Despite the inward-looking instincts of the ordinary Japanese, the Liberal Democratic government appears to appreciate that Japan ought to have fewer trade barriers than other countries, not more.

The Liberal Democrats are the most powerful party, in spite of scandals that toppled two prime ministers in 1989. The internationalist wing of the party is in the ascendant, which suggests that preserving good economic and military relations with the West will remain a priority. After all, insular or not, Japan has little choice: China is poor and has a stop-go economy, the Soviet Union is hostile and still occupies four Japanese islands. Japan depends too much on the Western world to want to go its own way.

The Economic Scene

Resources

Japan's four main islands and 4,000 smaller ones make up only 0.3% of the world's land mass – an area slightly smaller than California or Sweden – yet accommodate nearly 3% of the world's population. Despite hurricanes and earthquakes, a lack of land and geographical isolation, Japan has become Asia's only fully industrialized economy. Mount Fuji, an inactive volcano rising to 3,773 metres/12,370ft, presides over forested mountain ranges that cover over 70% of Japan's land area. Housing, industry and farming huddle on the coastal flatlands, principally in central-southern Honshu. The country's buoyant economy is almost totally dependent on imported fuel and raw materials.

Islands and regions

Japan's 2,995km/1,860 mile-long chain of islands stretches from the 24th parallel, off Taiwan, north to the 45th parallel, just below the USSR's Sakhalin Island.

Hokkaido is Japan's least populated island. Once a haven for outcasts, in the past century it has developed agriculture, leisure and beer-brewing. Just to the north are the disputed Kurile Islands, some of which have been occupied by the Soviets since 1945.

Honshu is where 80% of Japanese live, the majority concentrated in the plains of Kanto (Tokyo) and Kansai (Kyoto-Osaka), which have distinctive business cultures. Major ports and airports are in Honshu.

Shikoku used to be a comparative backwater, primarily devoted to agriculture and visited by foreigners for its picturesque character, but a new bridge linking it with Honshu has made it easily accessible.

Kyushu has a subtropical climate, and its people are reputedly the most outgoing. Bullet Train services to Hakata, near Fukuoka (which has a major airport), have aided the growth of Japan's Silicon Valley.

The Ryukyus were returned to Japan only in 1972, having been occupied by the USA since World War II, and are the poorest of all Japan's regions. These islands have a hybrid population and several are uninhabited; Okinawa is a major staging base for the US Air Force.

Raw materials

Although 33% of its GDP is derived from manufacturing, Japan is deficient in virtually all key industrial minerals and depends heavily on imports from the USA, Canada, Australia and the ASEAN countries. It has no bauxite or nickel and imports over 95% of the iron ore, tin and copper (as well as most of the lead and zinc) its factories need.

Energy

Japan is the world's largest importer of coal, natural gas and oil. It is almost totally dependent on other countries for oil, and imported 1.5bn barrels in 1987. Almost 70% comes from the Middle East, 18% from Southeast Asia; imports from China are rising steadily and now constitute 8%. Only 8% of Japan's natural gas needs and 19% of its coal needs are supplied by domestic sources.

Until nuclear fusion becomes a commercial reality in the next century, the contribution of local energy sources will remain at under 20%, mainly from hydroelectricity and nuclear fission, but also from limited geothermal and solar sources. Government policy is to reduce oil dependence to 50–60%, in favour of solid fuel, natural gas and local energy.

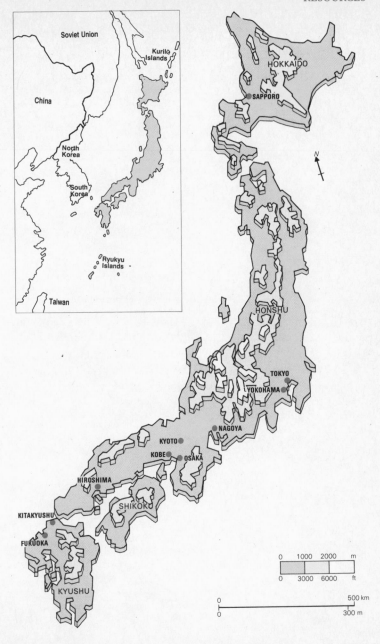

11

Forestry

The proportion of land covered by forests is among the highest in the world. The variety is considerable, from soft pines to cypress, cedar and a range of oaks. Ownership is fragmented. The principal problem is access: steep gradients make felling difficult and expensive. In addition, most forests were planted postwar and have yet to mature. As a result, Japan is only 30% self-sufficient and has become the world's largest net importer of timber – mainly unprocessed roundwood.

Agriculture

Despite surprisingly high self-sufficiency (70%) in foodstuffs, agriculture poses problems and will increasingly do so. Farms are very small (1.4ha on average) and inefficient by Western standards. The average age of farmers is over 50 and is rising, reflecting the unpopularity of farming as a livelihood and the movement of young people to the cities. Farms are often run by the women and old people, while the men work in industry.

The principal output of what is essentially a market garden sector includes rice, vegetables, melons and citrus fruits. Major imports include cereals and feed grains, poultry and dairy products. Although Kyushu can produce two crops a year, even rice is now imported; domestic rice prices are kept artificially high for political reasons. Protectionist measures are unlikely to stem the steady increase in imports, mostly from the USA.

Tastes have for some time been moving away from cereals in favour of meats, vegetables and dairy products. Domestic production has been unable to keep pace with demand or compete on price. Exports of foodstuffs are insignificant.

Fisheries

Japan is a voracious consumer of marine products, ranging from fish and seaweed to whale products. Among foodstuffs, imports of fish are second in value only to cereals; Japan has been a net importer since 1971 and the world's largest importer of fish since 1978. Fish stocks in the seas around Japan are becoming depleted, and Japanese fleets trawl the world causing flash points off the Kuriles with Soviet coastguards and with Greenpeace in whaling grounds, though whaling is to be phased out. Japan's imports have risen as 200-mile exclusive economic zones have been introduced by many countries, although in some cases Japanese fleets continue to fish in them under licence. Fish farming has developed to provide more freshwater supplies; coastal fish ranching is one attempt to restock local waters.

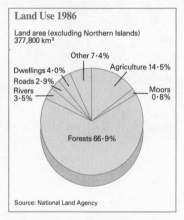

Land Use 1986

Land area (excluding Northern Islands)
377,800 km²

Other 7·4%
Agriculture 14·5%
Dwellings 4·0%
Roads 2·9%
Rivers 3·5%
Moors 0·8%
Forests 66·9%

Source: National Land Agency

Land use

Rising incomes have caused an increase in housing demand. The influx of foreign businesses in urban areas has been one factor in the rapid rise in office rents and land values. Urban land prices for the country as a whole rose 16% in the three years 1986–88, but in central Tokyo a 90% annual increase is not uncommon. Since 1955, urban land prices nationally have risen by over 6,000% (12 times the consumer prices index) and by twice that in Japan's six largest cities. Land reclamation adds only marginally to the available area.

The human dimension

Japan's population is expected to reach 130m in the next century. Today, with 123m, it has the world's seventh largest population, three-quarters of whom live in cities. Overall, there are 323 people per sq km/836 per sq mile, but if uninhabitable areas are excluded more realistic figures of 1,500/3,885 emerge, making Japan the world's most crowded country. The major business centres, Tokyo and Osaka, form an urban sprawl which is home to over 25m.

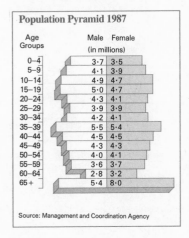

Population Pyramid 1987

Age Groups	Male (in millions)	Female (in millions)
0–4	3·7	3·5
5–9	4·1	3·9
10–14	4·9	4·7
15–19	5·0	4·7
20–24	4·3	4·1
25–29	3·9	3·9
30–34	4·2	4·1
35–39	5·5	5·4
40–44	4·5	4·5
45–49	4·3	4·3
50–54	4·0	4·1
55–59	3·6	3·7
60–64	2·8	3·2
65+	5·4	8·0

Source: Management and Coordination Agency

Population profile The average age is rising more rapidly than in any other industrial country. A comparatively smaller working population will, in the future, have to support a larger dependent population. One consequence is that the proportion of working women will continue to rise, particularly in the 25–43 age group, which has traditionally withdrawn from the labour force.

Trends The birth rate, 10.8 per 1,000, has fallen from 36.3 in 1870. The death rate is 6.5 per 1,000. The natural increase is just over 5 per 1,000. The rate of marriages, 5.9 per 1,000, is high for a developed country – the average age on marriage for

women being 25 years, for men 26–29 years. The low, but rising, divorce rate is 1.25 per 1,000 population, just over a quarter of the US rate.

Immigration and emigration Neither is significant in a permanent sense. Naturalization is rare, and immigration is neither commonplace nor encouraged. Overseas postings of businessmen and their families have increased markedly since the 1970s.

The working population

The labour pool of 60m is a bigger proportion of population than in the West. In 1960 nearly 50% worked on the land or in fishing. Today only 9% do so. The fastest-growing source of employment is the service sector, which now employs 58% of the working population, compared with 70% in the USA and 69% in Britain.

The proportion and number of working women have also grown and are high by international standards. However, women are poorly paid in comparison with men, and many work for low pay in family businesses. It is still widely expected that a woman will give up work on marriage and that those who do work after they are married will be content with part-time, low-paid jobs.

The skill base is very high by international standards, with nearly 94% continuing education after compulsory schooling, which ends at age 15. Half a million graduates enter the labour market each April, a high proportion of them engineers and business studies/economics graduates. Skill shortages are greatest in financial services and in foreign languages.

Unemployment has not been a problem, although there is much hidden unemployment and under-employment. In 1987 unemployment reached 3.1%, the highest official rate since 1953, when records were first kept, but it fell again in 1988 and was down to 2.3% by early 1989. Declining industries have tried to maintain the size of their permanent labour forces by diversification and by offering small (or no) pay rises.

The nation's finances

Japan has a strong economy in world terms, with low inflation and continuing growth, but its public expenditure has been deficit-financed since 1975. An antiquated fiscal structure, strong popular resistance to overdue tax reforms, and the government's attempt to spend its way out of recession in the late 1970s are at the root of current problems. Strong foreign pressure to reflate the economy has been largely resisted, but priority has been given to higher spending on defence and foreign aid. At home the government faces mounting welfare demands.

Deficit financing

Between 1969 and 1980 General Account expenditure grew in double digits annually. In 1975, after the first oil shock, the government issued its first "red bonds" to spend its way out of recession. Further huge bond issues followed, and by 1988 the national debt stood at 43.5% of GDP. In the 1980s public expenditure was cut in real terms, rising by 4.8% in 1988/89, with cuts in all major areas except defence and foreign aid.

Inflation

Following runaway inflation in 1973/74 (24.5% consumer, 31.6% wholesale), government policy has focused on controlling inflation. Japan now has the lowest inflation rate among developed countries – below 1% in both 1987 and 1988. Late-1980s price levels posed no threat to government or business, thanks to the fall in oil and commodity prices, low interest rates and the yen's appreciation.

Currency

The yen's exchange value has fluctuated considerably since it was floated in 1971. By international agreement the yen was effectively revalued in late 1985, rising some 30% against the US dollar by mid-1986. This was a long-overdue reflection of Japan's status as the world's second largest economy.
Lack of internationalization The yen finances only 2% of world trade, compared with 50% for the dollar (even Japanese traders invoice 70% of exports non-yen). As a foreign exchange market, Tokyo ranks only fifth. Despite the yen being a non-petro currency and lacking reserve currency status, and despite low interest rates, the underlying power of the economy has made it strong.

The system of public finance

Revenue is channelled through the General Account and the Fiscal Investment and Loan Plan (FILP). The General Account is responsible for about 70% of spending, and into this go all tax revenues and bond proceeds. FILP's revenues come from pension contributions and largely untaxed savings from the Postal Savings Bank, which has assets three times those of Citibank.
Fiscal policy The goal has been to balance the budget by 1990. The government is trying to cut public expenditure, close tax loopholes and introduce tax reforms. A consumption tax was introduced in April 1989.
Monetary policy is based on a wish to maintain yen strength at a realistic level and to contain monetary growth at stable rates. Broad money supply – M2 + CDs – rose by 10.4% in 1987. Upward pressure on interest rates is likely as deregulation proceeds.
Problems in the system Despite recent changes, the financial system lacks sophistication. There is no Treasury bill market, and a market for short-term government debt was created only in 1986. Commercial banks are loaded with government paper, and a high proportion of deposits are subject to regulated interest rates to provide cheap government funding.

Where the money comes from

Taxes account for almost 75% of General Account income, most of the rest coming from bond issues. Direct taxation provides 72% of tax revenue, income tax contributing the largest slice, followed closely by corporation tax. Individuals are lightly taxed – rates begin at 10%, and few people get beyond the 30% band – while corporations pay hefty rates of 37.5% upwards.

Among indirect taxes, liquor tax raises the most revenue, while stamp duties and gasoline, consumption, tobacco and inheritance taxes also make sizable contributions.

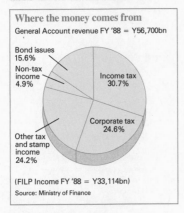

Where the money comes from

General Account revenue FY '88 = Y56,700bn

Bond issues 15.6%
Non-tax income 4.9%
Income tax 30.7%
Corporate tax 24.6%
Other tax and stamp income 24.2%

(FILP Income FY '88 = Y33,114bn)
Source: Ministry of Finance

Where the money goes

Servicing the national debt accounts for almost 20% of General Account expenditure. Grants to local government, of about Y11,000bn, provide over one-third of their income. FILP spends heavily on a deficient infrastructure (fewer than 60% of homes are on mains sewerage), on costly public and development corporations, and on state banks, which fund industry.
Welfare Spending is set to become the public sector's biggest headache. Most Japanese associate public welfare with "advanced country disease"; traditionally welfare has been the responsibility of employers. Companies offer guaranteed lifetime employment and provide assistance with medical, housing, education and pension costs. Low personal tax rates are possible because of minimal provisions for the sick, the unemployed and the elderly.
Education Spending is concentrated on 5–18 schooling, since most pre-school and higher education is privately funded.
Defence The USA, which has provided a defence umbrella since 1945, wants increased spending. A

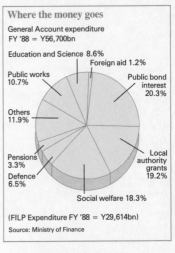

Where the money goes

General Account expenditure FY '88 = Y56,700bn

Education and Science 8.6%
Foreign aid 1.2%
Public works 10.7%
Public bond interest 20.3%
Others 11.9%
Pensions 3.3%
Defence 6.5%
Local authority grants 19.2%
Social welfare 18.3%

(FILP Expenditure FY '88 = Y29,614bn)
Source: Ministry of Finance

war-sensitive electorate, however, is loath to see spending exceed the unwritten postwar limit of 1% of GNP, the lowest among developed nations. It rose to 1.01% in 1988.
Foreign aid has been increasing but accounts for only 0.3% of GNP, lower than in most developed countries. Much of Japan's aid is viewed as self-serving and Asia-centred.

The political debate

Despite public resistance, there is a need for tax reform to cut the huge deficit. Business wants deep cuts in the public sector and privatization. The pressure for increased spending on health, welfare, defence and foreign aid will pose problems.

International trade

Japan's balance of payments, which showed the highest trade surplus ever recorded ($96bn) in 1987, has become a sore point in its relations with trading partners. No aspect, from yen policy to import promotion to export restraint or financial liberalization, has been immune from scrutiny, demand for reform and threats of protectionist retaliation. There has been movement: the yen's value has soared since late 1985, tariffs and quotas are now lower on average than in other industrial nations, and one-third of exports are subject to voluntary restraint.

Balance of payments

Like the yen, Japan's balance of payments has been on a roller coaster since the early 1970s. Deficits following the oil shocks have given way to seemingly in-built surpluses. The situation has been compounded by an American budget deficit which soaked up huge inflows of Japanese savings. The current account surplus in 1987 was $87bn. Following the world recession in the early 1980s, domestic demand was flat, and exports became the vehicle of growth, although by the end of the decade, this trend was beginning to be reversed.

Japan's trade

Japanese goods are substantially in surplus, whereas services are in deficit (though decreasingly so). Imports of low value-added fuels, raw materials and essential foodstuffs are shaped into high value-added manufactures for export. As a proportion of GNP, exports (11.5%), and imports (7.5%) are lower than those of several other leading industrial countries. Targeted

Main trading partners		
Country	% Exports	% Imports
USA	36.5	21.1
South Korea	5.8	5.4
Taiwan	4.9	4.8
West Germany	5.6	4.1
China	3.6	5.0
Australia	2.2	5.3
Canada	2.4	4.1
Saudi Arabia	1.4	4.9
UK	3.7	2.0
Hong Kong	3.9	1.0
Source: Ministry of Finance (1987)		

exports, though, are significant for the havoc they create abroad in selected industries and markets. The USA and the EC countries at the end of the 1980s were continuing to put pressure on Japan to reduce its bilateral surpluses, and the EC's recourse to anti-dumping measures has obliged many Japanese industries to step up their overseas production operations. Both Japan's exports and imports rank third in world terms, behind the USA and West Germany.

Top 10 exports	Top 10 imports
1. Road vehicles	1. Crude petroleum
2. Iron and steel	2. Natural gas
3. Chemicals	3. Electrical machinery
4. Consumer electronics	4. Petroleum products
5. Scientific instruments	5. Chemicals
6. Telecommunication equipment	6. Non-ferrous metals
7. Office equipment	7. Foodstuffs
8. Ships	8. Wood and lumber
9. Power-generating equipment	9. Iron ores
10. Synthetic fabrics	10. Transport equipment

Sources: Ministry of International Trade and Industry. Ministry of Finance

Major trading partners

The USA and Western Europe are Japan's most important markets, accounting for over half of exports. Developing countries absorb just under one-third (South Korea is the most important), while the Communist bloc accounts for only 5%, with China as the main market.

Almost half of Japan's imports come from developing countries; these consist largely of crude oil imports from the Gulf states and Indonesia, timber from Malaysia and South Korea, and Taiwanese foodstuffs. About 40% of imports come from developed countries, principally the USA, Australia and Canada, which are major suppliers of foodstuffs, industrial raw materials and coal. The Communist bloc supplied only 7% of Japan's imports in 1987, mainly Chinese oil and food.

Trade barriers

Liberalization since the 1970s has greatly reduced Japan's visible barriers. The major problems for foreigners seeking to export to Japan (see *Market entry*) are the strength of local competition, the unique qualities of the market and an assortment of invisible barriers.

The yen

Fluctuations in the yen have caused more problems to competitors than to Japan itself. When the yen has increased, Japan's larger firms have ridden the storm – albeit at reduced margins – because of their substantial edge in manufacturing efficiency and ability to sell on non-price factors.

Invisible trade

Japan still manages to earn only 70% of what it spends abroad on services. Most of its earnings from services come from net income on technology licences and from investment income on recycled trade surpluses. Losses from shipping are diminishing, but deficits from patent royalties and overseas travel are growing. Travelling Japanese spend four times more money overseas than do visitors to Japan.

Capital account

Capital outflows Japan has been a net exporter of capital since the early 1970s. By 1987, investment outflows were running at $10bn a month. The lifting of exchange controls and gradual liberalization of finance (non-yen lending has enabled Japanese banks to become heavily involved in international syndicated lending), combined with the recent massive current account surpluses and the need to invest in overseas plant (as a hedge against protectionist threats), have made Japanese capital a significant force overseas. Net overseas assets grew by 50% in 1987/88.

Capital inflows have increased since the 25% ceiling on equity holdings was removed and since firms have been free to borrow abroad. Over half the external finance for the corporate sector came from overseas in 1985. Japan has become a more popular choice for foreign institutions and investors. Tokyo's stock market has proved attractive and the bond market is booming.

Japan's Balance of Payments

($bn)	1975	1980	1987
Exports	54.70	126.70	224.60
Imports	49.70	124.60	128.22
Trade Bal.	5.03	2.13	96.39
Net Services	-5.35	-11.35	-5.70
Transfers	-0.36	-1.53	-3.67
Current A/C Balance	-0.68	-10.75	87.01
ST Cap Flows	-1.14	3.14	23.86
LT Cap Flows	-0.27	2.32	-136.53
E&O	-0.59	-3.10	-3.89
Overall Bal.	-2.68	-8.39	-29.54
Reserves	12.82	25.23	81.48

Source: Ministry of Finance

The Industrial Scene

Industry and investment

Japan is the second major industrial economy in the world and arguably the most dynamic. In the half century since the end of World War II, a war-shattered poor economy has been turned into a rich high-tech society that has not only caught up the rest of the industrial world but in many areas surpassed it. Broadly, there have been four phases: immediate post-war reconstruction; export-oriented high growth in the 1960s; slower growth following the oil shocks of the 1970s; and liberalization and restructuring of the domestic economy following the strengthening of the yen since 1985.

From textiles to high-tech

Japan has followed a classic path of industrial development. It started with fairly basic industries, notably textiles in the 1950s, moved on to steel and shipbuilding in the 1960s, and to cars, cameras and consumer electronics in the 1970s. In the 1980s, manufacturing industry moved a step up the technology ladder to semi-conductors, computers and robotics. In the 1990s, the new generation of high-tech industries will include electronics, communications and information, aerospace, biotechnology and new materials.

Dominance Japanese companies have taken a major global share of an increasing number of industries. Though they are falling back down the league table in the sunset industries such as steel and shipbuilding, they remain the largest producers of consumer electronics and the second largest producers of components. Japan has more than 95% of the world market for video cassette recorders, 85% for copiers and about 70% for both robots and facsimile machines.

How it was done

Between 1945 and the 1950s, low wages and strict direction of scarce capital were the key to the development of the economy. In the early years, wages were only 25% of American rates. This comparative advantage disappeared when wages doubled during the 1950s and then trebled in the 1960s.

Capital intensity High wage rates forced a move to substitute capital for labour, with the building of large-scale facilities for high-volume production, especially in steel and shipbuilding.

Targeting In the early 1970s, companies in Japan were ready to expand into international markets. Due to the strong presence of Western companies in existing markets they had to either find market niches where Western companies were weak or take on the high-volume segments where access was easiest. By reducing product variety, and applying more efficient production techniques, Japanese companies entered industry after industry.

Western weakness In most of these industries, Western companies were not mentally or organizationally prepared to stand and fight. They retreated from more and more segments of their markets, until many had no market left to speak of. The UK and US motorcycle industries are well-documented examples.

Trade friction The success of Japan in a number of high-employing manufacturing industries encouraged protectionist trade restrictions by the USA and Europe. That spurred Japanese companies to diversify into new industries and markets. In the early days the restrictions were against textiles, then against cars, semi-conductors and consumer electronics. Now the emphasis of American and European protection is shifting towards defence, high-technology and direct investment.

Unique blend The actions of MITI and other Japanese ministries in setting the direction of change since the 1950s cannot be ignored, though they are frequently overstated. Japanese bureaucrats have only ever been able to run with the tide of underlying economic change, although they have proved masters at getting the best out of it for Japan. It has been left up to individual companies to succeed as best they can in a highly competitive home market. Undoubtedly no other country has succeeded in creating as efficacious a blend of co-operation and competition. For all its direction of the economy, the government has shown great flexibility in adapting policies to meet a series of external threats to the economy arising from oil crises, declining industries, protectionism and, most recently, the appreciation of the yen and the pressure from foreign countries to open up the domestic market.

Technology and research

The Japanese are the magpies of the technological world. Their determined search for, and application of, technology from Europe and America and, increasingly, the ability to produce it at home, is another major factor responsible for the success of the Japanese economy. Japanese companies have become supreme in applying technology to develop new products, especially those that have a mass market. The disposable cartridge that Canon developed to turn the plain paper copier pioneered by America's Xerox into world-beating copiers was reworked to create the laser printer. Japanese firms are particularly adept at the incremental improvement of products by refining the technology involved.

R&D prominent Japan is a major spender on R&D. The emphasis has been heavily on the D, but it is shifting now more towards the R. Overall, R&D spending is increasing. From the equivalent of 1.5% of GNP 20 years ago, it has now reached around 3% and is forecast to go higher yet in the 1990s. As the Japanese economy has grown so much over that time, the absolute sums are huge. A firm like NEC, which ranks among the world's top ten in three of the swiftest-changing technologies, semi-conductors, computers and telecoms, is not uncommon in spending the equivalent of 10% of its sales on R&D and in being as assiduous in licensing foreign technology.

Most R&D spending in Japan is done through companies. A very low proportion, less than one-fifth, is funded by the government, reflecting the lack of a government defence programme in Japan comparable to that in the USA, where the government accounts for nearly one-half of all R&D. Japan's universities concentrate on teaching rather than research. For many companies, particularly electronics ones, their R&D bills are larger than their capital spending on plant and equipment. Unlike American firms, Japanese ones tend to concentrate on short-term product development rather than longer-term basic research.

Unstoppable momentum None the less, such levels of R&D spending have let Japanese companies overtake US firms in their technological expertise in areas such as lasers, video, digital electronics and flat-screen displays. A Japanese textile maker, Toray Industries, now leads the world in carbon-fibre technology. Mitsubishi Heavy Industries is reputed to be able to make aircraft wings from composites of carbon fibre better than any American aerospace firm.

The future

Having achieved so much in so short

a time, can Japanese industry maintain its momentum? It faces continuing and increasing protectionism. International competition is intensifying as other countries, especially those elsewhere in Asia, emulate it. Foreign governments are prising open its fortress home markets, which economic restructuring are making more important.

The generation of technology that underpinned Japan's export industries in the 1970s and 1980s is coming to its end. Employees are losing the work-all-hours attitudes of their parents and grandparents, and the cleverest among them are asking whether it is worth the slow ride up the escalator of seniority to the top jobs at the big companies. The close relationship between politicians, the bureaucracy and the industrialists of "Japan Inc" is increasingly questioned by many modern Japanese. The social glue that has held postwar Japan together and kept the country working hard for manufacturing industry is coming unstuck, at least at the edges.

Diversification Japanese firms have always sought to diversify into new products and markets as soon as existing ones seem mature or threatened. They ask what else they can make with their technology. An example is the brewing firm Kirin, which went into biochemicals because of its expertise with the enzymes in yeast.

Cost cutting Japanese firms are ruthless in reducing the break-even prices for products through the introduction of technology, constant re-designs, automation of production and shifting of low-tech component-making to lower-cost offshore centres. Crucially, this has helped insulate exporters against currency fluctuations. Japanese manufacturers got their break-even exchange rate down from an average of Y132 to the dollar in 1988 to Y105 to the dollar a year later. The robot maker Fanuc reckons it can survive with the dollar

at Y70. Japanese companies are equally assiduous in cutting the length of time it takes to get a new product from the drawing board to the shop shelf. Car makers have cut the time it takes to get a new model on the road to three years, faster than the five to seven years in Europe and America.

A new Japan The restructuring of the economy away from export-oriented growth to greater emphasis on domestic demand and the accompanying liberalization of the economy were under way for most of the 1980s as the trade-weighted value of the yen appreciated slowly but steadily, though the whole process received a sharp and public nudge forward from the Plaza Agreement to devalue the dollar against the yen in 1985. Industries such as bulk chemicals, shipbuilding and steel were already contracting. Lower-end consumer electronics and cars are going the same way. The injection of high technology and information services into many industries will more than offset the decline in others.

Foreign presence

The opening of the Japanese market has provided new opportunities for foreign firms in Japan. It remains a hard market to crack, however, though the rewards can be considerable for those who persevere and are prepared to commit the considerable resources required.

Direct investment

Foreign companies have had a stake in Japan since the last century: NEC started in 1899 as a joint venture involving a forerunner of ITT. A few years later, GE bailed out Tokyo Electric and took a stake in the company that was to become Toshiba.

Postwar Many of the major foreign success stories in Japan dated from the postwar period. In the early post-war years there were no restrictions on direct foreign investment in Japan if companies were prepared not to repatriate profits. Companies set up in this way included AMP and Coca-Cola. Joint ventures, of which Fuji Xerox was the most successful, were allowed to repatriate profits.

The door closes ... After 1964 all direct investment needed Japanese government approval. This was difficult to obtain unless key technologies were involved.

...and reopens By 1976 virtually all regulations had been removed and foreign companies could set up wholly owned subsidiaries or take over Japanese companies. Few have taken either option, particularly the latter because of expense and Japanese xenophobia. Even joint ventures have tended to be short-lived.

Restricted areas "National interest" still restricts foreign shareholdings in certain industries such as telecommunications, broadcasting and airlines.

Foreign penetration At the end of March 1988, the stock of foreign direct investment in Japan was worth $8.5bn, about one-seventh of the level of outward investment by Japanese companies. American firms accounted for nearly half of all foreign direct investment in Japan by value, and a quarter by volume. Some 2,600 firms in Japan had 25% or more of their equity owned by foreigners, a lower proportion than in America or many European countries.

Winning a market There are Japanese markets in which foreigners have strong or dominant positions, but they are mainly those in which there was no indigenous product, such as instant coffee, where Nestlé has two-thirds of the market, or certain premium consumer products where a foreign brand carries a cachet.

You don't have to be big The success of companies such as the UK's House of Hardy with fishing gear shows that small firms can make their mark in specialized fields.

Is it worth it? A numb⬛ ⬛oreign firms operating in Japa⬛ ⬛ ⬛gh

wholly owned subsidiaries or joint ventures are successful and highly profitable. The average operating profit of foreign firms in Japan, according to MITI, is 2.5 times that of Japanese companies. The 14th biggest company in the country ranked by earnings is IBM Japan. McDonald's has become one of Japan's largest fast-food chains, and has spawned local imitators.

Listening post Japan's strength in high technology and production techniques has prompted a number of foreign companies to increase the intelligence-gathering activities of their Japanese subsidiaries. Companies such as ICI and Nova have started to set up research laboratories in Japan.

Into the future The opening of the domestic market is encouraging more foreign firms to consider setting up local manufacturing and local sales operations to service it.

How to make it work

It is necessary to have clear aims in the Japanese market but not to expect quick results. Commitment, patience and a long-term strategy are the keys to success, together with management training for this specialized market and reasonable fluency in the language.

Taste is everything Different consumer habits and distribution practices have proved difficult for foreign firms to overcome, though not impossible. Most successful foreign firms have tailored their products to the local market in some way or other, such as green-tea flavoured ice cream, and found a partner to distribute their products whose own lines are not direct competitors.

Local talent It is essential if the venture is to be a success to hire talented local managers and sales people (chosen not just because of their fluency in English). Many of the best local affiliates of foreign companies, such as IBM Japan, have a distinctly Japanese feel.

The car industry

Japan's car industry established itself as a global force in the 1980s. For the 1990s, overseas production, a drive up-market with the emphasis on stylish designs, and the introduction of new technology will sustain the Japanese car makers in their competition with US firms for leadership of the industry worldwide.

The market

From small beginnings Before World War II, of the small number of cars in Japan, four out of five were either imported Fords or General Motors. After the war, the infant domestic industry was heavily protected. Annual production was raised from 32,000 vehicles in 1956 to 900,000 vehicles by 1966 and over 12m by 1986. By then, car exports accounted for about 20% by value of all Japanese exports.

Backyard sanctuary In 1988, for the first time in more than a decade, Japan's car makers got more than half their sales and operating profit from the domestic market rather than from exports. Abroad, they have been hit by the strength of the yen, tariffs, quotas and voluntary export restraints, and by tough competition from America's reviving Big Three and the low-cost South Koreans. The numbers of cars exported peaked in 1985. The subsequent decline has been partly offset by local production: domestic sales topped 6m vehicles a year for the first time in 1987.

Insignificant imports Car sales in Japan are overwhelmingly sales of Japanese cars. Although imports, particularly of luxury European cars such as BMWs and Mercedes, have grown rapidly thanks to market-opening measures and a booming domestic economy, imports still account for barely 2% of the market. In 1988, for the first time, these included Japanese cars built abroad, including Honda Accord Coupés from Ohio.

Fierce domestic market For Japanese and foreign car makers alike the Japanese market has become fiercely competitive, with many in the industry believing that the market is saturated except at the top end. Domestic sales forces have been revamped, sales promotion boosted, new models – especially stylish and luxury ones – introduced and cost-cutting at the factory has been relentless.

The companies

Nagoya-based Toyota is the industry leader and the world's third biggest car maker. Deeply conservative in its management and model lines, it has none the less a 40% market share and in 1988 rolled out its 60 millionth car. It has been putting money into its sales network in and around Tokyo, an area in which it has never been particularly strong. It was the last of the major Japanese car makers to move into overseas production, although it has joint ventures with GM and Volkswagen.

Nissan, the industry number two and fourth largest car maker in the world, has recovered from a rocky couple of years when it lost money after Toyota launched a price war to boost market share. A fearsome cost-cutting campaign and a stylish range of new cars, including the BMW-clone Cima range for the luxury end of the market, has restored its fortunes.

Honda is the most globally minded of the Japanese manufacturers, having pioneered overseas production, reverse imports and the use of a separate marque, Acura, to spearhead its drive up-market abroad. A post-war company that grew out of making motorcycles (in which it is still the world's number one), in many ways Honda seems as much a US company as a Japanese one. When all its North American factories are on stream, it will be America's number three car maker. At home, it is fighting it out with Mitsubishi Motors for the number three spot.

The smaller manufacturers are mostly associated with one of the bigger groups or foreign firms. The biggest of them is Mazda, in which Ford has a 24% stake. Ford seems to be trying to develop Mazda into a "Ford of Europe" for Asia. The two also have collaborative ventures in South Korea and Mexico. A grander coalition involving Mazda, Ford and Nissan is a conceivable future development. (Nissan and Ford have started to collaborate on building a light van in the USA.)

Isuzu Motors, which makes lorries and small cars, is tied to GM, which also has a stake in another minicar-producer, Suzuki. Daihatsu, another Japanese minicar maker, is in the Toyota group. Fuji Heavy, which makes Subaru minicars and four-wheel drive vehicles, is affiliated with Nissan.

Consolidation Japanese government officials have long nursed plans for consolidating the domestic industry into fewer but bigger groups. The emerging web of R&D, production and marketing alliances and affiliations, both domestic and international, is doing the job for them.

Transplants

Honda pioneered production in North America, but all the leading Japanese car makers have plants there now, either on their own or as joint ventures. When they are producing at full capacity in the early 1990s, they will be producing more than 1m cars a year, more than Chrysler now makes. That portends a bloody struggle for market share.

Japanese manufacturers see local production in the USA as essential to reduce costs while the dollar is weak, to ease protectionist pressures and to evade quotas on imports. For much the same reasons, they are setting up factories in Europe, too. On both continents, Japanese components makers are following in the car manufacturers' wake.

Exports Japanese factories in both the USA and Europe will be used to export to third markets and in some cases back to Japan. Honda America is planning to export 70,000 vehicles a year; it is already the leading "American" exporter to Japan's domestic car market, outselling both Ford and GM.

The future

The networks of alliances both domestic and international are likely to get more complicated as Japanese car makers make a smaller proportion of their vehicles at home for export and a larger proportion near the markets in which they are to be sold. They will also concentrate on moving up-market, abandoning the low end to South Korean firms such as Hyundai. Although car making is a relatively mature industry, new technology such as electronic control systems and new materials, in which the Japanese are at the forefront, will be used to add value to new models, while yet-more-sophisticated production and design engineering will be used to reduce product development cycles from the current four years to two.

Japanese automobile production 1988	
	(% of total)
Toyota Motor	31
Nissan Motor	17
Mazda Motor	10
Mitsubishi Motors	10
Honda Motor	10
Suzuki Motor	7
Isuzu Motors	4
Fuji Heavy Industries	5
Daihatsu Motor	5
Others	1
Total	100

Total production = 12.699m passenger cars and trucks.
Total exports = 48% of total production.
Source: Japan Automobile Manufacturers' Association

Heavy industry

Japan's heavy industries have been going through a period of major rationalization and restructuring since the mid-1980s. The combined pressures of falling world demand, protectionism in export markets and fierce competition from lower-cost producers in the newly industrializing countries, especially South Korea and Taiwan, have turned old export mainstays such as bulk chemicals, steel and shipbuilding into sunset industries for Japan.

Response to change

The heavy industrial giants that comprised Japan Inc in the 1960s and 1970s have shed capacity, moved up-market into speciality products and sought to diversify into new businesses for the home market. They have been helped by the sustained expansion of the domestic economy that was triggered by the government's Y6,000bn reflation package launched in 1986/87 to counter the high-yen recession.

Windfall benefits More important was the effect of the rising yen on cutting industries' import bill for raw materials. In the 30 months to March 1988, these were estimated to have fallen by Y29bn. Falling world oil prices and interest rates reduced costs further.

Cost cutting Sackings are socially unacceptable at big Japanese companies but this is not the case with early retirements and intra-group transfers. Nippon Steel, the world's biggest steel maker, cut 3,500 jobs this way in 1987. It aims to have reduced its once 54,000-strong work force by at least one-third by the early 1990s.

Offshore investment Production capacity was poured into lower-cost countries, and into the USA and Europe, to be nearer export markets or to gain technology. All the leading steel companies have joint ventures in the USA.

Moving up-market Shipbuilders, whose position as the world's number one was undermined by the collapse of demand for oil tankers in the 1970s, was further hurt by the spectacular rise of the South Korean industry. Firms such as Mitsubishi Heavy Industries, Ishikawajima-Harima Heavy Industries and Hitachi Zozen have switched to making cruise liners and military ships. Steel makers have moved into higher value-added speciality steels to offset industry's use of less steel per unit of output and the advance of cheaper steel substitutes. Chemicals companies have moved into fine and speciality chemicals, especially materials for bio- and other high-technology industries.

Government policy

The government has coordinated industry plans to reduce capacity and consolidate industries through the absorption of smaller firms by bigger ones. This was particularly effective in fragmented industries such as chemicals, but shipbuilding has seen its capacity reduced to 40% of its pre-1980 levels. The government has also provided subsidies in the form of low-interest loans to aid diversification.

Technological innovation The sunset heavy industries have had less scope for new product development than the lighter old-line export industries such as cameras and textiles. Instead they have concentrated on improving their production technology, mostly through more computerization and automation.

Diversification has been heavy industries' main hope for the new jobs that will let them switch workers from their dying businesses. Sumitomo Metal has gone into new-materials production; Nippon Steel into a range of new businesses from high-tech ceramics to importing super-minicomputers.

Defence and aerospace

Defence and aerospace could be the next big high-tech engineering industry to add to the list of cars, consumer electronics, robotics and semi-conductors which Japan has revolutionized.

Poised for take-off

The constitution forbids Japan going to war except if invaded and this, together with a government ban on arms exports, has prevented companies from gearing up for the production of large quantities of guns, tanks and defence electronics. However, by the end of the 1980s, interpretation of both these constraints had been modified to the extent that the defence industry had become one of MITI's priority sectors. Japan's arms industry, which still accounts for a mere 0.5% of industrial output, is poised to take off.

Spending Measured in dollars and on a comparable basis, Japan's defence spending is now probably higher than any other nation except for the USA and the Soviet Union. American pressure for "burden sharing" by its allies, and Japanese industries' desire to develop their own technologies, make it likely that defence spending will accelerate well into the 1990s.

Companies The list of big defence contractors includes most of the old heavy engineering groups such as Mitsubishi Heavy Industries, Kawasaki Heavy, Ishikawajima-Harima Heavy, Fuji Heavy and Sumitomo Heavy.

Still small In the world league, Japan's arms firms are still minnows. The leading company is Mitsubishi Heavy Industries, which accounts for about 30% of defence production. The top ten firms account for 80% of the business but they had contracts worth only Y787.2bn in 1987.

Aerospace

The government at present buys three out of every four Japanese aircraft made. The USA is sufficiently worried by Japan's potential prowess in building military aircraft, done in the past under licence from US firms, that it stopped the Japanese going it alone in building a new-generation jet fighter, the FSX, and insisted on joint development. Japan has already gone ahead with its own rocket-engine production because the USA denied it state-of-the-art technology. Under the US "Star Wars" project, a Japanese consortium is doing research into upgrading existing surface-to-air missiles to anti-ballistic ones.

Airliners Japan had a stab at making these in the 1960s with the 64-seat twin-prop YS-11 and then in the 1980s with a short take-off and landing 80-100 seater jet, the Asuka. Neither was a success. Only a few dozen YS-11s were built and the Asuka never got beyond the prototype stage. Japan's third try is a 75-seater short-haul airliner called the YSX, to be in service by 1994.

Technology

Technology is mostly licensed from the USA, but increasingly it is home grown. Japan can make its own missiles and has an air-to-surface missile reckoned capable of rivalling France's Exocet. It is also strong in fly-by-wire electronics aviation systems and laser technology. Missile-firing tanks are on the drawing board.

Space

Japanese spending on space is rising, but was worth only $1bn in 1989. The money is for launching a string of commercial satellites and an ambitious rocket development programme overseen by the National Space Development Agency. Japan's space programme is a decade behind the USA's and even Europe's and it lacks a rocket powerful enough to put satellites into commercially useful geostationary orbit. The first all-Japanese-developed rocket, the H-2, will be able to do so by the mid-1990s.

Consumer electronics

More than any other, the Japanese can be said to have made this area their own. From personal stereos to electronic breadmakers, they have set standards of quality, excellence and innovation that few other manufacturers appear able to match. Television, video and hi-fi are the mainstays of the business, but Japanese firms are now developing new applications and products which will enable them to consolidate their position and to commercialize the new generation of digital technology that will carry Japanese industry into the 1990s.

Market leaders

Through its National Panasonic, Technics, Quasar and other brands, Matsushita Electric dominates consumer electronics everywhere. The world's biggest maker of such goods dwarfs even its main Japanese rivals, Hitachi, Sanyo Electric, Sony, Sharp and Toshiba, in the $35bn worldwide consumer-electronics market, of which it has more than one-half. Its only serious non-Japanese rival is Philips. Matsushita is the market leader in a range of products from colour televisions to portable video cameras. Its VHS format for video cassette tapes won the day, after a 15-year battle, eclipsing Sony's Betamax format, despite being second into the market. Matsushita became the world's biggest manufacturer of video cassette recorders (VCRs), a $10bn-a-year business in Japan alone.

Diversification Matsushita gets about one-half of its $42bn annual sales (and four-fifths of its profit) from consumer electronics but, like its rivals, it is seeking to diversify further. Consumer-electronics markets are not growing so fast worldwide as are the markets for electronic components, office automation and industrial and professional electronics, which Matsushita is heading for; other consumer-electronics companies are concentrating on telecommunications and computers. In many of these markets the technology is interchangeable and the boundaries between them are blurring.

Standards A new battle for video standards is being fought out between VHS and Sony's newer and more compact 8mm tape. Smaller tape creates markets for new products such as the visual version of the personal stereo, Sony's Video Walkman, and hand-held video cameras-cum-recorders, called camcorders. There is now a compact version of VHS tape but which tape becomes the industry standard will probably be decided by the availability of software to be played on the hardware, such as films. Here VHS has a considerable lead.

Tomorrow's world

Digital technology Getting the hi-fi, video and television mainstays to do more will be achieved by getting them to work digitally, as computers do. This will make it easier to merge sound, vision and text into one. A digital textbook, for example, could provide a user with words, pictures and sound on any subject on a single compact disc.

The prospects opened up by this sort of multi-media product will force a convergence of the electronics, publishing and information-technology industries.

High-definition TV, with its super-sharp images, is the product on which the future of the consumer-electronics industry might turn in the 1990s because of its possible wide applications in personal computers, semi-conductors, telecommunications and manufacturing. The snag is that the Americans, Europeans and Japanese cannot agree on a world standard for transmission or format for the picture.

Computers

Japanese companies have been slow to find the international success in computers that they have had in other electronics fields, but it is coming ever faster as the computer and telecommunications businesses converge.

Hardware

Fujitsu is the largest domestic computer maker, and dominates in mainframes. It is a major maker of semi-conductors and of telecommunications equipment and is strong in office automation equipment such as word processors and personal computers (PCs). The market leader in personal computers, NEC, is one of the world's leading producers of semi-conductors. Second in both sectors of the market is IBM Japan. Other major mainframe producers include Hitachi, Toshiba, Oki Electric and Mitsubishi Electric.

Since PCs were introduced in the late 1970s, their use has grown swiftly: Japan never really took to typewriting because of the cumbersome nature of *kanji* typewriters. All the Japanese consumer-electronics makers produce Japanese and English word processors, using their LCD and printer technology. However, they have yet to capture world markets, although Toshiba has made headway with laptop computers.

Peripherals High quality and competitive prices have helped Japanese companies to win world markets for peripherals such as disk drives and printers, and for components and parts. Several US computer makers, including Hewlett-Packard and Apple, have established procurement offices in Japan.

Semi-conductors

Japan's leading microchip makers include NEC, Fujitsu and Matsushita Electric. They are investing heavily to strengthen their technological lead over American, South Korean and other competitors through the development of the new generation of 4-megabit dynamic random access memory (DRAM) chips.

Growing capacity The industry does not expect the increase in output to cause a repeat of the mid-1980s' crisis of excess supply that threw the industry into depression worldwide and sparked a trade row with the USA. Extra demand for chips for a range of new products such as digital television is expected to absorb the extra output.

Software

The software sector grew by 20–30% a year throughout the 1970s and 1980s. Annual sales are well in excess of $1bn, but the industry is fragmented, with more than 1,000 companies.

Most systems software is supplied by software houses affiliated to the leading computer makers. They also write some applications software, but nearly one-third of this is developed in-house by users. The Japanese preference has been for custom-written software but there is a trend towards buying-in applications software from independent suppliers who provide combined hardware and software packages. The spread of PCs is increasing the market for off-the-peg software packages, especially in robotics and financial services.

Government encouragement There is a shortage of programmers and systems analysts, and MITI has earmarked $100m to develop the software industry. The government is also encouraging the development of the TRON operating system designed to make computers easier to operate and to link together.

Foreign suppliers Japanese companies have turned to America and Europe for the shortages in expertise and software products that they lack. Trading companies have exclusive distribution agreements with foreign suppliers.

Automation

Japanese dominance in robotics has been swiftly and completely achieved. As robots became increasingly linked into complete automatic manufacturing systems, Japanese industry gained a further competitive edge.

Perspectives

True automation of the manufacturing sector has required the combination of several disparate elements. Computer-aided design and computer-aided manufacturing (CAD)/(CAM) systems are allowing rapid changes in product design. Increasingly intelligent robots translate these changes into flexible production processes, and the integration of computer and communications systems links the elements into powerful production systems.

The robot market

Japanese companies have taken a lead in world robot production ever since Japanese industry, faced with the need to cut costs in the wake of the 1970s oil crises, turned to greater automation as a solution. Japan has some 150,000 industrial robots installed, more than two-thirds of the world's total, and twice that many robots in all.

In the mid-1980s, the industry went through a slump as demand fell in both domestic and export markets. In the big Japanese market, demand dried up as manufacturers cut back their capital spending plans because of the impact of the high yen.

In Japanese industry, the use of robots, mostly for assembly, has spread far beyond the early big users, which were the car and electronics industries.

The companies

Fanuc, the dominant producer, was set up in 1972 as a spin-off from the computer-maker Fujitsu. It has three-quarters of the home market and half the world market for computer numerical control equipment, which is what turns a machine tool into a basic robot. The mid-1980s' slump has thinned a field of robot-making companies that had exceeded 300.

Overseas expansion With 20% of production exported, Japanese robot-makers have been setting up joint ventures and original equipment manufacturing (OEM) deals to penetrate the US and European markets. The best-known joint venture is that between Fanuc and General Motors, set up in 1982, and regarded as a spectacular success until GM, a major customer, cut its capital spending.

Growing lead It seems unlikely that the Japanese lead in robotics can be cut back in the foreseeable future by US or European competitors. Japanese companies are intensifying their R&D for new products, the acceptance of automation is higher in Japan than elsewhere, and the establishment by Japanese industry of offshore production, especially assembly, should help demand to recover.

CAD/CAM

American companies pioneered this technology in the 1950s and 1960s in the car, aerospace and shipbuilding industries. It is only since the 1980s that the Japanese market has established itself. Since then the Japanese robotics makers have been eroding the domination of the US companies and their products. New companies, including computer makers and companies such as Seiko Epson that have developed in-house software, have entered the market.

Peripheral strength Similarly, US dominance in CAD/CAM peripheral devices, such as plotters and graphic displays, is being rapidly eroded by Japanese manufacturers with their traditional strengths in this area.

Communications

The telecommunications and computer industries are converging in Japan, as they are everywhere, and computer-related information services are growing fast, in line with the rapid development of the computer industry. The advent of competing groups in telecommunications is spurring development that will transform this sector. Worth some $7bn in 1986, the Japanese telecommunications market is the world's third biggest after those of the USA and the Soviet Union.

Telecommunications

Japan formerly had separate domestic and international telecommunications monopolies, run by Nippon Telegraph and Telephone (NTT) and Kokusai Denshin Denwa (KDD) respectively; these monopolies were broken by legislation passed in 1984 as part of the government's programme to deregulate state-owned industries.

Once part of, and still close to, the Posts and Telecommunications Ministry, NTT is having about half its equity sold to the public in stages. Though it now has some 40 competitors in domestic services, NTT remains the dominant company in the industry. There is persistent talk of breaking it up on regional lines, as AT&T was in the USA, to stimulate more competition. Real competition exists only in the provision of long-distance services between Tokyo, Nagoya and Osaka.

New information networks are being developed. In particular, NTT is planning to replace all analog communications with a digital network, using optical-fibre cables and communication satellites, and introducing digital switching systems and exchanges. Telephone, data transmission, facsimile and video communication will be carried by the same integrated network under a concept called Information Network System (INS).

Competing services Challenging the still huge NTT, a number of so-called Type 1 common carriers have been licensed to provide trunk-line services on major routes using optical fibres, microwave radio or satellite links. Competing large-scale and small-scale value-added networks (VANs) have also been set up.

More suppliers For many years, NTT's domestic procurement has been a boon for the Japanese telecoms-equipment-making industry, particularly NEC, Hitachi, Fujitsu and Oki Electric. Under political pressure from the USA and as a result of the competitive pressures of denationalization and deregulation, NTT has started to procure more from abroad and from other domestic manufacturers.

Trade friction Telecoms equipment has become another frontier in the trade wars between the USA and Japan, and a growing source of friction between Japan and Europe. Japan runs a huge trade surplus (sufficient to cancel America's surplus in computers) and is accused by the Americans of protecting its domestic industry. Telecoms equipment production in Japan totalled Y2,100bn in 1988. Exports were worth Y676.3bn (nearly two-fifths of which went to the USA) but imports only Y49.6bn.

International expansion Japanese telecoms-equipment suppliers have used their strong domestic market as a launch pad for international sales since the start of the 1980s, first elsewhere in the region, then in America and Europe. Fujitsu and NEC now rank in the top ten of telecoms-equipment makers worldwide. Japanese firms as a whole have become the top exporters of products such as telephone sets, facsimile machines and satellite equipment. They are now moving into the market for central telephone exchanges and value-added services.

New materials

One of the key industries for the 1990s, new materials are seen as one way in which Japanese companies can maintain an edge in ever more competitive times. Japanese companies have been used by European and US firms as sales agents or licensees for new materials technologies but, despite having started late, Japanese companies are catching up, and are now at the forefront in applications technology, even though they still lag behind US firms in basic research. Japanese industry is concentrating on research into materials with higher or more specialist performance characteristics. Current research is concentrating on ceramics, metals, plastics and, particularly, composites.

Applications

The applications are widespread for new and advanced materials, which by no means comprise a distinct industry. The sectors are fragmented, the companies involved in developing the new materials are numerous and the technology in many cases is still at the development stage.

Electronics, car making and aerospace are the industries most likely to benefit from the main applications in the 1990s.

Key sectors

Composites are arguably the most important sector of the new-materials industry, with carbon-fibre composites the most important sub-sector. Japan accounts for nearly one-half of the non-communist world's production of carbon fibre. Its production capacity is being expanded rapidly to meet growing demand, particularly from the aerospace industry.

Toray Industries, the industry leader, and Toho Rayon, the number two, account for the bulk of the output. They were the first to market successfully polyacrylonitrile (PAN) carbon fibre, which was developed in the UK for the aerospace industry but then used under licence by the Japanese firms for sports goods such as fishing rods, tennis rackets and golf clubs. They subsequently developed carbon fibre to such an extent that they licensed their technology back to Europe. The wheel has now turned full circle again and the Japanese firms are concentrating on composites for the aerospace industry.

This sector is using increasingly larger components (the whole tail of Boeing's 7J7 aircraft scheduled for production in the early 1990s is to be made out of carbon fibre) and more sophisticated composites. Demand is expected to increase by at least 10% a year.

Fine ceramics This growing market is worth more than $8bn and is one of the largest of the new industrial materials sectors. Several hundred companies are involved. More than two-thirds of the market is for electro-ceramics: the electrical properties of fine ceramics make them ideal as packages for integrated circuits.

The insulating and structural properties of electro-ceramics also give them a growing role in specialized engineering sectors, where they are being used for cutting tools and other equipment for making semi-conductors. Great hopes are being held for the development of ceramic car engine parts.

Engineering plastics High heat resistance is the significant feature of engineering plastics. Their main applications are in the car, computer and home electrical appliance industries. The market already exceeds $1bn a year. Competition is intense, with more and more companies seeking niches in specialist rather than general-purpose engineering plastics.

Biotechnology and pharmaceuticals

Biotechnology has been identified as one of the key industries for the 1990s, partly for its potential application to other industries from foods to pharmaceuticals. There is plenty of R&D, much of it advanced, but also acceptance that extensive commercial pay-offs may not come until the next century.

Government backing

Japan's serious interest in biotechnology started in the early 1980s when MITI chose recombinant DNA technology (whereby genes from different organisms are joined to produce new features), bioreactors, mass cell culture and biochips (semi-conductors using biotechnology) as research subjects for its programme. The future industrial ministry set up a biotechnology department in 1982 and has sponsored biotech-based research into new fuels, water recycling and marine life.

The Science and Technology Agency has been doing genetics research as part of its life sciences projects; the Agriculture Ministry has carried out research into the use of biotechnology in plant breeding; and the Health Ministry has drawn up guidelines for the manufacture of foods and pharmaceuticals using biotechnologies. Other areas of biotechnological research in which official and quasi-official bodies are involved include bioholonics and information transmission, and medical fields such as cancer treatment and vaccines.

Total spending on biotechnology R&D has been running at about $400m a year. The main channel for government funds is the Japan Key Technology Centre, a joint venture set up by MITI and the Posts and Telecommunications Ministry.

The companies

The big spending on biotech research is by companies, which account for around four-fifths of the total. Unlike in the West, where small start-up companies are formed to take advantage of advances in the science, much Japanese biotech R&D is being carried out inside big industrial groups. The $30m Protein Engineering Research Institute was set up by a consortium led by Mitsubishi Chemical, Takeda Chemical and Toray.

Biomedicines are one of the leading and most competitive sectors of the Japanese biotech industry, and the one in which the first commercial products have arrived, such as Sumitomo Pharmaceuticals' recombinant DNA anti-cancer drug, launched in the late 1980s. The confidence of this sector is indicated by the activities of Chugai Pharmaceutical, which has been researching into gene-engineering technology. It spent Y10bn to set up the then largest biotech-medicines factory in Japan.

Biochips Japan's big electronics groups have been spending heavily on R&D into ways of applying biotechnology to the computer and semi-conductor businesses. Japan's research in this area is among the most advanced in the world.

Biofood Research into developing new foods and plants has become the latest focus of the biotech industry. These are seen as the long-term answer to the problem of how to make Japan's inefficient and over-protected agriculture economically viable. Brewers such as Kirin see in this sector possibilities for applying their fermentation-enzyme technology.

In the longer term

Starting with applications in pharmaceuticals and clinical diagnostic testing, commercialization of new developments will slowly fan out into other areas, including bulk chemicals, food, agriculture, energy and water treatment.

Leading companies

The list of the top ten Japanese industrial companies by assets provides a snapshot of the changing industrial structure of Japan, as well as a reminder of the enduring and adaptable strength of the big industrial groups. The steel and heavy engineering groups were slipping down the rankings by the end of the 1980s, while the telecommunications and electronics companies were on the rise.

Nippon Telegraph & Telephone

The biggest telecommunications company in the world by far, in terms of stock-market capitalization, Nippon Telegraph & Telephone (NTT), or Nippon Denshin Denwa, ranks second in the world only to AT&T by size of business. It is the biggest commercial employer in Japan, with a staff of nearly 300,000 and is expanding into international services through subsidiaries. Until 1986, the company was state-owned, with a monopoly of domestic telecommunications in Japan; it still dominates the business, and plays an important role as catalyst for Japanese makers of telecommunications equipment.

Hitachi

An exemplar for post-war Japan, Hitachi (Hitachi Beisakusho) is switching away from its traditional strengths in making heavy electrical equipment, industrial plant, chemicals, wire and cable, and shipbuilding into aerospace, computers and information and communications systems. Under Katsushigo Mita, the company revamped its marketing and distribution, recognizing that its future lay no longer in "old boy network" sales to Japan's large industrial groups.

Matsushita Electric Industrial

One of the world's largest consumer electronics manufacturers, Matsushita Electric Industrial (Matsushita Danki Sangyo) is the nucleus of the Matsushita group. Its best-known brand names are National Panasonic, JVC, Technics and Quasar. Since its founder, Konosuke Matsushita ceased to play an active part in the company in the mid-1980s, it has slipped from top spot among Japanese manufacturers and is trying to reorganize itself to regain the flair it feels it has lost.

Toyota Motor

Japan's largest car maker, with a 40% domestic market share, Toyota (Toyota Jidosha) is also the world's number three car maker. Deeply conservative and still run by the Toyoda family, it was the last of the Japanese car firms to move into overseas production in the USA and Europe. Financially very strong, it is sometimes nicknamed the Toyota Bank.

Nissan Motor

Nissan Motor (Nissan Jidosha) ranks one below Toyota in both Japanese and world car making. Under Yutaka Kuma, its president, the company has recovered from a sticky patch and in the process has shaken off a reputation for dull vehicles, particularly with its new top-of-the-range models. Nissan is developing a separate sales network for those in the USA. The company has been strengthening its ties with America's Ford for the development of a multi-purpose vehicle. It is also well known for its aeronautics and space technology.

Toshiba

Japan's number two all-round electrical and electronic engineering group is recovering from sanctions imposed against it by the USA in 1987, following illegal exports to Communist countries by its machine-tools affiliate. Strong in the nuclear power industry, it cooperates with America's General Electric in nuclear power generation. Toshiba also has foreign tie-ups with West Germany's Siemens in semi-conductors and with Italy's Olivetti in computers.

Nippon Steel

The world's largest steel maker, Nippon Steel (Shin Nippon Beitetsu), is the most blue-blooded of the industrial aristocracy that used to make up "Japan Inc." Hurt by the stronger yen, lower-cost competition from South Korea and falling worldwide demand, the company has been restructuring painfully by cutting back its workforce and closing mills. It has a joint venture in the USA with Inland Steel, aimed at producing steel for the car industry. As well as developing steels with other speciality uses, the company has been diversifying into electronics, data communications, new materials and theme-park development.

NEC

One of the world's leading producers of semi-conductors, NEC (Nippon Denki) stands at the point where the computer and communications industries converge. The company's sales of computers and communications equipment account for three-quarters of group sales. It is the leading producer of Japanese personal computers. Fifteen years ago NEC would not have ranked among the top 20 Japanese industrial companies but many think it is now heading for the top three.

Mitsubishi Heavy Industries

Japan's largest heavy engineering group, and the core of the old-line Mitsubishi combine, Mitsubishi Heavy Industries (Mitsubishi Jukogyo) is the industry leader in the shipbuilding, aircraft, power plant and other heavy engineering sectors but it is having to reorganize to keep pace with a changing economy.

NKK

Another Japanese steel maker that has had to restructure in the face of a deteriorating competitive environment. NKK (formerly Nippon Kokan) nevertheless remains one of the world's top five. Known for its steel pipes and steel for shipbuilding, it owns 50% of America's National Steel.

The top ten companies (year ended March 1989)

	Assets (Ybn)	Net Profit (Ybn)	Sales (Ybn)	Exports as % of sales	Employees ('000)
NTT	10.6	30.6	5.7	N/A	276.7
Toyota	5.5	38.0	6.7	34	65.4
Hitachi	3.2	100.4	3.2	25	76.5
Nissan	3.1	63.6	3.6	42	52.8
Nippon Steel	3.0	62.7	2.4	26	58.2
Matsushita Electric	2.9	128.5	4.1	34	41.4
Heavy Industries	2.9	49.3	1.7	22	44.4
Toshiba	2.7	61.3	2.9	31	69.2
NKK	2.2	42.0	1.3	27	23.8
Fujitsu	2.0	51.5	2.0	18	50.9
Mitsubishi Electric	2.0	32.5	2.2	21	47.7

Source: Fortune International

The Political Scene

The government of the nation

The present-day Japanese political system owes much to the changes made by the Americans during their postwar occupation and the subsequent modifications made by the Japanese themselves.

The American model

The USA revamped the extremely centralized and bureaucratic Japanese political structure that had survived World War II. A new constitution, a reduced role for the Emperor, a considerable decentralization of government and a major programme of social, political and economic reforms were introduced to demilitarize and democratize the country.

Japanese changes Since the Occupation forces left in 1952, the Japanese have continually modified the American reforms. Nearly 40 years of conservative rule have been largely responsible for a growing re-centralization of economic and political power. The main elements in the power structure are the Liberal Democratic Party, the bureaucrats of the major ministries and the large industrial companies (see *The reins of power*).

A new constitution

Three principles form the basis of the 1947 constitution: a shift of sovereign power to the people, with the Emperor the symbol of the state; a declaration of pacifism and renunciation of war; and a respect for human rights.

Checks and balances The constitution attempted to divide and balance the powers of the legislature, the executive and the judiciary. The Diet (parliament) makes the laws, while executive power resides in a cabinet nominally responsible to the Diet and forming the pinnacle of Japan's government institutions. Judicial power is vested in a Supreme Court and four types of lower court: High, district, family and summary.

The legislature

The House of Representatives and the House of Councillors, both of them elected bodies, form the Diet. The Americans favoured a single-house legislature, but the Japanese insisted on a second house.

House of Representatives Members face an election whenever the prime minister dissolves the house. This must be done at least every four years and in practice happens every 2–3 years. Standing committees, corresponding approximately to the Cabinet ministries, have become the most important method of operation.

House of Councillors This house was set up to provide a check on the House of Representatives, but it is largely a rubber-stamp institution with few actual powers. The LDP lost control of this House for the first time in 1989. The term of office is six years, with half the house running for election every three years.

Elections

The 512 members of the House of Representatives are elected from 130 multi-seat constituencies, with three to five members from each constituency. Each voter has one vote. Elections to the 252-seat House of Councillors follow a mixed system; 100 candidates are elected from national constituencies, with the remaining 152 elected from 47 local multi-seat constituencies.

Gerrymandering The electoral boundaries are heavily weighted in favour of the rural districts. Because the ruling LDP has its power base in the rural constituencies, a redrawing of the boundaries is unlikely, despite court rulings declaring some results of the 1983 elections unconstitutional.

The executive and judiciary

Prime minister As the leader of the majority party, the prime minister is in control of the Diet, at least in principle. He is also leader of the Cabinet, responsible for the appointment of ministers, and can influence the judiciary through the appointment of judges. He is the supreme centre of power under the constitution, though in practice his actions are limited by the exigencies of party politics.

Cabinet The parliamentary cabinet system is the basis of the executive arm of the government. Most of the 20 or so ministers are members of the House of Representatives, and all have to be civilians. Apart from a few top jobs, ministries are regularly re-allocated to senior party members, most of whom will serve at least one stint.

Supreme Court Set up to guard the constitutional rights of citizens against the excesses of government, the Supreme Court has not had the desired impact. Justices are appointed by the prime minister, and 40 years of conservative consensus have ensured the Supreme Court's unassertive character. Much of its time has been spent solving disputes concerning the constitutional status of the military, but it has avoided making political decisions.

Local government

Japan's local government is organized in a two-tier system, with the 47 federal prefectures mediating between central government and the city, town and village assemblies.

Coping with development Local administrations have had to cope with the effects of Japan's rapid industrial development, which has produced a dramatic shift of population to the cities. Central government, however, has provided the funding for many of the necessary public works and major projects. During the Tanaka premiership in the early 1970s these large-scale projects were used to consolidate the power of the ruling faction of the LDP in the regions, but specific support for the regions is now much reduced.

Political issues

Electoral reform Efforts to reform the electoral system and prevent clashes between members of the same party in multi-seat constituencies have so far failed. The desire of many – especially the opposition parties – to eliminate the imbalance between the rural and urban constituencies also remains unfulfilled; Prime Minister Nakasone introduced a bill for the reform of constituencies, following the adverse court rulings in 1983, but dropped it for lack of support from his own party.

Campaign funds Enormous sums – $1–4m – are spent in trying to win a seat in an election. This encourages corruption and factionalism; candidates needing cash are recruited by party factions. The ties of money are strong, and attempts at reform have been unsuccessful. The Recruit corruption scandal in 1989 brought down the government (see *Party politics*).

Defence The anti-military consensus in Japan is under pressure from the USA, which feels that Japan should contribute more to its own defence. Voluntary restraints keep spending low, but the issue is at the forefront of political debate (see *International alignments* and *National security*).

Finance The significant upward revaluation of the yen since 1985 has had a mildly depressive effect on the economy. There is conflict between those who wish to reflate the economy and more conservative elements wishing to cut the government budget deficit.

Internationalism For a major economic power, Japan has only limited interest in international affairs; domestic issues are paramount with the electorate.

Party politics

Japan's political parties are all relatively recent creations, the results of mergers and breakaways. The main interest centres on the factional infighting of the Liberal Democratic Party, which has been in power since its formation. Opposition is weak and divided, though the better showing of the socialists in the 1989 House of Councillors elections suggests that this may be changing. The LDP rarely uses its majority to force through unpopular legislation. Here, as elsewhere in Japanese life, consensus is of the essence, and opposition parties can wield power by boycotting, or threatening to boycott, Diet proceedings; a suitable compromise is usually arranged.

Liberal Democratic Party

A merger of the Japan Democratic Party with the Liberal Party in 1955 led to the formation of the LDP, which is particularly strong in the over-weighted rural constituencies. Its politics are broadly conservative.
Factionalism From the first, the LDP has been a collection of competing factions based on key political personalities. The factions have changed over the years but remain a central element, influencing the election of the party president (i.e. the prime minister), the appointment of ministers and party officials, and the selection of candidates in national elections. This factionalism encourages nepotism and corruption. On the plus side it lends the party a chameleon quality, enabling it to change its stance and leaders to adapt to shifts in the mood of the electorate.
The factions There are five main factions. The two largest, the Takeshita and Suzuki factions, are known as the mainstream factions. The others are named after Nakasone, Fukuda and Komoto. The factions are not ideologically based; rather they depend on ties of loyalty, marriage and cash. They are the money-brokers, collecting cash from party supporters and disbursing it to candidates.
Nakasone – winner yet loser It is ironic that having led the LDP to a landslide victory in 1986, Nakasone found his position weakened by the resurgence of the Tanaka faction,

which won sufficient seats to make it by far the largest. When ill-health removed Mr Tanaka from politics, Noboru Takeshita succeeded him, defeating the other principal contenders, Shintaro Abe, the former foreign affairs minister, and Minister of Finance Kiichi Miyazawa. In 1989, all of the powerful LDP leaders were hit by the Recruit company scandal, in which a commercial company allegedly gave them, their family or aides, discounted shares in the hope of political favours. Prime Minister Takeshita was obliged to resign in favour of a lesser-known figure, who in turn resigned after allegations concerning his private life. Toshiki Kaifu was appointed Prime Minister in August 1989.

The Japan Socialist Party

The JSP was born of a merger of many diverse elements. It was the majority party in 1947 and led the subsequent coalition government which was brought down by dissenters within the JSP's own ranks. After 1947 it went downhill in electoral terms, though remaining the largest of the opposition parties progressively losing support in the large cities and having increasingly to rely on support from the small town and country constituencies.
Union party The trade unions have a strong control over the JSP. The Sohyo union group, the largest in Japan, contributes 75% of party funds.
Policies Although it is traditionally a

Marxist-Leninist party, its erstwhile leader Masashi Ishibashi attempted to move the JSP towards the middle ground. It remains committed to "unarmed neutrality" and would scrap Japan's defence forces.

New leader Despite Mr Ishibashi's policy changes, the JSP continued to lose seats. Only under his successor, Takako Doi, the first woman party leader in Japan, did the JSP begin to stage a comeback, winning seats at the Liberal Democrats' expense in the 1989 House of Councillors election. While meeting resistance from the unions and left-wingers, she offered voters a very moderate version of socialism.

Komeito
Also known as the Clean Government Party, the Komeito grew out of the Soka Gakkai, a group linked to the Shoshu Buddhist sect. Since its formation in 1964, the Komeito has established itself as the second largest opposition party and would be a key element of any opposition coalition. Its highly disciplined organization prevents the factionalism apparent in the other political parties.

Turning its back on Buddha The Komeito has publicly distanced itself from the Soka Gakkai during the last 15 years, though strong links remain. The Komeito began as an anti-corruption party with leftish leanings, but has shifted ground to the middle of the road. It supports small businesses and is concerned with local improvements, especially in the inner city areas where its main strength lies.

Japan Communist Party
Efficiently organized at the grass-roots level and soundly financed, the Japan Communist Party is the most extreme of all parties, with a Marxist-Leninist philosophy and links with the Soviet Union. For many years its existence was turbulent, marked by mass arrests and subsequently a purging of its leadership by the American Occupation forces, as well as by internal divisions. The JCP reached its zenith in 1972 when it was the second largest opposition party. The prospects for political influence are small, except for the nuisance value of its strong rump in the Diet. Opposition parties have kept their distance, due both to a strong ideological distaste and to a belief that future election prospects would be damaged by any connection or cooperation.

Democratic Socialist Party
Formed in a right-wing breakaway from the Japan Socialist Party in 1960, the DSP soon gained, and kept, the backing of the Domei, the second-largest union group. Despite this, the party has never made much of an impact.

United Social Democratic Party
The smallest of the opposition parties to have made any impact at all, the USDP was formed in 1978, through defections of moderates within the JSP. The subsequent right-ward shift of the JSP has left the USDP isolated, and its role will continue to diminish.

Future possibilities
A coalition of the JSP, the Democratic Socialists and the Komeito – a possibility striven for by the parties concerned for over 10 years – represents the only alternative to a continuation of LDP rule, and then only if the LDP continues to be dogged by scandal and factional rivalry.

State of the parties
(after July 1989 elections)

	Representatives	Councillors
LDP	295	109
JSP	85	72
Komeito	55	21
JCP	27	14
DSP	28	10
Others	72	6
Total	512*	251

* including vacant seats

The reins of power

Power in Japan is highly centralized, a coalition between the LDP, the ministry bureaucrats and "big business" (see *Power in business*). Business provides considerable funds to the LDP, although its power is not as great as might be expected, due to the demands of the many sectional interests on which the LDP is electorally dependent.

The prime minister's power

The power vested in the prime minister by the constitution is tempered by the political realities of the LDP. In his appointment of ministers, for example, he is restricted by the need to please all the factional interests. The same restraints apply to any attempts to force unpopular legislation through the Diet. The biennial elections for party leader prevent any individual from building a significant power-base.

The power of ministers

Ministers derive their power from their position in the party rather than from their ministry. Most serve only for a year, and even those who last longer rarely stamp their authority on the ministry. The prime minister rotates available ministerial posts in order to balance factional elements within the government, and to reward loyalty and repay political debts.

A few charismatic leaders are able to tie the interests of their various ministries to their own political ambitions, but most ministers take advantage of their positions only to repay favours in their constituencies. Agriculture and Construction are among the most prized "pork barrel" ministries.

The power of the ministries

While the prime minister appoints the ministers and parliamentary vice-ministers, the ministries make appointments below this level. The ministers' and prime minister's power in setting policy is thus severely restricted.

The Agriculture and Education Ministries are most closely controlled by the LDP, while the Ministry of Finance and MITI are the most independent – and powerful.

Centres of power Postwar constitutional reforms have done little to break the power of the civil service. The bureaucrats are largely responsible for drafting legislation, controlling budgets and setting policies.

Ministry power struggles

The main struggles for political power in Japan are those within and between the ministries.

Internal factions Within the ministries, each year's intake from Tokyo University forms a faction that struggles to achieve the positions of section chief and, ultimately, administrative vice-minister (the senior civil servant). The personnel chief may use his position to improve the chances of contemporaries by moving promising members of other classes into unpromising positions.

Culling the old Promotion up to section chief is based on a strict system of seniority. In some ministries only one member of the same entering class can become vice-minister, all the others being asked to resign. This early retirement, coupled with low pension provisions, leaves bureaucrats free and willing to enter industry or commerce (see *Government and business*), as well as public corporations or politics.

Brother against brother Struggles between the individual ministries can be severe as they attempt to extend their responsibilities. Even ostensibly independent agencies, such as the Economic Planning Agency and the Science and Technology Agency, are battlegrounds where the ministries fight to control certain key appointments. Many of the main claims have already been staked out, but changes in the industrial and economic structure are opening up new avenues for rivalry.

Key ministries

Ministry of Finance Employing 76,000, this is the most powerful of the ministries, with a key role in the function of government, and is run by an enormously influential clique of arch-conservatives. Its most important role is the preparation and implementation of the national budget. Negotiations with other ministries and with the Cabinet and LDP members concerning the precise allocations lead sometimes to changes designed to accommodate special interests. Control of the budget gives the Ministry of Finance considerable influence over other ministries.

Dedicated to a policy of fiscal austerity, and exercising direct control of interest rates and the financial and banking systems, it plays the dominant role in deciding the extent of liberalization of the financial sector.

Ministry of International Trade and Industry MITI's financial structure gives it a greater independence from the Ministry of Finance than that of any other ministry. Despite receiving only a small part of the budget, it has been instrumental in setting the direction of Japan's postwar economic development. In this function, its control of a number of key public corporations, such as the Export-Import Bank and the Japan Development Bank, were crucial, as was its control of the foreign exchange budget in the 1960s.

More recently it has concentrated on the reorganization of dying industries. However, its power has waned slightly as the private sector has placed less reliance on help from government.

Ministry of Foreign Affairs This is not as important in Japan as in most industrialized countries, reflecting Japan's concentration on domestic affairs. It has a low budget and a small staff.

Bureaucrats in government

The ministries' hold over government has been assisted by the number of their members who have entered politics. As many as one-third of LDP Diet members at a time have been former career bureaucrats, and many of the postwar prime ministers have been ex-ministry officials.

Paradoxically, in recent years this trend has tended to weaken the hold of the bureaucracy over the legislature. Ex-bureaucrats in the Diet have made it more competent and confident about legislation. Instead of bills being drafted by the ministries, debated by the Diet and passed by the committees, more are being initiated by the politicians themselves on behalf of the interest groups they represent.

Additionally, the policy affairs councils of the LDP are growing more confident in making alterations to bills drafted by the civil service before they come up for debate.

Into the future

The liberalization of the economy and the growth of powerful independent industrial corporations have weakened the control of the ministries, especially in the case of MITI. The authoritarian style of government in Japan has moderated, reflecting the changed circumstances of the country itself. At the same time, less respect is accorded the civil service now than formerly, and the politicians' argument that their public accountability justifies their taking on more responsibility is gaining strength.

Considerable power is nevertheless retained by the ministries, although pressures on them have increased from all sides. The prime minister and the Cabinet have improved their own position in the decision-making process but must still share power with the bureaucracy.

International alignments

Alignment with the USA was thrust upon Japan by the realities of defeat and occupation. More recently this policy has been fuelled by a desire to match the world's major economic power. While relations with China have improved since its split with the USSR, those with the Soviet Union remain distant. Perhaps Japan's largest international problem is its success in Western markets, which leads to friction with the USA and the European Community.

The United States

With US help Japan rebuilt its economy after the war and was accepted back into the international community. The USA is Japan's largest trading partner, and it provides vital defence cover. However, traditional US industries have suffered from Japanese competition, and trade imbalances in Japan's favour have led the Americans to apply pressure on Japan to open up her home markets. Anti-Japanese feeling sometimes runs high in the States, but the strategic value of US bases in Japan militates against a permanent rift.

The Soviet Union

No peace treaty has been signed following World War II, but the two countries maintain diplomatic relations. These can be rather strained due to the USSR's annexation in 1945 of the four small Kurile Islands nearest to Japan. Siberian raw materials and Japanese technology seem made for each other, but it is difficult to see the USSR giving up its bases on the Kuriles. A more enlightened Soviet leadership could change the nature of Asian politics and make Japan less dependent on the USA.

China

Japan's long-standing adversary, China, was recently, for a few years, its second largest trading partner but now ranks fifth; a formal peace and friendship treaty was signed in 1978. China's response to growing imbalances in trade – unilateral cancellation of contracts – has caused some friction. Memories of Japanese aggression fuel Chinese suspicion of Japan.

ASEAN

Japan has endeavoured to take the lead in the Pacific Basin, although a formal concept has yet to evolve. A third of Japan's foreign aid goes to the six nations in ASEAN, to which it also lends diplomatic and technological support. However, Japan's tendency to discriminate against manufactured exports in favour of ASEAN's raw materials causes some resentment.

Europe

With no strategic links between Japan and Europe, relations centre around trade, which has proved a constant source of tension. Japan has come to terms with individual countries, in some cases voluntarily restricting its exports; with the EC as a whole, however, growing trade imbalances have led to conflicts in GATT. Nothing less than Japan setting and meeting an increased import target is likely to satisfy the Community, but frictions have been eased by Japanese manufacturing investment in the EC.

International acceptance

Japan has progressively re-entered the international community through its membership of the UN, IMF, GATT, and OECD. Within the UN, it has not taken the leading role its economic status would suggest, and although it participates fully in the international economic community – it is the second largest subscriber to the World Bank – its continual trade surpluses have put it at odds with fellow members of GATT.

National security

Japan's national security is highly dependent on US assistance. The defence forces, restricted by low government spending levels, would not be sufficient to repulse any serious military attack on Japan.

Constitutional constraints

The postwar constitution explicitly stated that Japan would "forever renounce war as a sovereign right of the nation and the threat or use of force as a means of settling international disputes." In addition, Japan, with its unique experience of nuclear warfare, adopted in 1967 its three non-nuclear principles, stating that it would never produce, possess, or allow to be introduced any nuclear weapons.

Defence

Japan's self defence forces were created from the Police Reserve Force in 1954. Since then the LDP has continued a policy of limited non-nuclear defence under the US nuclear umbrella. Currently the self defence forces have 155,000 personnel in the Ground Force and 44,000 each in the Air and Maritime forces. There are also 55,000 US servicemen, stationed at two naval bases, two air bases and at the marine base on the island of Okinawa.

Civilian control The self defence forces are administered by the Defence Agency (not by a ministry – an indication of their lesser status), which is composed of civilians. The three services are run individually and take orders only from the Cabinet.

Self-imposed limits Pacifism runs deep in Japan, and despite US pressure the LDP had (until 1986) kept spending within a limit of 1% of GNP. With Japan's GNP being so high this still amounts to a substantial sum – the sixth largest military budget in the world. Defence spending restrictions and a ban on the export of weapons have prevented the emergence of a defence industry. The USA acquires much of Japan's defence-linked technology under the security treaty, making Japan an R&D annex to the US military-industrial complex.

Intelligence services

In the early postwar years Japan relied heavily on US intelligence to counter Soviet, and later Chinese and North Korean, infiltration and subversion. However, a country with no offensive military forces and no defence ministry cannot be thought of as having any secrets; and it is not illegal for foreign nationals to collect military information in Japan, unless it relates to US equipment.

There are several agencies with their own independent intelligence services – the Ministry of Justice, the Defence Agency and the Police Agency, among others – but no secret service as such. The uncovering of a Soviet spy ring in 1980 led to the leader, a naval officer, being charged with the theft of official papers and receiving the maximum possible sentence – one year's imprisonment.

The police

Japan has an exceptionally low crime rate. The police force is very efficient and fairly large, with one officer to every 30 households. Each prefecture runs its own force, and all are coordinated by the Police Agency.

There are around 35,000 far-left activists in Japan. In 1986 there was renewed activity by the Chukakuha (Core faction), who made token rocket attacks on the Tokyo Economic Summit. Narita airport, the site of riots in the early 1970s, is being expanded, and a resurgence of trouble is expected. However, the crack national anti-riot police rarely let any situation get out of control, and the strict security at Narita makes it one of the world's safest airports.

The Business Scene

Government and business

Government and business are closely allied in Japan. The post-war dominance of the government in aiding and directing industrial recovery and development with subsidy, regulation, market protection and binding advice (known as administrative guidance) is beginning to give way to a more liberal and equitable situation.

Elected politicians

The LDP has kept itself in power by ensuring an atmosphere in which business could prosper. Money talks in Japanese politics, and business has provided the funds that support the LDP (and, to a lesser extent, the main opposition parties too). Not only does the leadership strive to support business as a whole, but individual members of the Diet repay those companies who have supported them by speaking up for industrial interests and pressure groups, especially those based in their home constituencies. Scandals occasionally erupt when politicians go too far, but successive attempts to rid the Japanese body politic of the influence of big money have been half-hearted and ineffective.

Support from Keidanren and Keizai Doyukai (see *Power in business*) for impending legislation is important. If the business community objects to proposed legislation, its criticisms are usually heeded.

The public sector The government is progressively privatizing a number of state corporations. In 1985 Japan Salt and Tobacco and Nippon Telephone and Telegraph were privatized, after strong US pressure on Japan to liberalize markets. Privatization Japanese-style is a slow process, with the government taking up the whole of the share issue and releasing it onto the market in stages.

Japan National Railways, under its new name of Japan Railways (JR), was privatized in April 1987 and split into seven independent operating companies.

The civil service

State control over the economy has been exercised largely through the ministries, particularly MITI and the Ministry of Finance and, in the agricultural sector, the Ministry of Agriculture and Forestry. Administrative guidance has been backed up by financial controls and subsidies. Influence, rather than direct action, remains the preferred method. In recent years the success of the economy and gradual de-regulation have reduced the ability of government to direct business.

Negative assistance Besides receiving direct help from MITI and the Ministry of Finance, Japan's industry has been helped in the past by other ministries' erection of obstacles to foreign products. Foremost among these has been the Ministry of Health and Welfare, which is responsible for setting testing standards for all imported foods, drugs and chemicals. Its refusal to accept foreign test results, insisting on replication in Japan and setting standards different from those pertaining worldwide, allowed local industry to get established, though here too attitudes and practices are changing.

Monopoly legislation Based on US anti-trust laws, this was introduced in the Anti-Monopoly Act of 1947, amended in 1953 and toughened in 1977. The act is enforced by the Fair Trade Commission (FTC) which, like other Japanese government departments, has quasi-judicial and quasi-legislative powers. Its administrative guidance must be adhered to.

There is no strong anti-monopoly tradition in Japan; indeed MITI encouraged co-operation and mergers to strengthen the world trading position of Japanese companies. The 1977 amendment, though, permits the FTC to break up companies with more than a 50% share of a market, or two companies with more than a 75% share. This tough line is seldom taken, since any break-up has to be made with the co-operation of MITI.

The FTC is also empowered to outlaw mergers that seek to restrain competition or to threaten national security, public order and safety, or the running of the economy. Although there are still areas where cartels are possible, even encouraged, heavy fines can be imposed on companies guilty of parallel pricing.

Bureaucrats in business
Amakudari, or "descent from heaven," describes the practice of bureaucrats from government ministries taking up senior management positions in private industry on their retirement. The considerable licensing and approval authority of the ministries is one reason why companies are prepared to accept and even embrace this practice. Contracts and awards are often made to those companies with ex-bureaucrats on the board.
Contacts In Japan many of the top politicians, bureaucrats and senior executives are graduates of Tokyo University. Informal meetings with former classmates add another dimension to communications between business and government.

Aid and subsidies
The era when the government disbursed large sums of money through MITI for the promotion of industry in general and exports in particular is over. JETRO, the arm of MITI concerned with external trade, is now principally concerned with the promotion of imports (see *Market entry*). Current government aid to industry, in the form of long-term low-interest loans and the reduction or deferral of taxation, as well as direct subsidy, is limited to specific industries and certain areas to ease the process of restructuring. It is not used to prop up "lame duck" industries.

Legislation drafted by MITI seeks to create hi-tech industrial centres in rural areas, by providing sites, discretionary funding and other incentives, especially for priority industries such as those related to energy conservation, pollution control and biotechnology. Tax exemption is granted on real estate sales to any firm moving from central Tokyo.

Long-term low-interest loans are available from the Japan Development Bank; again, rural developments are favoured, as are urban renewal, hi-tech industries and energy projects.
Local government The prefectures have joined forces with MITI's Industrial Location Guidance Division to promote decentralization by sponsoring tours for foreign companies and media. More than half of Japan's 47 prefectures offer packages of subsidies to foreign firms setting up factories or offices (see *Other sources of finance*).

Unravelling the bureaucracy
Japanese government ministries operate like independent fiefdoms, competing with each other for influence. Public rows between ministries are not uncommon. The bureaucracy is labyrinthine, but Japanese officials are at least approachable. The key level is *kacho* (section head); it is here that policy is formulated. Foreign companies wanting background on their own fields will find that English-language publications such as the *MITI Handbook* and *Organization of the Government of Japan* provide, in most cases, the basic information for identifying the contact point. These publications and others are available from Japanese embassies and offices of JETRO worldwide.

Power in business

Power in the post-war Japanese business community is concentrated in four main organizations: the Keidanren, Keizai Doyukai, Nikkeiren and Nissho. Representing the business community's interests, they put pressure on the LDP, on government ministries and on labour. They are also influential in trade discussions with other countries.

The zaikai

The power brokers of the Japanese financial and business world are known collectively as the *zaikai* (*zai* meaning "money", and *kai* meaning "world"). Its members are the top management of the major industrial and financial corporations.

The pre-war *zaibatsu* – Mitsubishi, Mitsui, Sumitomo and others – were disbanded during the US occupation but form the basis of the post-war *keiretsu gaisha* (see *The business framework*). The pre-war generation of business leaders was for the most part purged, and a new generation took the helm to guide Japan's post-war industrial success. Their views are still highly valued, and they remain in positions of influence, sitting on government advisory committees and policy-making bodies well into their 70s and 80s.

Power and influence The *zaikai*'s power is based on generous funds, personal connections between themselves and with politicians and bureaucrats, and organizational muscle. The four main business organizations – Keidanren, Keizai Doyukai, Nikkeiren and Nissho – exert considerable influence on the government's policy decisions. Part of their role is to encourage politicians to guard the capitalist system. To this end they channel hefty donations to political parties, mainly the LDP .

Overseas diplomacy As part of the establishment, *zaikai* leaders have regular breakfast meetings with LDP leaders, sit on government councils and meet visiting world leaders. A network of committees and conferences keeps them in touch with overseas business leaders, especially the Americans. Senior *zaikai* members often lead government-instigated missions abroad.

Tax reform The *zaikai* were strong supporters of the tax reforms introduced in April 1989 (see *The nation's finances*), including the 3% consumption tax and (not surprisingly) the reduction of corporate and income taxes. Nissho initially opposed the introduction of a new indirect tax, fearing its effects on the small businesses it represents, but was won over by government concessions on the scope of the new tax.

Keidanren

The Federation of Economic Organizations (Keidanren) is the most powerful of the business organizations and acts as the headquarters of the business community. Its members are the major trade associations as well as prominent companies in virtually all fields of industry and commerce. Its organizational strength revolves around 48 standing committees, which address specific problems, and a full-time secretariat of 170 people.

Objectives Keidanren's role, first, is that of a pressure group representing the business community's interests. Second, it undertakes private-level diplomacy to resolve international problems in conjunction with similar business organizations overseas. And third, it acts as the business community's public relations office, to inform both the Japanese public and overseas opinion.

Its PR arm – the Keizai Koho Center – organizes seminars, sponsors TV programmes, conducts surveys, advertises in the press, organizes speakers at international conferences and publishes numerous magazines and booklets in both Japanese and English.

Policies Recognizing that any moves to shut Japan out of foreign markets would do great damage to its members and to the economy as a whole, Keidanren has been at the forefront of pressure to open Japan's markets to imports of manufactured goods and to ease trade friction with other countries. On the home front Keidanren is lobbying for cuts in government expenditure, simplified formalities for obtaining government approval, privatization and flexible implementation of anti-monopoly policy.

New leaders Age and seniority are considered great assets in Japanese business. Yoshihiro Inayama, honorary chairman of Nippon Steel, was 82 when he stepped down as chairman of Keidanren in May 1986 after his third two-year term. The current chairman, Eishiro Saito, honorary chairman of Nippon Steel, took his place at the age of 74.

Keizai Doyukai

The Japan Committee for Economic Development (Keizai Doyukai) was formed in 1946. Its two distinguishing features are, first, that its members are individuals rather than corporations and, second, that it is a policy-oriented organization. Its 1,000-plus members are mainly managing directors, chairmen or presidents of big corporations.

Objectives It acts as a forum for *individual* views on the economy and on management philosophy, addressing itself to medium- and long-term structural problems. It has long-standing ties with overseas economic organizations and regularly dispatches study missions abroad. Since its members are individuals, Keizai Doyukai sometimes submits proposals and reports that conflict with the majority of the business community and the government.

Policies Keizai Doyukai believes strongly in the free enterprise system, advocates liberalization of trade and capital in Japan, and is much concerned with lessening international trade friction.

A new engine The present chairman is Takashi Ishihara, also chairman of Nissan Motor. His main task has been to revitalize a once progressive but ageing organization.

Nikkeiren

The Japan Federation of Employers' Associations (Nikkeiren) represents employers' interests in the fields of labour and wage negotiations. It was set up in 1948 to counteract the growing strength of the union movement. Through prefectural and trade associations it represents over 30,000 companies which employ around 30% of the workforce. Its president is Eiji Suzuki, chairman of Mitsubishi Chemical Industries.

Objectives With the more peaceful labour situation in Japan since the 1960s, Nikkeiren has softened its stance towards labour. It now aims to improve management-labour relations through social education of employers, corporate training of workers and publicity for employers' policies.

Advisory role Nikkeiren is campaigning to keep average wage increases in line with productivity improvements. It does not negotiate directly with workers but issues guidelines on wages and conditions which, set alongside union recommendations, are influential in the annual wage negotiations.

Nissho

The Japan Chamber of Commerce and Industry (Nissho) is a federation of nearly 500 local chambers of commerce and industry. Established in 1878, it is the oldest and biggest business organization with 11,000 staff and branches overseas.

Objectives Nissho not only represents its chambers but acts on behalf of the small- and medium-size business sector. Its views are therefore not always in line with those of Keidanren, representing big business. Its chairman is Rokuro Ishikawa, chairman of Kajima Corporation.

The business framework

The Western executive approaching the Japanese market is faced with daunting paradoxes. High-profile, traditional corporate structures intimidate with their behind-the-scenes deals, yet there is a profusion of non-corporate enterprises competing in a more familiar fashion. Great stress seems to be laid on non-aggressive business conduct, yet competition is patently ferocious, both domestically and internationally.

Company size

The high-profile empires are the exception. Most of Japan's 6m businesses are small, though a large proportion of them are linked directly or indirectly to the corporate sector. Some 30% of Japanese workers are engaged in long-term employment in the highly productive, high-technology industries for which Japan is best known. The other 70% have a far lower degree of security as employees of smaller, less efficient operations offering few of the financial and social benefits of the well-known corporations. About 75% of businesses have fewer than 100 employees, whereas the ten largest each employ more than 40,000.

Corporate attitudes

Japanese attitudes towards takeovers differ radically from those in the West, where the large fish gobble up the small fish as fast as they can, and with impunity. Among Japanese companies, the hostile takeover is considered immoral. It is fiercely resisted on the rare occasions when it does occur. Friendly mergers and acquisitions do, however, take place to save companies from bankruptcy.

The same moral imperatives that restrain takeovers also inhibit Japanese companies from headhunting one another's key employees. These attitudes are part of the traditional values which still regard the company as a human community rather than a mere legal entity or set of assets. Private companies have public-service ethics. *Competition* can be fierce – but a sense of balance and restraint should not be lost. Opponents are not to be destroyed, and litigation is avoided

except as a last resort (see *The law*). "Face" is an intrinsic factor in business success. Bankruptcy involves a heavy loss of face and is avoided at all costs among major companies. There is nevertheless a high bankruptcy rate among small businesses.

Company ownership

The structure of company ownership is much more internal than in the West, with finance coming predominantly from borrowing and reinvestment of profits. Borrowing on the capital markets as a source of finance is increasing. Shares are allotted to employees rather than floated on the market. Some 80% of quoted firms prefer to generate share capital in this way, so that in a real sense the company is run by and belongs to its members. For example, in what the president of the zip manufacturer YKK calls the "cycle of goodness," the firm's employees deposit 10% of their wages in return for shares. Dividends are low: partly for tax reasons, Japanese investors look for capital growth rather than dividend income.

Large individual shareholdings within a company are rare. Even in family corporations like Matsushita and Honda, the founding fathers hold less than 5%, and only one in 30 companies has a shareholder with more than 10% of the equity.

The AGM is a speedy formality lasting on average less than an hour. Despite changes in the law in 1982 designed to outlaw the practice, some companies still hire *sokaiya*, heavies with nominal shareholdings, whose job is to shout down the queries of troublesome shareholders at the annual meeting. Individual shareholders, who hold just under 25% of all shares, exert little influence.

Japan's "dual economy"

A salient feature of Japan's economy is the interdependence of the highly visible corporate sector and the less publicly visible small businesses which service them on a subcontract basis – the so-called "dual economy." The Japanese categorize businesses according to differences not only in size of capitalization and workforce, but also in their terms and conditions of employment, the source of their finance, and their public standing.

Large corporations About a quarter of the labour force works for the *dai kigyo*. These are the 1% of businesses employing more than 500 workers. (See *The Japanese at work* and *Corporate hierarchies* for aspects of the corporate psyche.)

Medium and small firms Known as the *chu-sho kigyo*, these companies are the ones in which probably the greatest initiatives and risks are taken. Future Sonys or Hondas begin here. The grouping includes entrepreneurial operations designed to exploit gaps in the market not yet filled by the big corporations.

Often with fewer than 100 employees, *chu-sho kigyo* provide the contractors and subcontractors so essential to the efficiency of the major manufacturers. Unlike the big corporations, these smaller firms are usually non-unionized and do not offer the security of lifetime employment.

In the automobile industry the majors depend on the small business sector to manufacture and supply parts for the highly successful "just in time" (JIT) delivery system, thereby saving warehouse costs and over-stocking problems, as well as reducing the payroll. Space is at a premium in Japan. Firms such as Nissan and Toyota have even exported the JIT system to their overseas operations.

Japanese cars contain about 70% bought-in parts, compared with 50% in the US industry. Quality control is achieved by close cooperation between manufacturer and parts supplier right through the product design and development stages. Some majors have strong equity positions in their key suppliers, and some firms, such as Toyota, even share research facilities with suppliers. Staff visit one another's plants, and there are regular joint meetings.

Although small and medium-sized businesses provide the cutting edge in high technology, their existence is precarious. Bankruptcy rates are higher and credit notes longer as their size diminishes.

Family enterprises The smallest businesses of all, making up 80% of the total, are the *rei-sai kigyo* or family enterprises. These are often registered as public companies, though they may have fewer than ten employees. Family firms dominate retail distribution.

Corporate networks

Cartels are an integral aspect of business in Japan. They are well established and usually legitimate, since neither the government nor the business community accepts the idea of free competition as understood in the USA and Europe (see *Government and business*). Japanese traditions call for a high degree of collusion and collective action, often under the state's leadership.

The automobile and steel industries serve as classic examples of market bypassing. They make periodic agreements dividing up steel demand between a limited number of steel producers in negotiated proportions, at pre-agreed prices. Outsiders have no chance to tender.

Industrial groups These are the descendants of the prewar *zaibatsu* groupings (see *Power in business*). The present-day groups, known as *keiretsu gaisha*, are generally based around a trading company (*sogo shosha* – see below) and a major bank, and have associated companies in a wide range of industries.

Each major company holds equity in several of the others, both directly and through others in the group, although the individual percentages are small, often in the order of 3–5%. Traditionally, the banking member has exerted considerable influence as the major source of finance for most of the group's members, but this situation is gradually changing as bonds replace bank finance.

The relationships among the members of a group are often flexible enough to allow alliances between members of different groups, particularly on large-scale deals and overseas business. However, the inertia and set trading patterns of the powerful groups can prove inefficient because they hinder competition and make it difficult for newcomers to break into a market that is carved up among entrenched interests.

The sogo shosha

The general trading companies known as *sogo shosha* are a major force in Japanese industry and commerce. The largest of them are Mitsubishi Corporation, Mitsui & Co, C. Itoh & Co, Marubeni Corporation, Sumitomo Corporation, Nissho Iwai Corporation, Tomen, Kanematsu-Gosho, and Nichimen. Between them they handle more than half of all Japanese trade, internal and external.

The *sogo shosha* are the traditional corporate go-betweens, purchasing raw materials and selling them on to manufacturers, buying back the manufactured products and selling them into the distribution chain, and acting as matchmaker and often partner in business deals.

Company types

Public limited liability company (*kabushiki kaisha* or kk). This is the most popular form of incorporation among Japanese and foreign firms. Seven promoters put up a minimum Y350,000 and form a board consisting of at least three directors and a statutory auditor.

Private limited companies (*yugen gaisha*) are generally very small family businesses. They have a maximum of 50 company members, each with limited liability, and require only one director. Minimum capital is Y100,000. Foreign firms rarely opt for this form because of its small-business image.

In 1989 the Diet was debating legislation to increase minimum capital requirements to Y20m for a *kabushiki kaisha* and to Y5m for a *yugen gaisha*.

Partnership companies may have either limited (*goshi gaisha*) or unlimited liability (*gomei gaisha*). Neither form is widely used by foreign businesses. There is no partnership law and few relevant provisions in the Civil Code.

Sole proprietorships (*hitori kaisha*) are uncommon, but are found among small retail outlets. They have high tax rates and a "small" image.

Self-employment (*jiei gyosha*) is very common, especially among professionals, and is an option for foreigners in service industries, though not usually for those in professions, due to legal restrictions.

Establishing a presence

The process of establishing a presence in Japan entails careful study. Companies planning to set up in Japan should seek expert advice from international accountancy and consultancy firms.

Foreign exchange controls and legal barriers to direct investment from overseas are no longer problems, but the prospective entrant needs to choose the correct business "face."

A liaison office (*renraku jimusho*) is not much more than a local base and mail drop. It is a useful – and tax-free – presence but must be registered. Its temporary nature makes local recruitment difficult, and swift upgrading is recommended.

A branch office (*shiten*) is a step up, but still regarded as temporary. The registration fee is Y30,000, and the

legal costs Y400,000–750,000. Bank and securities companies require Ministry of Finance licences. Expect close scrutiny by the tax authorities.
Joint ventures ease problems of language, bureaucracy and market complexity. Pioneered by leading multinationals such as Xerox and Union Carbide, joint ventures are increasingly used by smaller firms in commercial and consumer services. Problems include incompatibility of partners' long-term objectives, and difficulty in attracting good staff.
The wholly owned subsidiary (genchi hojin) is the most permanent form of presence in the market and in time can lead to almost complete localization. Costs are considerable, and time lags from investment to profit are long. With all-Japanese staff and Japanese business methods, *genchi hojin* can be attractive employers for the growing numbers of Japanese educated abroad, who may find it hard to fit into a major Japanese company.

Checking possible partners

Investigating a potential partner can be difficult, especially since much of the published material is available only in Japanese, but thorough investigation and then protracted negotiation are essential.
Embassy commercial departments in Tokyo not only have good, current information on many Japanese companies but can put you in touch with clients who have dealt with the companies and with the relevant trade associations.
Overseas chambers of commerce in Tokyo are also a good source of similar information and contacts. JETRO can also help.
Private investigators (koshinsho) and *"research officers" (chosa jimusho)* will go beyond public information – as they do when investigating possible marriage partners.
City banks will provide substantial amounts of key information about companies they are linked with through the *keiretsu gaisha* system if

they scent new business from you. A foreign company's own bank is also a good source of information.
Company directories are a good source of publicly available information, since companies are legally required to disclose detailed information on their finances (see *Business media*). It is however of little use writing direct to Japanese companies, as they rarely respond to unsolicited letters. Introductions should be sought through the intermediaries suggested above.

Legal considerations

Incorporation normally takes one month from the completion of all paperwork, which is entirely in Japanese. Articles of association for public companies need to conform to a highly standardized format to pass official scrutiny. Incorporation of a public company will cost Y1–2m in legal fees and Y500,000 or 0.7% of paid-in capital for registration.

Japanese firms have no company secretaries or treasurers, but statutory auditors instead. Large companies must have two, as well as independent auditors.

Financial considerations

Although accounting principles are broadly similar to American ones, tax returns must effectively be prepared by Japanese accountants. Dealing with tax officials is an arcane art beyond the skills of all but local tax specialists (see *Accountants*).

Tax authorities are strict about accepting deductions for bad debts; depreciation rates are much slower (an office building depreciates over 60 years). There is no allowance for capital gains; gains from the sale of property can be taxed at 65–70%.

From 1 April 1989 the basic rate of corporation tax was reduced from 42% to 40%. A further reduction to 37.5% was due from April 1990. Allowances for business entertainment decline as the capital size of a company increases (zero above Y50m).

Employment

Japan's much-vaunted system of lifetime employment and paternalistic labour relations is still generally true for regular employees in major companies, although it does not apply throughout Japanese industry, nor has it always been a feature of Japanese employment practice. Demographic pressures (with the ageing of the Japanese population), the need for greater diversity and flexibility in business operations, and changes in employees' expectations are all exerting pressures for change. A greater degree of job mobility is emerging, though this is nowhere near Western levels and changing jobs in mid-career is still unusual and slightly suspect. Following some slackness in the labour market in the economic slowdown of 1985-86, the economic recovery and improved business prospects from mid-1987 led to increased job openings, larger numbers in work and falling unemployment. The Ministry of Labour predicts that by the year 2000 Japan could be experiencing a shortage of nearly 1m workers.

Employment patterns

Japan's employed labour force totals just over 60m, of whom 60% are male and 40% female. The proportion of women and of temporary and part-time employees (often one and the same) is increasing faster than the overall growth in the workforce. Foreigners occupy a very tiny fraction of the total workforce, although some Japanese companies now have a policy of recruiting more foreign staff at managerial level. Skill shortages are forcing a review of Japan's closed-door policy towards migrant workers from other Asian countries.

Japan's unemployment rate reached a peak of 3.1% in May 1987, but has since fallen back to around 2.5%. A number of factors keep unemployment low in Japan: economic growth and diversification, with companies moving into new areas of business as old lines become unprofitable, a high proportion of self-employed or family workers (18% of the workforce), high levels of hidden unemployment or underemployment, and the lifetime employment system which makes firms unwilling or unable to dispense with redundant workers (the latter are known as *madogiwa-zoku*, or those who sit by the window, with nothing much to do except read newspapers).

Japan's employment structure, like that of other industrialized countries, is gradually changing in favour of the service industries. About 58% are engaged in this sector, with 33% in manufacturing and 9% in agriculture, forestry and fisheries.

Recruitment

Prospective employers are ultimately more interested in character than in individual skills or hard-won academic qualifications. They are looking for people who will fit into the company "team" and make its goals and interests their own. For both parties, it is generally a lifetime commitment.

"Virgin" workers, who expect to be engaged for life, sit a company examination and attend interviews during the autumn recruitment drive, for vacancies becoming available in the following spring. Major companies have long practised *aota-gai* ("buying up the harvest before the season"), luring students into employment agreements well before graduation. The recruitment process may well include an investigation of the applicant's personal and family background which Westerners would find intrusive.

The *shin'nyu-shain*, or new employees, join their companies in

Pointers for prospective employers

Working for a foreign firm has until recently been regarded as mildly unpatriotic and risky. The higher salaries, faster promotion and greater responsibilities offered by foreign firms are not always enough to overcome the fear of being fired or left without a job if the company pulls out of Japan. Working for a foreign firm may spoil a worker's chances of getting a later job with a Japanese company.

Although "headhunting" is rare, and changing firms in mid-career can cost the Japanese considerable loss of lifetime earnings, a growing number of foreign firms are attracting specialists with a track record. This trend will develop as Japan's growing recruitment-services industry matures. In the current economic climate, major corporations are now seeking to place prematurely retired top executives – lifetime employees – with other companies. Foreign firms can also draw on the experience and invaluable contacts of retired civil servants. They have also tapped into Japan's great under-utilized resource: the female workforce.

Students returning to Japan after being educated overseas have fewer inhibitions about working for a foreign company. Many have excellent language and cross-cultural skills.

Foreign employers should take Japanese recruits back to home base for training. It enables them to understand better what the company is trying to do in Japan.

April. There are formal welcoming ceremonies at which the new recruits are instructed in the company ideals and what is expected of them. There follows a period of training –

including such subjects as how to address superiors and how to greet guests – during which the company spirit is inculcated, turning the recruits into model company men (or women). This is an important time for the new recruits, since those who joined the company together will move through the company as a cohort, developing strong personal ties but also, as some start to edge ahead of others, some rivalries.

Temporary workers have none of the privileges of lifetime staff and can be released at any time. It is they who bear the first brunt of any downturn in the company's fortunes.

Post-retirement applicants An increasingly important group are those workers over 55 who have been retired and who still wish – or, for financial reasons, need – to work, sometimes part-time, sometimes in a different field.

Agency recruitment is rarely used by large companies when seeking long-term staff, and speculative applications are uncommon. Personal recommendation is important for an applicant.

Employment legislation

The Labour Standards Law, Trade Union Law, Labour Relations Adjustment Law and Equal Employment Opportunities Law govern Japanese employment practices formally. Custom and convention determine attitudes and practice. In the matter of redundancies, for example, employers go to extraordinary lengths to avoid lay-offs, and when all else fails will attempt – often successfully – to place their workforce *en masse* with another company or an affiliate.

New employees are designated as either *permanent* or *temporary*. Permanent workers normally serve a 2–6 month probation, following which they are entitled by law or practice to expect lifetime employment unless their contract stipulates a specified period or they breach contract. Temporary staff have short-term contracts, which if renewed regularly could imply a lifetime obligation. Provided it is not contrary to the terms of an individual contract, dismissal with 30 days' notice or pay in lieu is legal, but it is very rare and is regarded as unethical.

Working hours
Annual working hours average 2,111 (including overtime), 500 more than in West Germany and 200 more than in the USA. Despite efforts and exhortations by the Japanese government to reduce working hours, partly in response to foreign criticism that "the Japanese work too hard," the number of hours worked by the average Japanese employee remains stubbornly high. There are various reasons for this: the reluctance of, in particular, small and medium-sized companies to introduce the five-day working week (though this is becoming the norm in the big companies), Japanese workers' apparent reluctance to take all the holidays due to them (on average they take only 50% of entitlement), and the preference of companies to regulate output through overtime rather than by lay-offs or new hirings.

Unions
Some 12.2m of Japan's 45m dependent employees belong to nearly 35,000 unions throughout Japan. Overall, numbers are about what they were when unions were helped back to their feet by postwar reforms. But the unions' inability to win substantial pay increases has brought the level of unionization down from 35% in 1975 to 26.8% in 1988. It is lower than in Western Europe, somewhat higher than in the USA.
Enterprise unions More than 90% of union members belong to enterprise, or company, unions. Each plant has its own union association which negotiates locally on some issues and combines with associations in the company's other plants to represent the workforce nationally. There are a few Western-style unions, such as the

teachers' union (*Nikkyoso*) and the Japan Seamen's Union, but they are rare.
Union attitudes are remarkably cooperative by Western standards, reflecting both the failure of direct action immediately after the war and the unions' subsequent ability to negotiate settlements higher than the level of inflation in the years of high growth and full employment. Brief stoppages (often for no more than a few hours) are little more than a symbolic flexing of industrial muscle.

At the national level Japanese trade unionism is undergoing a change, with the establishment in 1987 of the Japanese Private Sector Trade Union Confederation (known as *Rengo*). Two other federations, *Domei* and *Churitsu Roren* voluntarily dissolved themselves to join *Rengo*, and the once powerful General Council of Trade Unions of Japan (*Sohyo*), consisting mostly of public sector unions, was expected to do the same during 1989.
Wage bargaining, known as *shunto* or the "spring wages offensive," takes place in April (private sector) and May (public sector). This is preceded by four months of public posturing by pundits, academics and leaders of employers' federations, which moves both sides towards norms for pay and bonuses. All unions then settle within a fairly small range determined by the industry leaders (the increase in the 1989 *shunto* averaged 5.2%).
Disputes Japan loses fewer days in disputes than other major industrialized countries, with the exception of West Germany. Disputes are settled by collective bargaining or, failing that, by a professional mediator.

Labour costs
These have risen rapidly in postwar Japan, linked closely with increases in national product. Annual increases of up to 15% were common before the first oil shock, but they fell to single figures in the early 1980s, and since then have continued to fall slightly.

Direct earnings vary by as much as a third between the small and big business sectors; effective earnings in terms of benefits vary even more. In big businesses, labour costs for the permanently employed are particularly high. Average Japanese incomes overtook those of the Americans in 1986.

Remuneration packages include three elements in addition to basic pay – bonuses, allowances and fringe benefits – which can double annual earnings. For the permanently employed, most of these benefits are linked to seniority rather than performance, but Western job evaluation techniques are starting to be used in some companies.

Starting pay School-leavers entering at 18–19 start at Y1.5–2m a year; graduates start at Y2–2.5m. Apart from sales-oriented employment, most Japanese take a long-term view, regarding monthly income as an instalment of lifetime income. An employee's starting wage is based on job classification, age, education, experience and sex. Starting salaries for female graduates joining a major corporation are about 3% below those of their male counterparts, and as their careers progress, the differential increases considerably. Women are expected to resign on marriage or the birth of the first child, often re-entering the workforce later as part-time employees. All employees receive gradual increases until their early 30s, when the likelihood of remaining for life with the company, combined with increased family commitments, produces a substantial boost in male pay levels. Pay levels peak for most men between 47 and 50, with an average private-sector wage of Y8m.

Bonuses are paid in cash twice a year, in June and December. Although introduced as an incentive, they are now regarded as an entitlement. Effectively they are a means of deferring higher basic pay. They are on average 2–4 times the worker's basic monthly wage, depending on the size and profitability of the firm.

Allowances paid on top of the basic wage are significant in boosting effective income by up to 20–30%. They are a vital element in the seniority wages system. Some relate to personal circumstances: housing, commuting costs, marriage, family and educational commitments. Others are related to work: payment in lieu of direct remuneration for overtime, unsocial hours and posts of responsibility.

Fringe benefits paid in kind are the preserve of larger firms, which can afford low-cost housing for new recruits, sports and recreational facilities, subsidized holidays at company resorts, cheap loans and private medical insurance.

Executive salaries Even the most senior managers rarely earn more than six or seven times the salary of those just beginning their careers. Presidents of small and medium companies earn Y10–15m, directors of larger companies up to Y20m. The biggest payers are finance, banking and insurance companies, followed by the *sogo shosha* and the manufacturing industries. Senior civil service jobs offer more prestige than cash – top earnings being Y10–15m. The highest earners of all are doctors.

Personal taxes

Personal tax levels are the lowest among advanced countries, though big earners pay more than in the West, with the exception of Scandinavia. Japanese pay two types of direct taxes (on worldwide income): national income tax and local inhabitants' tax. Foreign residents staying for less than five years pay only income tax and only on income earned in and/or remitted to Japan from abroad.

Tax rates Income tax rates range from 10% to 50%, with a minimum taxable income of Y3.19m. Average incomes lie in the 20%–30% range. Local inhabitants' tax rates range from 4.5–17%, and the average taxpayer is in the 8–12% band.

Financial institutions

What was a highly rigid financial system is evolving into a fast-moving and internationally competitive one. Japanese banking is emerging as a strong force in the international financial community, and the Tokyo Stock Exchange (TSE) has assumed a firm place in the 24-hour global trading network. As Japanese banks and securities houses aim for a major presence abroad commensurate with Japan's economic and financial strength, they increasingly pose a competitive threat to the US and European financial services industries.

Postwar isolation

Japanese companies' access to capital in the postwar years was rigidly controlled by the Ministry of Finance. The Ministry and the central bank, the Bank of Japan, set limits on how much money the banks could lend in each quarter. Japan was, in effect, a closed society financially.

Opening the economy Inward investment was eased in the late 1970s, but foreign exchange controls were not abolished until 1980. Significant liberalization in the financial sector began only in 1984, but has proceeded rapidly since. This has included a lifting of the interest ceiling on large deposits, easing of restrictions on the issue of short-term certificates of deposit, partial liberalization of the Euroyen market and concessions to foreign securities houses (see *The markets*).

Pressures within the system

Savings The Japanese have an exceptionally high savings rate, at 16–20% of disposable income, with total savings representing some 1.8 times annual income. This is the highest rate in the industrial world (over two and a half times the US level) and is due to the high cost of housing, the need to prepare for retirement, an inadequate system of social security, and the practice of paying lump sum bonuses.

The Japanese saver now has a wide range of instruments in which to invest. The abolition in April 1988 of the *maruyu* tax exemption for small savings up to Y3m, coupled with deregulation in the permitted size of

transactions on the TSE, caused a massive outflow of private savings into the stock markets.

Article 65 of the Japanese Securities and Exchange Law, based on the US Glass-Steagall Act, maintains a strict separation between banks and securities dealers. This has been breached by some foreign banks, which can own up to 50% of a securities house; Japanese banks are restricted to a 5% share. Foreign exchange dealings remain in the hands of the banks, hampering the securities houses in currency swap dealings.

Government influence Until the early 1970s the government did not run a deficit and kept interest rates artificially low. Long-term government borrowing was minimal and financial institutions were protected. The oil shock of 1973 and subsequent deficit spending changed this. The process continued through overseas pressure for access to Japanese financial markets, an increasingly international outlook from Japanese industry and finance, and a surplus of funds within Japan seeking investment opportunities.

Interest rates After the 1979 oil crisis the Bank of Japan used interest rates, rather than credit ceilings, to control the money supply and inflation. There has been continued foreign pressure on Japan to liberalize interest rates, with some success.

To cope with increasing funding costs, Japanese banks introduced in January 1989 a new short-term prime rate, initially set at 4.25%, 0.875% above the previous rate.

The banks

Japanese banks are strictly divided according to their functions and permitted methods of raising funds although – like the formal separation of banking and securities business – the system is beginning to fray round the edges. They have played an active role in the industrial development of modern Japan, both in the provision of finance and in their shareholdings in the major companies. Of the world's ten largest banks, in terms of assets, nine are Japanese.

Types of bank

Long-term credit banks The three long-term credit banks were set up in 1952, in the face of an underdeveloped capital market, to provide inexpensive long-term funding for Japanese industry. They were given the right to raise money through the issue of five-year debentures. Although they can offer short-term loans, they are barred from soliciting funds from small depositors. With Japanese industry now mature, and likely to seek long-term funding by bond issues, the original *raison d'être* for these banks has almost gone, and they are seeking new roles. Their know-how and expertise, however, has stood them in good stead, especially in their underwriting of Eurobond issues.

The Industrial Bank of Japan, which has retained its right to underwrite public sector bonds, is the largest, with total fund volume of around $224bn; the Long Term Credit Bank has a fund volume of over $144bn and the Nippon Credit Bank just over $94bn.

City banks The 13 city banks are commercial banks, with 3,243 branches and half the total assets of all Japanese banks. They operate in the retail end of the market. Deregulation has squeezed their profits. Fixed low-interest rates for deposits cannot attract all the individual and company business they would wish, and they have to make up the shortfall in the money markets at higher rates. At the same time, loan income has fallen because of high corporate liquidity and the trend towards raising money on the securities market.

In Japan city banks have turned covetous eyes on the lucrative securities market and, as a sop, the government in 1984 allowed them to become secondary dealers in government bonds.

In terms of assets, Japanese banks are among the strongest financial institutions in the world. Of the top ten world banks ranked by asset size, nine are Japanese (the other is France's Crédit Agricole, in eighth place). This reflects the way the dynamism of the Japanese economy has been translated into the prosperity of its financial institutions. Ranked according to the BIS-inspired "Basel rules" on capital ratios, due to come into effect in 1992, Japanese banks do slightly less well, though they still occupy six of the top ten positions.

Regional banks The 64 regional banks vary considerably in size, from the bank of Yokohama which, with

City banks' assets 1988	
	$bn
Dai-ichi Kangyo Bank (DKB)	352
Sumitomo Bank	335
Fuji Bank	328
Mitsubishi Bank	318
Sanwa Bank	307
Tokai Bank	213
Mitsui Bank*	196
Bank of Tokyo	171
Taiyo Kobe Bank*	163
Daiwa Bank	149

Source: The Banker

* Mitsui Bank and Taiyo Kobe Bank have announced plans to merge in April 1990, to form the Taiyo Kobe Mitsui Bank.

funds of nearly $63bn, is as big as a small city bank, to the bank of Saga with only some $7bn. They have their headquarters in the major prefectural towns and cities and a total of over 7,000 branches nationwide. They have no separate legal status from city banks, to whom they are important suppliers of funds. They take short-term deposits, mainly from individuals, and finance local industry. Regional banks are responsible for 40% of local government finance and also provide fiscal services, disbursing subsidies and handling pensions. Some of the larger regional banks are involved in international expansion.

Trust banks The seven trust banks have total assets of $835bn; the largest of them, Mitsubishi Trust and Banking, accounts for $186bn. They undertake a wide range of asset management activities. Most importantly, they share with insurance companies a legal monopoly on the running of private pension funds, a huge growth area. The trust banks also take part in regular lending and in real estate broking. They are funded by deposits, savings and the money markets. High asset management fees made them staid and complacent, and in 1985 the government allowed in five American and four European banks to act as trust banks.

Sogo banks The 68 mutual savings and loan banks, known as *sogo banks*, with a total fund volume of $365bn (just over 8% of Japanese banks' total), provide financing for small businesses. Since February 1989 they have been permitted to convert themselves into ordinary (city) banks, and 52 have applied to the Ministry of Finance to do so. They will compete primarily with the regional banks but, being weaker in terms of profitability, asset base and capital ratios, they will not have an easy task.

Foreign banks In keeping with the new opportunities in the Japanese market, foreign financial groups have set up or extended their Japanese presence. More than 80 foreign banks are operating, with about 3% of the total market. A quarter of these are American, but the largest in terms of fund volume are French. Banque Nationale de Paris and Société Générale both exceed Citicorp, the largest US bank.

Foreign banks are seeking footholds in corporate finance and fund management rather than retail banking, though Citibank is said to have ambitions in this area; their special interest is in securities, the richest financial market in Japan. Those without a banking licence in Japan could apply for a securities licence; UK merchant bankers S G Warburg followed this route.

Offshore banking The Japanese offshore banking market, open to all foreign exchange banks in Japan, began trading in December 1986. The main benefit was to the regional banks, which can operate on an equal footing with the city banks for international syndication and bond issues.

Choosing a bank
Japanese banks have enormous amounts of cheap money at their disposal, and the desire to build long-term relationships with their clients makes them very competitive. They can usually offer cheaper loans than the local branches of the foreign banks, and they fully understand the intricacies of the Japanese financial system. The banks often fulfil the advisory function that is the province of accountants in other countries.

Investment capital The long-term credit banks offer competitive rates for the financing of investment in Japan. It is also worthwhile consulting the regional banks in the area in which investment is planned, especially if your company is small or medium-sized. The regional banks are also the experts on local government grants and subsidies. If money is to be raised by a stock flotation, one of the securities companies should be approached (see *The markets*).

The markets

Financial deregulation has initially favoured the securities markets, and the top securities houses are at the forefront of Japanese finance. Bond markets are underdeveloped compared with the frenetic equity markets, but Japanese companies are very active in overseas bond markets. The most recent addition to the markets is financial futures.

Securities market

Strict separation between commercial banking and the securities business assisted four securities houses to become dominant in both broking and underwriting.

The houses The Big Four – Nomura Securities, Daiwa Securities, Nikko Securities and Yamaichi Securities – together account for 44% of equity-trading and 80% of bond-trading in Japan. Nomura is twice the size of the others, with shareholders' funds of well over $4bn and a market capitalization of over $35bn. Daiwa's strength is in its links with institutional investors. Nikko is strong in bonds, while Yamaichi's specialities are corporate finance, mergers and acquisitions. Between them, the Big Four account for an estimated 45% of share trading on the Tokyo Stock Exchange.

In April 1985 security houses were allowed into lending, using local government bonds as collateral. At the same time they were freed to deal in certificates of deposit, foreign CDs, and commercial paper.

Foreign entrants After pressure from overseas governments, 22 foreign brokers had been admitted to the Tokyo Stock Exchange by mid-1989. Several others were still awaiting admission, expected in 1990.

The Japanese abroad The major securities houses have intensified their own overseas challenge. Nomura is well established in the USA and has been active in the UK since deregulation in October 1986, while Daiwa is participating in US trust business. Massive profits in their home markets mean that the Big Four can be very competitive in overseas money markets, risking losses to build market share.

The stock market

Japan's stock markets, of which Tokyo is by far the largest, account for 42% of total world stock market capitalization, compared with 32% for the USA and 9% for the UK. The Tokyo Stock Exchange (TSE) is the second largest in the world in terms of total equity, after Wall Street. In terms of trading volume, however, its average monthly volume far exceeds New York's.

Institutional stockholding Since the war, banks, life insurance companies and major non-financial companies have built up interlocking shareholdings. Japanese companies tend to hold on to shares long-term for capital appreciation and as a sign of the cooperative relationships between companies. This institutionalizes the market and minimizes takeovers.

At one time companies owned more than 60% of shares and accounted for just 10% of turnover. Since any stock must have a minimum annual turnover to be listed, companies simply swap portfolios, and many shares never come on to the open market. Individual shareholders do not account for more than a quarter of total holdings.

Gains before dividends Trading on the Tokyo Stock Exchange is concerned with the making of tax-free capital gains rather than earning dividends. Yields can be lower than 1%. It is a speculator's market, where the prices of shares bear only a passing resemblance to the economic fundamentals of a company.

Making a profit in capital gains involves moving in and out of shares quickly, and trading volumes occasionally reach Y2,000bn a day. Ramping is endemic in the market.

With such dedicated chasing, the market can get overheated, and collapses do happen. Such is the basic strength of the economy, however, that the market tends to bounce back. Tokyo was, for example, much less affected by the "crash" of October 1987, and recovered more quickly, than other world stock markets.

Self-regulation Following several scandals in 1987–89, and given the need for greater cross-border surveillance as world stock markets become more integrated, there have been moves towards stricter regulation of the stock market and provisions have been introduced to deal with insider trading. The market nevertheless remains substantially self-regulating, with social sanctions preferred to legal ones.

Commissions under fire Foreign brokers have had only a small impact on the TSE. They are, however, inducing large Japanese life insurance houses to purchase Japanese equities in London or New York at negotiated commissions, thereby undercutting Tokyo's fixed rates (0.25–1.25%). This could put pressure on the TSE members to reduce commissions.

A secure future? It was at one time supposed that any revision of the law separating the banking and securities business would await revision of the equivalent US Glass-Steagall Act (see *Financial institutions*). With the increasing internationalization of the Tokyo markets, however, and growing confidence, Japan may move in that direction independently, sooner rather than later. When the legislation is revised, the securities houses will face their biggest threat. The banks will move in, though whether via merger, acquisition, or competition remains to be seen.

Bond markets

Companies and successive Japanese governments have become major issuers on bond markets that were once dominated by the long-term credit banks. A medium-term government bond market was not introduced until 1980.

Samurai, sushi and shogun Strong growth has been seen in samurai and sushi bonds. The former are issued by foreign companies in yen on the Tokyo market, whereas the latter are issued by Japanese companies in dollars. Less popular are shogun bonds – dollar bonds issued by overseas companies on the Japanese market.

Yen Eurobonds Since 1984, foreign and Japanese companies have issued yen denomination bonds on the Euromarkets. Japanese securities houses dominate these issues with cut-price rates.

Financial futures

The TSE trades futures contracts in 10-year and 20-year Japanese government bonds (introduced October 1985 and July 1988 respectively) and the TOPIX stock index (introduced September 1988).

There were a number of developments in Japan's financial futures markets in June 1989. Banks were for the first time permitted to trade government bond futures on behalf of individuals and institutions, having previously been able to do so only on their own account. Also, banks and securities companies were allowed to start trading overseas financial futures.

June 1989 also saw the opening of the Tokyo International Financial Futures Exchange (TIFFE), trading futures contracts in three-month Euroyen and Eurodollar interest rates and yen futures. The same month, the Osaka Securities Exchange started trading stock options based on the Nikkei average of 225 stocks.

Commodities

Markets exist in a wide range of commodities. The Tokyo Commodity Exchange for Industry (TOCOM) is the largest, resulting from the 1984 merger of gold, rubber and textile exchanges. It trades platinum, gold and silver futures contracts, and started admitting foreign members in April 1989.

Other sources of finance

Until a few years ago there were few alternative sources of finance available to the overseas businessman in Japan. Recently this position has eased, as Japan has come to welcome foreign business.

Setting up a factory

Companies considering building a factory in Japan have a range of tax and financial incentives available that stand comparison with those of other industrial nations.

Labour subsidies In areas where employment prospects are poor, an employment promotion subsidy, averaging around $150 per person per month, is available for the first year. If employees are transferred, moving expenses are also subsidized.

Relocation subsidies Incoming companies and those already in Japan might consider moving to a designated industry induction area in order to obtain an industrial relocation promotion subsidy.

Cheap public money Low-cost loans for companies locating in the regions, or for ecologically beneficial factory improvements, are available from the government-run Japan Development Bank and Hokkaido-Tohoku Development Finance Public Corporation.

Tax reductions A number of tax incentives are available under various Regional Development Laws. At their best, these give incentives for relocation of business assets, special depreciation and reduction of local taxes – specifically reduction of enterprise tax, fixed asset tax, real property acquisition tax and special land-holding tax.

Technopolis Many of the prefectural and municipal authorities have schemes to attract industry. Most significant are the localities chosen by MITI as sites for the so-called Technopolis programme. By the 1990s, 19 high-technology towns, combining factories, universities and living quarters, will have been built.

Alternative finance

Venture capital is still fairly new in Japan. Efforts by MITI and others to establish a venture capital market on the US model are hindered by the conservatism of the financial community; venture capital as it is understood in the USA and Europe is unlikely to become a major force in Japan.

Government research programmes R&D funding is usually available only to Japanese companies. A few opportunities do exist, especially if the field of research is demonstrably of use to Japan. Foreign companies, however, may not wish to share the fruits of their research efforts with Japanese companies or agencies.

Some useful contacts

MITI Industrial Location Guidance Division, 1-3-1 Kasumigaseki, Chiyoda-ku, Tokyo ☏ (03) 501 0645.
Bank of Japan Exchange Control and Foreign Investment Division, 2-2-1 Nihonbashi-Hongokucho, Chuo-ku, Tokyo ☏ (03) 279 1111.
Center for Inducement of Industry to Rural Areas Zenkoku Choson Kaikan, 1-11-35 Nagata-cho, Chiyoda-ku, Tokyo ☏ (03) 580 1668.
Hokkaido-Tohoku Development Finance Public Corporation Koko Building, 1-9-3 Otemachi, Chiyoda-ku, Tokyo ☏ (03) 270 1651.
Japan Development Bank Planning Department Bureau for Regional Development, 1-9-1 Otemachi, Chiyoda-ku, Tokyo ☏ (03) 270 3211.
Japan Industrial Location Center 1-4-2 Toranomon, Minato-ku, Tokyo ☏ (03) 502 2361/2366.
Japan Regional Development Corporation Sales Promotion Division, Toranomon Mitsui Building, 3-8-1 Kasumigaseki, Chiyoda-ku, Tokyo ☏ (03) 501 5211.

Introductions to these contacts are best sought through your bank or embassy commercial department.

Insurance

A rapid increase in assets, and the need to diversify their investment portfolios, is turning Japanese insurance companies – particularly the life insurers – into major players in the international financial markets. At home, they are coming into competition with the Japanese banks.

Life insurance

Over 300m life insurance contracts are in force, an average of 2.5 policies per person with a per capita value of Y10m. Both per capita figures are the highest in the world. The total value of life insurance policies in force is Y1,232,000bn, placing Japan in first place in the world (having overtaken the USA in 1987). Just over 90% of Japanese families have life insurance cover.

The companies There are 25 life insurance companies with total assets of just on Y100,000bn. Nippon Life Insurance dominates with about 20% of the market. Just over half its size are Dai-ichi Mutual and Sumitomo.

Forces of change The ageing of the Japanese population, the abolition of the *maruyu* tax exemption system (see *Financial institutions*) and the general increase in Japanese consumers' financial awareness have acted as a spur to the life insurance companies' business, producing year-on-year increases of over 20%. Single-premium, high-interest endowment policies have proved popular, and the value of both personal and corporate annuity pensions is also increasing rapidly. Deposit funds have been sucked out of the banking system, increasing competition with the banks (especially the trust banks), and prompting the Ministry of Finance to ask the life insurance companies to exercise restraint. The life insurers' mutual society status at present hinders their full participation in the banking and securities markets.

Investment portfolios The Japanese life insurers have traditionally been, and remain, comparatively weak in asset management. However, the sharp growth in their asset base is forcing change upon them. Investment portfolios are made up primarily of securities (46% of the total, including 14% in foreign securities) and loans (35%, and decreasing as a proportion of the total). Investment in property, especially overseas, is becoming a major element.

Annuity insurance Life insurance is a major form of saving, accounting for 19% of personal savings. Annuity insurance, benefiting from the inadequacies of the public pension scheme, is the leading form of life insurance.

Non-life insurance

If the natural risks of earthquake, fire and typhoon are excepted, Japan is a low-risk society, and non-life insurance premiums are correspondingly low. The 23 casualty and liability companies have assets of Y20,000bn, one-fifth of those held by the life companies. The largest non-life companies are Tokio Marine and Fire (with 17% of the market), Yasuda Fire and Marine (13%), Taisho Marine and Fire (9%) and Sumitomo Marine and Fire (7%). The non-life insurers traditionally sell only one-year policies, but have plans to introduce pension schemes with a 20-year maturity, challenging the life insurance companies in this increasingly important area of business.

About half of the industry's business is accounted for by instalment-type policies which provide a wide range of flexible cover and can be tailored to suit individual customers' needs.

Liquid assets The non-life insurers' assets tend to be concentrated in short-term investments providing high liquidity but at a level of risk most Western insurance companies would consider inadvisable.

The law

The Western executive has to be aware of Japanese law and should take expert advice, but it is ultimately much more important to be familiar with Japanese attitudes to the law. The legal niceties need to be taken care of but the success of an enterprise will depend on the will to co-operate and the ability to be flexible about legal detail, as opposed to the desire to gain ground.

The Japanese approach

Much Japanese law is framed in written codes introduced in the late 19th or early 20th century, based in part on the French Civil Code but mostly on the analagous German Legal Codes of the time. This "dry" framework of law sits awkwardly on Japanese shoulders and the tendency is to take a more comfortable "wet" approach which enables legal relationships to be varied as circumstances change and which avoids conflict. This approach is grafted into the codes by liberal use of the principles of "abuse of rights," "good faith" and "changed circumstances" contained in broad abstract terms in the Civil Code and Commercial Code. Except in new fields of law, the Japanese do not base legal decisions on precedents, preferring to treat each case as a new one, to be decided on its merits.

The courts

The American occupation of Japan resulted in the Constitution of 1947, which placed a Supreme Court as the apex of a pyramidal judiciary. A Chief Justice designated by the Cabinet and appointed by the Emperor presides. The Cabinet also appoints the other 14 justices of the Supreme Court, which in its turn nominates the list from which are chosen the lower court judges. Other than some of the Supreme Court judges, all judges are career bureaucrats who have graduated from the Legal Research and Training Institute operated by the Supreme Court, and therefore have virtually no independent experience in business or as practising attorneys. All judges are appointed on ten-year engagements,

and they can be removed prematurely from office only by public impeachment.

Beneath the Supreme Court are eight High Courts and the district courts, one for each of the 46 prefectures except Hokkaido, which has four. The bottom layer of the pyramid consists of a large number of family courts, specializing in domestic and juvenile cases, and summary courts that handle certain claims of less than Y900,000.

Litigation

Wherever possible, disputes are settled without recourse to the courts. This is because a lawsuit results in a decision which can be construed as penalizing one or other of the parties involved. The penalized party loses face, as does the other party for causing the penalty to be enacted.

Procedure and style There are 2,800 judges. They operate with a lack of courtroom fireworks which owes something to the fact that there are no juries, the jury system having been instituted and then quite quickly abandoned after World War II. Details of cases are often thrashed out in chambers, specifically to avoid courtroom surprises. Trials are conducted on a discontinuous basis through periodic hearings on single issues, following the German procedural style. Very few independent discovery procedures exist. Evidence discovery takes place, to the extent that it exists, only through the presiding judge. There are no class action suits but a representative party may be appointed for cases involving numerous parties, such as pollution litigation. Judges are reassigned to new posts every two–three years; the judge assigned to any one case will therefore change at least once and possibly several times during the life of that case.

Mediation Many cases are subject to forms of mediation, which may replace or complement court proceedings. Arbitration (*chusai*) is an alternative to litigation. However, conciliation (*chotei*) is a preliminary part of litigation, and compromise (*wakai*) may take place either prior to or during litigation. Mediation may take place in or out of court and can be handled by quasi-legal professionals skilled in fields such as contracts, patents or tax law. Their findings are often legally enforceable.

The profession

Prospective Japanese lawyers must either be graduates of undergraduate law faculties or pass a preliminary examination before taking the entrance examination to the Legal Research and Training Institute. This demanding examination requires mastery of 1,000 civil code laws and a great deal of archaic specialist legal terminology. Of those who sit the examination, only about 2% pass and enter the institute for a two-year professional training course.

Working practices The qualified lawyer wishing to work as an attorney is most likely to be self-employed, either working as an individual or joining a law associate practice with other self-employed lawyers. Only about ten attorneys have permission from their local bar association to work as in-house counsel but many attorneys serve as outside counsel to corporate clients. Corporate legal departments have increased dramatically, and are usually staffed by graduates of law faculties who have not attended the institute and thus are not licensed attorneys. However, these legal department personnel usually have substantive legal education and increasingly have been sponsored by their companies for postgraduate courses in the USA

and elsewhere. Since such people often specialize full time in legal work for their companies, they often become as knowledgeable and effective as licensed attorneys.

Complaints The profession is regulated by the Japan Federation of Bar Associations (*Nichibenren*) and by local bar associations, which consider (free of charge) complaints from clients on such matters as negligent advice.

Costs Litigation in Japan is both extremely expensive and extremely time consuming. A judgment may sometimes be reached within a year but may often extend to three or four years and exceptionally up to ten years. Appeals can increase these delays. Bringing a civil damage suit requires payment of a court fee which is often substantial, sometimes leading to piecemeal litigation to avoid a large initial fee, and the losing party must usually bear additional court costs; each party must pay its own lawyer's fees. In domestic litigation, lawyers usually charge on a lump sum or contingency basis but in commercial cases an hourly fee (Y10,000–40,000) is common. Fees for leading Japanese law firms in Tokyo are midway between top London and New York rates.

Contracts

One of the greatest problems for the Western business person approaching Japan is the status of the business contract. Where the Westerner's final goal in negotiations is often a watertight contract, the Japanese businessman places little confidence in contracts as guarantees of business relationships, preferring to see how cooperative ventures develop. The Japanese contract is deliberately vague, and often no longer than a single page. Large companies, such as Sony, like to boast of the millions of dollars worth of business they have carried out in the past without any written contracts at all. Increasingly, however, major Japanese companies prefer and are well used to typical

Western legal contracts in international transactions.

Flexibility Though more common these days, contracts are still not viewed as serious restriction on freedom of action. Flexible terms are preferable to what could, in changing circumstances, become punitive formulae. In this situation the Japanese will renegotiate rather than feel tied.

Jurisdiction International financial contracts are traditionally negotiated under English or New York law. With commercial contracts it generally depends who initiates them. A joint venture or licensing agreement initiated by a foreign firm will usually fall under the law of its country or state. If you are dealing with a Japanese firm that has no international assets, it is wise to negotiate under Japanese law as there are no reciprocal enforcement treaties between Japan and other countries. The Japanese Code of Civil Procedure Article 200 provides for enforcement in Japan of judgments issued by foreign courts, but requires reciprocal treatment for Japanese judgments in the relevant foreign country. Under Japanese legal principles, a contract can provide for both a choice of law and a choice of jurisdiction. Also, it may be possible to obtain a guarantee under your own law from the Japanese firm's bank or an associated company.

Aspects of business law

Statutes covering business are comprehensive, and Japanese courts have a reputation for integrity and for enforcing individual rights. (See *Government and business* for details of the Fair Trade Commission and anti-monopoly legislation; see *Employment* for relevant labour law.)

Industrial property rights Japanese law specifically protects five kinds of industrial property rights: patents, utility model, design, trademark, and rights in computer software.

Patents are granted for new and highly developed industrial inventions which have not had any public airing in Japan, or written publicity in Japan or abroad. Uniqueness and technical sophistication are stressed in patent requirements.

Utility models are defined as "technical ideas by which a law of nature is utilized" and may relate to design or construction methods. They are easier to register than patents, and unsuccessful patent applications can be adapted to utility model applications within three months of the patent application's failure.

Design applications seek registration of "the shape, pattern or colour or combination thereof of an article" and are successful only where the design is new and unpublished worldwide.

Trademark restrictions are long and complex, and set out in the Trademark Law. Trademarks and trade names should be registered as early as possible, by the exporter rather than the Japanese agent, who would technically retain control otherwise.

Rights in computer software are protected under copyright principles. Japan is a signatory to the Berne Convention and the Universal Copyright Convention. Registration of computer software program copyrights has been available in Japan since 1987 but has not been used to any great degree.

All categories of industrial property should be registered through a specialist Japanese patent attorney. All documentation is in Japanese.

Consumer laws Western business people hoping to operate within Japan need to be aware of the rigorous legal standards now applicable through consumer protection and anti-pollution laws.

The Consumer Products Safety Law of 1973 covers safety standards, inspection requirements, product recall, registration of manufactures and the approval of model specification. It also provides for compensation to be paid to consumers injured by defective goods.

Judgments on compensation can be extremely harsh against erring companies.

Confidentiality is a problem during business negotiations, as protection against disclosure is vague and limited, and at an early stage Japanese negotiators expect to discuss far more detailed technical and cost information than would be common in the West. There is provision for non-disclosure in agreements with employees. It is not unknown for *sokaiya* extortionists to infiltrate companies to gain information which they can then threaten to reveal unless payment is made, even though changes in the Commercial Code in 1981 were intended to put an end to such abuses.

Using a lawyer

For any matter under Japanese jurisdiction it is obligatory to use a lawyer qualified at the Japanese bar. With the exception of a few Americans, who set up before restrictions on foreigners were imposed in 1955, this will be a Japanese lawyer. Some 500 Japanese lawyers have studied and practised abroad, many in the USA, and several are members of the English and American bars.

Under new legislation, which came into force in 1987, foreign law firms are beginning to open offices in Japan. They are, however, restricted to advising on their own national law or, with permission, the law of other overseas countries, but not that of Japan. The international firms, many of which are associates or partners of Japanese law firms, have liaison lawyers able to brief Japanese lawyers and work in conjunction with them on translating paperwork.

The regularly updated, six-volume *Doing Business in Japan*, published by Matthew Bender, is a legal reference work for the executive, with translations of relevant laws and an informative commentary, but should be used with care.

In business negotiations the use of

a Japanese lawyer will reassure prospective partners, where the introduction of Western legal advisers might be seen as a poor indication of future co-operation.

Selecting a lawyer Those expecting to use legal services in Japan should consult international law firms and their own bar association before departure. These will be able to make recommendations, but consult your embassy and chamber of commerce in Japan, who will be more familiar with the relative competence and experience of individual Japanese law firms. Having shortlisted firms, visit each to gain a first impression.

The language barrier is a major impediment to consistently high-quality legal advice. For foreign companies the best sort of Japanese law firm is one that is in partnership with an international law firm or one that employs foreign legal assistants who are relatively fluent in Japanese. These assistants often act as go-betweens and may actually conduct the bulk of a foreign client's business. However, the relationship requires tact, and foreign clients should show deference to their Japanese lawyers in personal conferences and should address correspondence to them with a copy to the assistant.

Local offices of *Nichibenren* will also recommend law firms. Contact: *Nichibenren* 1-1-1 Kasumigaseki, Chiyoda-ku, Tokyo 100 ☎ (03) 580 9841.

Patent attorneys

These are Toyko firms experienced in handling foreign business.

Asamura Patent Office Room 331 New Otemachi Building, 2–1 Otemachi 2-chome, Chiyoda-ku, Tokyo ☎ (03) 211 3651.

Nakamura, Yamamoto, Takeda and Partners Shin Tokyo Building, 3–1 Marunouchi 3-chome, Chiyoda-ku, Tokyo ☎ (03) 211 8741/5.

Sugimura International Patent and Trademark Agency Bureau 7th Floor, Kazan Building, 2–4 Kasumigaseki 3-chome, Chiyoda-ku, Tokyo

☎ (03) 581 2241.
Tokyo Aoyama Law Office 4th Floor, Room 410 Aoyama Building, 2–3 Kita Aoyama 1-chome, Minato-ku, Tokyo ☎ (03) 403 5281. Partners: Baker & McKenzie.
(See also *Top law firms*).

Top law firms

These are firms experienced in handling foreign business, arranged alphabetically by cities. Japanese law firms are not permitted to have branch offices and it is therefore necessary to deal with a different firm in each city.

Minoru-Shimizu Ueno Building, 1-34 Daimyo 2-chome, Chuo-ku, Fukuoka ☎ (092) 741 2951.

Kumo Kono 1-19 Motomachi, Naka-ku, Hiroshima ☎ (082) 221 3766.

Akira Kobayashi Room 206 Sky Mansion, 561-4 Komano-cho, Nakamichi-sagaru, Marutamachi-dori, Kamigyo-ku, Kyoto ☎ (075) 256 0715.

Adachi, Henderson, Miyatake and Fujita 10th Floor, Time & Life Building, 3-6 Otemachi 2-chome, Chiyoda-ku, Tokyo ☎ (03) 270 7461 (member of English bar).

Anderson, Mori and Rabinowitz 6th Floor, AIU Building, 1-3 Marunouchi 1-chome, Chiyoda-ku, Tokyo ☎ (03) 214 1371.

Braun Moriya, Hoashi and Kubota Room 911 Iino Building, 1-1 Uchisaiwai-cho 2-chome, Chiyoda-ku, Tokyo ☎ (03) 504 0251 (member of English bar).

Nakagawa Godo Law Office, 6th Floor, Akasaka Nakagawa Building, 11-3 Akasaka 3-chome, Minato-ku, Tokyo ☎ (03) 589 2921.
Associates: Clifford-Chance.

Tokyo Aoyama Law Office
4th Floor, Room 410 Aoyama Building, 2-3 Kita Aoyama 1-chome, Minato-ku, Tokyo ☎ (03) 403 5281. Partners: Baker & McKenzie. Note: This firm is also a leader in the field of Japanese industrial property rights.

Accountants

Accountancy as a profession is still in its infancy in Japan. Though attitudes are changing, it is still regarded as something of a Western obsession. The country's position as the world's largest net creditor and the home of many multinationals has required the adoption of Western standards but the profession has yet to mature to self-sufficiency.

Beginnings

In 1948 the Ministry of Finance established the Japanese Institute of Certified Public Accountants (JICPA) on the American model. JICPA was made responsible for issuing guidelines on acceptable accounting practices. Auditing began in the 1950s, though at a low technical level. Certified Public Accountants (CPAs) worked on an individual basis until 1966 when the law was changed to permit the formation of audit corporations (*kansa hojin*), the Japanese equivalent of the Western accounting partnership.

Company framework

International accountancy firms established themselves in Japan in the 1960s, as emergent Japanese industry sought overseas finance. The new domestic audit corporations sought affiliation with these major accounting groups. Few audit corporations have developed their internal capacity to meet international reporting requirements; most perform domestic audits while their international affiliates maintain essentially separate offices for international business. A continuing wave of mergers is creating larger audit corporations, some affiliated with two or three international accountancy firms.

The profession

To qualify as a CPA a candidate must pass a series of three examinations, followed by three years in an audit corporation or with an individual CPA. Standards are rigorous, with pass rates as low as 10% or less. There are currently some 8,000–9,000 CPAs in Japan.

Regulation The government is the major influence on financial reporting. The Commercial Code, operated by the Ministry of Justice, covers all Japanese companies. The code places stress on the protection of creditors, putting more emphasis on balance sheet strength than on measurement of income. The Securities and Exchange laws, operated by the Ministry of Finance, apply only to the 2,800 or so publicly traded companies. An advisory body, the Business Accounting Deliberation Council (BADC), prepares a set of accounting and auditing principles for all publicly traded companies.

Status Accountancy is a low-status profession in Japan compared with the West and it is rare for the financial managers of Japanese companies to be members of JICPA.

Activities are generally restricted to auditing, bookkeeping and taxation work. Insolvency is the prerogative of the legal profession. Bankers traditionally fill the management consultancy role, though the international accountancy firms are trying to raise their profile as consultants in Japan. Large Japanese audit firms too are trying to increase their consultancy capabilities.

Audits

Business in Japan tends to be debt-financed rather than equity-financed, so the auditor's usual role of protector of the shareholders' interests is not so important.

The statutory examiner The Commercial Code requires that the financial statements of all companies must be reported on by a statutory examiner (*kansayaku*). His brief is to audit the performance of the directors rather than the financial condition of the company. In larger companies the *kansayaku* has to be, or be assisted by, a CPA. In general, only in the

publicly traded companies is there a legal requirement for an audit by an independent CPA or audit corporation; certain firms classified under the Commercial Code as large companies, regardless of whether or not they are publicly traded, are also subject to this legal requirement.

A different approach While Western multinationals see auditing as a central management tool and employ one firm worldwide, Japanese multinationals tend to leave the choice of accountants for their overseas operations in the hands of local management.

Audit standards are not so rigorous as in the West, and audits are often done very quickly. The quality of auditing in Japan has recently been brought into focus by the collapse of large companies such as Sanko Shipping and Osawa Trading. It is unheard of for an audit corporation to be sued on the collapse of one of its clients.

Fraud Large-scale fraud is rare and embezzlement is often handled in-house. To save company face, offenders may be pensioned off or moved to another job rather than fired or prosecuted.

Company reports

Company reports of the major companies are usually available in English and Japanese versions. The English versions are drawn up in formats that will be familiar to most Westerners.

Tax laws There is a tendency for accounts to be kept in line with Japan's complex tax laws, sometimes at the expense of giving a true picture of the underlying commercial realities. For example, the tax laws permit only a certain percentage of outstanding debts to be written off as bad debts in each year. The auditor, rather than examining the possibility of each debt being paid, will simply record the permitted percentage. The same principle applies to depreciation of assets, amortization, and profit from instalment sales. In recent years a shift has begun towards reporting based on commercial actualities rather than the maximization of tax benefits.

The almighty tax inspector

Company bookkeepers are trained in-house and have very high standards of efficiency. The critical test of their efficiency is not, however, the twice-yearly audit – most Japanese companies work on a financial year beginning on the first of April – but the enormously thorough tax inspections every two or three years. There is a large tax bureaucracy in Japan and it descends in force for an inspection, which may last for weeks and even months. The tax inspectors are believed to have a fixed budget of extra tax to find, and they will stay until they find it. Bookkeepers will leave errors for them to find.

Using audit corporations

The largest audit corporations all have international affiliates, staffed by expatriate accountants familiar with the Japanese business scene. Some will be Japanese speakers.
Services for the visitor Audit corporations or their international affiliates can provide the visiting executive with valuable introductions and advice. Local branches of international accountancy firms can usefully be consulted before you set out for Japan. When in Japan, Japanese or expatriate staff may join you at meetings to help with discussions, give advice and interpret the mood of the meeting.
Setting up in Japan An accountant is indispensable. Apart from offering advice on legal matters and taxation, they can help find offices and are essential for dealing with Japanese red tape. International affiliates will provide a Western audit as a management tool.
Fees Statutory audits are carried out for a fixed fee based on a percentage of assets. Fees for other services are high to cover the cost of maintaining the necessary expatriate staff.

Top audit corporations

Showa Ota Hibiya Kokusai Building, 2-2-3 Uchisaiwai-cho, Chiyoda-ku, Tokyo 100 ☎ (03) 503 1100. Regional offices: Fukuoka, Hokoriku, Kansai, Nagoya, Nara, Niigata, Sapporo, Sendai. 169 partners. Affiliates: Ernst & Young.
Chuo Audit Corporation Kasumigaseki Building 25F, 2-5 Kasumigaseki 3-chome, Chiyoda-ku, Tokyo 100 ☎ (03) 581 6281. Regional offices: Fukuoka, Hiroshima, Kyoto, Nagoya, Osaka, Yokohama. Over 150 partners. Affiliates: Coopers & Lybrand International.
Tohmatsu, Awoki & Sanwa M.S. Shibaura Building, 4-13-23 Shibaura, Minato-ku, Tokyo 108 ☎ (03) 457 1691. Regional offices: Fukuoka, Hiroshima, Kobe, Kyoto, Nagoya, Nara, Osaka, Sapporo, Sendai, Takamatsu. 141 partners. In October 1989 it was announced that a new international firm, DRT, was to be created by a merger of Deloitte Haskins & Sells International, Touche Ross International and Tohmatsu.
Asahi Shinwa & Co Nissei Building, 1-18 Agebacho, Shinjuku-ku, Tokyo 162 ☎ (03) 235 8551. Regional offices: Hiroshima, Kanazawa, Kobe, Kyoto, Nagoya, Oita, Osaka, Sapporo, Sendai, Takasaki, Tokuyama, Wakayama, Yonago. 133 partners. Affiliates: Ernst & Young, Grant Thornton International, Binder, Dijker Otte.
Century Audit Corporation Japan Red Cross Building, 1-2-3 Shiba Daimon 1-chome, Minato-ku, Tokyo 105 ☎ (03) 578 1910. Regional offices: Chiba, Fukuoka, Kobe, Kyoto, Matsue, Nagoya, Osaka, Sapporo, Sendai. 118 partners. Affiliates: KPMG, Moore Stephens.
Shinko Audit Corporation Shin-Aoyama Building Twin-West, 20th Floor, 1-1 Minami-Aoyama 1-chome, Minato-ku, Tokyo 107 ☎ (03) 475 1711. 69 partners. Regional offices: Kumamoto, Nagoya, Osaka, Yokohama. Affiliates: Price Waterhouse International.

Advertising and PR

Japan's gross advertising expenditure ($30bn a year in the late-1980s) is second only to that of the USA, and continues to grow at a pace at least matching GNP growth. The major advertising media, accounting for about two-thirds of all expenditure, are television, newspapers, magazines and radio, with the balance taken up by other forms such as direct mail and billboards. The industry is dominated by Dentsu Inc., the country's largest advertising agency. Public relations is relatively underdeveloped as a separate marketing tool, but is growing in recognition and importance.

The advertising agencies

Dentsu, which is majority-owned by the Kyodo News Service, had 1987 billings of $6.8bn, compared with $4.9bn for its nearest international rival, Young and Rubicam, with which it nevertheless has a number of international business tie-ups. Dentsu accounts for about one-quarter of total Japanese advertising expenditure. Its supremacy in the domestic market was achieved by its being one of the first agencies to recognize the importance of commercial television. It arranged finance for new television ventures, in some cases taking a shareholding in the station concerned, and even supplying staff. This gave – and gives – Dentsu access to large blocks of prime television advertising, forcing large companies to use Dentsu.

Number two The next largest agency, Hakuhodo, is only just over one-third of Dentsu's size, with 1987 billings of $3bn, representing 10% of total Japanese advertising expenditure.

The rest The remaining Japanese advertising agencies are minnows by comparison with these two. The combined market share of numbers three to ten is still only two-thirds that of Dentsu. Many would argue, however, that what the small agencies lack in size they make up for in creative talent.

Development of an industry

Modern advertising in Japan dates from the introduction of commercial radio in 1951 and commercial television in 1953.

Radio's decline From a high point of attracting more than 17% of total advertising revenue in 1956, radio has steadily lost ground to television as an advertising medium, and now attracts only about 4.5% of all advertising. Radio received a small fillip from the advent of car radios, new FM stations and the ubiquitous personal radio, and the medium provides some opportunities for reaching particular segments of the market.

TV's rise Television achieved first place as an advertising medium in 1975. It now accounts for some 30% of the market. There are more than 100 commercial stations in operation. The major national commercial networks are Nihon TV (NTV), Tokyo Broadcasting System (TBS), Fuji TV and Asahi TV. The country's public-service broadcasting corporation, NHK, does not take advertising.

Newspapers and magazines

Newspapers have about 25% of the total advertising market, and magazines about 6.5%. Like radio, magazines can be effective in reaching specialized audiences. About one-third of newspaper advertising volume is accounted for by the five major national dailies.

Other advertising outlets The so-called "new media" – such as teletext and cable TV are taking a still small, but rapidly increasing, share of total advertising.

The clients

Advertising in Japan is very much a seller's market. Since advertising space is controlled by a small number of agencies, Japanese companies usually find themselves using the same agencies as their competitors. The large agencies claim to protect clients' interests by placing competing accounts in separate divisions.

Major sectors With the market for many highly advertised consumer durables nearing saturation, other sectors are taking a larger share. Food, beverages and tobacco are still top of the list, with 17.5% of total advertising expenditure. Other major sectors include services and leisure, with 12%, and distribution/retail and cosmetics/toiletries, with 7% each. But advertising by the real estate and housing industries, banking and insurance, and the energy sector (especially gasoline) is rising rapidly.

Costs The cost of advertising in Japan is, predictably, high in absolute terms, though less so in terms of "opportunities to see" (OTS).

Television advertising takes two forms: programme sponsorship, and spot commercials during station breaks. Rates vary considerably depending on programme, broadcast area, and time of day. As a rough guide, a 15-second commercial at prime time would cost Y750,000, excluding production costs – although the real cost would inevitably be much higher, since one slot would not constitute a viable advertising campaign. A half-page black and white advertisement in *Nihon Keizai Shimbun* costs Y6.2m–Y7.6m.

Dentsu's *Japan Marketing/Advertising Yearbook* is an invaluable guide to facts, figures and trends.

Style

Japanese advertising takes a much softer approach than the hard sell of many American and European advertisements. Its primary objective is to create a bond between the reader/viewer and the product or service being offered, and to reinforce familiarity with the supplier. Overt references to price or special product features are considered tasteless and unnecessary.

An oddity (to foreigners) of Japanese advertising is the frequent use made of Western models and scenes of Western life-styles, especially on television. These are thought to promote a "chic" modern image.

Advertising by foreign companies

At an estimated $325m, advertising in Japan by foreign companies is still tiny in comparison with the total market, but is increasing quite fast.

Because of the high cost, and the peculiarities of the Japanese advertising market, foreign companies are best advised to undertake advertising only as part of a co-ordinated marketing, advertising and public relations programme.

Public relations

The Japanese public relations industry is relatively immature. The oldest indigenous public relations company, International Public Relations (now owned by Shandwick of the UK), was founded in 1959 and has a staff of about 120. All other PR companies in the market are either small (46 of the 78 members of the Public Relations Society of Japan have fewer than 20 employees) or are primarily advertising agencies offering PR services to clients.

Two factors are starting to lead to a greater recognition of the value of PR. One is the entry into the market of American and European companies, through subsidiaries or link-ups with Japanese partners. The other is the move by many large (and some small) Japanese companies overseas, where they must adopt Western-style PR techniques to compete effectively and gain local recognition.

Many foreign companies in the past have given low priority to PR in Japan. As a result, many which are household names in their home country are almost unknown in Japan. This will inevitably affect overall business performance in the market; it will also make it harder to attract good staff.

Market entry

In the initial postwar period of industrial expansion, the Japanese economy was heavily protected by exchange controls, import quotas and high tariffs. Would-be exporters found it one of the toughest markets in the world to crack. In the last few years, many of these formalized barriers to trade have been removed as the Japanese have responded to pressure from their major trading partners to reduce Japan's huge visible trade surplus; the Japanese take the protectionist threat to their own exports very seriously. Since the G5 Plaza agreement in 1985 the value of the yen against the dollar has soared, although this is somewhat offset by a very low level of inflation in Japan and a marked consumer preference for home-produced goods. The new, advantageous terms of trade and the liberalization of most controls on imports make exporting to Japan less difficult than it has been, but some barriers remain.

Barriers and openings

Between 1981 and 1985 the Japanese government introduced a number of "market-opening" packages designed to promote imports into Japan and remove trade barriers. The last of these was a three-year Action Programme introduced in July 1985. The cumulative effect of these measures was to reduce the average Japanese import tariff to below the OECD average and to relax a number of certification procedures.

On top of these measures came the Maekawa Report (named after the former Bank of Japan governor who chaired the committee which drafted it). This called for a "historic transformation" in Japan's economic structure from one dependent on exports to one led by domestic demand. The report's other main recommendations included phasing out declining industries, increasing overseas investment, encouraging imports of manufactured goods and agricultural products, liberalizing Japan's financial markets, international cooperation to solve problems such as Third World debt, and changes in fiscal and tax policies.

Although many foreign observers saw the Maekawa Report as an exercise in window-dressing to placate Japan's trading partners, most have been surprised and impressed at how effective it has been in changing attitudes and shaping government policy. Real progress has been made in removing many of the formal and conscious barriers to imports.

Direct foreign investment began to be liberalized in the early 1970s and controls remain in only a few strategically sensitive sectors. Exchange controls were removed in 1980, the same year that foreign firms were finally allowed to use the JIS (Japan Industrial Standard) mark on their products. Further financial liberalization, initiated in 1984, is proceeding slowly but surely (see *Financial institutions*).

Import quotas have largely disappeared. Those that remain are concentrated in the politically sensitive agricultural sector – the ruling LDP is heavily dependent on the farming vote. Beef, citrus fruits and juices are among the products affected. Not all quota levels are published.

The average tariff is about 2%, and most machinery imports are subject to zero duty. A small number of industries are still protected by high tariffs. Among these are leather footwear, confectionery and biscuits. The introduction of the 3% consumption tax on 1 April 1989 has eliminated the high (5–30%) commodity tax on luxury goods.

Technical standards and certification procedures are in many instances unique to Japan, and have formed a barrier to trade in the past, but have been considerably relaxed as a result of the market-opening measures referred to above. Generally accepted international standards do not necessarily apply; foreign laboratory data and quality certificates are not always accepted. The time and money involved in setting up a Japanese test may prove prohibitive. Rather than maintain a list of banned products, the Japanese policy is one of "positive listing" – only those items listed are allowed in. Finding out why a product is not listed can be difficult, and altering the situation more difficult still.

Japanese government tenders generally meet GATT guidelines, although in some industries – notably construction – tender rigging and cartels pose obstacles to the foreign bidder.

Customs procedures can be elaborate, time-consuming and tedious. Variations in interpretation of the customs regulations can be found at different ports.

The Office of Trade Ombudsman investigates complaints of discrimination against imported products in favour of domestic ones, and can claim reasonable success in clearing up misunderstandings. Cases may also be submitted to your Trade/Commerce Department at home, your embassy in Japan, or a JETRO office.

Invisible barriers Despite liberalization of trade and the government's import promotion measures, some features of the Japanese economy still militate against the exporter. The days of protectionism have left Japanese consumers with an underdeveloped appetite for imported manufactures, except in the field of high quality consumer goods. The Japanese consumer manufacturing sector is highly efficient and competitive; a premium is placed on design innovation and rapid product development.

The way in

Japan is a special market. It is not for novices – successful experience in other export markets is a must if simple mistakes are to be avoided. It is important for the would-be exporter to adapt his approach to suit a unique trading environment and to take the time necessary to develop a successful business relationship with the Japanese.

Research is vital. You need to establish market potential and the best means of market entry. Check whether product modifications have to be made to meet exacting Japanese technical standards and increasingly individualized tastes.

A niche market Mass marketing is rarely an option. Japanese consumers are most particular about what they buy. Buying is not just about design, quality and price, but about lifestyle. Japan is a niche market where imported products fill gaps rather than set trends. For all their efficiency, the Japanese are not leaders in everything. They have weaknesses, for example in some areas of technology. But they are quick to recognize these and to put considerable resources into catching up.

Filling that gap Once the exporter has identified a gap in the market, he must be sure that he is able to commit adequate time and resources to the gradual building-up of market share. The whole approach should be geared to becoming established in the market and then staying there. Diligence and persistence are qualities much admired in Japan.

Food for thought The Japanese often genuinely believe that their products are superior, and frequently they may be right. Justified or not, the most commonly voiced complaints about imported goods are: that prices are too high compared with domestic products; that the goods are not adapted to local tastes in their marketing, packaging and content; that there is insufficient after-sales service; that instructions in Japanese are inadequate, or lacking completely; and that the goods are inadequately stocked.

Entry options There are many ways to get a foothold in the Japanese market apart from direct export to a retail, wholesale or industrial customer. Sales can be made through a Japanese general trading company or a specialist importer. Goods can be shipped in bulk for packaging and/or assembly in Japan, or manufactured there under licence – in this case you should make sure that your industrial property rights are fully protected. Other possibilities are joint ventures or the setting up of a representative office (see *The business framework*) to establish a "face" in the market. Expatriate staff should be committed to the market long-term, receive language training and have full support from their home office.

Two fundamentals should be borne in mind in dealing with the Japanese: the importance of personal relationships and the extended time-scale in which business is conducted. The Japanese are interested in the person with whom they are dealing. They will judge his company and his product by the way he conducts himself. An open and co-operative nature will count for more than a slick sales presentation. An aggressive and impatient manner will not win friends. The building of relationships contributes to the length of time it takes for things to happen. The Japanese will want to be convinced of your long-term commitment to the relationship before becoming involved; they cannot be hurried. Japan is perhaps the most competitive market in the world and one of the most affluent. It requires wholehearted commitment and considerable patience.

Getting to know the market
Complex and daunting though the market may be, copious advice, information and assistance are available from various sources. At home, government trade, industry

and commerce departments will have Japan desks. Some capital cities have Japan Associations, formed by business people who deal regularly with Japan – a good source of contacts – and Japanese Chambers of Commerce. In Japan, your embassy's official commercial section or trade centre will be a source of information, as will Japanese and overseas chambers of commerce.

JETRO, the Japan External Trade Organization, now concentrates heavily on the promotion of imports into Japan and on technical and industrial exchanges and investment. It has 30 offices in Japan and 78 overseas and can provide advice, market information and other forms of assistance. It also maintains specialist libraries and data banks. JETRO's head office is at 2-2-5 Toranomon Minato-ku, Tokyo 107, though normally it is best to contact your local JETRO office first.

General trading companies There are 13 such companies, known as *sogo shosha* (see *The business framework*). The nine largest handle about half of Japan's total trade. They dominate commodity and capital goods imports into Japan. Previously specialists in high-volume trade, they are now looking increasingly for higher value-added business such as the high-tech and communications sectors. All offer market intelligence based on worldwide local office networks.

Specialized traders (*senmon shosha*), who number 8,000, are smaller than the *sogo shosha* and specialize in particular product areas; they, too, have deep knowledge of their fields.

Nissho, the Japanese Chamber of Commerce and Industry, represents 1.2m businessmen in Japan and has overseas representation and ties with local chambers of commerce.

Japanese embassies, though principally concerned with trade policy, sometimes have attached to them officials from *Keidanren*, an employers' organization which represents more than 1,000 Japanese industrial associations.

Distribution

Japan's distribution system is notorious for its complexity and, by Western standards, inefficiency. Despite some recent streamlining it is likely to remain so for the forseeable future. Successful foreign companies have learned to work with the system, with all its failings, rather than fight it.

Coping with the system

Distribution is multi-stage, with up to three levels of wholesaling to service the small stores that predominate in Japanese retailing. Dealing directly with the distribution network is nearly impossible for the prospective exporter, at least in the initial stages, because of the importance of inside knowledge and personal connections.

The key to success generally is a good agent. He may not be the wholesaler or distributor himself but will handle importation and will set up marketing and distribution. He will aim to build up sales over a long period, to establish and maintain a satisfactory market share. To do this he will need support. The exporter must be prepared to make regular visits to the market, changes to the product and/or its packaging and presentation, and contributions to advertising and other expenses.

Retail outlets Department stores are the major force in the distribution of top quality products, accounting for an estimated 50% of all sales of imported consumer goods. They often run promotions of foreign products to introduce new lines and gauge customer reaction. For a small exporter with limited ambitions in the market, department stores will often be the best route in. Most of them have overseas buying offices. To achieve significant sales across a broader range of stores, however, a local agent is usually necessary.

Chains of speciality shops may also provide a good route. However, while it is sometimes possible to service a department store adequately from outside the country, it is effectively impossible to do the same for numerous speciality stores.

Industrial goods The distribution chain for industrial and capital goods is likely to be shorter but the technical support required becomes a major consideration. Selling from a distance without a local agent able to provide after-sales and technical back-up is unlikely to result in consistent sales.

The agents The major importers who will act as agents are the huge general trading companies (*sogo shosha*), such as Mitsubishi and Mitsui, who handle an enormous range of products and have offices worldwide (see *Market entry* and *The business framework*). Below them are numerous smaller trading companies and specialist importers. Both have representatives in major centres abroad, and may well have the right strengths and connections for your product.

Choosing the right agent may take a year or more of thorough research, correspondence and discussions at home before meeting a few potential agents in Japan to ascertain exactly where their distribution channels lead. At the start it is worth getting both a broad overview and recommendations from organizations such as JETRO, the Japanese Chamber of Commerce and Industry, international banks and relevant government departments. Your embassy in Tokyo can give specific advice on the Japanese market, and institute inquiries to identify suitable agents or distributors. Dodwell Marketing Consultants' *Retail Distribution in Japan* is an invaluable guide to the retail network.

Talk to a range of agents from the giants down to the small specialist. In order to maintain confidence it is often unwise to negotiate with several agents simultaneously – news can travel fast. Changing agents in Japan can be extremely difficult, so it is essential to make the right choice.

Business Awareness

Business in Japan is as much about building human relationships as negotiating contracts. Many Westerners find dealing with the Japanese a unique and difficult experience because, despite government efforts at internationalization, Japan remains an insular society, psychologically open to new techniques but sociologically closed.

The main difficulty that outsiders from both the West and East face is the very fact that they are outsiders, or *gaijin*. The trick of succeeding in business is not to become an insider – that is an impossibility – but to prove you are a reliable person. The Japanese are intensely loyal to existing suppliers – because they know and trust them – and, as a newcomer, your first step must be to build an atmosphere of trust and friendliness. Personal rapport is the *sine qua non*.

The Japanese at work

The Japanese are generally regarded as workaholics. There is an element of truth in this. Workers put in on average 2,111 hours per year, about 500 more than their West German counterparts and about 200 hours more than US workers. The government aims to reduce hours worked to 1,800 by 1992, but this seems unattainable on present trends.

But do the Japanese actually work harder? In a sense they do: their commitment to the company is greater. In the corporate sector, particularly, the job comes first, ahead of family, holidays and other commitments. On the other hand, they generally work less hard during the course of the day – notably in offices – and their productivity, by Western standards, is lower. Manufacturing productivity still lags behind the West in many areas and has only recently overtaken the USA in certain industries, largely due to high investment in new technology.

The working week The norm is still a five-and-a-half-day week, though the trend, particularly among large firms, is towards a five-day week. In small businesses managers may get a two-day weekend (a "thinking holiday") once a month. Japan's labour law sets 46 hours a week as the upper limit without overtime pay, reduced from 48 hours in April 1989, though this

has had a negligible effect on the actual hours worked.

Business hours Office hours are 9–5 or 5.30. Factories start at 8 and work for 8 $\frac{1}{2}$ hours. Shift-working is less common than in the West.

Punctuality The importance of this is emphasized by time clocks or sign-in books for all staff in offices, factories and shops. The Japanese are good time-keepers. Senior staff often turn up early.

Setting the mood The day often begins with limbering-up exercises (*taiso*) for everyone from the chairman down. This may be followed by a section leader's pep talk.

The office day The desire for consensus means that much of the day is taken up with "desk conferences." People consult frequently with both senior and junior colleagues. The open-plan nature of the offices – senior executives usually sit with juniors – contributes to this cross-flow of ideas. Executives tend to spend less time on administration than in the West.

Lunch breaks are staggered from 12–2. Everyone takes a brisk 30min break in the staff canteen or at his or her desk or at nearby restaurants. Lunchtime drinking is frowned upon and Western-style business lunches are rare (see *Business meetings*).

Going home Factory and shop workers and many who are not in

lifetime employment leave on the dot, contributing to the frenzied rush hour between 5 and 6. Lifetime employees – *salarymen* – often work late into the evening, but few executives take work home, even at weekends.
Increasingly, some executives are prepared to risk future promotion for more home life, and will leave work promptly.

After hours Though most Tokyo workers have a long journey home – 90mins is the norm – few senior executives or junior *salarymen* rush straight home. If they are not working late, they rush for the bars where much serious drinking and informal business discussion take place. Top executives mingle readily with juniors. No ambitious *salaryman* turns down an invitation. It is an extension of the working day in which discussion is franker, though off-the-record and best not referred to the next day. Visiting businessmen are expected to take part and it is an ideal opportunity for cementing relationships. This blending of business and pleasure is aided by substantial tax-free entertainment allowances. There is a second rush hour at 11.30pm as businessmen stagger for last trains or taxis.

Weekends are spent at home, though a visitor may be invited for a round of golf or to a baseball game or sumo on the Saturday. Sunday is a day of rest with the family. Visitors are unlikely to be invited home (see *Invitations, hospitality and gifts*) and it is unwise to phone Japanese contacts at home, either at weekends or in the evenings.

Holidays Manual and shop workers and those in small companies get only a few days' leave plus 13 days of public holidays. New Year and May's Golden Week are the major public holidays. Many Japanese – particularly executives – take only 60% of their holiday entitlement and few executives take more than 10 days. Company holidays – three days away with family and/or colleagues – are common in larger companies.

The salaryman's work ethic

To succeed in a Japanese company a *salaryman* must combine sensitivity, tact, flexibility and, above all, enthusiastic commitment.

One of the group The old adage "the nail which sticks up gets hammered down" neatly sums up corporate thinking. The work group rather than the individual is the key unit. Authority is more diffuse and control over budgets, resources and decision-making more collective than in the West. Individual talent is more highly prized in small, newly established firms, but the corporate world still values those skilled at working harmoniously with others.

Other awareness Japanese culture emphasizes "other awareness" before self-concern. One consequence is that the company time/my time distinction has been deliberately and shrewdly blurred by management. An evening spent with clients, or playing mahjong with a senior, or drinking with colleagues is all part of a day's work.

Commitment Japanese come of age at 20, but a more significant rite of passage occurs when entering full-time employment for the first time (generally at 22 in the corporate sector). One then becomes a *shakaijin* (a member of society) and is expected to put responsibilities and obligations before personal wishes and individual rights. Some *shakaijin* pack away their bluejeans – a potent libertine symbol – as a demonstration of their commitment. Commitment is more generally expressed through correct dress, punctuality and flexibility, and by taking holiday cues from senior management.

Flexibility Apart from areas where technical skills are essential, Japanese corporations recruit non-specialists for career posts. Career employees are the elite and, as generalists, must demonstrate flexibility – about what they do and where they may be asked to do it. Companies are increasingly training workers for possible future foreign postings.

Corporate hierarchies

Hierarchy is fundamental to Japanese thinking. Industries are ranked in terms of status, prospects and performance, as are the companies that make them up, and these rankings are widely known. Corporations have greater status than medium-sized and small companies. Within a firm, seniority is important, and older staff normally have higher rank.

Understanding rank

Kaicho	Chairman
Shacho	President
Fuku shacho	Vice president
Senmu torishimariyaku	Managing director
Jomu torishimariyaku	Senior executive director
Torishimariyaku	Executive director
Kansayaku	Statutory auditor
Sodanyaku/Sanyo	Non-executive director
Bucho	Dept manager
Bucho dairi	Deputy dept manager
Bucho hosa	Assistant dept manager
Kacho	Section manager
Kakaricho	Supervisor
Hancho	Foreman

Visitors may come across other titles, for companies often create them to satisfy an executive's ego. The chairman (often a past president) is the company figurehead and the president is the chief executive. Large corporations have many vice presidents and managing directors. The statutory auditor protects shareholders' interests (see *Accountants*). *Sodanyaku* are often retired senior executives.

Titles denote status in relation to other ranks, rather than a specific job. The Japanese like to deal with those of equivalent status: a *bucho* in the medium-sized sector would expect to deal with a *kacho*, or his deputy, in the corporate sector.

Middle management are the key players. Ranging from section manager to department manager, they have wide experience and usually 15–20 years' service. In Japan's system of bottom-up management, these are the people, especially in large corporations, who must be won over to any proposed new plan or concept.

Managers must ensure that their team feels part of decision-making, and they work hard to motivate subordinates. They look after staff welfare both inside and outside of the office.

When approaching a company, avoid going over the heads of middle management. These are the people who implement decisions. You will meet top management when a decision has percolated upwards – timing is all.

Decision-making

Top management initiates decisions on matters of strategy but many other decisions are formulated in the lower ranks, through a lengthy process known as *nemawashi* – consensus-building.

Nemawashi occurs formally at meetings between managers and informally in discussions with junior colleagues. The details of a plan are ironed out in verbal agreements before it is drafted.

The draft, or *ringi-sho* – a decision-requesting circular – is passed to each manager involved for approval and comments. A final draft is submitted to directors. Once the plan is sanctioned, instant action is required by the staff, who are already aware of what it entails.

Ringi-sho are used widely in large corporations, sometimes to rubber-stamp decisions already taken. Decisions can, however, be made without *ringi-sho* at management meetings. In small and medium-sized companies *ringi-sho* are often not used.

Women in business

Although changing slowly under the influence of Western ideas, sexual role stereotypes remain strong in Japan and women in management are rare. Although younger Japanese men – those in the postwar generation – accept that *foreign* women do business, older men may require some convincing.

Women in the workforce

Japanese women make up 40% of the total workforce, but only 6% of the managers and officials. Of these, most are in small businesses and are concentrated in a handful of industries – design, PR, fashion, cosmetics and advertising. In the large trading companies, banks and securities houses women in upper and middle management are almost unheard of.

Short careers Large companies, though they may take on female graduates, neglect their business training as it is assumed – and often required – that they will leave on marriage or at least on the birth of their first child. The long hours of the *salaryman* are seen as incompatible with the roles of wife and mother. Women running their own small businesses are typically single or divorced. Equal opportunity legislation was passed in April 1986, but the law lacks teeth, and its effects have so far been negligible.

The overseas businesswoman

A polite respect will be afforded the visiting businesswoman as a matter of course. However, in the masculine world of Japanese big business, the Western businesswoman must prove she is at least the equal of the men. As with visiting male executives she must be fully briefed and professional in presentation and manner, taking particular care to dress in a conservative business-like style. In addition, she must emphasize her business qualifications and show she has the full backing of her company. If her company is not well known, gaining business respect may be a struggle. Persistence, however, will pay off.

Male and female colleagues in the same delegation should emphasize the working arrangement when setting up a visit, or they may find the man scheduled for meetings while the woman is set for a round of sightseeing.

Chivalry towards women is a foreign concept to the Japanese, where the custom is for men to take precedence. Men will grab seats on public transport and go through doors first. Westernized Japanese do try to adapt, holding doors open and helping women into their coats. Their efforts may be unwelcome but should not be spurned. Be prepared to give way when jammed in a doorway.

Socializing Most Japanese men are not accustomed to socializing on an equal footing with female colleagues. However, a foreign businesswoman can become "one of the boys" fairly easily, providing her business credentials are established at the outset, and so long as she takes care not to flaunt her femininity. The key to acceptance is to join in. Be prepared to answer personal questions: if single, why not married; if married, who is looking after the home. These questions may be among the first you are asked, and a ready supply of stock answers is useful, the lighter the better.

Drinking Some Japanese might feel ill-at-ease inviting visiting businesswomen to the essentially male environment of the drinking clubs. It is in the informal atmosphere of the clubs that many business relationships are cemented, however, so if you are keen to join your hosts make this clear to them. It is inadvisable to drink anything stronger than your hosts, as this may cause them loss of face.

Business meetings

Meetings, formal and informal, are the essence of Japanese business. Western business people, especially first-time visitors, can be taken aback by the amount of detailed information they are expected to have at their fingertips and by the time taken to come to a decision. Meetings are not about decisions and conclusions; their purpose is the exchange of plans and information and the building of relationships. The key to successful negotiation is planning and preparation at home, and flexibility and patience in dealing with the Japanese face-to-face.

Planning and preparation

Information Japanese in middle management are experienced non-specialists, exceptionally well briefed about their company and the markets in which it operates. They will expect the same from visitors. Be prepared to answer searching questions about your company's size, finances, affiliations, work force, plant, production, markets, competition and strategy. Be especially sure of production capacity and delivery dates. It is best to talk about concrete facts rather than vague future plans, as asking for a reaction to an idea can leave your audience nonplussed.

You should be armed not only with information on the companies you are dealing with and their competitors but with details of relevant design standards and tariffs.

Materials The Japanese are happier with the concrete and visual than the abstract and spoken. Company reports and corporate brochures detailing the history, standing and aims of the company are much appreciated, as are reference lists of international customers. Material written in English is acceptable, while brochures printed in Japanese are a large plus. English material with a summary insert in Japanese are a happy compromise. It is best to have Japanese translations and printing done in Japan, as those done elsewhere can be embarrassingly inept.

Visual aids Photographs, videotapes and short audio-visual presentations are welcome. Be sure to check with your agents that compatible VCRs, projectors and so on are available at the companies to be visited.

Business cards (*meishi*) are indispensable in establishing the credentials of you and your company. It is best to arrange with a Japanese representative to have a supply printed and ready for your arrival. JAL and other airlines also provide this service. Your *meishi* should carry your name, company and precise title on one side, and a correct Japanese translation on the other. Any additional information that helps to define your status – qualifications, membership of professional bodies, and so forth – can be added to the Western side. Take advice from Japanese friends and colleagues on the layout of the other side. *Meishi* are of a standard size (90mm x 55mm) and should be impressive without being ostentatious.

Arranging meetings Introductions through a go-between are helpful in setting up initial meetings. This may be an individual or government agency. In either case, try to keep a flexible programme. Unless you insist, your agent will totally fill your agenda from 9–6 or later. The Japanese are very accommodating to the Western visitor, and will make every effort to set up follow-up meetings at short notice if required. Those who suffer from jet-lag should arrange enough time to recover.

The meeting

Getting there The big cities are notoriously difficult to get around, and the taxi drivers rarely know the way. Your hotel will provide a map and directions in Japanese for the driver if required. Always allow plenty of travelling time; the Japanese value punctuality, often arriving up to 30 minutes early at meetings.

The venue Japanese offices are open-plan. Only rarely will a Japanese meet an outsider at his desk. Meetings generally take place either in a separate conference room or mini-lounge among the desks.

The people Even if your appointment is with one person, the meeting will not be one-to-one. Depending on your status, and the topics to be covered, as many as a dozen might turn up. It is wise, if possible, to take along at least one other person. This will ease the strain. You will be greeted by your contact in the company, who will introduce his colleagues by their family name, in order of seniority. The suffix "-san" added to a name implies respect. To refer to Moto as Mister Moto is fine, but Moto-san is better. As "-san" is an honorific, you should never use it for yourself; say "I am Brown" not "I am Brown-san". You may be greeted with a bow or a proffered hand. Take your cue from this, and return the gesture, remembering to bow from the hips and to use only light pressure in the handshake.

Exchanging cards is an important formality on first meeting. This initial ritual exchange of information, establishing relative status, helps get the relationship off to a good start. Visitors go first; after the bow or handshake proffer your card smoothly, holding it so that it can be read immediately. Showing the English side shows respect for your opposite number's linguistic ability. Courteously study the card you receive in exchange. This is a gesture of respect and enables you to fix name and rank in your mind. Repeat the surname to ensure you have the correct pronunciation and ask for a translation of titles if none is offered.

Lay the cards in front of you in seating order for reference. The Japanese are very formal in business

situations and will almost always be known by their family names; you, in turn, will be addressed by yours. You should not use forenames or suggest they use yours.

Present your card only to those to whom you are introduced at meetings. At future meetings present your card only to people you have not met. Only when your own status changes through promotion, should you pass out a new card to those you have already met.

Treat cards with great respect. Don't bend them or shove them unceremoniously into a pocket. Other people's cards should not be passed on without their permission.

Seats are allocated according to status. Generally, guests sit on the seats farthest from the door. Wait until you are given a seat before sitting down. The Japanese team will sit together on one side of the table and the visitors will be placed opposite; this is customary rather than confrontational, and is generally true also for seating at meals.

The working language is almost always Japanese. Be sure to check this. As your host may have no command of spoken English and you probably have none of Japanese, your relative linguistic abilities are best clarified in advance. Do not be surprised if a man who can entertain you in English prefers to do business through an interpreter.

Professional interpreters The Japanese company may take responsibility for providing interpreters. This is satisfactory for initial courtesy calls, but for more detailed or technical discussions you should take either a professional interpreter or a Japanese-speaking colleague with you (see *Language*).

In many cases your Japanese hosts will understand English well enough not to need everything you say interpreted, but when speaking themselves will prefer to speak through an interpreter. Get the interpreter to check occasionally that you are being understood. Sometimes

Japanese contacts who you know can speak and understand English perfectly well will still prefer to use an interpreter, especially if the subject under discussion is a difficult or important one. This is done to avoid the danger of misunderstanding, but also as a (quite legitimate) tactic to give time for reflection between statements. If you are using an interpreter, give him or her time – remember it can take around twice as long to say something in Japanese as it does in English – and be prepared to repeat yourself. Talk in short "thought blocks", not rambling sentences or discontinuous phrases.

Informal conversation begins the meeting, setting the tone. Be prepared to chat about the weather, your impressions of Japan, your family, sport, anything but business. Let your hosts initiate this conversation.

Who speaks? Everyone at the meeting will have their say, but not all of them will necessarily have it at the meeting. The senior personnel are the main channels of communication and the juniors defer to them. Although there is no formal chairman of the meeting, those wishing to speak will need to catch the eye of the senior Japanese. He himself may speak little, preferring to listen and to judge. The Japanese are likely to break off and talk among themselves in Japanese. No discourtesy is intended, but without an interpreter present you may be missing vital information on how the meeting is going.

Speaking in meetings You should keep to short sentences and clear concepts; slang, jargon and buzz-words should be avoided. Jokes and facetiousness do not readily translate into Japanese and tend to be misunderstood. Interrupting is considered rude, as is directness in disagreement and correction. If you feel that one of your hosts has not understood, or is drifting from the point, do not leap in to correct him but wait patiently until he has finished before beginning "Yes, but...."

Preface a divergent point of view with "Perhaps" or "Maybe" or "I wonder if..." or "It may seem from your point of view." Do not say "No." 'Let me think it over" or "I'm not sure" are usually understood as meaning "No." The Japanese do not say "No"; instead rejection is inferred by a lukewarm tone of agreement.

When talking technicalities, beware bland answers of "Hai, hai" (I am listening, I hear you, I understand). This may indicate that you are *not* understood, and your hosts are merely being polite. Take a different approach, ask the same questions in a different way to check.

Visual aids Sketching on a pad or a blackboard is an invaluable aid to any presentation, as it is a universal language; be prepared to improvise to get your point across. Long speeches are best avoided lest they give the impression that you are trying too hard.

A printed list of your main points can be circulated at the meeting. Japanese read English far better than they understand the spoken word.

Silence is no embarrassment to the Japanese. Indeed, they savour moments of silence in a meeting to reflect on what has been said and the atmosphere in which it has been said. Do not fill in these "awkward" pauses.

The right attitude Business meetings can seem both baffling and agonizingly slow. This is par for the course and is no reflection on you or your proposals. The Japanese are a very patient people and it is important to approach meetings in this spirit. It is essential to let matters take their course; and useless to force the pace. It is permissible, though, to show a degree of keenness. After all, your hosts are also eager to do business.

Above all, however, you must avoid getting excited or showing any strong emotion.

Strategy Little or no hard business will be done at the first meeting. The visitor's main aim should be to establish himself as the sort of person that the Japanese like to do business with: reliable, flexible, interesting and interested. Answer questions about your business as fully as you can. There is no loss of face in not knowing the answer to more off-beat questions; promise to find the answer as soon as possible, and do so. Avoid the hard sell as it is always counter-productive, but take the opportunity to outline firm future plans. Remember the Japanese are more concerned with quality than price; show that you are ready to adjust prices and product specifications to suit their markets. Show an interest in the people and in their company and its products.

Taking the hint Politeness is so deeply engrained in the Japanese character that even if they are totally uninterested in your product they will not say so. Signs of lack of interest include evasiveness, monosyllabic answers and a tendency to stop asking questions. On the other hand, you may realize that they are not the right customers for your product. In neither case should the meeting come to an abrupt end. See it through and maintain a polite interest.

Success in dealing with the Japanese is more to do with the negotiator than the product. Be sensitive to the mood of the meeting, gauge what is expected of you, and avoid making extravagant promises.

The end of the meeting is usually timetabled but they can often overrun. If your hosts show no signs of stopping, the meeting will continue. If there are long silences and a lack of questions the meeting is winding down. The proceedings end when your hosts initiate a round of courteous thank-yous and hopes to meet again. If the next appointment is not fixed, now is a good time to do it. Gather up the *meishi* you have been given and keep them for future reference – it is a good idea to invest,

as do the Japanese, in a custom-made holder. *After* the meeting make notes on each card – for example vegetarian, non-smoker – and you will build up an invaluable data-bank on the most important aspect of Japanese business: people.

Minutes are not kept and circulated by the Japanese. This leaves room for discussion, with nothing cut and dried, and is appreciated by the Japanese. It is often a good idea, though, to circulate a note of the points covered as an early-warning system to prevent possible misunderstandings.

Other venues can be suggested for subsequent meetings. Meetings at your hotel are fine, with the proviso that they do not take place in your room, as this might embarrass the Japanese. Also, an invitation to an hotel might suggest an offer of hospitality.

Business lunches are getting-to-know-you affairs, not used for hard discussions. The visitor should not suggest a lunchtime meeting unless he knows the Japanese well. There is little lunchtime drinking, and meals start at 12.00 or 12.30, and rarely take longer than an hour. If you are in a meeting that is scheduled to end at lunchtime, your hosts may invite you to lunch. This is a courtesy, and not an invitation to continue the business of the meeting during the meal.

Decisions should never be expected at first meetings. Perhaps a trial order might be made at a second meeting. Although the Japanese are adjusting to Western time-scales, you should be prepared for a wait of two years or more before beginning business in earnest, and up to five years before a firm business relationship is established.

Keep in touch During this time you should maintain constant communications with the Japanese and make at least one visit a year to Japan; as many as two or three visits might be needed in the first 18 months.

Dressing for business

Western executives visiting Japan need to be more aware of their dress and physical appearance than they might be at home. People are judged by appearances much more in Japan than in the West, and your hosts' evaluation of you for the vital "right attitude" will include a careful, though unobtrusive scrutiny of your clothing and grooming.

The ubiquitous suit

Uniformity within the group is prized by the Japanese. Factory workers all wear company overalls or smocks, and even office workers may wear a uniform. At Sony, for example, everyone, up to and including the chairman, dons a Sony jacket for the working day. A more widespread convention is the ubiquitous dark business suit (*sebiro* or "Savile Row"), worn with a crisp, white shirt, sober tie and black shoes.

Expensive Western tailoring is appreciated by the Japanese. Visiting businessmen should wear conservative colours and styling, avoiding flagrant checked suits or shirts that might appear too casual. Take all the clothing you need with you, for it can be difficult to find the right size in Japan (especially in footwear). Slip-on shoes are most convenient.

Smart clothing is essential. The Japanese do not wear or appreciate "old but comfortable" clothing. Adapt your wardrobe to the level of company hierarchy you will be dealing with. Most Japanese businessmen aged over 40 are not fashion-conscious, and they dress like American politicians or British City businessmen. Younger Japanese businessmen are still conservative, but will be more aware of fashion than their elders.

Japan's weather in summer is hot, humid and hard on clothing. To appear in battle-fatigued garb at a business appointment would be disastrous, so take advantage of hotel facilities such as two-hour suit renovating services. The Japanese carry umbrellas rather than raincoats, and it is wise to do the same. The summer visitor should pack enough shirts for at least two changes a day, plenty of underwear and socks, and at least two suits. The Japanese are obsessive about personal cleanliness and tidiness. Short, well-groomed hair, frequent showers, and a constant supply of clean clothing, preferably with a high cotton content, are all good investments.

Western women have to be careful not to overwhelm their hosts. Make-up, jewellery and perfume should all be used sparingly. Avoid high heels if they make you tower over your hosts. Women are seldom found at executive level, so business dress should be restrained to reduce the "threat." Trousers should not be worn. Accessories can be upmarket; fashionable Japanese women spend a lot on items like Louis Vuitton handbags and Yves Saint Laurent shoes. Styles associated with teenagers, such as dresses and tights in pink or red, or with *femmes fatales*, such as split skirts or plunging necklines, should be avoided. Dark colours – traditionally worn by women over 40 – may give a woman the desired mature image. Shaggy or way-out hairstyles are not appreciated.

High fashion is increasingly important among the young and affluent, and those doing business with highly image-conscious sectors might well find their opposite numbers decked out in the creations of Japanese designers with international reputations, such as Mitsuhiro Matsuda or Rei Kawakubo. In general, however, the visiting business traveller should only step outside convention on the golf course, where chic wear will be the latest thing from the golf pro's shop – casual, elegant, and probably very expensive.

Invitations, hospitality and gifts

The Japanese are the world's most assiduous business hosts, and unless you make arrangements to the contrary, you are likely to be entertained every evening, often at short notice. This is partly because the Japanese are naturally hospitable and wish to shield a foreign visitor from any difficulties in coping with their culture. On a less altruistic level, they enjoy the prestige attached to entertaining visiting Westerners and the opportunity to demonstrate the size of their expense account. But it is mainly because the Japanese prefer to do business with people that they not only know, but also like; and the relationship is deepened by after-hours contact, where conference-room defences and formalities can be dropped.

Being entertained

Breakfast meetings are unusual, except among US residents, and lunches are normally brief abstemious affairs. Most business entertaining takes place after office hours, and may start as early as 6pm.

A typical evening may begin at your hotel, or in a small bar directly after work, then move on to a restaurant. Thereafter, if it is not too late, you will go on to a hostess bar before being delivered back to your hotel in a taxi, by someone often a great deal more inebriated than you (the Japanese have a notoriously low alcohol threshold). (See *Planning and reference* for more information on bars, restaurants and types of cuisine.)

Some bars that cater for expense-account drinkers charge astronomical prices. But if you are taken to any bar, it will be as a non-paying guest and your hosts will order all the drinks. The usual drinks are beer (*biru*), sake (*o-sake*) or whisky and water (*mizuwari*).

Dinner Rather than select your own meal – in many cases this will be impossible as the menu will be solely in Japanese – it is tactful and in keeping with the harmony of the evening to allow your host to order on your behalf. Seldom will a Japanese person be so inconsiderate as to have you presented with anything too difficult. Perceptions differ, of course, and your host may be surprised if you balk at the idea of eating live prawns.

The best advice is to abandon preconceptions and be adventurous, following your host's suggestions and expressing delight at the different dishes. Those with dietary preferences or allergies should make these clear to their hosts *before* any invitation is accepted. (See *Manners and conversation* for details of mealtime etiquette.)

Hostess bars The most common venue for business entertaining is a hostess bar, presided over by mama-san, a Japanese woman of indeterminate age but indisputable authority, and served by hostesses whose fundamental role is to boost male egos, giggling prettily and flirting mildly at an hourly rate. The Japanese like to eat while drinking, so rice biscuits and other snacks will be served up periodically.

You may be entertained by your usual contact on his own, but more often he will be accompanied by one or more colleagues.

The conversation veers between small talk and general business discussion and should be seen as an opportunity to forge links of friendship. Business matters may be discussed, but without too much prejudice on either side. Binding offers and agreements are left to daytime meetings. Confidences exchanged during social drinking sessions should not be referred to at subsequent business meetings.

Other entertainment

As you get to know your contact

better, you can venture forth to enjoy some of the rich variety of entertainment on offer. You may like to use the opportunity to watch some sumo wrestling; grapple with the formalities of Noh traditional theatre; or even indulge in the unique pleasures of a *karaoke* ('empty orchestra") bar, where you must take your turn singing along to a backing tape of a popular song. There is an innocence to these quaintly Japanese pastimes that makes them easier to enjoy than you might expect.

Whether you will be invited to explore further or whether you need to make the suggestion yourself depends on the individual you are dealing with and the length of time you are spending there. It is best to allow a couple of evenings of traditional wining and dining to pass before broaching the topic, but most business hosts will welcome the opportunity to take you off the beaten track.

If an invitation is issued for a weekend, it may include one of any number of sporting events. It is a signal honour to be invited to play golf, and it demonstrates the importance of your host if he is in a position to issue such an invitation.

Less innocent recreation is available but is unlikely to be offered. You can ask, but this may cause embarrassment and you should judge the situation carefully.

An invitation home

On rare occasions, or if a relationship has progressed well beyond normal courtesies, you may be invited for an evening meal at a Japanese person's home.

You should ascertain who is the lady of the house (often your host's mother or mother-in-law) and arrive with a gift for her. A small present from home would be most appreciated, but a box of chocolates or a bunch of flowers is quite appropriate.

All but the most senior and highly-paid executives will be found to live in surprisingly humble and usually overcrowded circumstances.

Remove your shoes at the door. Except in *tatami* (straw mat) rooms, you will be lent a pair of slippers for indoor use. The living-room will be sparsely furnished, and you will join the family sitting cross-legged around a low central table. Most hosts will be able to offer you a folding back-rest, to ease the discomfort of this position.

Conversation As at business meetings, conversation will seem stilted and slow-moving, unless you have already adjusted to the pace. The usual exchange of toasts will typically be followed by a leisurely meal of sushi, perhaps preceded by an informal tea ceremony, and proceedings will be brought to a close at about 11 with coffee or yet more green tea.

As elsewhere, you will be guided through the necessary formalities, and allowances will be made for your gaffes. Expect to be charmed by the simplicity of it, but remember that it is a great honour to be invited home, and you should show that you appreciate this.

Returning hospitality

The tireless generosity of the Japanese can become embarrassing, since circumstances often make it very difficult to reciprocate.

The standard recourse is to arrange a dinner for your Japanese colleagues. But instead of inviting just the one or two senior personnel who have been working on the deal, it can make – if at all appropriate – a favourable impression to ask up to, say, half a dozen others who have been associated with the work. The Japanese may well protest this is not permitted; that allowing a foreign guest to pick up a bill is virtually a sackable offence; don't take them literally.

Do not attempt to invite the wives: although some Westerners have succeeded in scoring points for this unwarranted courtesy – quaint and eccentric in the eyes of the Japanese – it is just as likely to cause embarrassment. Do not invite anyone outside the immediate circle of acquaintance in the company.

Choose an evening towards the end of the visit and inform everyone verbally, with ample notice, of the invitation; there is no need to issue formal invitations.

It is inappropriate to build an evening around an event such as a baseball game or theatre – and logistically difficult. Anyway, the Japanese are used to thinking of a business dinner as a semi-ceremonial occasion whose purpose is to cement a relationship. It is sound practice to repay hospitality at a restaurant with non-Japanese cooking where you can remain in charge.

After the meal it is good form to acquiesce in transforming the evening into a Japanese one by agreeing to adjourn for *nijikai* – the second round. This will typically be in a neighbourhood bar, perhaps followed by a hostess bar, where once again it will be your turn to be entertained at their expense.

Gifts

The giving and receiving of gifts is an important element in the development of good will in Japanese business relationships.

Receiving Gifts will be produced not in the conference room, but after hours, either to mark the successful conclusion of a phase of the business, or more likely towards the end of your visit. The gift should not be opened in front of your host (unless you are asked to do so), but you should express suitable thanks, with further thanks at a later date. If the present is a company tie or cuff links, wearing it at the next meeting will be much appreciated.

Giving Westerners are excused the strict Japanese formalities that govern the value and timing of reciprocal gifts, and it is the spirit of the giving that counts.

It is important to bring in your full allocation of duty-free Scotch whisky, which is expensive in Japan. These three bottles are ideal gifts for important contacts, to be handed over on or soon after your first meeting. Name brands generally carry more weight than lesser-known single-malts.

Once you have exhausted your limited supply, the matter becomes more difficult. Your opposite number is likely to have the latest model of every imaginable consumer durable, so calculators and electronic executive games are out.

A stock of company gifts is a good idea – especially good quality, name-branded Western goods, which carry a status out of proportion to their cost at home. Swiss Army knives, Dunhill or Zippo lighters, English leather wallets, silk ties, and almost anything with a Harrods, Nieman Marcus or similarly well-known label will make a good impression.

Give with style The wrapping of the gift is very important. Anything purchased in Japan will be wrapped at the store for you, and many hotels offer a wrapping service for things you may have brought with you. Proffer a gift with style, rather than slipping it unceremoniously across the table, and avoid praising the value of your gift.

The timing of the gift-giving is dependent on circumstances and can usually be managed as a direct response to any gift you may receive. However, if this might be awkward, it is as acceptable to send a gift by post after your return home.

Gift or bribe? The Japanese are conventionally more generous than Westerners, and a gift of surprisingly high value is considered quite normal. Provided it can reasonably be interpreted as a gift to ease the progress of a major deal, the question of bribery should not arise.

Cash handouts are to be avoided. The best advice is to stick to gifts that are relatively inexpensive but foreign-made.

The business media

An extremely wide range of English-language material is available for the business traveller to Japan, some of it extremely valuable. The offerings in other languages are much more limited.

Japanese-language media

The dailies Selling almost 70m copies, Japan's daily press has the largest circulation per head of population in the world. Sales of the morning editions of the leading nationals, *Yomiuri Shimbun* (9m), *Asahi Shimbun* (8m), *Mainichi Shimbun* (4m) and *Sankei Shimbun* (2m) are exceeded only by the Soviet Union's *Pravda* and *Investia*. All are "quality" papers and publish seven days a week. They are free of party political affiliation, but generally lack incisive investigative-type reporting.

The leading business paper is *Nihon Keizai Shimbun* (often abbreviated to *Nikkei*), with a morning circulation of nearly 3m. It is very influential, and is required reading for senior Japanese business people and bureaucrats.

The main business magazines are *President*, *Nikkei Business*, *Will*, *Economist* (no relation to London's *The Economist*), *Shukan Diamond* and *Shukan Toyo Keizai*.

English-language media

The dailies The daily newspapers available in English are the *Japan Times* (the most widely read), *Mainichi Daily News*, *Daily Yomiuri* and *Asahi Evening News*. They are very much aimed at the foreign community and visitors, and their circulations are below 60,000. Although useful for keeping up with the main domestic and foreign news stories, they clearly cannot match the coverage provided by the Japanese-language press.

The *Japan Economic Journal*, published by the Nihon Keizai Shimbun, has comprehensive coverage of Japanese economy and business, and is invaluable to foreign business people interested in Japan.

Monthlies *Tokyo Business Today*, with a circulation of about 30,000, has a number of good topical articles of interest to the foreign business person. The *Journal of Japanese Trade and Industry*, *Economic Journal Industria*, and *Business Japan* are also useful.

Directories Company directories include the invaluable twice-yearly *Japan Company Handbook* and its accompanying *Second Section Firms*, Nihon Keizai Shimbun's *Japanese Companies Consolidated Data*, and the *Japan Business Directory* from the Diamond Lead Company. The *Japan Economic Almanac* from Nihon Keizai Shimbun is an excellent review of industry. Also useful is the Oriental Economist's *Japan Economic Yearbook*.

Cable TV Japan Cable Television (JCTV) broadcasts English-language programmes, available in leading hotels and modern apartments. No TV station broadcasts regularly in English, though there are bilingual English/Japanese newscasts on the main TV channels.

Databases

There are a number of databases providing on-line information in English on Japan's financial, securities and commodities markets, as well as general economic, industrial, company and marketing news. The *Nikkei* NEEDS database, for example, is capable of storing over 5m news items, and its QUICK real-time stock quotation and market information service feeds some 40,000 terminals in 100 cities worldwide. Other providers of English-language database services (all available outside Japan) are: Com-net (Comline News Service of Tokyo); Jiji-Win, which is offered outside Japan through Reuters; Telerate Japan; NRIE (Nomura Research Institute); and PMS International (Daiwa Securities).

Cultural Awareness

A historical perspective

A major effect of Japan's defeat in the Pacific War was to sever it from its lengthy and often illustrious history. This was the first occasion on which Japan had been conquered, and it continues to reel from the shock. Much that is mysterious about modern Japan may be clarified by a nodding acquaintance with the nation's history.

The China impact: c600–800

Japan entered the mainstream of world history in the late 6th century when official support for Buddhism and the sophisticated Chinese culture that followed in its wake produced radical changes.

An emperor is made The title emperor was applied for the first time to the leader of the dominant Yamato clan, and the myth-makers invented the genealogy of the emperor's descent from the Sun goddess. Chinese political institutions and land reforms were also imported.

Culture China's influence went beyond attempts to unite the state under the figurehead of the newly fashioned imperial house. From China, too, came writing, literature and the visual arts. These the Japanese assimilated, assessed, remodelled – and, in many cases, rejected; for they were not mere imitators. Located at Nara for most of the 8th century, the imperial capital was moved at the end of the century to Heian (now Kyoto).

Heian period: c800–1200

The period of foreign influence was followed by an era of reappraisal and an assertion of things Japanese.

Politics and culture Politically, the Heian period saw emperors manipulated by nobles of the Fujiwara family. Although the imperial family was never to regain the political power it had enjoyed in Nara, it would not be destroyed. For successive regimes imperial sanction became the mark of legitimate rule. Culturally, the Heian period was one of superb aesthetic refinement which left an enduring stamp on Japanese artistic ideals. The *kana* scripts were devised; poetry and prose – no longer in Chinese – flourished, and the world's first and Japan's best-loved novel, *Tale of Genji*, was written. But while the refined, humane courtiers composed poetry, the neglected provinces became increasingly ungovernable. The Taira and Minamoto, two warrior families of noble descent, were commissioned to quell provincial unrest. A string of military successes brought them onto the national stage. Formerly servants of the court, they soon became its masters.

Kamakura period: c1200–1300

Military government and martial values characterize the Kamakura period and all periods until 1868.

The shoguns The Minamoto, the first of Japan's shoguns, established headquarters at present-day Kamakura, far from the debilitating influence of Kyoto. But the shoguns, like the emperors who remained in Kyoto, soon became puppets of counsellors who ruled in their name. It is clear that the modern Japanese aversion to individual responsibility and decision-making has a very long history. Culturally, Kamakura was coloured by the less-refined taste of warriors, as reflected in stirring war epics like the *Tale of the Heike*.

Invasion At the end of the 13th century, the stability of Kamakura Japan was rocked by two massive invasion attempts. The failure of these attempts to conquer Japan can be attributed less to the fierce fighting of the Japanese than to *kamikaze*, or "divine winds," which on both occasions destroyed the Mongol fleet.

Pyrrhic victory In the short term, victory over the Mongols was pyrrhic. The cost of maintaining armies on the alert until the death of Kublai Khan bankrupted the Kamakura regime. In the long term, these victories persuaded the Japanese that Japan was divine and invincible, a conviction that survived intact until Japan's surrender at the end of World War II.

Muromachi period: c1300–1600

The Kamakura regime was overthrown by samurai of the Ashikaga family who set up headquarters in the Muromachi sector of Kyoto. The grip of the Ashikaga shoguns on the nation was never strong, and incessant warfare scarred their rule.

Zen culture A renewed interest in trade with China characterizes this anarchic period. Foreign trade led to economic growth and enabled towns such as Osaka to expand. Once again, Kyoto saw the flowering of a dazzling culture. This time, however, it was centred on the court of the shogun and not that of the emperor. Ashikaga culture was a mixture of Chinese influence, traditional Japanese taste, and warrior asceticism. The period saw the refinement and development of many of modern Japan's aesthetic pursuits – the tea ceremony, flower-arranging, gardening, ink-painting, calligraphy and the Noh theatre. All bear the mark of Zen Buddhism.

Unification Not until the end of the 16th century did a warrior powerful enough to topple the Ashikaga emerge from the anarchy of provincial warfare. The man was Oda Nobunaga. If Nobunaga quarried the stones for Japan's later unification, his brilliant successor, Hideyoshi, shaped them. Hideyoshi is remembered, too, for his disastrous invasion of Korea in 1592. This left a legacy of bitterness that survives today in Korean-Japanese relations. It was his successor, Tokugawa Ieyasu, who set the stones of unification in place.

Edo period: c1600–1867

Ieyasu was appointed shogun in 1603. He made the small fishing village of Edo (modern Tokyo) his headquarters. From here the Tokugawa guaranteed Japan's peace for over 200 years.

Christianity Europeans had arrived and begun trading in Japan in the mid-16th century. But soon European missionary success was seen as a threat to the state unity that European muskets had helped achieve. Christianity was all but eradicated in the early 17th century and all foreigners, except the Dutch and the Chinese, were expelled.

State and society The isolationist Tokugawa regime was a police state, which bound the regional lords to Edo, both by a hostage system and by the enforcement of crippling financial contributions. Oaths of loyalty to the shogun also bound them. This loyalty was rationalized by Confucian ethics, which emphasized a man's duties to his lord and the supreme importance of harmony within society. The ethics of modern Japan are deeply rooted in the Confucian ideals inculcated during the Edo period. Tokugawa society was strictly hierarchical: the samurai, idle now in peacetime, occupied the top rung. Beneath them were the peasants. The despised money-handling merchants were at the bottom. Social harmony depended on there being no social mobility, but the reality was different.

Edo culture Most that is memorable in Edo culture was inspired by the rise of the merchant class: the Kabuki and puppet theatres, haiku poetry, and the woodblock prints of Hiroshige and Utamaro. The trading houses of Mitsui, Mitsubishi and Sumitomo all sprang up in the expanding and changing economy of the early Edo period.

Stability threatened The real power of the money-lender merchants was painfully evident to the samurai class, who were increasingly in their debt. By the end of the Tokugawa period, the samurai and their government were impoverished. But pressures were not solely financial. Ideologically, there was a dangerous new questioning of the imperial family's right to rule, and curiosity about the outside world (always a Japanese trait) was fanned by information seeping in via Dutch traders in Nagasaki. These pressures alone were not sufficient to bring down the Tokugawa; however, in combination with the new 19th-century threat from the West, they were.

Collapse The American Commodore Perry prised open Japan in 1854, but the beleaguered Tokugawa were caught between those who favoured isolation and those who thought the Tokugawa stood in the path of modernization. A brief civil war ensued, and control of the court was seized by enemies of the Tokugawa.

The modern period

In the Meiji Restoration, Edo was renamed Tokyo and became the seat of the Emperor Meiji.

Meiji rule The Meiji government's aims were twofold: spiritual unity of the nation under imperial rule and "pure Shinto," and political, economic and military modernization. It was to prove a poisonous mixture. Westernization was forced on Japan, and the Prussian-inspired Meiji Constitution was promulgated in 1889. With the state guiding industrial growth, as it does today, Japan became a powerful constitutional monarchy. Termination in the 1890s of unequal trade treaties with the West was followed by Japan's defeat of China in 1895, and then the astonishing victory over Russia in 1905. Annexation of Formosa, parts of Russia and then Korea followed. In less than 50 years Japan had developed from a feudal state to a respected and feared world power. Culturally, it produced novelists of world stature, such as Natsume Soseki, who combined Western realism with Heian sensibility.

Militarism Japan's support of the Allies in World War I brought her rich material rewards. But success on the world stage convinced many Japanese that they were divinely called to lead the rest of Asia to greater prosperity. The depression of the early 1930s and the perennial problems of scarce resources and over-population were at the root of Japan's expansionist ideals. In 1931 it invaded Manchuria, and the military came to dominate policy-making. The attack on Pearl Harbor in 1941 was the natural consequence.

Defeat and Occupation In 1945 the Pacific war was ended by the atom bomb, with Japan conquered and occupied for the first time in its history. The Allied Occupation, under General MacArthur, gave Japan a "peace constitution" which forbade it to make war and banned state involvement with Shinto. It also guaranteed freedoms of speech and religion and universal suffrage, and introduced an extensive land reform programme.

Postwar prosperity The Liberal Democrats, in power since 1955, gave Japan political stability. This and the government's close involvement in industry have ensured Japan's continued material prosperity. The spiritual void, in the painful postwar years, is perhaps best demonstrated in the novels of Mishima Yukio.

Future challenges Postwar Japan has shown that affluence is not the exclusive property of the West. Moreover, democracy and freedom can thrive in Asia, and Westernization does not necessarily entail the loss of traditional values. However, over-population and lack of natural resources continue to cause concern. Japan's greatest challenge, though, is that of overcoming its historical sense of isolation – and, hence, uniqueness – in order to play a fuller and more active role in the international community.

Important events in Japanese history

660BC	Legendary Jimmu Tenno founds the present imperial dynasty.
AD300	Yamato period begins.
mid-6thC	Buddhism introduced.
710–94	Nara period; Chinese influence strong.
794–1185	Heian period; imperial capital established at Heian (Kyoto).
1192–1333	Kamakura period; Yoritomo becomes first shogun.
1227	Zen introduced to Japan.
1274&1281	First Mongol expedition, Second Mongol expedition.
1333–1573	Muromachi period.
1338	Ashikaga Takauji is appointed shogun.
1404	Japan's trade with China is officially inaugurated.
1467	A century of civil war begins.
1542–3	Portuguese (first Europeans) reach islands of southern Kyushu.
1549	Francis Xavier, first Christian missionary, lands at Kagoshima.
1573	The Ashikaga are overthrown by Oda Nobunaga.
1582	Nobunaga is assassinated.
1590	Hideyoshi unifies much of Japan.
1600	Will Adams, first Englishman, arrives in Japan.
1603–1867	Edo period. Tokugawa Ieyasu is appointed shogun.
1609	Dutch establish a trading "factory" at Hirado.
1612–38	Christians throughout Japan persecuted.
1639–1854	Japan sealed off to all trade except with Dutch and Chinese.
1853	Commodore Perry's US fleet sails into Tokyo Bay.
1854–5	Reluctant trading treaties with USA, Britain, Netherlands, Russia.
1868–1912	Meiji period; Japan's modernization begins. Edo renamed Tokyo.
1871	Samurai class abolished in Meiji Reforms.
1871–3	French-style education system and Gregorian calendar adopted.
1889	First constitution establishes national Diet; first general election.
1894–5	Japan victorious in first Sino-Japanese War; Taiwan occupied.
1902	Alliance with Britain; Japan fights alongside Allies in World War I.
1904–5	Russo-Japanese War; Asia's first modern defeat of European power.
1910	Korea annexed as a colony.
1912	Death of Meiji emperor; Taisho period begins.
1923	Great Kanto earthquake levels Tokyo; 100,000+ killed.
1926	Showa period begins (under Emperor Hirohito).
1931	Manchuria invaded.
1937	Marco Polo Bridge Incident begins second Sino-Japanese War.
1940	Tripartite Treaty with Germany and Italy signed.
1941	Pearl Harbor attacked on 7 Dec; Japan enters World War II.
1945	Atomic bombs dropped on Hiroshima and Nagasaki. Unconditional surrender to Allies on 2 Sep; Emperor renounces divine descent.
1945–52	Japan occupied. Reform Constitution promulgated in 1947.
1951	Peace Treaty ending Occupation; first Security Treaty with USA.
1954	Liberal Democratic Party formed; postwar domination begins.
1956	Japan joins the United Nations.
1964	Tokyo Olympics signal international reacceptance.
1969	Japanese economy overtakes Western Europe's.
1976	Prime Minister Tanaka indicted in Lockheed bribes scandal.
1978–9	Second oil crisis.
1980	Foreign exchange controls lifted.
1983	Deregulation and liberalization of financial system begun.
1989	Death of Showa Emperor Hirohito. Heisei period begins under Emperor Akihiro.

Beliefs, attitudes and lifestyles

The Japanese are a strictly ordered people who, by and large, cling to traditional values that are rigid enough to impose harmony and foster a way of working in groups and, paradoxically, flexible enough to adjust to modern influences. Individuality is not encouraged, yet the individual founders of major industries are much admired.

Tradition and modernity coexist in the major religions – Shinto and Buddhism – which, along with Confucian ethics, retain a strong hold on the Japanese consciousness and which, instead of clashing with the new materialism in Japan, contrive to lend it an air of spirituality.

Insularity

Japan opened its borders over 100 years ago, but it remains in many ways a sealed society. Outside Tokyo and other major cities, where Westerners nowadays pass almost unnoticed, even a Japanese-speaking visitor will feel very foreign indeed.

The face the Japanese show to foreigners, however, could hardly be kinder. You will find that passers-by will even shed their usual reticence to offer help and advice to a bemused Westerner.

But a Westerner can no more join this closed society than he can avoid looking conspicuously different. The very word for foreigner – *gaijin* – translates as "outside person." The Japanese view themselves as superior, not only to Westerners but also to other Asians.

The heirs to a hierarchy

A strictly defined pecking order is an important part of Japanese social as well as business life; and an almost unquestioning obedience to authority is an important element in their ability to work in teams and to make decisions as a committee. Juniors automatically respect and obey their seniors in business, as youngers do their elders in the larger context (though less so than in the past).
The group mentality The roots of Japanese conformity are pragmatic. Many years of severe overcrowding have taught them to avoid open conflict at almost any cost.

The Japanese enjoy doing things in groups. Thus it is rare to see individuals jogging in the park but common to see large groups taking their exercise *en masse*. You will see many examples of this in business and in social activities.

Prized qualities are those attained and proven within the group: a good reputation, integrity, loyalty and trustworthiness. The strategy of "divide and conquer," even on a small business scale, is not likely to be successful.

Life in the herd can seem oppressive to Western eyes, but the Japanese are predominantly a good-humoured people – remarkably so, considering the stresses of the hyper-competitive business world.

An aesthetic society

Much of Japan's cultural heritage may have been borrowed, but it has been assimilated and refined to a high degree of elegant simplicity.

This refinement pervades many aspects of Japanese life: its fine art; its simple houses and spartan furnishings; and, of course, the spare and polished ritual of the tea ceremony.

Traditional theatre flourishes in various forms, including the highly-stylized Noh theatre, bunraku puppet theatre, and Kabuki.

Paradoxically, the characteristic Japanese good taste vanishes in relation to Western objects. For example, some hotel lobbies are painfully gaudy, and the Japanese have an inexplicable fondness for plastic flowers and other kitsch.

Japanese TV is often bizarre.

Respectably dressed presenters front programmes that are frequently erotic, violent or even pornographic. On game shows, for instance, participants go through rituals of humiliating self-abasement. Similar violence – also frequently pornographic – is evident in the comics widely read by businessmen on trains.

Traditional good taste reasserts itself in Japanese fashion, which vies with that of Paris, Milan and New York in its combination of striking colours and bold but simple themes.

Religion

Although commonly denied by the Japanese, religious conviction is an integral part of their life, and is approached in a matter-of-fact manner. To Westerners, Japanese religions seem inordinately flexible and multi-faceted. It is common, for example, to follow both the Shinto and Buddhist faiths, each one serving a different area of spiritual life.

More remarkable still is the way the old religions fit into modern life, just as Shinto temples take their place comfortably among modern skyscrapers.

Shinto, "The Way of the Gods," is the predominant religion but is not one of particular piety or reverence. The main concern of Shinto is to obtain the approval of the gods for projects ranging from a birth or marriage to a sporting endeavour; from a journey to a new business enterprise. It is quite common for a new business venture to be blessed either by a visit to a nearby shrine, or by a visiting Shinto priest.

Buddhism Whereas Shinto takes care of daily life, Buddhism takes care of death. It is normal custom to be married Shinto but buried Buddhist; and most Japanese families have their own domestic Buddhist shrine dedicated to the ancestral spirits.

Other religions The spiritual tolerance of Japan allows other religions to take their place with no great clashes. These range from Christianity (a growing force) and Judaism to the many sects of Buddhism, including the main Zen sects of Soto and Rinzai.

Present-day society

The real conflict in modern Japan is between its traditional lifestyle and the fast-food culture imported from the USA. In Tokyo, especially, the younger generation has embraced Western fads and fashions with great enthusiasm. To the bulk of society this is a worrying phenomenon.

The new attitudes are expressed in an erosion of the extended family and in freer sexuality among the young. Perhaps in future these aberrations will be absorbed, as others have been in the past, in the same way that highly competitive commercialism coexists with a spirit of respect for others – just one of many paradoxes that modern Japanese take in their stride.

The growing middle class Class divisions are closely related to material success, but are not as pronounced as in some parts of the Western world, with the majority of the population fitting happily into a homogeneous middle/working class.

Subdivisions within this group are defined by the status of a person's job, and by his income. A white-collar worker is higher up the pecking order than a blue-collar labourer; but in the modern industries the distinction between clerk and assembly-line worker is no longer so clear-cut.

There is, nevertheless, a powerful elite, largely composed of the wealthy heads of industry. The emperor and imperial family are still revered, but more popular idols include film and pop stars, sumo wrestlers and top golfers.

Standards of living are high in terms of material possessions, from cars to hi-fi systems, but low in terms of living space. Apartments are very small – a couple with children may live in one large room with a kitchenette and bathroom.

The family

The pressures of work mean that the male breadwinner is usually absent six days a week, often from early in the morning until late at night.

As a result, domestic life, in this ostensibly male-dominated society, is basically maternalistic; and although a Japanese woman is subservient to her husband's wishes, she rules in his absence, controlling all major family matters, including the finances. It is usual for him to hand over to her the whole of his wage packet, receiving an allowance for his expenses.

Thus a Japanese child's life takes place in a calm and well-ordered environment. Typically, he will live with his parents and one or the other pair of grandparents.

Love and marriage Marriages often result from introductions arranged by families, for it can otherwise be difficult to meet a suitable partner. The resulting marriage is usually a love match, however, and the practice of formally arranging a marriage is dying out.

Unless the wife is one of the new breed of career women, she will be consigned to the family home, to take second place to her mother or mother-in-law.

Premarital sex is probably not much more common than it was in the past, but it is more openly accepted.

Beyond the family

Pubic hair is erased from Western men's magazines, but pornography in Japan is alive and well, to an extent not commonly seen in the West.

Prostitution is illegal, but there is, nevertheless, a flourishing sex trade which thrives on the custom of middle and upper management and is priced accordingly.

In the larger cities there are bars where bizarrely under-dressed waitresses serve drinks, "soapland" parlours offering erotic massage, and "love hotels," which have fantasy rooms catering to young couples, adulterers and prostitutes alike with legendary discretion. Homosexuality is tolerated, and there is an active gay scene in Tokyo.

Geishas There are still many geisha girls – who are not prostitutes, although some may fill the role of expensive mistress. Regular geisha entertainment is very expensive, perfectly innocent and somewhat like a formalized children's party. Westerners, who may be invited as a special treat, tend to find it boring.

Leisure

As a nation of workaholics, the Japanese take their leisure seldom and generally in large groups.

Weekday evenings are usually a time for working men to enjoy themselves, drinking with their fellows in the cities or, more rarely, taking their families out, sometimes to the theatre, more often to a meal.

Sundays are family days, when the breadwinner takes his wife and children on an outing. This may be simply a walk in the park or a trip to another branch of the family, or to the recently opened Disneyland near Tokyo. The Japanese are voracious sightseers, both at home and abroad, and flock to popular tourist sites on holidays and at weekends.

Under company patronage, a Japanese *salaryman* can even play golf, a game that is a Japanese obsession, yet is limited as a rule to those wealthy enough to afford the exorbitant club membership and green fees. Many keen Japanese golfers seldom, if ever, play anywhere except in a multistoried driving range.

Tradition rules

The Japanese may be shy with foreigners, but they have few inhibitions when in their own groups. Their long, highly cultured, independent history has fitted them well to adapt to and cope with the strains of modern living. In spite of the many changes in their society, it is still the traditional values that really matter in Japan.

Education

The child crouched over his desk in the examination hall wears a white headband inscribed with the message "sure victory in exam." Exams are at the heart of Japanese education, which is highly competitive from the earliest age. Pressures on children are intense, and there is growing demand for changes in both the style of education and the syllabus.

The importance of education

The Japanese are dedicated to their children's education. About 10% of Japan's GNP is spent on private and state education, and parents, particularly mothers, devote themselves to facilitating and overseeing intensive routines of extra study to give their offspring the edge in the series of qualifying exams that culminate in university or college entry at the age of 18. Mothers will attend school when children are ill so that they can take notes to be written up and learned by the invalid. To avoid disrupting the children's schooling, families sometimes split up when the father is posted elsewhere in Japan or overseas. This feverish competition for academic success has as its goal a secure job in a high-status industry or profession.

The education system

The Japanese state school structure is based on the US model. The system is styled "6-3-3-4," with six years at elementary school, for 6- to 12-year-olds; three years at junior high, up to the age of 15, when compulsory education ceases; three years at senior high, which is completed by over 90% of all pupils; and a four-year university degree course. Over 35% of Japanese students go to university, although not all courses last four years; there are many two-year junior colleges, especially for girls.

Schools

Japanese schooling is motivated by Confucian ideals of unceasing learning and punctuated by frequent exams. Great stress is placed on learning by rote, and progress is usually at the pace of the slowest, with streaming almost nonexistent because of the problems of "face" implicit in such categorizing. Mixed-sex and mixed-ability classes of up to 50 pupils are not unusual. Children work a 5 1/2-day week, with a total of 240 school days per year (most Western children put in about 200 days).

Rigorous examinations are taken in the top grade of each level of school to determine which candidates attend the most favoured establishments.

Early schooling Prestigious private universities have their own feeder systems, for which ferocious competition starts at a tender age. Ambitious parents start the process earlier than the state system, sending their children to private nursery schools at the age of three. The most sought-after nursery schools have entrance exams.

Modern business requirements have invaded even the preschool sector, and some nursery schools introduce their tiny charges to computers.

Nursery and elementary schooling is dominated by the learning of the 96 *kana* (phonetic symbols) and the almost 2,000 *kanji* (Chinese characters) necessary for general reading. As a result, the country's literacy rate is close to 100%.

High school In addition to Japanese and Chinese literature, the curriculum includes linear algebra, inorganic chemistry, mechanical and electronic physics, statistics, and calculus. English instruction, which begins at 12, is geared to passing exams rather than to communicating.

Private tuition With the competition for success so intense, there has arisen a large private educational sector. *Juku*, or private crammers, cater particularly for 12- to 15- year-olds seeking coveted places in the best senior high schools. Urged on by their *kyoiku mama* ("education mothers"), some youngsters get up as early as 4.30am, travel to the crammer, put in an hour's work, go to their state school and complete a normal day, then return to the crammer for another session, getting home as late as 11pm in some cases. Weekend time, too, may be sacrificed to the cramming of work already covered by the formal syllabus. As the time for university entrance approaches, the pressures intensify even further.

Technical colleges have not been a great success. They teach trades and practical subjects, but most 15- year-olds opt for senior high schools, because employers prefer to teach their own trades.

University entrance In the February of their senior year, high school students take the university entrance exams. Around 38% pass first time; those who fail go on in most cases to do a further year or two at a crammer before re-taking the exams. Every candidate takes the common entrance exam, consisting of multiple-choice questions in seven subjects. This is followed by exam papers for the specific university. A good memory is the main factor in success. Personality is not a factor: there are no interviews for university places.

Universities Only a quarter of Japan's 460 universities are public – either national or municipal. The remainder are private institutions, only the best of which can compete with the leading public universities. At the top of the pyramid is the state-run Tokyo University, whose prestigious law faculty has provided all but one Finance Minister. Most top people in government or business are graduates of the national universities in Tokyo or Kyoto, or the private Tokyo universities, Keio and Waseda.

Starting a career Once at university, most students are past the ordeal of exams. Acceptance at a top university is virtually all that's required for a high-status job. A good degree is

unimportant, since major companies, using recent graduates as talent scouts, compete for students from the elite universities, recruiting them well before graduation. (See also *Employment.*) It is here that Japan's old-boy network (*gakubatsu*) has its roots.

Postgraduate courses at universities are dominated by engineering (50%) and medical or technical subjects. An increasing number of Japanese students are doing postgraduate studies overseas.

In-house training by major corporations is substantial. Vocational courses can be taken in a variety of subjects with a view to switching direction, or just improving general knowledge of the industry. Where technical changes have affected jobs, state subsidies encourage retraining within the company.

The educational debate

A British government report in the mid-1980s commented that "the purpose of Japanese education is clear cut. It provides what the dominant voices in industry and commerce want, in the national interest, and generally does so to their satisfaction."

However, many Japanese fear that the emphasis on rote learning has sacrificed education to mere ability to pass exams. Teenage suicides and a growing trend of classroom violence are blamed on postwar Occupation education policies which eradicated *shushin*, the moral education that was the essence of traditional schooling, with its emphasis on loyalty, filial piety and nationalism.

What is clear is that education will become the subject of increasing political debate, not least because policy makers fear that the present system is stunting originality and creative thought. They are beginning to realize that what is good for the multinationals now may not, in the long run, be good for the nation.

Language

The Japanese language seemed so complex to a 16th-century Jesuit that he dubbed it "the Devil's tongue." Contrary to popular myth, however, modern spoken Japanese is not impossibly difficult. Pronunciation is relatively easy, not tonal like Chinese, a language to which Japanese is *not* structurally related. The grammar is manageable, though sentence structure differs fundamentally from English and other European languages. There are, however, two devilish areas: the written word, and respectful forms of speech.

The written word

Japanese may be written in three directions (left to right or right to left horizontally, and right to left, reading down vertically) and in four scripts.
Hiragana A phonetic system whose 46 symbols represent the 46 sounds of Japanese. It is used principally for writing prepositions and assorted word endings.
Katakana Another phonetic system with 46 symbols. It is used principally for imported words and is standard in telegrams and in much advertising.
Kanji Pictograms of Chinese origin, representing nuggets of meaning. In, for example, "I am learning Japanese," "I," "learn" and "Japanese" will be in *kanji*, while "am ...ing" and particles modifying the subject and object will be in *hiragana*.

The sound of *kanji* can be transcribed in *hiragana* (and often is, when the writer forgets a *kanji*); but Japanese is not easily read without *kanji*, since homonyms abound (the word *sei*, for example, has 12 meanings). Some 2,000 *kanji* are required for daily use (professionals will use perhaps twice this number) and countless compounds also exist.
Romaji Japanese written in Roman script. It is much used in advertising.

The language of respect

The special style of speech used to show respect to social superiors and strangers is in a state of disarray. It can be so complex that the Japanese regularly misuse it. There are, for example, at least nine different words for "I," the appropriate one depending on the relative status of the speaker and listener. For foreigners, an appropriate facial expression is a good substitute for the correct form of words.

Borrowed words

The number of words adopted from other languages is staggering. Formerly Japanese borrowed from the Chinese both the *kanji* and their pronunciation, but English is now the major source. Some 25,000 English words, such as *takushi* (taxi) and *esukareta* (escalator), are in daily use. Most, however, are rendered unrecognizable to the Westerner by unpliable Japanese lips or by the phonetic system (neither of which can distinguish "b" from "v," "l" from "r" and "s" from "th"). Words are also dramatically changed by the Japanese passion for truncation, which produces such variants as *terebi* (television), *suto* (from *sutoraiki*, strike) and *depato* (department store).

Getting by without Japanese

For most of your stay you will probably be chaperoned by an English-speaking company man (very few Japanese, incidentally, speak any other foreign language). Coping alone in Japan without the language is not impossible, since the Japanese are always helpful. Your main problem will be locating places, since most signs and place names are in *kanji*, *hiragana* and *katakana*. However, English translations are increasingly found in Tokyo, Osaka and Kobe, and on highways, subways and JR stations. Also, despite an ability to read and correspond in English, most Japanese do not speak it. If in difficulties, approach a young person, who is more likely to be conversant with English, or write your question clearly. The Japanese are touched when foreigners try to speak their language, and mastery of a few everyday phrases will enhance your standing.

Interpreters

Rather than go it alone, you may wish to employ an interpreter (see *Business meetings*). Interpreters can be contacted through your agent or embassy, or through major hotels, travel agencies and specialist agencies (listed in *City by city*). Standard rates for student and professional respectively are around Y25,000 and Y80,000 daily, plus expenses.

Your interpreter will probably be a woman. Brief her fully in advance. At the meeting, seat her where she can hear easily. Speak slowly and clearly and allow adequate pauses. Write out

large numbers and check frequently that she has understood. Don't overwork your interpreter or interrupt when she is listening, and avoid arcane terms, jargon, slang and questions phrased in the negative. For example, the reply to "Don't you smoke?" will be "Yes (you're right, I don't smoke)," rather than "No," as in English.

It may sometimes seem that the length of the interpretation bears little resemblance to the length of the original statement. This is caused both by differences in the make-up of English and Japanese, and by the need sometimes to explain the context, or cultural differences.

It is useful to discuss the results of the meeting afterwards with the interpreter, who will be able to tell you of any non-verbal communications you may have missed, and explain what expressions of interest or support can be taken at face value, and what are merely courtesies intended to avoid causing offence.

Japanese phrases

The English phrases here have Japanese translations in *romaji* (Romanized Japanese) and a guide to pronunciation in brackets. In phrases with ... insert the appropriate name or word, or a word or phrase from this list.

Basic courtesies

Yes, please	*O-negai shimasu* (oh-nehguy shemass)
No, thank you	*Kekko desu* (kek-kaw dess)
Excuse me/sorry/ Please do!/Come in!	*Sumimasen* (suememahsen)
Here you are	*Hai dozo* (high dawzo)
After you!	*O-saki ni dozo* (oh-sahkey nee dawzo)
Thank you	*Arigato gozaimasu* (arigahtaw gozighmass)
It's my/It was a pleasure	*Do itashimashite* (daw eetahshemahshtay)

Greetings and farewells

Good morning, Mr/Mrs/Miss ...	*...-san, o-hayo gozaimasu* (...-san, oh-highyoh gozighmass)
Good evening, Mr/Mrs/Miss ...	*...-san, konban wa* (konban wah)
Hello, Mr/Mrs/Miss ...	*...-san, konnichi wa* (kon-nichee wah)
I am pleased to meet you	*Hajimemashite* (hahjemaymahshtay)
How are you?	*O-genki desu ka* (oh-genkey dess kah)
Very well, thank you	*O-kage sama de* (oh-kahgay sahmah day)
My name is John/Jane Smith	*John/Jane Smith to moshimasu* (toh mawshemass)

This is my business card	*Watakushi no meishi desu ga* (wahtahkshe no mayshe dessoo gah)
I look forward to doing business with you	*Yoroshiku o-negai shimasu* (yoroshekoo oh-nehguy shemass)
Shall we go for a drink/meal?	*Nomi/Shokuji ni ikimasho ka* (nohmee/shokoojee nee ikimahshaw kah)
Thank you for ...	*... arigato gozaimasu* (arigahtaw gozighmass)
Today	*Kyo wa* (kyaw wah)
Last night	*Yube wa* (youbeh wah)
The other day	*Senjitsu* (senjitsoo)
Please accept this (gift)	*Kore o dozo* (kawray oh dawzoh)
That's very kind of you	*Domo arigato gozaimasu* (dawmow arigahtaw gozighmass)
Please give my regards to ...	*... ni yoroshiku* (... nee yoroshekoo)
Excuse me, I must leave	*Shitsurei itashimasu* (shitsueray eetashimass)
Goodbye	*Sayonara* (sahyohnahrah)
Goodnight	*O-yasumi nasai* (oh-yahsueme nahsigh)
See you tomorrow	*Mata ashita* (mahtah ahshtah)
Thank you for taking care of me/us	*O-sewa ni narimashita* (o-sehwah nee narimashtah)
Let's meet again	*Mata o-ai shimasho* (mahtah oh-eyeshemahshaw)

Eating or drinking out

... please!	*... kudasai* (koodasigh)
How about ...?	*... ikaga desu ka* (eekahgah dess kah)
This	*Kore* (kawray)
Breakfast	*Choshoku* (chohshoku)
Coffee	*Kohi* (kawhe)
Tea (English-type)	*Kocha* (kawchah)
Juice	*Jusu* (joosoo)
Beer	*Biru* (beeroo)
Scotch	*Sukotchi* (skotchee)
Whisky with water and ice	*Mizuwari* (meezoowahree)
Rice wine	*O-sake* (oh-sahkeh)
Cigarettes	*Tabako* (tahbahkoh)
Menu	*Menyu* (menyou)
Another one	*Mo hitotsu* (maw hetotsu)
A little more	*Mo sukoshi* (maw skoshee)
The bill	*O-kanjo* (oh-kanjaw)
What is this?	*Kore wa nan desu ka* (kawray wah nan dess kah)
That looks delicious	*Oishiso desu ne* (oisheesaw dess nay)
It tastes delicious	*Oishii desu* (oishee-ee dess)
That was delicious	*Oishikatta desu* (oisheekat-tah dess)
Cheers!	*Kanpai* (kanpigh)
Bon appétit!	*Itadakimasu* (eetahdahkeymass)
Thank you for the meal	*Go-chisosama deshita* (gocheesawsama deshtah)
Where is the toilet?	*O-tearai wa dochira desu ka* (oh-tayarigh wah docheerah dess kah)

Small talk

| Do you speak English? | *Eigo ga dekimasu ka* (aygo gah dekeemass kah) |
| I speak only a little Japanese | *Nihongo wa sukoshi shika dekimasen* (neehongo wah skoshee shkah dekeemahsen) |

Japanese is very difficult	*Nihongo wa totemo muzukashii desu* (neehongo wah totehmow moozookashee-ee dess)
How do you say ...... in Japanese?	*...... wa Nihongo de nan to iimasu ka* (wah neehongo day nan toh ee-eemass kah)
What does ... mean?	*... wa do iu imi desu ka* (wah daw you eemee dess kah)
Are you married?	*Kekkon shite imasu ka* (kek-kon shtay eemass kah)
I'm married	*Watashi wa kekkon shite imasu* (wahtahshe wah kek-kon shtay eemass)
I'm single	*Dokushin desu* (dokooshin dess)
Have you any children?	*Kodomo wa imasu ka* (kodomow wah eemass kah)
You're very good (eg at English or golf)	*O-jozu desu ne* (oh-jawzoo dess nay)
Not really	*Chigaimasu* (cheeguyeemass)
What lovely weather!	*Ii o-tenki desu ne* (ee-ee oh-tenkey dess nay)
It's hot, isn't it	*Atsui desu ne* (atsooee dess nay)
It's cold, isn't it	*Samui desu ne* (samooee dess nay)
Do you understand?	*Wakarimasu ka* (wakahreemass ka)
Yes, I do (understand)	*Hai, wakarimasu* (high, wakahreemass)
No, I don't (understand)	*Ie, wakarimasen* (ee-eh, wakahreemasen)
Yes, that's right	*Hai, so desu* (high saw dess)

Asking directions

Excuse me, where is the ...?	*Sumimasen, ... wa doko desu ka* (suememahsen, ... wah dohkoh dess kah)
Excuse me, is there a ... near here?	*Sumimasen, kono chikaku ni ... arimasu ka* (suememahsen, kohnoh chikahkoo nee ... ahreemass kah)
Taxi rank	*Takushi noriba* (takshee noreebah)
Station	*Eki* (ehkey)
Subway station	*Chikatetsueki* (chickahtetsooayki)
Hotel/Japanese-style hotel	*Hoteru* (hohtehroo)/*Ryokan* (ryohkan)
Pharmacy	*Yakkyoku* (yak-kyohkoo)
Post office	*Yubinkyoku* (youbinkyohkoo)
Police box	*Koban* (kawban)
Public toilet	*O-tearai* (oh-tayarigh)
Public telephone	*Koshu denwa* (kawshoo denwah)
Travel agent	*Kotsukosha* (kawtsoo kawshah)
I'd like to make an international call	*Kokusai denwa o-negai shitai n'desu ga* (koksigh denwah oh-nehguy shtay'n dess gah)

Taxis and trains

To ... please	*... made o-negai shimasu* (... mahday oh-nehguy shemass)
The airport	*Kuko* (kookaw)
Please let me/us off here	*Koko de oroshite kudasai* (koko deh oroshteh koodasigh)
How much is it?	*Ikura desu ka* (eekoorah dess kah)
A single/return to ..., please	*... made katamichi/o-fuku o-negai shimasu* (... mahday kahtahmitchee/awfookoo oh-nehguy shemass)
First class	*Guriin ken* (green ken)

Manners and conversation

Etiquette is the indispensable lubricant in a society as hierarchical, and as crowded, as Japan's. Although the foreign visitor is not expected to be conversant with all the traditional courtesies, a willingness to learn is important. The essence of etiquette lies in the preservation of surface harmony. Humility, reserve, patience and tolerance are all qualities that contribute to this. Effusive apologies (for even minor errors) and effusive thanks (for even minor favours) also oil the wheels. Displays of anger, disappointment or frustration serve only to disrupt the surface harmony – often to the Westerner's disadvantage – and should be avoided.

Conversation

Be sensitive to status, and always address the most senior of your hosts, who may not be the best English-speaker. Listen rather than lecture, and when you speak, do so with modesty and reserve. Silent pauses in conversation are not feared but savoured in Japan. It is not Japanese practice to use first names, and it is best not to do so even if invited to, except in the most informal situations.

Clarity and tact Get into the habit of speaking carefully and clearly (but not patronizingly so), at least until you have gauged the English-speaking ability of your host. It is often wise to ask the same question twice, in a different way, to ensure understanding, but avoid constant (and especially ever-louder) repetition of questions and statements. This may require you to pretend that your host has understood when you have good reason to believe otherwise, but it saves face and maintains the harmony. Informal notes confirming the points discussed can be exchanged after any meeting (most businessmen are able to correspond without difficulty in English, though not in other European languages).

Yes? "Yes" (*Hai, hai*) very rarely means "Yes, I agree." It means "Yes, I'm listening," or "I see." The written word is always the surest indication of an affirmative answer.

No? "No" (*Ie*) is considered too blunt to be used often. Vaguer expressions such as "Maybe" or "Let's think about it" are most common. You, also, should use these less direct terms. A Japanese businessman will, for example, often appear to go along with what you say, especially if you pursue a point with vigour, even when he disagrees. His purpose is to maintain harmony. Try to take an indirect approach yourself until mutual trust has been established. Take care to conceal frustration and anger at the length of time it takes to make decisions. This is the way business works in Japan.

Sensitive subjects No topics are taboo. The political scene, sex and religion are less sensitive subjects in Japan than in many Western societies. The following, however, *are* sensitive: the role of MITI in Japanese industry, dumping, the Japanese work ethic, housing conditions, militarism and World War II, attitudes towards – and the status of – women, and the treatment of the Korean and *B'rakumin* (outcast) minorities. The Koreans, for example, are discriminated against in Japan, especially when it comes to marriage. People of Korean ancestry are usually careful to hide the fact.

It is a common Western gaffe to suppose that the Japanese worship their ancestors; they do not, but they do honour their memory.

Opening gambits Topics of endless interest include the family (family snaps always make useful conversation openings), the weather, sport (baseball, golf and sumo are avidly followed) and, above all, your impressions of Japan. Some familiarity with Japan's culture, its history (with the exception of World War II) and places of historical interest creates a very favourable impression.

Small talk Serious business negotiations will often begin with less serious conversation. Let your hosts initiate these informal exchanges and decide what topics are appropriate to the situation. This is the first step in building a successful business relationship.

Intimate questions Foreign visitors should be careful not to take umbrage at the intimate nature of certain questions on age ('How old are you?"), money ('How much do you earn?") and marital status ('Why are you not married?").

Humour Despite the stereotype of the Japanese as a race both serious and single-minded in its devotion to work, they have a great sense of fun. Although jokes as such are not told in Japan, the Japanese are certainly able to appreciate the funny side of things. Men laugh openly in Japan, but etiquette requires women to cover their mouths when they laugh. Raucous laughter should be confined to drinking establishments.

Body language

Harmony may be disturbed by transmitting inappropriate non-verbal signals or by failing to interpret signals received.

The bow As a Westerner, you may often be welcomed by a handshake, but the bow is the accepted form of greeting and farewell. If greeted with a bow, try to return the depth and intensity of the host's bow. The arms should be kept fairly straight with palms flat against the thighs. The eyes are lowered, as well as the upper body. Often you may be greeted with a compromise combination of a slight bow and handshake. The weak, almost reluctant, handshake of many Japanese should not be mistaken for weakness of character.

Physical contact Public displays of

affection for the opposite sex, such as kissing, hugging and holding hands, are both rare and generally frowned upon. Male displays of camaraderie, such as back-slapping, vigorous handshakes and arm-touching, should also be avoided.

Personal space The Japanese tend to require more personal space than Westerners, so when conversing take a position a little farther from your host than normal.

Eye contact should not be insisted on, as it often is in the West. It may be considered impolite and an infringement on personal space. A demure, downward look is not a sign of weakness or dishonesty.

The smile expresses pleasure, joy and affection, but it may also conceal embarrassment, frustration and discontent. The ubiquitous smile may be less a sign of affirmation or approval than of self-control.

Western ways

Because Western non-verbal language differs from that of the Japanese, there is much that may confuse. The Westerner should remember not to exaggerate emotions or those gestures that accompany them.

Shrugging The Japanese do not shrug their shoulders or understand what may be meant by it.

Winking While younger men may wink at women, the "affectionate wink" between friends will not be understood and is best avoided.

Pointing Avoid pointing, since it is thought too direct. The Japanese use the whole hand, palm up, in a horizontal, wavy motion in the general direction of the object, place or person being referred to.

Beckoning The Japanese beckon with the motion that in the West suggests "Go away." It is exactly the opposite of the Western beckoning action, with the fingers pointing down from the extended hand.

Nose blowing Handkerchiefs are used for wiping the fingers and the brow but almost never the nose. Paper tissues are used instead. The Western use of handkerchiefs for nose-blowing is considered extremely unhygienic. The Japanese will sniff, snort and spit with relish, but loud nose-blowing will certainly cause offence.

Dress Both men and women should avoid loud colours and flashy styles. For women, skirts and dresses are acceptable but trousers are generally best not worn in a business context. Classic restraint is preferable to glamour.

Japanese behaviour

Foreign visitors will need to adjust their expectations of what is acceptable social behaviour.

Chivalry has yet to reach Japan. Businesswomen should not expect seats to be offered or doors to be opened, since men precede women in everything. Likewise, the foreign businessman should not insist on Japanese women accepting chivalry. It may cause embarrassment, especially among the older generation. Indeed, the modern Japanese seem increasingly to place youth before age. It is not uncommon for a frail old lady to be deprived of a seat by a healthy young child.

Pushing and shoving Although strict codes of etiquette govern behaviour within any identifiable group, in the outside world anarchy sometimes reigns. Pushing and shoving in crowds, particularly in the subway, and reluctance to form orderly queues are both commonplace. Try to suppress any annoyance.

Excuse me "Excuse me, I'd like to get past" is often expressed non-verbally, by a combination of a bow and a karate-chop movement of the hand, repeated several times over.

Urination Urinating and spitting in public do not always cause the offence they do in some Western nations.

Women beware Japan is one of the safest places in the world, but this applies primarily to men. On crowded and late-night trains it is not uncommon for women (including foreign women) to be harassed.

Harassment can take the form of staring and attempts at touching. Curiously, Japanese society seems to turn a blind eye to such male harassment (perhaps because Japanese women are reluctant to make a scene). Most offensive approaches can be stopped instantly with shrieks of anger.

Mealtime etiquette

To order steak when your hosts suggest raw fish disturbs the harmony; to refuse to try a dish may offend. The rule is to conform. In all things follow your host, who will take pleasure in teaching you. Let him decide the menu. He will say *itadakimasu* ('bon appétit") before beginning the meal, and you should reply *itadakimasu*. Remember either to say *go-chisosama deshita* ('Thank you") at the end of the meal or to express effusive thanks in your own language.

Chopsticks Take your cue from the host and remove the wooden sticks from the paper sleeve, splitting them if necessary. Mastery of chopsticks is guaranteed to impress your hosts. Those less dextrous should practise in private or enter into the fun of being shown in public. Alternatively, ask for a fork. Never point chopsticks at anyone, never leave them crossed and never stick them vertically in the rice bowl. Align them neatly on the china chopstick rest.

Bowls Follow your host, who will first take the lid off his rice bowl and place it to the left. Next he will remove the lid of the soup bowl and place it to the right. The rice and soup bowls can both be held in the hand while eating. When drinking soup it is not impolite to slurp a little. Use both hands when holding out a bowl to have it refilled.

Alcohol Women traditionally pour for men and inferiors for superiors. Having had wine or beer poured for you, take the bottle and offer to pour in return. The host may offer you the cup from which he has drunk, carefully wiping it first. If this honour is extended to you, accept the cup graciously and raise it with both hands to be filled. If you are teetotal or just dislike sake, it is sufficient to bring the filled cup to your lips without drinking. An ability to consume vast quantities of alcohol is much admired, but when you have had your fill, do not leave the glass or cup standing empty or it will be refilled.

Toasts It is common practice to propose toasts, usually at the beginning of a meal. Etiquette is the opposite of that in the West, however, and the person being toasted should always drink the toast along with those who have proposed it.

Smoking The Japanese tend to smoke more than Westerners, and the conference room and drinking establishments can be very smoky places. Some Japanese smoke during meals. If you are a nonsmoker, do not be offended if your permission is not requested. If you are a smoker do not be offended if a cigarette is not offered to you. Cigarettes are considered very personal things.

The bill It is not necessary to offer to pay or split the bill in any establishment. To insist may offend. A return invitation to a Western-style restaurant or bar is the best way of repaying hospitality.

Living Japanese-style

Special care is called for when visiting a Japanese home (a rare honour) or a Japanese-style inn, or *ryokan*.

Shoes Remember to take your shoes off before entering a Japanese house or inn (slip-on shoes save time). Turn them around to face the door so that they will be easy to put on when leaving. You will then shuffle to the main room in "corridor slippers," provided at the entrance. Remove the slippers before entering a matted room (clean socks save embarrassment!). Use the corridor slippers again to take you to the toilet, where you must change into toilet slippers. Do not forget to remove your toilet slippers on leaving the toilet.

The toilet Toilets are usually squat-style, sometimes with no lock on the door. Knock on the door, and if it is engaged you will hear a counter-knock.

Bathing The Japanese bathe for relaxation as well as cleanliness. You will find Japanese-style baths in some hotels, in all inns, in the still-popular public baths and in all households. Although the bath is private, one is expected to use it in the prescribed manner; ignorance of bathing etiquette is unforgivable. First remove your clothes in the antechamber and place them in the basket provided. You will be given a hand towel to take into the bathroom. Squat on a stool and, with the bowl provided, scoop water from the tub and pour it over you. Using the hand towel and soap, wash your body thoroughly before rinsing off with water scooped from the bath. Only now can you step into the bath. You may take your well-rinsed hand towel in with you. Often the water is extremely hot. Add a little cold water from the tap if you wish. To avoid getting scorched, it is best to slip into the tub gently and keep still once you are in.

Never get into the bath without cleaning yourself first; don't use soap in the bath and don't pull out the plug. Others will be using the bath after you. After relaxing in the bath, climb out and wring your hand towel dry. With this you are expected to dry yourself. There may be a cotton kimono provided in the antechamber. If there is, slip it on over your underwear, wrapping the left side over the right (only corpses have their kimonos wrapped right over left!) and tying it with a sash.

Baths are to be enjoyed, so don't hurry excessively or you may offend your host.

City by City

Introduction

To the travelling executive, Japan can appear to be one immense city. The urban sprawl begins with Tokyo, which merges imperceptibly into Kawasaki and Yokohama – enormous cities in their own right – to form one of the biggest conurbations in the world. This megacity spreads westward along the Pacific coast, in an industrial belt that runs through Nagoya, Osaka and Hiroshima to the far tip of Honshu and, almost without interruption, on across the water to Kitakyushu, Fukuoka and beyond.

The cities within this 885km/550-mile urban landscape are those that the business traveller is most likely to visit, for it is here that Japan's main commercial and industrial centres are concentrated. The ten cities selected for this guide all have a population of 1m or more, and all but one – Sapporo, a refreshingly provincial, northern city – fall within the southern urban area.

The endless urban wilderness may leave the business traveller wondering what has happened to the mysterious Orient. It is, of course, still there, hidden just beneath the surface. Even in a cosmopolitan centre such as Tokyo, the plastic cherry blossom lining the street or the bowing elevator girls remind you with a jolt that this is Japan.

Japan's intercity transport system is excellent. The Bullet Train links every major city except Sapporo, and that omission will be remedied in the near future. It takes, for example, just seven hours from Tokyo to Fukuoka. The major cities are also linked by efficient airlines. Internal flights are only marginally more expensive than the Bullet Train and, frequently, a journey is cheaper by air than by train.

Finding your way around the cities is likely to be your major problem. Japan's address system is notoriously difficult to understand. An address may appear in English as, for example, 4-14-3 Ginza or 14-3 Ginza 4-chome, which are in fact the same; "chome" means district and the other numbers refer to blocks. However, the address of a place often seems to bear little relationship to its location. The easiest course is to take with you the name and address of your destination in Japanese (and phone number, in case of crisis) and let the taxi driver worry about finding it. Be patient; he, too, may have little idea where it is, but he will consult a policeman or call for directions. If you travel by subway (thus avoiding the traffic jams) telephone ahead to get exact directions, including the number of the subway exit and the appearance of the building.

Your difficulties will be eased by the helpfulness of the Japanese people. Japan may appear to be a land of cities, but what other country has cities where people look at you askance if you check a restaurant bill? The streets are safe, public transport runs exactly on time, public phones invariably work and the people are scrupulously honest.

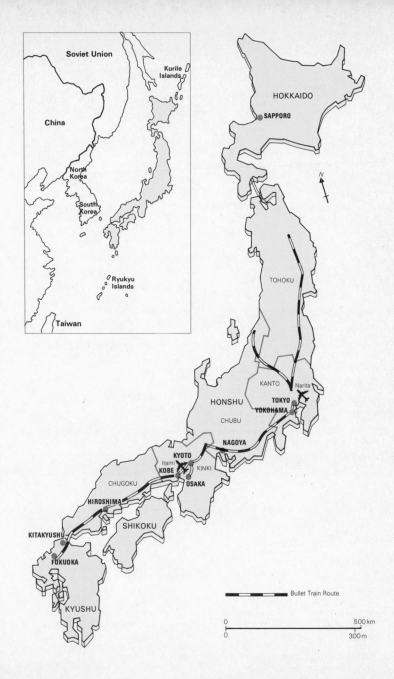

| | Soviet Union |
| Kurile Islands |
| China |
| North Korea |
| South Korea |
| Ryukyu Islands |
| Taiwan |

N

HOKKAIDO

SAPPORO

TOHOKU

KANTO
Narita

HONSHU

TOKYO
YOKOHAMA

CHUBU

NAGOYA

KYOTO

Itami

KOBE

KINKI

OSAKA

CHUGOKU

HIROSHIMA

SHIKOKU

KITAKYUSHU

FUKUOKA

KYUSHU

Bullet Train Route

0   500 km

0   300 m

TOKYO

City code ☎ 03

Tokyo sprawls over more than 2,000 sq kms/800 sq miles and has a population of nearly 13m. Government, industry and commerce, including most major companies and the stock market, are based here; and it is also the centre for sports, education and the arts. At the hub of the city are the commercial areas, with the residential areas lying on the periphery. Heavy and light industries, located in the coastal area, include electrical appliances, electronics, optical products, precision engineering, textiles, printing and publishing.

When shogun Tokugawa Ieyasu took the minor castle town of Edo as his capital in 1590, it marked a major transition in Japan's development, from a country dominated by the decadent Kyoto aristocracy to a modern commercial state. During the 250-year rule of the Tokugawas, Edo grew into the largest city in the world (in 1700 the population reached 1m). To service the enormous population of *daimyo* and samurai warlords, forced to spend part of each year there under surveillance, Tokugawa brought merchants and artisans to the city, and set about the reclamation of the eastern marshes (the present Tsukiji, Shimbashi and Nihonbashi districts) for their use. Theoretically one of the lowest classes in the rigid Tokugawa hierarchy, the merchants actually became more and more prosperous, and the impoverished samurai had to come to them for money.

In 1868, Emperor Meiji abolished the shogunate and moved his court from Kyoto to Edo, renaming it Tokyo (Eastern Capital). The city began a period of rapid modernization to bring it into line with the West. The *daimyo* left, and the merchants, now able to move freely, settled in the hilly areas in the western part of the city.

Tokyo continues to grow and change. The main area of expansion at present is around Shinjuku and out into the western suburbs where there is still empty land for building. In 1991 the metropolitan government will move from Marunouchi to Shinjuku, where a new City Hall, designed by Kenzo Tange, is under construction. There are plans for a high-speed underground road link between Shinjuku and Otemachi and talk of a Bullet Train station here sometime in the future. Tokyo Bay and the whole Tokyo waterfront are also being redeveloped, largely as a resort area, although many of the financial institutions of Kabutocho are also expanding into this area.

Arriving

From 1992, business travellers arriving at Narita International airport will be able to enjoy the facilities of a second passenger terminal. However, Narita still remains singularly inconvenient, located a gruelling 66 kms/40 miles from Tokyo. The previous international airport, Haneda, a mere 15mins from town, now handles mainly domestic flights. There is a limousine bus connecting the two airports, which takes about 90mins, and a new helicopter link with 8 flights a day.

Narita airport

Narita is a highly efficient modern airport, designed to ensure the smoothest possible passage for the traveller. Immigration procedures are extremely rapid, signs are in English as well as Japanese and even the porters are friendly and helpful. The only complaint is the time it takes to get to Tokyo. Facilities include a wide range of good-quality restaurants, coffee shops and bars, most of them open until 8pm; VIP lounges for first class passengers; plenty of useful shops, including a branch of Mitsukoshi and shops selling electronic goods, woodblock prints and kimonos; several banks, open from 7.30am to 11pm. JAL Cargo Services ☎ (0476) 32 3350. Airport information ☎ (0476) 32 2800.

Nearby hotels Narita Prince 560 Tokko, Narita ☎ (0476) 33 1111 ⟨TX⟩ 3762147 fax (0476) 33 1108; *Narita View*, 700 Kosuge, Narita ☎ (0476) 32 1111 ⟨TX⟩ 3762123 fax (0476) 32 1078; *Narita Nikko*, 500 Tokko, Narita ☎ (0476) 32 0032 ⟨TX⟩ 3762165 fax (0476) 32 3993; *ANA Hotel Narita*, 68 Horinouchi, Narita ☎ (0476) 33 1311 fax (0476) 24 1050.

City link The easiest way to cover the 66kms/40 miles into Tokyo is to be met, or to dig deep into your wallet for the taxi fare. Failing that, the comfortable limousine bus is a good alternative. The journey by road takes 60–75mins; allow an extra 30mins in rush hours.

Taxi and limousine There are always plenty of taxis. A chauffeur-driven limousine can be arranged at the limousine bus desk.

Car rental Major firms have offices at Narita.

Bus There are buses direct to 30 major hotels, departing between 6am and 10pm. Alternatively, take the bus to the city air terminal, from where you will have to take a taxi.

Train The Keisei Skyliner is fast, reliable and cheap. Comfortable, air-conditioned trains depart every 30mins between 8am and 10pm, with a journey time of exactly 1hr. However, Keisei Narita station is a bus ride from the airport and you will need to take a taxi or subway from the Tokyo terminal, Keisei Ueno, to your hotel. There are also stopping trains on the Keisei and JR lines, which take slightly longer.

Haneda airport

Most domestic flights use Haneda, and there are connections with every major city. Facilities are somewhat more basic than at Narita, and you will have to walk across the tarmac to your plane. There are several restaurants, coffee shops and bars on landside, open until 8.30pm; a few shops with a limited range of goods – mainly local foods, tea and cakes; and a bank, open until 4.30pm. Airport information ☎ 747 8000.

Nearby hotels Haneda Tokyu, 2-8-6 Haneda Kuko, Ota-ku ☎ 747 0311 ⟨TX⟩ 2466560 fax 747 0366.

City link Monorail is the best way to get into Tokyo. Trains depart for Hamamatsucho on the Yamanote line, every 6–7mins between 6.40am and 11pm. The journey takes 16mins. There are no porters or trolleys.

Taxi It takes about 45mins to get to Tokyo station by taxi.

Bus The limousine bus departs every 40mins and stops at the main hotels in Shinjuku. There are also buses to Narita and Yokohama.

Railway stations

Bullet Trains heading west from Tokyo run from Tokyo station; those heading northeast depart from Ueno station.

Tokyo station Built in 1914, Tokyo station is vast and labyrinthine, with north, central and south exits connected by a passageway. The Marunouchi subway line is at the north exit of the station, and the south exit connects with Daimaru department store and a large underground shopping mall. The Bullet Train tracks are at one side. When you surrender your Bullet Train ticket, retain the remaining ticket, which enables you to transfer to other JR lines and get off at any JR station in Tokyo. Inquiries ☎ 212 4441 or 4456.

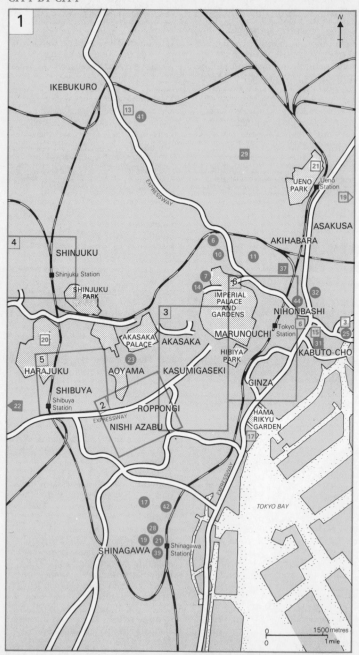

HOTELS | Map

		Map
1	Akasaka Prince	3
2	Akasaka Tokyo	3
3	ANA	3
4	Capitol Tokyo	3
5	Century Hyatt	4
6	Edmont	1
7	Fairmont	1
8	Ginza Tobu	6
9	Ginza Tokyu	6
10	Grand Palace	1
11	Hilltop	1
12	Hilton	4
13	Imperial	6
14	Kayu Kaikan	1
15	Keio Plaza	4
16	Marunouchi	6
17	Miyako	1
18	New Otani	3
19	New Takanawa Prince	1
20	Okura	3
21	Pacific Meridien	1
22	Palace	6
23	President	3
24	Roppongi Prince	2
25	Royal Park	1
26	Seiyo Ginza	6
27	Shiba Park	3
28	Takanawa Prince	1
29	Tokyo Prince	3
30	Yaesu Fujiya	6
31	Atagoyama Tokyo Inn	3
32	Gimmond	1
33	Ginza Daiichi	6
34	Ginza International	6
35	Ginza Marunouchi	6
36	Ginza Nikko	6
37	Mitsui Urban	6
38	Shimbashi Daiichi	6
39	Shinagawa Prince	1
40	Shinjuku Washington	4
41	Sunshine City Prince	1
42	Takanawa	1
43	Tobu	5
44	Tokyo City	1
45	Tokyo Station	6

RESTAURANTS | Map

		Map
1	Al Porto	2
2	Apicius	6
	Attore (hotel 26)	6
3	Bistrot de la Citè	2
4	Borsalino	2
5	Brasserie Bernard	2
6	Cay	5
7	Chez Inno	6
8	Chianti	2 & 3
9	Daini's Table	5
10	Hiramatsu	2
11	Ile de France	2
	Imari (hotel 12)	4
12	Joel	5
	Keyaki Grill (hotel 4)	3
	La Belle Epoque (hotel 20)	3
13	L'Affresco	6
14	La Granata	3
15	La Rochelle	5
16	La Terre	3
	La Tour d'Argent (hotel 18)	3
17	L'Ecrin	6
	Les Saisons (hotel 13)	6
18	L'Orangerie de Paris	5
	Maxim's de Paris	
	(building 12)	6
19	Metropole	2
20	Mireille	2 & 3
21	Moti	3
22	Pachon	1
23	Petit Point	2
24	Queen Alice	2
25	Sabatini Aoyama	5
	Sabatini di Firenze	
	(building 12)	6
26	Spago	2
	Star Hill (hotel 4)	3
	Tohkalin (hotel 20)	3
27	Edogin	6
28	Fukuzushi	2
29	Goemon	1
30	Hayashi	3
31	Inagiku	1
32	Inakaya	3
33	Isehiro	6
34	Kocho	6
35	Kushinobo	3
36	Kyubei	6
37	Matsuya	1
38	Mon Cher Ton Ton	2
	Nadaman (hotel 18)	3
39	Nambantei	2
40	Sushi Bar Sai	5
41	Sushi Sei	3
42	Takamura	2
43	Tempura Tenichi	6
44	Yama-no-chaya	3
45	Zakuro	3

BUILDINGS | Map

		Map
1	Central Post Office	6
2	Chamber of Commerce	6
3	City Air Terminal	1
4	Immigration Office	3
5	Japan National Tourist	
	Organisation	6
6	Japan Travel Bureau	1
7	JETRO	3
8	MITI	3
9	Mitsukoshi Department Store	6
10	National Diet	3
11	Seibu/Hankyu Department	
	Store	6
12	Sony Building	6
13	Sunshine City Convention	
	Centre	1
14	Takashimaya Department Store	6
15	Tokyo Stock Exchange	1
16	Tokyo Tower	3
17	Tokyo Trade Centre	1
18	Tourist Information Centre	6
19	Asakusa Kannon Temple	1
20	Meiji Shrine	1
21	Tokyo National Museum	1

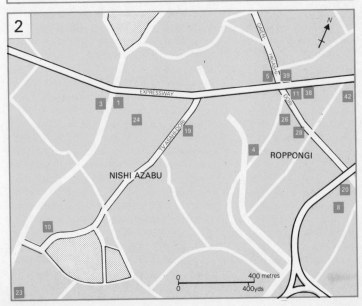

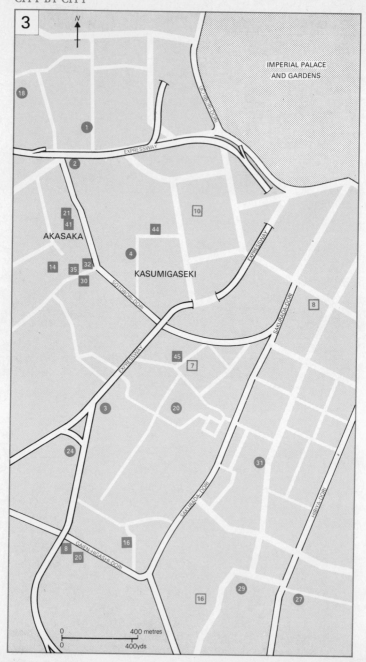

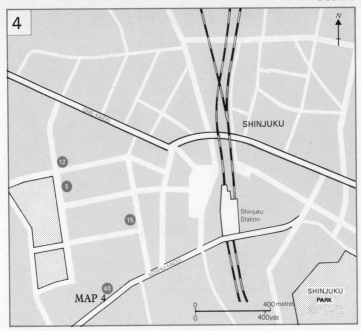

MAP 4

MAP 3

⬤ **HOTELS**

1 Akasaka Prince
2 Akasaka Tokyu
3 ANA
4 Capitol Tokyo
18 New Otani
20 Okura
24 Roppongi Prince
27 Shiba Park
29 Tokyo Prince
31 Atagoyama Tōkyō Inn

⬛ **RESTAURANTS**

8 Chianti
Keyaki Grill (hotel 4)
La Belle Epoque (hotel 20)
14 La Granata
16 La Terre
La Tour d'Argent (hotel 18)
20 Mireille
21 Moti
Tohkalin (hotel 20)
Star Hill (hotel 4)
30 Hayashi
32 Inakaya
35 Kushinobo
Nadaman (hotel 18)
41 Sushi Sei
44 Yama-no-chaya
45 Zakuro

⬜ **BUILDINGS**

7 JETRO
8 MITI
10 National Diet
16 Tokyo Tower

MAP 4

⬤ **HOTELS**

5 Century Hyatt
12 Hilton
15 Keio Plaza
40 Shinjuku Washington

⬛ **RESTAURANTS**

Imari (hotel 12)

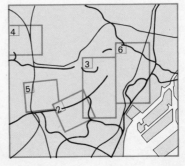

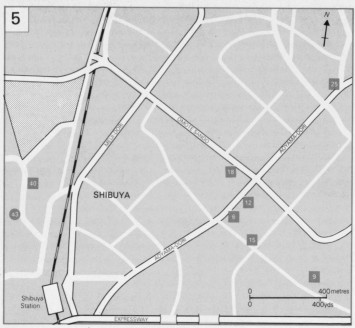

MAP 5

● HOTELS

43 Tobu

■ RESTAURANTS

6 Cay
9 Daini's Table
12 Joel
15 La Rochelle
18 L'Orangerie de Paris
25 Sabatini Aoyama
40 Sushi Bar Sai

MAP 6

● HOTELS

8 Ginza Tobu
9 Ginza Tokyu
13 Imperial
16 Marunouchi
22 Palace
26 Seiyo Ginza
30 Yaesu Fujiya
33 Ginza Daiichi
34 Ginza International
35 Ginza Marunouchi
36 Ginza Nikko
37 Mitsui Urban
38 Shimbasi Daiichi
45 Tokyo Station

■ RESTAURANTS

2 Apicius
  Attore (hotel 26)
7 Chez Inno
13 L'Affresco
17 L'Ecrin
  Les Saisons (hotel 13)
  Maxim's de Paris (building 12)
  Sabatini di Firenze
    (building 12)
27 Edogin
33 Isehiro
34 Kocho
36 Kyubei
43 Tempura Tenichi

□ BUILDINGS

1 Central Post Office
2 Chamber of Commerce
4 Immigration Office
5 Japan National Tourist Organisation
9 Mitsukoshi Department Store
11 Seibu/Hankyu Department Store
12 Sony Building
14 Takashimaya Department Store
18 Tourist Information Centre

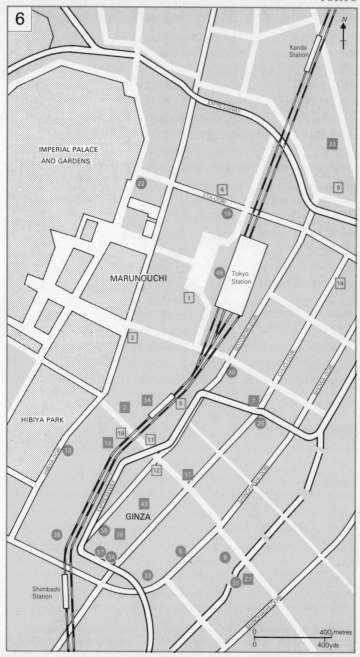

6

N

IMPERIAL PALACE
AND GARDENS

Kanda
Station

33

9

22

ETA-DORI

4

16

MARUNOUCHI

45　Tokyo
Station

1

14

2

30

SOTOBORI-DORI

CHUO-DORI

SHOWA-DORI

34

2

5

7

26

HIBIYA PARK

18

13

11

HIBIYA-DORI

12

17

SHINOBASHI-DORI

43

13

GINZA

38

36

36

37

34

8

9

33

35

27

EXPRESSWAY

Shimbashi
Station

SHINOBASHI-DORI

0　　　　　400 metres

0　　　　　400yds

Getting around

Tokyo's streets were first laid out in irregular zigzags to confuse the enemy, and it is still notoriously difficult to find your way around. Taxi drivers will know hotels and major landmarks but otherwise will be as baffled as you are. Japanese usually draw maps for each other. The best procedure is to consult your hotel concierge or to phone your destination and find out the nearest subway or train station and the direction from there. Tokyo policemen in small neighbourhood police boxes are helpful and usually speak some English. As a last resort, telephone the TIC's Travel Phone ☎ 502 1461. A map of Tokyo including subway and train routes is essential; the TIC issues several good ones, and maps are available at hotels. Travel in Tokyo during the rush hours (7.30–9.30am and 5–7pm) by any mode of transport is to be avoided if at all possible.

Taxis Cabs are clean and taxi drivers generally courteous. Unfortunately, almost none of them speak English, and even if they did, they would still not know the way. It is always worthwhile having the name and address of your destination in Japanese; ask your hotel concierge to write it for you. Tokyo's streets are full of taxis – simply flag one down. A red light means "for hire." There are ranks at hotels, stations, department stores and on main streets such as the Ginza. Beware of the passenger door, which opens and closes automatically. Tipping is not customary. Although subways and trains are faster than taxis for daytime travel, taxis are the only form of transport late at night, when public transport closes down. After 11pm you may need to hold up two or three fingers (to show that you will pay two or three times the fare) to get a taxi to stop.

Driving The roads are crowded, the traffic system is complicated and road signs are in Japanese only. The main car rental chains have branches in the

city, but driving will only add to the difficulties of coping with Tokyo's boisterous complexity.

Walking It is possible, interesting and, apart from a few streets around Shinjuku, completely safe to walk around Tokyo; but distances are enormous.

Bus Even for those who speak Japanese, the buses are fairly confusing and to be avoided.

Subway Tokyo's subways are clean, safe and the quickest, most efficient way to get around, although some of the lines are more convenient than others. With the aid of a map, the system is reasonably easy to use. The major lines, each a different colour, are operated by Teito Rapid Transit Authority. You can transfer easily and conveniently between the Chiyoda (green), Ginza (orange), Hibiya (grey) and Marunouchi (red) lines. Connections are more difficult on the Hanzomon (purple), Tozai (pale blue) and Yurakucho (yellow) lines. There are also three Toei lines run by Tokyo Metropolitan subways. Trains run every 2–3mins from 5am to midnight, more frequently in rush hours and less frequently in early morning and late evening.

Subway stations are marked by a dark blue circular symbol. Buy your ticket from a machine, some of which will change a Y1,000 note. If in doubt, buy the cheapest ticket and pay the difference at the fare adjustment office at your destination. Platforms are signposted in English, with the terminal, the preceding station and the next one all indicated. Subway system maps in stations are usually in Japanese only, with a blank red square to indicate where you are. At large subway stations there are maps of the many exits, again only in Japanese; the company you are visiting should tell you the letter and number of the exit.

Train The JR trains are all colour-coded. The most useful are the Yamanote line (green) which circles the city, with 29 stops, including Tokyo, Ueno, Shinjuku, Shibuya,

Shinagawa and Hamamatsucho, and the Chuo line (orange) which cuts across, linking Tokyo station with Shinjuku and the western suburbs. The Sobu line (yellow) follows the same line across Tokyo as the Chuo, stopping at every station. The train is somewhat more difficult to use than the subway, since most signs are in Japanese only. Beware of boarding an express, which will speed you out to the western suburbs without stopping. Some of Tokyo's stations are vast, extremely crowded and very confusing; Shinjuku, probably the largest station in the world, is notorious.

Area by area

Tokyo grew up around Edo Castle, gradually expanding into a huge metropolis. The Imperial Palace is still the heart of the city; in its shadow is Marunouchi, the main business and administrative district. However, central Tokyo has reached its limits. The development of a New Metropolitan Centre in west Shinjuku began in 1971 and today it is one of the capital's key business areas. Most of Japan's high-tech and computer companies – whose laboratories and factories are based in satellite industrial parks still farther out to the west – have offices in Shinjuku; and the city government, in spite of much opposition in Marunouchi, will move there in 1991.

Marunouchi Marunouchi is the business centre of Tokyo and business heart of the nation. Strategically located around Tokyo station, to the southeast of the Imperial Palace, it extends north to Otemachi and south to Nihonbashi. It is an area of trim office blocks, their height limited by earthquake regulations, and neat tree-lined avenues, full of hurrying business people by day and completely deserted at night. Here you will find the headquarters of most major Japanese companies, including trading and financial firms and insurance companies, and the offices of international corporations, banks and airlines.

Nihonbashi The first of the merchant areas to be reclaimed from the sea, Nihonbashi is an important mercantile and commercial district. Banks, including the Bank of Japan, and national government offices are concentrated here, as is the main branch of Mitsukoshi, Japan's most prestigious department store.

Kabutocho Japan's premier financial district is on the other side of Nihonbashi. It houses the Tokyo stock exchange.

Ginza The Ginza is Japan's most famous shopping district, full of expensive shops, famous department stores and restaurants, as well as art galleries, theatres and cinemas. The San-Ai Building, at the main Ginza crossing, stands on one of the most expensive pieces of land in the world. On Sundays the main street is closed to traffic and crowded with pedestrians. At night Ginza dons a sybaritic aspect and is revealed as the home of some of Japan's most expensive hostess clubs, the scene of lavish expense-account entertaining by Japanese executives.

Kasumigaseki Kasumigaseki is the country's administrative centre, full of government offices, ministries and agencies. Here you will find the National Diet and the prime minister's official residence.

Akasaka This is an area of high-class entertainment of all varieties. The small, exclusive *ryotei*, where politicians and company directors dine to the accompaniment of geisha entertainment, are concentrated here, and Akasaka's cabarets, nightclubs, discos, bars and restaurants are among the smartest in town. Dominating the bustling side streets is the TBS television headquarters, and up the hill are two of Tokyo's best hotels, the New Otani and the Akasaka Prince.

Roppongi At night Roppongi's neon-lit main street is packed with pleasure-seekers. You can eat, drink and dance in its restaurants and discos until morning. The crowds here are younger and more international than in Akasaka. Just off the main street are expensive residential districts and embassies. To the south is Shiba with its large and pleasant park. Towards Akasaka, near the prestigious Okura Hotel, is the Ark Hills development, a centre for foreign companies, such as Bank of America and IBM. There are also cultural facilities such as a concert hall and broadcasting channel.

Nishi Azabu Nishi Azabu is host to some of Tokyo's most stylish and fashionable bars and restaurants. Just down the road is Hiroo, where many of the resident foreign executives live.

Aoyama Aoyama, between Shibuya and Akasaka, is full of sophisticated and expensive boutiques, antique shops and restaurants. Much of it is residential, and there are several embassies.

Shibuya Shibuya is Tokyo's fashion centre and the haunt of trendy young Japanese. The denizens of nearby Harajuku are even younger and considerably more outrageous.

Shinjuku Shinjuku, boasting one of the world's largest and most confusing stations, is one of Tokyo's liveliest areas. The main streets are full of department stores and boutiques. Kabukicho, up by the station, a maze of tiny streets bright with neon, is Tokyo's amusement centre and a place to explore Japan's phenomenal range of pleasures of the flesh – strip shows, "pink" cabaret, "soapland" massage parlours and more besides. In parts of Kabukicho it is sensible to be a little wary at night. You may bump into not only the executives you did business with in the morning, but also the *yakuza*,

the Japanese Mafia. In west Shinjuku, on the other side of the station, is the New Metropolitan Centre with its skyscrapers (theoretically earthquake-proof). High-tech and computer companies such as Computervision and Canon are based here. The New Sumitomo, a high-tech business centre with Japan's biggest concentration of computer hardware and software companies is also here.

Shinagawa There is not much in Shinagawa besides hotels, but it is a pleasant and green district with plenty of space and trees. Along the coast lies the Keihin industrial belt, full of factories and warehouses.

Other areas Akihabara is Tokyo's electronics district. Ueno is where the national museums are located. Ikebukuro, a student area and a major shopping district, is the home of Sunshine City, a vast convention complex. There are plans to turn the area into a cultural centre.

The suburbs

Most of Tokyo's residential areas are outside the city centre in the suburbs, and many people commute from as far as Saitama and Chiba. The western suburbs, out from Shibuya and Shinjuku, are the fashionable ones. Setagaya, sprawling out west of Shibuya, and Mejiro, on the Yamanote line, are traditionally the places where old families and the very rich live, whereas Denenchofu and Jiyugaoka are for those who are both well-off and stylish. The up-and-coming areas are west of Shinjuku, in the direction of the developing industrial zones. Quiet residential areas such as Kichijoji and Kokubunji are rapidly becoming boom towns, with land prices rocketing.

Hotels

Tokyo's hotels rank with the best in the world, from the grand old hotels like the Okura, still the top as far as prestige is concerned, to ultra-modern international-style hotels such as the stunningly designed Akasaka Prince. In spite of the city's reputation for high prices, Tokyo's hotels are no more expensive than those of New York or London. There are many moderately priced hotels conveniently located for the business centres and even – appropriate to Tokyo as electronic leader of the world – futuristic high-tech hotels.

Akasaka Prince *Y/////*
1-2 Kioicho, Chiyoda-ku, 102
☎ *234 1111* ⊠ *2324028*
fax 262 5163 • *AE DC MC V* •
678 rooms, 82 suites, 7 restaurants,
2 bars, 3 coffee shops/tea lounges
The decor is stunning in this very modern and fashionable hotel, designed by Kenzo Tange. The spacious rooms are completely white and very stylish, with huge windows and vistas over the city. In spite of its glamorous style, the Akasaka Prince is notably business-oriented, with a well-equipped Executive Service Centre and spacious executive suites on four floors; it is possible to reserve an entire floor complete with meeting rooms. 24hr room service, concierge and travel desk, limousine bus to airport • business service centre with extensive facilities, 33 meeting rooms (capacity up to 1,600).

Akasaka Tokyu *Y////*
2-14-3 Nagatacho, Chiyoda-ku, 100
☎ *580 2311* ⊠ *2224310*
fax 580 6066 • *554 rooms, 2 suites,*
2 restaurants, 2 bars, 2 coffee
shop/tea lounges
Hidden behind a long arcade of fashionable shops and directly opposite Akasaka Mitsuke station, the Tokyu is better known as the "Pyjama hotel" because of its striped exterior. It is not in the same class as the other Akasaka hotels. The rooms are acceptable, but basically one stays here for the location and the price. Secretarial services, 4 meeting rooms (capacity up to 220).

ANA *Y/////*
1-12-33 Akasaka, Minato-ku, 107
☎ *505 1111* ⊠ *2424625*
fax 505 1155 • *AE DC MC V* •
867 rooms, 33 suites, 5 restaurants,
3 bars, 2 coffee shops
In the Ark Hills business complex, the ANA is an American-designed luxury hotel. It features an enormous lobby overflowing with greenery, a waterfall and a stream, and attractive bedrooms (all with minibar) each with a view of Mount Fuji, Tokyo Bay or the Imperial Palace. There is an executive floor. For enthusiasts of the game *Go*, there is a salon devoted to it on the top floor. Travel desk, shopping arcade • outdoor pool, sauna, massage (men only) • business service centre with extensive facilities, 20 meeting rooms (capacity up to 2,200).

Capitol Tokyu *Y/////*
2-10-3 Nagatacho, Chiyoda-ku, 100
☎ *581 4511* ⊠ *2223605*
fax 581 5822 • *AE DC MC V* •
461 rooms, 18 suites, 4 restaurants,
1 bar, 3 coffee shops
Some people still consider the Capitol Tokyu, the old Hilton, to be the best hotel in Tokyo, and certainly it is among the top, although foreigners rate it more highly than Japanese. The decor is quiet and classic with many Japanese touches, a huge flower arrangement in the lobby, and spacious bedrooms, all with minibar. There are executive suites on two floors. The Keyaki Grill (see *Restaurants*) is much used by foreign executives and diplomats, and the Star Hill (see *Restaurants*) is one of Tokyo's best Chinese restaurants. 24hr room service, theatre bookings and travel information, arcade of shops including hairdresser, chemist and bookshop, bus to airport • pool • secretarial services, 10 meeting rooms (capacity up to 1,000).

Century Hyatt *Y////*
2-7-2 Nishi Shinjuku, Shinjuku-ku,
106 ☎ *349 0111* ⊠ *2325231*
fax 344 5575 • *AE DC MC V* •
780 rooms, 20 suites, 6 restaurants,
5 bars, 1 coffee shop
Located among the Shinjuku skyscrapers, the Century Hyatt is particularly popular with American

business travellers. The executive floor, the Regency Club, offers a private lounge, conference facilities and a helpful concierge. There is a rooftop pool with spectacular views, and a popular disco, the Samba Club. 24hr room service • pool • secretarial services, 20 meeting rooms.

Edmont *Y*////
3-10-8 Iidabashi, Chiyoda-ku, 102
☎ *237 1111* TX *2324510*
fax 234 4371 • *AE DC MC V* •
JR/Seiyo • *450 rooms, 2 restaurants, 2 bars, 2 coffee shops/tea lounges*
The Edmont, opened in 1985, was Seibu's first venture into hotel-building, and as with their department stores, the concept has been carefully developed. The customer being wooed is the travelling executive: each bedroom is equipped like a mini-office, with a large desk on which a fax machine or word processor can be installed on request; and there is a seminar room with audio-visual equipment.
Members of the Edmont Club can use a private lounge with secretarial services. Unfortunately, the hotel is somewhat off the beaten track, at Iidabashi. 17 meeting rooms.

Fairmont *Y*/
2-1-17 Kudan Minami, Chiyoda-ku, 102 ☎ *262 1151* TX *2322883*
fax 264 2476 • *AE DC MC V* •
240 rooms, 2 restaurants, 1 bar, 1 coffee shop
Many European businessmen name the Fairmont as their favourite low-budget hotel. It has a pleasant air of comfortable restraint and is set in a quiet backwater surrounded by avenues of cherry trees beside the Imperial Palace moat. The twin and double rooms are much more spacious than the singles. 9 meeting rooms (capacity up to 50).

Ginza Tobu *Y*/////
6-14-10 Ginza, Chuo-ku, 104
☎ *546 0111* TX *2523388*
fax 546 8990 • *Ramada Renaissance* • *AE DC MC V* • *197 rooms, 9 suites,*
3 restaurants, 1 bar, 1 tea lounge
The Ginza Tobu opened in 1987 and is still gleaming and immaculate. The staff are smiling and eager to please. The rooms, though small, are equipped with all the latest high-tech – three telephones per room, for example, one of which may be used for sending fax communications. There are two executive floors and a small executive lounge. 24hr room service. Travel desk. Secretarial services. 6 meeting rooms.

Ginza Tokyu *Y*////
5-15-9 Ginza, Chuo-ku, 104
☎ *541 2411* TX *2522601*
fax 541 6622 • *AE DC MC V* •
444 rooms, 3 suites, 4 restaurants, 1 bar, 2 coffee shops
European and American business travellers make up nearly half the clientele of this exceptionally popular moderately-priced hotel in Higashi Ginza, which is within walking distance of Marunouchi. The rooms are soundproofed and efficiently furnished, with a good-sized desk. Service is brisk, efficient and friendly. Travel desk, shops • men's sauna, massage • secretarial services, 11 meeting rooms (capacity up to 350).

Grand Palace *Y*////
1-1-1 Iidabashi, Chiyoda-ku, 102
☎ *264 1111* TX *2322981*
fax 230 4985 • *Friendship, affil.*
Palace Hotel • *AE DC MC V* •
483 rooms, 4 suites, 7 restaurants, 2 bars, 1 coffee shop
Pleasantly located close to Kitanomaru Park and the Imperial Palace, and right above Kudanshita subway station, only two stops from Marunouchi, the Grand Palace is a tranquil hotel, popular with visiting foreign executives. The friendly staff aim to make the hotel like a home for the business traveller. The twin rooms are considerably more spacious than the singles. Travel desk, arcade of shops, hairdresser • jogging in Kitanomaru Park • secretarial services, 25 meeting rooms (capacity up to 1,000).

Hilltop [Y]//

1-1 Surugadai, Kanda, Chiyoda-ku,
101 ☎ *293 2311* ⊠ *2226712*
fax 233 4567 ● *AE DC MC V* ●
74 rooms, 1 suite, 4 restaurants,
2 bars, 1 coffee shop

A long-time favourite of writers and
artists, the Hilltop is a faintly
eccentric, lovely old hotel. The 1930s
atmosphere has been lovingly
preserved, from the ceramic borders
along the corridors to the velvet
curtains, tasselled lampshades and
heavy wooden furniture in the
bedrooms. In keeping with the plan
of the founder, a wealthy
philanthropist, health-giving negative
ions are circulated around the rooms.
The Tempura Yamanoue restaurant is
well regarded. There is also a more
down-to-earth business annexe.
1 meeting room (capacity up to 100).

Hilton [Y]////

6-6-2 Nishi Shinjuku, Shinjuku-ku,
106 ☎ *344 5111* ⊠ *2324515*
fax 342 6094 ● *AE DC MC V* ●
788 rooms, 53 suites, 4 restaurants,
2 bars

The curving Hilton opened in 1984
among the skyscrapers in the
developing business area west of
Shinjuku station. It offers all the
standard Hilton facilities, and foreign
executives, particularly Americans,
make up a large proportion of the
guests. The bedrooms, all with
minibar and in-house movies, are
exceptionally large and attractively
furnished with Japanese touches
including paper *shoji* windows and
Nishijin silk framed on the walls. The
executive suites have a private lounge
and check-in counter and a helpful
concierge. The Imari Restaurant (see
Restaurants) is popular for business
dining and there is a fine Chinese
restaurant, Dynasty. 24hr room
service, travel desk, shops, pharmacy,
hairdresser, hotel bus to Shinjuku
station, Narita and Haneda ● fitness
centre with sauna, gym, massage,
pool, tennis courts ● business service
centre with extensive facilities, 11
meeting rooms (capacity up to 1,300).

Imperial [Y]////

1-1-1 Uchisaiwaicho, Chiyoda-ku, 100
☎ *504 1111* ⊠ *2222346*
fax 581 9146 ● *AE DC MC V* ●
1,065 rooms, 75 suites, 12 restaurants,
3 bars, 2 coffee shops

Founded in 1890, the Imperial is
Japan's oldest Western-style hotel.
For prestige it is second only to the
Okura, and for quality many would
now give it top place. The style is
solid and traditional, from the
imposing lobby to the impeccably
furnished bedrooms with views over
the Imperial Palace and Tokyo Bay;
the rooms in the Tower block are
particularly popular. The Executive
Service Lounge is the best in town,
and the Old Imperial Bar (see *Bars*) is
one of Tokyo's most popular meeting
places. The Imperial also boasts
Tokyo's only non-smoking coffee
shop. Les Saisons (see *Restaurants*) is
a favourite for business lunches. The
Imperial is conveniently located close
to Ginza and within walking distance
of the major trading companies.
Concierge, theatre and travel
bookings, 2 shopping arcades, beauty
salon, post office, medical and dental
clinics ● indoor pool, sauna, massage,
jogging ● business service centre with
extensive facilities, 26 meeting rooms,
including the vast Fuji conference
room with 6-channel translation
facilities (capacity up
to 2,000).

Kayu Kaikan [Y]/

8-1 Sanbancho, Chiyoda-ku, 102
☎ *230 1111* ⊠ *2323318*
fax 230 2529 ● *Okura* ● *AE DC MC V*
● *116 rooms, 11 suites, 2 restaurants,*
1 bar, 1 coffee shop

The Kayu Kaikan is a rare find, in
spite of its rather inconvenient
location, near Hanzomon. Owned by
the Ministry of Foreign Affairs and
managed by the Hotel Okura, it
offers exceptionally spacious (if
somewhat spartan) rooms and fine
cuisine prepared by Okura chefs,
along with a serene, peaceful
atmosphere, all at budget prices.
Service is pruned to a minimum.

Hotel guests have access to the Executive Service Salon at the Okura. No room service • 5 meeting rooms.

Keio Plaza ⓨ////
2-2-1 Nishi Shinjuku, Shinjuku-ku, 160☎ *344 0111* ⓉⓍ *J26874 fax 344 0247* • *InterContinental* • *AE DC MC V* • *1,485 rooms, 23 suites, 17 restaurants, 10 bars, 2 coffee shops/tea lounges*
The first skyscraper in Shinjuku and Japan's tallest hotel, the Keio Plaza opened in 1971. The rooms on the upper floors have views across Tokyo to Mount Fuji and have to be reserved well in advance. The Keio Plaza has all the features of a deluxe international-style hotel. The rooms are spacious, with a separate dressing area and in-house movies, and there is an executive floor and a business service centre. The vast convention complex is geared to cater for meetings and conferences, large or small. Concierge, travel desk, theatre bookings, arcade of shops, hairdresser, medical and dental clinics, courier service, florist, pharmacy, hotel bus to airport • outdoor pool, men's sauna, jogging, concessionary rates at Do Sports Plaza and Sakuragaoka Country Golf Club • business service centre with extensive facilities, 32 meeting rooms (capacity up to 2,000).

Marunouchi ⓨ///
1-6-3 Marunouchi, Chiyoda-ku, 100☎ *215 2151* ⓉⓍ *2224655 fax 215 8036* • *AE DC MC V* • *198 rooms, 2 suites, 4 restaurants, 2 bars, 1 coffee shop*
In a prime location, between banks and offices around the corner from Tokyo station, the Marunouchi is a solid, well-established hotel, designed to suit the needs of the travelling executive. The lobby and bedrooms are appropriately sober in decor, and service is brisk and efficient. Foreign executives make up a large percentage of the clientele. Shuttle bus to airport • 6 meeting rooms (capacity up to 200).

Miyako ⓨ////
1-1-50 Shiroganedai Minato-ku, 108☎ *447 3111* ⓉⓍ *2423111 fax 447 3133* • *AE DC MC V* • *475 rooms, 25 suites, 6 restaurants, 1 bar, 2 coffee shops*
In an exclusive residential district and built around a beautiful Japanese garden, the Miyako has an air of quiet distinction. Service is impeccable, and the tastefully decorated bedrooms, many overlooking the garden, are exceptionally spacious. The location, however, is rather inconvenient. Shops, hotel bus to railway stations and Ginza • health club with sauna, pool, gym; jogging • 13 meeting rooms (capacity up to 1,000).

New Otani ⓨ////
4-1, Kioicho, Chiyoda-ku, 102☎ *265 1111* ⓉⓍ *J24719 fax 221 2619* • *Sheraton* • *AE DC MC V* • *2,057 rooms and suites, 23 restaurants, 5 bars, 5 coffee shops/tea lounges*
An immense hotel, the second largest in Asia and one of the largest in the world, the New Otani lacks the prestige of the Okura or the Imperial, but is still the choice of many Japanese and foreign executives. It is a mini-city, with more than 100 shops selling luxury goods and many excellent restaurants, including the spectacular Tour d'Argent (see *Restaurants*), and Nadaman (see *Restaurants*). There is also Japan's first women-only floor, a non-smoking floor and facilities for the disabled. Some of the rooms (all with minibar) in the older main block are rather small; foreign executives usually prefer the spacious rooms in the newer Tower Block, overlooking the beautiful 10thC Japanese garden. There are two executive floors in the Tower Block and an executive lounge. Theatre bookings, travel desks, free shuttle bus to Aoyama, Azabu, Ginza and Otemachi • Golden Spa health club, outdoor pool, jogging • business service centre with extensive facilities, 48 meeting rooms (capacity up to 10,000).

New Takanawa Prince *Y*/////
3-13-1 Takanawa, Minato-ku, 108
☎ *442 1111* ⊠ *2427418*
fax 444 1234 ● *AE DC MC V* ●
968 rooms, 32 suites, 6 restaurants,
1 bar, 1 coffee shop
Separated from the older Takagawa
Prince by a large and beautiful
Japanese garden with winding paths,
a lake and a teahouse, the New
Takanawa was designed by Togo
Murano, and in typical Prince fashion
incorporates many innovative
features. Not only can you open the
windows (unusual for Tokyo), but
each of the enormous and attractive
rooms has its own private balcony
overlooking the garden. The
Executive Floor includes a large and
well-equipped business service centre,
a variety of meeting rooms and a
lounge. Guests have access to the
sports facilities at the nearby
Shinagawa Prince Hotel. 24hr room
service, travel desk, shops,
hairdresser, shuttle bus to airport ●
pool, jogging ● business service
centre with extensive facilities, 20
meeting rooms (capacity up to 5,000).

Okura *Y*//////
2-10-4 Toranomon, Minato-ku, 105
☎ *582 0111* ⊠ *J22790*
fax 589 0373 ● *AE DC MC V* ●
826 rooms, 62 suites, 6 restaurants,
4 bars, 2 coffee shops
Set in a Japanese garden with a carp-
filled pond and a waterfall topped
with a shrine, the Okura is designed
and furnished with restrained
elegance. The emphasis is on service,
and the Okura is geared particularly
towards fulfilling the foreign
executive's every need. The Executive
Service Centre is considered by many
to be the best in the city, and the
bedrooms, all with minibar, are large
enough to work in. The rooms have
all been newly renovated by British
designer David Hicks. Tohkalin (see
Restaurants) is generally agreed to be
the finest Chinese restaurant in
Tokyo, and La Belle Epoque (see
Restaurants) is popular for business
entertaining. The many luxury shops

include branches of Takashimaya,
Mikimoto and Hanae Mori. Even the
sauna and massage are famous, and
the pool and gym are excellent.
Complimentary entrance to the Okura
Art Museum in the grounds. Theatre
bookings, travel arrangements, arcade
of shops ● health club with indoor
and outdoor pools, sauna, gym,
platform tennis, jogging course ●
business service centre with extensive
facilities, 36 meeting rooms (capacity
up to 3,000).

Pacific Meridien *Y*////
3-13-3 Takanawa, Minato-ku, 108
☎ *445 6711* ⊠ *22861 fax 445 5733*
● *AE DC MC V* ● *913 rooms, 41 suites,*
5 restaurants, 4 bars, 2 coffee shops
Set in a Japanese garden which once
belonged to the Imperial family, the
Pacific Meridien is an enormous
luxury hotel a minute's walk from
Shinagawa station. The rooms are
spacious and well designed,
overlooking the city and Tokyo Bay.
There are special rates for Pacific
Club International members. The
luxury shops include a branch of
Takashimaya. Of all the Shinagawa
hotels, the Pacific is the most popular
with foreign executives. Arcade of
shops, hairdresser, pharmacy, shuttle
bus to airport ● pool, steam bath,
men's sauna, jogging ● secretarial
services, 19 meeting rooms (capacity
up to 3,000).

Palace *Y*////
1-1-1 Marunouchi, Chiyoda-ku, 108
☎ *211 5211* ⊠ *2222580*
fax 211 6987 ● *404 rooms,*
7 restaurants, 2 bars, 1 coffee shop
The Palace is the choice of many
visiting foreign executives and is
recommended by resident
Westerners. Superbly situated
opposite the Imperial Palace, on the
edge of the Marunouchi business
district, it is set well back from the
road, behind an attractive plaza. The
style is low-key and sober. The
bedrooms are a good size and all
soundproofed. One floor is reserved
for non-smokers. Arcade of shops,

hairdresser, airline offices •
secretarial services, 18 meeting rooms
(capacity up to 500).

President *Y*/
2-2-3 Minami Aoyama, Minato-ku, 107
☎ *497 0111* TX *25575 fax 401 4816*
• *AE DC MC V* • *212 rooms,*
2 restaurants, 1 coffee shop
Close to fashionable Omotesando, the
President sports a marble staircase,
grand piano and life-size ceramic St.
Bernard in its lobby, and is generally
agreed to be the best low-budget
hotel in town. The rooms are small
but pleasantly furnished. Limited
hotel parking • 1 meeting room
(capacity 150).

Roppongi Prince *Y*///
3-2-7 Roppongi, Minato-ku, 106
☎ *587 1111* TX *2427231*
fax 587 0770 • *AE DC MC V* •
216 rooms, 4 restaurants, 1 bar,
2 coffee shop/tea lounges
The Roppongi Prince was designed
by noted architect Kurokawa, clearly
in playful mood. Both physically and
conceptually built around the central
pool, it has a starkly minimalist
decor, with waterproof silver sofas in
the black-and-white bedrooms and
Escher optical illusions incorporated
into the stairwell and the bar. The
hotel is located very close to the Ark
Hills complex. 24hr room service •
heated outdoor pool • 4 meeting
rooms (capacity up to 120).

Royal Park *Y*///
2-2-1 Nihonbashi Kakigaracho,
Chuo-ku, 103 ☎ *667 1111*
TX *2523788 fax 665 7212* •
AE DC MC V • *439 rooms, 11 suites,*
6 restaurants, 1 bar, 3 coffee
shop/tea lounges
Close to the Kabutocho business
district and right next to the city air
terminal, the new Royal Park (opened
June 1989) is designed specifically
with the requirements of business
travellers in mind. The rooms are a
reasonable size and well-equipped and
there is a nonsmoking floor and 2
executive floors. Arcade of shops •

fitness club with pool, gym and
jacuzzi • business service centre with
limited facilities, 10 meeting rooms
(capacity up to 1,300).

Seiyo Ginza *Y*/////
1 Ginza, Chuo-ku, 104
☎ *535 1111* TX *2523118*
fax 535 1110 • *Preferred Hotels* •
AE DC MC V • *30 rooms, 50 suites,*
4 restaurants, 1 bar, 1 tea lounge
The Seiyo is not as exclusive as it
used to be. It now caters not only to
film stars and the ultra rich but also
to top-ranking executives. It is small,
intimate and very classy. Service is
superb; the staff guest ratio is 3:1.
The bathrooms are palatial, with huge
bath, separate shower, remote control
video and steam bath. It is also home
to an Italian restaurant, Attore, which
many consider to be Tokyo's best (see
Restaurants). 24hr room service • 1
shop (a branch of Harry Winston's,
the New York jeweller) • fitness
room • business services installed in
your room on request, 2 meeting
rooms (capacity up to 150).

Shiba Park *Y*///
1-5-10 Shiba Koen, Minato-ku, 105
☎ *433 4141* TX *2422917*
fax 433 6327 • *AE DC MC V* •
384 rooms, 16 suites, 3 restaurants,
1 bar, 1 coffee shop
This unpretentious, economical hotel
is linked to the Imperial and has a
reputation for excellent service.
English-speakers are plentiful, and
many of the guests hail from New
Zealand, as does one of the staff. The
popular bar, Fifteen's, is hung with
rugby club shields. The hotel features
a popular Chinese restaurant, the
Peking. 18 meeting rooms (capacity
up to 330).

Takanawa Prince *Y*/////
3-13-1 Takanawa, Minato-ku, 108
☎ *447 1111* TX *2423232*
fax 446 0849 • *AE DC MC V* •
384 rooms, 34 suites, 6 restaurants,
3 bars, 2 coffee shops
Linked to the New Takanawa Prince
by a large landscaped Japanese

garden, the Takanawa Prince was built in 1970 and has recently been renovated. The decor is businesslike, solid and unfussy, and the rooms are spacious with windows opening onto the garden. It is popular with business travellers. 24hr room service, travel desk, shops, hairdresser, shuttle bus to airport • 2 pools • business service centre with extensive facilities (in New Takanawa Prince), 29 meeting rooms (capacity up to 1,000).

Tokyo Prince Hotel *Y* ////
3-3-1 Shiba Koen, Minato-ku, 105
☎ *432 1111* TX *2422488*
fax 434 5551 • *AE DC MC V* •
484 rooms, 7 restaurants, 3 bars,
1 coffee shop
While the top executives stay at the Okura, younger Japanese businessmen choose the Tokyo Prince; politicians and financiers often hold receptions and meetings here. Situated in the middle of parkland, it has a European ambience and decor with a comfortably antique flavour. The Beaux Séjours is popular for business lunches. 24hr room service, concierge, theatre booking, shopping arcade, direct bus to Narita • pool, jogging, golf driving range and bowling alley nearby • business service centre with limited facilities, 25 meeting rooms (capacity up to 2,400).

Yaesu Fujiya *Y* /
2-9-1 Yaesu, Chuo-ku, 104
☎ *273 2111* TX *2223801*
fax 273 2180 • *AE DC MC V* •
373 rooms, 4 suites, 3 restaurants,
1 bar, 1 coffee shop
The Yaesu Fujiya is a branch of the hundred-year-old Fujiya Hotel in Hakone and has a particularly appealing atmosphere reminiscent of a resort hotel, although catering mainly for business travellers. The staff are friendly and the rooms pleasant. The hotel is within walking distance of Ginza, Marunouchi and Tokyo station. Japanese television only. 2 meeting rooms (capacity up to 380).

OTHER HOTELS

Atagoyama Tokyu Inn *Y* // *1-6-6 Atago, Minato-ku, 105* ☎ *431 0109* TX *2425179 fax 431 0434* • *AE DC MC V*. Near the Shimbashi and Toranomon areas.

Gimmond *Y* *1-6 Nihonbashi Odenmacho, Chuo-ku, 104* ☎ *666 4111* TX *2522317 fax 666 3040* • *AE DC MC V*. Popular with Japanese businessmen, comfortable rooms and a central location.

Ginza Daiichi *Y* // *8-13-1 Ginza, Chuo-ku, 104* ☎ *542 5311* TX *2523714 fax 542 3030* • *AE DC MC V*. A popular mid-range hotel, convenient for the Ginza.

Ginza International *Y* / *8-7-13 Ginza, Chuo-ku, 104* ☎ *574 9843 fax 289 0478* • *AE DC MC V*. In the main Ginza entertainment area, near Shimbashi station. The rooms are spacious for the price.

Ginza Marunouchi *Y* / *4-1-12 Tsuliji, Chuo-ku, 104* ☎ *543 5431* TX *2522214 fax 543 6006* • *AE DC MC V*. A branch of the popular Marunouchi Hotel, near Higashi Ginza station.

Ginza Nikko *Y* // *8-4-21 Ginza, Chuo-ku, 104* ☎ *571 4911* TX *2522812 fax 571 8373* • JAL • *AE DC MC V*. Popular with Japanese businessmen.

Mitsui Urban *Y* / *8-6-15 Ginza, Chuo-ku, 104* ☎ *572 4131* TX *2522949 fax 572 4254* • *AE DC MC V*. A superior business hotel near Shimbashi station.

Shimbashi Daiichi *Y* / *1-2-6 Shimbashi, Minato-ku, 108* ☎ *501 4411* TX *2222233 fax 595 2634* • *AE DC MC V*. Near Shimbashi station. Quiet but cramped rooms.

Shinagawa Prince *Y* / *4-10-30 Takanawa, Minato-ku, 108* ☎ *440 1111* TX *2425178 fax 441 7092* • *AE DC MC V*. Popular business hotel at Shinagawa station.

Shinjuku Washington *Y* / *3-2-9 Nishi Shinjuku, Shinjuku-ku, 106* ☎ *343 3111* TX *2322101 fax 342 2575* • *AE DC MC V*. Reasonable-size rooms, equipped with space-age gadgets.

Sunshine City Prince *Ɏ//* *3-1-5 Higashi Ikebukuro, Toshima-ku, 107* ☎ *988 1111* ⊠ *2723749 fax 983 0115*. Located inside the Sunshine City Convention Centre.
Takanawa *Ɏ* *2-1-17 Takanawa, Minato-ku, 108* ☎ *443 9251* ⊠ *2422553 fax 443 9025* • *AE DC MC V*. A bit faded, but rooms are spacious for the price.
Tobu *Ɏ//* *3-1 Udagawacho, Shibuya-ku, 151* ☎ *476 0111* ⊠ *2425585 fax 476 0903* • *AE DC MC V*. A better-than-average business hotel in Shibuya.
Tokyo City *Ɏ* *1-5-4 Nihonbashi Honcho, Chuo-ku, 104* ☎ *270 7671 fax 270 8930* • *AE DC MC V*. In the Nihonbashi business area.
Tokyo Station *Ɏ//* *1-9-1 Marunouchi, Chiyoda-ku, 100* ☎ *231 2511* ⊠ *2312511 fax 231 3513* • *AE DC V*. At Tokyo station.

Clubs

The *Tokyo Club* (Kasumigaseki) ☎ 580 0781 is the most prestigious club in Japan and has reciprocal arrangements with Britain's Oxford and Cambridge clubs. It is an excellent place to entertain Japanese colleagues. Among the resident Western community, the *American Club* (Kamiyacho) ☎ 583 8381 is most used; it has reciprocal arrangements with clubs all over the world, including the London, Sydney and Hong Kong American Clubs. The *Foreign Correspondents' Club* (Yurakucho) ☎ 211 3161 is a popular gathering place, particularly at lunch time, and many resident Western executives are members. Guest membership is available on the introduction of a member. There are bars, a library and a workroom with telex and fax.

Restaurants

In Tokyo the business traveller is spoilt for choice. For entertaining, top foreign executives use the grand French restaurants in the Okura and New Otani hotels or in the Ginza, while their Japanese counterparts – if the expense account will run to it – choose among the exclusive *ryotei* in Akasaka. Young Western businessmen on a tighter budget gravitate to Roppongi, while those who want to impress with their grasp of the local scene follow the fashionable Japanese to Aoyama and Nishi Azabu. Although in other Japanese cities there are few really excellent Western-style restaurants, in Tokyo the most exciting and popular cuisine is a fusion of Western and Japanese: non-Japanese dishes – usually French, but also Italian or Chinese – prepared *kaiseki*-style, light and mild in flavour.

NON-JAPANESE
Al Porto *Ɏ/*
3-24-9 Nishi Azabu, Minato-ku ☎ *403 2916* • *closed Mon* • *AE DC MC V*
Al Porto's stylish and well-heeled clientele includes young Western executives with plenty of savoir-faire, who bring their Japanese clients here. The dining room is tiny and like a Victorian parlour, with engravings on the walls and heavy draperies. Owner/ chef Kataoka serves superb Italian cuisine, *kaiseki*-style.

Apicius *Ɏ////*
B1 Sanshi Bldg, 1-9-4 Yurakucho, Chiyoda-ku ☎ *214 1361/1362* • *closed Sun* • *AE DC MC V* • *jacket and tie* • *reservations essential*
Apicius has something of the air of a gentlemen's club. In the heart of the Yurakucho business district, it is one of the city's most famous venues for business entertaining. The cuisine is French of the old school, with one of the best cellars in Tokyo. The decor is similarly restrained in flavour and the walls are hung with originals.

Attore *Y*|

B1 Ginza Saison Theatre, 1 Ginza, Chuo-ku ☎ *535 1111 ext 2156 • AE DC MC V • reservations recommended*
Attore, in the basement of the immensely luxurious and prestigious Hotel Seiyo Ginza, is, appropriately, one of the city's top Italian restaurants. The elegant dining-room is spacious and quiet and the scene of much business entertaining and there is also a café area for less formal meals, from where you can watch the chefs at work in the kitchens. The cuisine is spectacular – northern Italian, immaculately fresh ingredients imaginatively prepared.

Bistrot de la Cité *Y*|

4-2-10 Nishi Azabu, Minato-ku ☎ *406 5475 • closed Mon • AE DC V • reservations essential*
Some of the best French food in the city is to be found in this tiny cramped bistro in the heart of Nishi Azabu. The cosmopolitan clientele is here primarily for the cuisine (Chef Tamura's fish and seafood dishes are famous) and also for the atmosphere – pure Paris, from the walls hung with yellowing and lithographs and prints to the charming waiters in long black aprons. Not a place for a business lunch but an excellent place to relax with colleagues.

Borsalino *Y*|

6-8-21 Roppongi, Minato-ku ☎ *401 7751 • closed Sun L, Mon • AE DC MC V*
Borsalino is a haunt of the smart set, both Japanese and Western. The fashionably minimalist interior, all white walls, black seating and silver wall lights, tends to distract one from the excellent cuisine. The chef cooks light Italian food in the *nouvelle* idiom, using imported Italian ingredients. The wines are all Italian.

Brasserie Bernard *Y*|

7F Kajimaya Bldg, 7-14-3 Roppongi, Minato-ku ☎ *405 7877 • AE DC MC V*
Brasserie Bernard serves classic French cuisine at prices that are reasonable for Tokyo. The setting is rustic French, with low ceilings, wooden beams and shelves of wine (all French). The clientele, almost entirely Western, comes here as much for the lively atmosphere as for the food. Brasserie Bernard has proved so popular that owner/chef Bernard Anquetil has opened two more branches, in Ginza and Kobe.

Cay *Y*|

B1 Spiral Bldg, 5-6-23 Minami Aoyama, Minato-ku ☎ *498 5790 D only; closed Sun • AE DC MC V*
"Ethnic" food has been the rage for several years. Of the multitude of fashionable Vietnamese, Thai and Cambodian restaurants which have sprung up, Cay has lasted the longest. The food here is Thai via California, with plenty of coconut milk; the decor all light and space – palm trees, wicker, ceiling fans and huge pale murals; and the clientele is well-heeled, fashionable and sophisticated. The bar is also famous.

Chez Inno *Y*|||||

3-2-11 Kyobashi, Chuo-ku ☎ *274 2020 • closed Sun L • AE DC MC V*
At the Tokyo station end of Ginza, half hidden among offices, is a discreet marble doorway with "Chez Inno" carved into the lintel. It leads to a small restaurant which has one of the highest reputations in Tokyo. Chef Innoue Noboru spent seven years in France and cooks the lightest and most superb *nouvelle cuisine* imaginable. The decor, like the cuisine, is understated but classy, making this a particularly impressive place to entertain business clients. Set price menu available.

Chianti *Y*|

3-1-7 Azabudai, Minato-ku ☎ *583 7546 • AE DC MC V*
While the city sprouts new Italian restaurants, Chianti remains eternally fashionable. The food is distinguished and many of the city's movers and shakers can be found among the clientele.

125

Daini's Table Y|

6-3-14 Minami Aoyama, Minato-ku
☎ *407 0363* • *AE DC MC V* •
reservations essential
Daini's clientele is as stylish as its
decor. The cuisine is *nouvelle*
Chinese, *kaiseki*-style, tiny portions of
many different Shanghai dishes,
served on black and red lacquerware.
The severely minimalist interior, with
curving walls and rows of spotlights,
is set off by a large lacquered screen
at one end of the room.

Hiramatsu Y|||

5-15-13 Minami Azabu, Minato-ku
☎ *444 3967* • *closed Mon* • *AE DC
MC V* • *reservations recommended*
Hiramatsu, one of Tokyo's most
highly rated young chefs, has opened
a chic new restaurant among the
embassies and business residences of
Hiroo. The first floor consists of
private rooms for business
entertaining, while the second is
grand and airy, tastefully decorated in
whites and greys, and looks out onto
trees and greenery. Here Hiramatsu
continues to conjure up the delicate
French cuisine which has made him
so popular.

Ile de France Y||

*Com Roppongi Bldg, 3-11-5 Roppongi,
Minato-ku* ☎ *404 0384* • *closed Sun* •
AE DC MC V
André Pachon came to Japan from
Carcassonne in 1972. He now has two
fine restaurants, Pachon and Ile de
France. His cooking is
uncompromisingly French, and the
selection of cheeses is said to be the
best in Tokyo. The restaurant is
decorated in rustic French style, with
copper pans hanging on the
whitewashed walls. The faithful
clientele, largely foreign executives,
often drop in for a working lunch.

Imari Y|||

*2F Tokyo Hilton International, 6-6-2
Nishi Shinjuku, Shinjuku-ku*
☎ *344 5111* • *AE DC MC V*
The restaurant houses many antique
Japanese objets d'art and a

magnificent collection of Imari
porcelain. Chef Siegfried Jaeger's
cuisine is classic French, but he
reveals his Austrian origins in his
famous cakes and pastries. The wine
list is extensive and the service
impeccable. Diplomats and executives
are among the clientele, and Imari is
popular for high-level business
entertaining.

Joel Y|||

*2F Kyodo Bldg, 5-6-24 Minami
Aoyama, Minato-ku* ☎ *400 7149* •
AE DC MC V • *reservations essential*
Joel Bruant was sent to Japan in 1972
by his mentor, Paul Bocuse, and
continues to excite the palates of
gourmets of all nationalities in his
small restaurant in Omotesando. Both
the cuisine and the decor are classic
French of the highest quality; Many
businessmen, both Japanese and
Western, pay their clients the
compliment of entertaining them
here.

Keyaki Grill Y|||

*B1 Capitol Tokyu Hotel, 2-10-3
Nagatacho, Chiyoda-ku* ☎ *581 4511
ext 3210* • *AE DC MC V* • *reservations
essential*
Under Austrian chef Karl Hoermann,
the distinguished Keyaki Grill
continues to maintain its reputation as
one of Japan's finest hotel restaurants.
The standard of cooking is uniformly
high, the wine list superior and
service incomparable. The clientele,
largely businessmen, many of them
Western, make full use of the quiet
Keyaki for business entertaining.

La Belle Epoque Y|||

*12F Hotel Okura, 2-10-4 Toranomon,
Minato-ku* ☎ *505 6073* • *AE DC MC V*
• *reservations essential*
La Belle Epoque, at the top of the
Hotel Okura, is stunningly baroque
in style, with a rich Art Nouveau
decor of purples, golds and wrought
iron lamps. Partitions of stained glass
between tables give a degree of
privacy. The clientele is cosmopolitan
and has included the Prince and

Princess of Wales. The chef, Philippe Mouchel, studied with Paul Bocuse, and cooks a lighter version of traditional French cuisine.

L'Affresco *Y*/

B2 Hibiya Chanter, 1-2-2 Yurakucho, Chiyoda-ku ☎ 581 7421 • AE DC MC V
L'Affresco, in the basement of the newly opened Chanter Building in Yurakucho, is Tokyo's first Venetian restaurant and features the distinguished cuisine of Alzetta Ettore, the chef of the Venice Summit. It is a favourite for business lunches among resident Westerners. There are frescoes of Venice all along the walls and chandeliers of Venetian glass.

La Granata *Y*/

B1 TBS Kaikan Bldg, 5-3-3 Akasaka, Minato-ku ☎ 582 3241 or 3243 • AE DC MC V
The interior of this very popular restaurant is like an Italian farmhouse, with heavy wooden beams, plaster walls and a huge brick hearth for grilling the home-made sausages. In the evening local Italians mingle with the Akasaka media people, and Western businessmen bring their Japanese colleagues here to dine. The cuisine is Roman, and the wines, imported direct from Italy, inexpensive.

La Rochelle *Y*//

B1 Aoyama Ohara Bldg, 5-7-17 Minami Aoyama, Minato-ku ☎ 400 8220 • closed Sun • AE DC MC V
La Rochelle, with its pink walls and antique dressers, feels like a provincial French restaurant. Here Hiroyuki Sakai, trained as a *kaiseki* chef, wields his magic knife. His hors d'oeuvres, each a minuscule work of art, are legendary among gourmets.

La Terre *Y*/

1-9-20 Azabudai, Minato-ku ☎ 583 9682 • closed Sun • AE DC MC V
A tiny, friendly restaurant hidden away at the top of a flight of steps near the Okura, La Terre, with its pink check tablecloths and red chairs, has a very French atmosphere. Customers include diplomats from nearby embassies, Japanese businessmen and resident Westerners. In the spring time you can eat outside under the beautiful cherry blossoms.

La Tour d'Argent *Y*/////

2F Hotel New Otani, 4-1 Kioicho, Chiyoda-ku ☎ 239 3111 • D only • AE DC MC V • jacket and tie • reservations essential
Duck is the dish to eat in this extremely expensive branch of the three-star Paris Tour d'Argent which opened in 1985. The setting is truly palatial. You step through the marble-lined reception area hung with portraits of 16thC French dignitaries into a vast, high-ceilinged dining room with massive chandeliers, spun gold draperies and dark blue china printed with the Tour d'Argent motif. The duck is flown over from Paris, and each diner receives a "duck number," a centuries-long tradition. This is dining on the highest level, and both the setting and the cuisine will be regarded as a great compliment by your Japanese guests.

L'Ecrin *Y*////

B1 Mikimoto Bldg, 4-5-5 Ginza, Chuo-ku ☎ 561 9706 • closed Sun • AE DC MC V • reservations essential
A top-class Ginza restaurant, L'Ecrin has the reputation of being one of Tokyo's finest. The Paris-trained chef, a member of the Académie Culinaire, prepares classic French cuisine of the old school, and the wine list is outstanding. The discreet service and aristocratic atmosphere, with its plush red carpets and elegant Art Nouveau decor, make it an obvious choice for business entertaining. At lunch time you will find many top Japanese executives here.

Les Saisons Y////

Imperial Hotel, 1-1-1 Uchisaiwaicho, Chiyoda-ku ☎ *504 1111 ext 5882* ● AE DC MC V

Les Saisons is indisputably *the* place for power breakfasts. Most of the day's deals, it's said, are concluded here by 9 am, among the potted palms and Mediterranean lighting. The cuisine, under Chef Ishikawa Hichio, is equally light and sunny.

L'Orangerie de Paris Y///

5F Hanae Mori Bldg, 3-6-1 Kita Aoyama, Minato-ku ☎ *407 7461* ● *closed Sun D* ● AE DC MC V

L'Orangerie, in trendy Harajuku, serves elegant French cuisine, and an excellent buffet-style Sunday brunch.

Maxim's de Paris Y/////

B3 Sony Bldg, 5-3-1 Ginza, Chuo-ku ☎ *572 3621* ● *closed Sun* ● AE DC MC V ● *reservations essential*

An 80% scale replica of the Paris original, Maxim's is undoubtedly one of Japan's top French restaurants. The cuisine, though expensive, is well worth it, the setting is magnificent, and the wine list one of the finest in the city. The cosmopolitan clientele includes diplomats, visiting executives and connoisseurs of the famous cakes. There is a private room appropriate for large-scale business entertaining.

Metropole Y///

6-4-5 Roppongi, Minato-ku ☎ *405 4400* ● AE DC MC V

The Metropole is a Chinese restaurant, its decor a cross between a Victorian theatre and an English club. At the front is a well-stocked bar with an 18thC library on the balcony overhead. The restaurant itself is like a stage, with red velvet curtains and a backdrop, changed regularly. The customers are mainly young and professional.

Mireille Y/

3-1-6 Azabudai, Minato-ku ☎ *586 9050* ● *closed Sun* ● AE DC MC V

European businessmen are prominent among customers at the wooden tables in Mireille's whitewashed basement room. Both decor and cuisine are authentically Provençal, and the chef is well known for his subtle use of herbs, garlic and fresh local ingredients.

Moti Y

2F Akasaka Floral Plaza, 3-8-8 Akasaka, Minato-ku ☎ *584 3760 or 582 3620* ● AE DC MC V

Generally reckoned to serve the best value and most authentic Indian food in Tokyo, the Moti, in Akasaka, is popular among diplomatic and business circles and with Westerners, both visiting and resident. The 13 chefs are all from North India and include specialists in tandoori and curry. The Moti is a convivial place to dine alone or with colleagues, but probably somewhat noisy and cramped for a working lunch. There is also a branch in Roppongi (☎ 479 1939) and near Akasaka TBS (☎ 584 6649).

Pachon Y///

29-18 Sarugakucho, Shibuya-ku ☎ *476 5025* ● *closed Sun* ● AE DC MC V

André Pachon's second restaurant (see *Ile de France*) is indisputably one of the city's best French restaurants. Pride of place goes to the huge stone fireplace, with iron grill and bellows, where M. Pachon's nightly roast includes sides of beef, pheasant, marinated duck and fresh local fish. In summer you can dine outside on the veranda.

Petit Point Y///

TGK Bldg, 4-2-48 Minami Azabu, Minato-ku ☎ *440 3667* ● AE DC V

Petit Point, named after the chef's mentor, the great Fernand Point, is considered one of the best of the new-wave French restaurants. Owner/chef Kitaoka, a long-time resident of Paris, cooks authentic French cuisine with Japanese flair; his ten-course *Plaisirs de Table* is particularly celebrated. The tastefully decorated interior is European in flavour, with dried flowers, Toulouse-Lautrec prints, Victorian brass curios and fringed lace curtains. The clientele ranges from executives to artists, with a large proportion of Westerners.

Queen Alice [Y]/
3-17-34 Nishi Azabu, Minato-ku
☎ *405 9039* ● *closed Mon* ● *AE DC V*
● *reservations essential*
Queen Alice is the creation of young owner/chef Yutaka Ishinabe. He has turned the dining room of his house in Nishi Azabu into a conservatory, full of trailing vines and huge potted palms. On fine days you can dine outside. Japanese professionals and well-informed Westerners book well in advance to savour the cuisine, a marvellous fusion of French *nouvelle* and *kaiseki*.

Sabatini Aoyama [Y]///
B1 Suncrest Bldg, 2-13-5 Kita Aoyama, Minato-ku ☎ *402 3812* ● *AE DC MC V*
A re-creation of the Rome Sabatini, Sabatini Aoyama occupies a vast vaulted cellar, with heavy wooden beams, candelabra and a stone chimney with charcoal barbecue. The cuisine is classic Roman, with much fresh seafood. The clientele, generally affluent, professional and cosmopolitan, either love or loathe the strolling musicians who serenade them with guitars. For casual meals, the Pizzeria Romana Sabatini (☎ 402 2027) offers pizzas and pastas at reasonable prices.

Sabatini di Firenze [Y]//
7F Sony Bldg, 5-3-1 Ginza, Chuo-ku ☎ *573 0013 or 0014* ● *AE DC MC V*
The setting is magnificent in this branch of the Florence Sabatini, with marble floors, carved beams and panelling, huge bouquets of fresh flowers and heavy flowered draperies. At lunch time the restaurant is crowded with businessmen. Dinner is more leisurely. The food is, needless to say, excellent, with Tuscan specialities, and the wines, all Italian, are surprisingly inexpensive.

Spago [Y]//
5-7-8 Roppongi, Minato-ku
☎ *423 4025* ● *AE DC MC V*
A branch of the Los Angeles Spago, this outpost of the USA is the inspiration of American chef Wolfgang Puck. Spago serves California cuisine, a mix of many culinary traditions, with *nouvelle* influence notably strong. Of the clientele, Westerners, mainly businessmen, outnumber Japanese. The staff are notably pleasant and competent and business dining here is guaranteed to run smoothly.

Star Hill [Y]//
B1 Capitol Tokyu Hotel, 2-10-3 Nagatacho, Chiyoda-ku ☎ *581 4511 ext 3220* ● *AE DC MC V*
Star Hill has an air of restrained opulence, with a red and gold decor. The cuisine is predominantly Cantonese, although the menu includes dishes from Shanghai and Peking. During the week the restaurant is the scene of much business entertaining, and reservations are essential for the private rooms. There is a good-value all-you-can-eat buffet at weekends.

Tohkalin [Y]///
6F Hotel Okura, 2-10-4 Toranomon, Minato-ku ☎ *505 6068* ● *AE DC MC V*
Long rated Tokyo's best Chinese restaurant, Tohkalin is the first choice of many businessmen, both Japanese and Western, for a working lunch or dinner (there are nine private rooms set aside for the purpose). The cuisine is mainly Cantonese and the surroundings tastefully opulent in the Chinese fashion, with red carpets and delicate gold screens.

JAPANESE
Edogin [Y]/
4-5-12 Tsukiji, Chuo-ku ☎ *543 4406* ●
closed Sun ● *AE DC MC V*
Edogin is a famous old sushi shop, a Tokyo institution, occupying almost a whole street on the way to Tsukiji fish market. The friendly staff, sporting Wellington boots and white

caps, serve up superbly fresh sushi straight from the market. The sushi is not only tasty but also enormous; the staff boast that they serve the biggest pieces of fish in town.

Fukuzushi $\boxed{Y}$/
5-7-8 Roppongi, Minato-ku
☎ *402 4116* • *AE DC MC V*
Fukuzushi is sushi for sophisticates. In the heart of Roppongi, it features an elegant black bar where you sip cocktails and watch videos, before retiring to the main restaurant – all shades of black, white and grey – to dine on sushi which many swear is the best in town. The atmosphere is as restrained as the decor – a highly suitable place for having a business dinner.

Goemon $\boxed{Y}$/
1-1-26 Komagome, Bunkyo-ku
☎ *811 2015* • *closed Mon*
At Goemon, the speciality is tofu – beancurd, delicately flavoured and highly nutritious – prepared in an amazing variety of ways. The setting is equally traditional, a rambling Japanese house with tiny tea rooms where you sit and look over the garden. This is a place to relax and discover one of the delights of Japanese cuisine, in company with off-duty Japanese businessmen and gourmet members of the foreign community.

Hayashi $\boxed{Y}$/
4F Sanno Kaikan Bldg, 2-14-1 Akasaka, Minato-ku ☎ *582 4078* •
closed Sun • *AE DC MC V*
On the 4th floor of a rather nondescript building amidst the glitz and neon of Akasaka is a restaurant which feels like a corner of old Japan or a country inn a hundred miles from Tokyo. Hayashi has rough, smoke-blackened walls, bamboo ceilings and tables which double as charcoal hearths. The restaurant specializes in sumiyaki, charcoal-grilled dishes. Motherly waitresses in cotton kimonos serve you with quail, venison, fish, chicken (every

imaginable part) and vegetables, which you grill yourself over the charcoal. Hayashi is hardly the place for a business dinner; but you may well be brought here by Japanese or Western colleagues and will be very welcome on your own.

Inagiku $\boxed{Y}$///
2-9-8 Nihonbashi Kayabacho, Chuo-ku
☎ *669 5501* • *closed Sun* • *AE DC MC V*
Inagiku is one of Japan's most famous and high-class tempura restaurants, patronized by the rich and famous and recommended by the top hotels. The rooms and service are immaculate. Your fellow diners are likely to include managing directors with their foreign guests or high-powered foreign executives from nearby Nihonbashi.

Inakaya $\boxed{Y}$/
3-12-7 Akasaka, Minato-ku
☎ *586 3054* • *AE DC MC V*
Inakaya, a venerable establishment, is full of shouting and merriment. Customers sit around the hearth on which the chefs grill meats, seafoods and vegetables, which they pass across on wooden paddles. Among the clientele are entertainers, media folk and foreign visitors, brought by Japanese friends or colleagues to enjoy the lively atmosphere and Japanese country cooking. There are also two branches of Inakaya in Roppongi: 7-8-4 Roppongi, Minato-ku ☎ 405 9866 and 1F Reine Bldg, 5-3-4 Roppongi ☎ 408 5040.

Isehiro $\boxed{Y}$/
1-5-4 Kyobashi, Chuo-ku ☎ *281 5864*
• *closed Sun* • *AE DC MC V*
Down a back alley just behind the business area of Nihonbashi is a little restaurant which has been serving *yakitori* since 1922. At lunch time local businessmen and Westerners, crowd in to savour the skewers of finest Shamo chicken, grilled over charcoal and served at budget prices. In the evening the tiny upstairs rooms are reserved for business entertaining.

Kocho *Y*/////

*B2 Shin Yurakucho Bldg, 1-12-1
Yurakucho, Chiyoda-ku ☎ 214 4741 •
closed Sun • AE DC MC V •
reservations essential*
Kocho is famous for three things.
First, for Chef Goto's beautiful and
intricate *kaiseki* cuisine. Second, for
the wondrous Japanese garden in
which it is located – thick shady
bamboo groves, trickling streams,
waterfalls and tiny wooden houses
with tiled eaves, all growing
miraculously in this basement deep
beneath the Yurakucho business
district. Third, Kocho is famous for
the welcome which it affords to
Westerners. You may well be
entertained here by your Japanese
hosts; but you will be equally
welcome on your own.

Kushinobo *Y*

*3-10-17 Akasaka, Minato-ku
☎ 586 7390 • AE DC V*
Kushinobo serves *kushi-age*, tiny
portions of fish, meat and vegetables
in apparently endless variety, strung
on to skewers and crisply deep-fried
in batter. The atmosphere is lively
and friendly and Westerners are
welcome. An interesting place for a
culinary adventure on a night off.

Kyubei *Y*/////

*8-5-23 Ginza, Chuo-ku ☎ 571 6523 •
closed Sun • AE DC MC V*
Ginza businessmen literally rub
shoulders in this tiny, intimate sushi
shop; the two floors together hold a
total of 20. Kyubei is quite unlike the
usual noisy neighbourhood sushi
shop. The staff are well aware of its
status as possibly Tokyo's best, and
the quality of the sushi more than
justifies the steep prices. There are
branches of Kyubei in the Okura, the
New Otani and the Keio Plaza.

Matsuya *Y*

*1-13 Sudacho, Kanda, Chiyoda-ku
☎ 251 1556 • closed Sun*
In the grey business district of
Kanda, in a street of highrise office
blocks, is a small wooden house with

the legend (in Japanese) outside it:
"handmade noodles." Matsuya has
stood here for over 60 years, ever
since the great earthquake of 1923,
and it serves only one dish – soba,
buckwheat noodles. The noodles are
made on the premises – by a young
man who rolls out the dough at
lightning speed – and businessmen
come from miles around to lunch
here.

Mon Cher Ton Ton *Y*////

*3-12-2 Roppongi, Minato-ku
☎ 402 1055 • AE DC MC V*
Part of the Seryna complex (see
below), Mon Cher Ton Ton is a
sophisticated *teppanyaki* restaurant. In
its cavernous basement room,
customers sit around gleaming steel-
topped tables on which four chefs fry
up finest Kobe beef and seafoods.
There are side rooms specifically for
business entertaining, which makes
up a large part of the custom.

Nadaman *Y*/////

*Hotel New Otani, 4-1 Kioicho,
Chiyoda-ku ☎ 264 7921 • AE DC
MC V*
Sazanka-so Nadaman, modestly
located in a small but exquisite
Japanese house in the garden of the
New Otani, is one of Japan's most
exclusive *ryotei*. If you are fortunate
enough to be invited, regard it as a
supreme compliment. Fellow diners
will be from the top strata of
Japanese society. You can savour
Nadaman's famous Kansai-style
kaiseki cuisine in a more relaxed
atmosphere in a branch on the 6th
floor of the New Otani, overlooking
the spectacular garden. At lunch time
there is a good value mini-*kaiseki*.
There are also branches of Nadaman
in the Imperial Hotel and in Osaka,
Nadaman's birthplace, at the Royal
and the Tokyu.

Nambantei *Y*/

*4-5-6 Roppongi, Minato-ku
☎ 402 0606 • AE DC MC V*
Nambantei means "the inn of the
Southern barbarians," and it was they

– that is, the Portuguese – who introduced *yakitori* to Japan. Customers sit around open charcoal grills where the young chefs in dark blue *happi* coats grill not only skewers of chicken but many different types of meat and vegetables, seasoned with spices or marinaded and served with rich sauces.

Sushi Bar Sai [Y]/
2F Rambling Core Andos Bldg, 1-7-5 Jinnan, Shibuya-ku ☎ *496 6333* ● *AE DC MC V*
Sushi Bar Sai serves sushi in the modern idiom, California-style, using *tofu* and meat as well as the more traditional ingredients. The sushi is served *nouvelle cuisine*-style, in the exact centre of fine Arita and Kiyomizu dishes, and the decor is fashionable high-tech. Sushi Bar Sai is much patronized by young businessmen, both Japanese and Western.

Sushi Sei [Y]
Akasaka branch: 3-11-14 Akasaka, Minato-ku ☎ *586 6446* ● *closed Sun; Aoyama branch: 5F Bell Commons, 2-14-6 Kita Aoyama, Minato-ku* ☎ *475 8053*
To be good, raw fish must be perfectly fresh; and those who line up at Sushi Sei are evidence of the quality here. In true sushi bar style, the chefs keep up a noisy repartee which in no way impairs the lightning precision with which they press fish onto rice. Those jaded palates for whom sea urchin, yellowtail, ark shell and bonito are no longer exciting can try whole squid, grilled and stuffed with rice, or live prawns, beheaded before your eyes and still twitching on their rice balls. And it's inexpensive.

Takamura [Y]///
3-4-27 Roppongi, Minato-ku ☎ *585 6600/6620* ● *closed Sun* ● *AE DC MC V* ● *reservations essential*
At Takamura, the only sound is the wind rustling in the bamboos and the plop of water in the stone pool. You follow a path of stone steps lit by paper lanterns through a bamboo grove to a small Japanese house with earthern walls and woven bamboo ceilings – amazingly, only a few minutes' walk from the main Roppongi crossing. The cuisine at Takamura is Kyoto-style *kaiseki*, an endless succession of tiny dishes served by kimono-clad waitresses. Entry to Takamura is by introduction only and the diners, many of whom are Western, come from the top levels of business and politics; your hotel should provide an introduction for you.

Tempura Tenichi [Y]//
Namiki-dori, 6-6-5 Ginza, Chuo-ku ☎ *571 1949* ● *AE DC MC V*
Tempura Tenichi was founded by the present owner's father in 1930, and has been one of the best and most popular tempura restaurants in Tokyo ever since. In addition to sake, French wines, carefully selected to go with tempura, are served; and a Chagall hangs beside a Japanese flower arrangement. The upstairs rooms are reserved for the most distinguished customers, top politicians and company directors, who entertain their guests with tempura *kaiseki*. There are another nine branches in Tokyo, and several throughout the country.

Yama-no-chaya [Y]//
2-10-6 Nagatacho, Chiyoda-ku ☎ *581 0585* ● *closed Sun* ● *reservations essential*
Squeezed in between the Capitol Tokyu and Hie Shrine, just behind the Diet, this little Japanese house is reached via a thatched gate and some stone steps leading through a garden full of bamboos and the song of birds and frogs. The house was built in 1923, and here Madame Endo, the present owner's grandmother, used to entertain. In 1950 they began serving eel; and their eel is legendary. If you are lucky, your Japanese colleagues may bring you here; it is a popular place for business entertaining.

Otherwise you will have to reserve well in advance for one of the four small rooms.

Zakuro ¥//
1-9-15, Akasaka, Minato-ku
☎ *582 2661 3 • AE DC MC V •*
reservations essential for dinner
Zakuro's shabu-shabu is reputed to be the best in town. It opened in 1955 and has huge beams, like a Japanese farmhouse, and whitewashed walls hung with Munakata prints; the fine handcrafted pottery includes some of Hamada's. There is an English-speaking adviser, Shizue Mogi, who will plan your business dinner for you and ensure that it goes off perfectly. Service is reckoned to be among the best in Japan. There are several other branches of this high-quality chain in Tokyo, including Ginza (Sanwa Ginko Bldg, Ginza ☎ 535 4421), Akasaka (TBS Bldg, Akasaka ☎ 582 6841) and Kyobashi (1-7 Kyobashi ☎ 563 5031).

Bars
In Tokyo there are three main areas for those all-important after-hours drinking sessions. Ginza's elite and astronomically expensive hostess clubs are for executives, mainly Japanese, on maximum expense accounts. Here, your professional status and credentials are rated by which bar you patronize, and you are likely to be rubbing shoulders with politicians, industry magnates and entertainers. Only the top Western executives are taken to these clubs; it is unlikely that you would be allowed to enter on your own. Akasaka, too, has high-class geisha and hostess bars, less expensive than Ginza, but still far from cheap. For a relaxed evening, you can join the international set in Roppongi, which has a huge concentration of bars and discos, or slip down to one of the stylish and fashionable bars in Nishi Azabu. Shinjuku is for very late night drinking, in an environment that is relaxed, to say the least. The standard pattern is drinks in a hotel bar before

dinner and a hostess bar afterwards; your Japanese colleagues will take you to their favourite. Most bars are open until 1 or 2am; some stay open later.

Much of the city's wheeling and dealing goes on in hotel bars, of which the most popular – practically mandatory for early evening drinks – is the Imperial Hotel's *Old Imperial Bar*. Affectionately known as the Frank Lloyd Wright Bar, it is an exact reproduction, down to the wood panelling and leather armchairs, of the bar in Frank Lloyd Wright's lamented Art Deco Imperial. In the Okura, the *Orchid* and *Highlander* (said to stock over 200 varieties of Scotch whisky) are also well-used. The New Otani's *Outrigger* serves tropical cocktails while the *Virgo* on the 40th floor has spectacular views over the city's neon. The bars in the Capitol Tokyu, Tokyo Prince, Palace and Marunouchi hotels are also popular with visiting executives.

Outside the hotels, the foreign business community is likely to be found in the newly opened *Foreign Traders' Bar* (in the American Club), which many claim to be the best in town. It is certainly one of the largest, with a selection of drinks as impressive as the clientele, a poker table, a darts board, and an atmosphere more reminiscent of New York than Tokyo. Other favourites of the foreign business community include *Bauhaus*, 4-5-3 Roppongi, known as Bond House because of the preponderance of bond dealers, and *Bei Rudi*, a German beer hall almost next door to the American Embassy.

A relatively new development in Tokyo is Western-style bars where the emphasis is on the quality and variety of drinks available and on the interior – often dramatic and created by a well-known international designer. The clientele is usually a cosmopolitan and sophisticated mix of Westerners and Japanese. One of the most stylish is *Le Club*, B1 Plaza Kay, 5-1-1 Minami Azabu, the creation of alternative ikebana master Koichi Saito. Elegant young black-clad barmen serve an extensive, carefully selected range of high class drinks in an austerely elegant setting, with a spotlight picking out the master's flower arrangement on the shiny black bar. Just across the road, *I Piselli*, 1F Nikko Palace, 5-2-40 Minami Azabu, used to be the trendiest bar in town and is still very popular. The drinks on offer include Wild Turkey and I.W. Harper 12-year-old bourbon. *Ex*, B1 Junikagetsu Bldg, 1-18-7 Jinnan, Shibuya-ku, is famous for its cavernous interior and is the haunt of the Shibuya fashionable, while at *Radio Bar*, B1 Villa Gloria, 2-31-7 Jingumae, the tuxedoed barmen shake up your cocktail with immense panache. *Café Mystique*, on Meiji-dori, Harajuku, is worth visiting for its magnificent interior alone (designed by Philippe Starck). It is a favourite hangout of the Tokyo fashionable, as are *Café Bonggo* (designed by Nigel Coates), in the Parco Building in Shibuya, and *Café Seed* in the Seed building next door. For those who require entertainment with their drinks, there are charming hostesses as well as beautifully executed erotic paintings at *Harrington Gardens The Club*, 3F Harrington Bldg, 7-7-4 Roppongi.

Altogether less sophisticated are the foreigners' bars where weary expats gather. The most popular is probably *Maggie's Revenge*, Takano Bldg, 3-8-7 Roppongi, which has Australian beer as well as spirits and cocktails. The *Charleston Club*, 3-8-1 Roppongi, and *Henry Africa's*, 2F Hanatsubaki Bldg, Roppongi, are old-timers but still well-used, while *Mr Stamp's*, 4-4-2 Roppongi, has a fine collection of wines and a singularly knowledgeable wine steward.

Finally, at the bottom of the scale for sophistication, but worthy of investigation both as a Japanese phenomenon and for a pleasant evening's drinking, is *Golden Gai*, "Golden Alley," a maze of back lanes in the Shinjuku area, where every door opens into a tiny bar big enough to seat six at the most.

Entertainment

Tokyo is the nation's centre for entertainment, as for everything else, and a sizable proportion is in English, or accessible to the Western visitor. The traditional arts such as Kabuki continue to flourish here, and Western artists of all varieties, from ballet companies and orchestras to rock stars, are frequent visitors. At the far end of the spectrum, you may be lucky enough to catch a performance of one of Tokyo's very lively, and frequently outrageous, avant garde theatre groups. *Tokyo Journal* will keep you up to date with what's on. There are also several free English language publications such as *Tour Companion* and *Tokyo Weekender*, available in hotels. Make reservations through your hotel or at *PIA*, *Saisons* or *Play Guide* ticket agencies in main stations and the ground floor or basement of department stores. Your Japanese colleagues will be able to help you locate entertainment of a rather less sophisticated variety. If left to your own devices, make your way to Kabukicho's Sakura-dori, in Shinjuku.

Theatre Tokyo is the home of Kabuki. For maximum enjoyment of these spectacular dramas, bone up beforehand with *The Kabuki Handbook*, which gives detailed descriptions of the highly complicated plots. The actors to see are the immensely popular Tamasaburo, the celebrated player of female roles, and his consort, Takao, who appear at the *Kabuki Theatre*, 4-12 Ginza. This is the place to see the best, classic Kabuki. Performances, usually three or four plays, start at 11am and 4.30pm and last up to 5 hours. Cheap tickets to watch a single play are available on the day, and there are English-language programmes and earphone guides. The programme changes once a month. The innovative and energetic Ennosuke and his troupe usually perform at the *Shimbashi Embujo*, 6-8-12 Ginza, or the *National Theatre*, 4-1

Hayabusacho, Chiyoda-ku, which also shows modern Japanese dramas.

Each school of Noh has its own theatre in Tokyo. The Kanze, the oldest and most popular school, is based at *Kanze Nohgakudo*, 1-16-4 Shoto, Shibuya-ku. The other main schools are the Hosho, at *Hosho Nohgakudo*, 1-5-9 Hongo, Bunkyo-ku, and Kita, at *Kita Nohgakudo*, 4-6-9 Kami Osaki, Shinagawa-ku. The *National Noh Theatre*, 4-18-1 Sendagaya, Shibuya-ku, opened in 1983. As far as most Japanese are concerned, Shakespeare is considerably more interesting than traditional Japanese theatre, and can be enjoyed in Japanese or English at the newly-opened *Tokyo Globe Theatre*, 3-1-2 Hyakunincho, Shinjuku-ku ☎ 360 1151. Bright pink and designed by celebrated architect Arata Isozaki, it is a noteworthy site.

Ballet The world's great ballet companies frequently visit Tokyo, and the Matsuyama Ballet Company performs ballets choreographed and directed by, and sometimes featuring, Rudolf Nureyev.

Cinema There are plenty of foreign movies in Tokyo, most of which are original language with Japanese subtitles. Japanese films by internationally famous directors such as Kurosawa are shown with English subtitles at one or two cinemas. The most popular foreign movies show all over town and play for months, but there are many small cinemas, listed in the local press, which show revivals and serious films.

Music Japan's musical luminaries range from internationally acclaimed composer Toru Takemitsu to synthesizer magicians Ryuichi Sakamoto and Kitaro, and with luck you will be able to see one of these play. The choice of music in Tokyo is immense. There are some excellent local orchestras such as the NHK Symphony (considered the best), Tokyo Philharmonic and Yomiuri Symphony, as well as visiting international orchestras. Several international rock bands have made

their name in Japan, and regularly perform here, together with Japanese rock artists. There are also concerts of traditional Japanese music, including the immensely popular *enka*, sung with a throb in the voice, as well as the more familiar classical koto and shamisen music. Concert tickets rapidly sell out, and should be bought as far in advance as possible.

Nightclubs Much of Tokyo's entertainment finishes early. Films, plays and concerts end by 9pm and most restaurants have closed by 10pm. For late night entertainment, Roppongi is the place to go; you will also find pockets of activity in Akasaka and Shibuya, and Shinjuku never sleeps. Tokyo's sophisticated cabarets are for the affluent or those on liberal expense accounts. Among the best are the *New Latin Quarter*, 2-13-8 Nagatacho, Chiyoda-ku, an elegant cabaret and hostess bar, and *The Crystal Room*, a theatre-restaurant in the New Otani Hotel. Japanese colleagues might entertain you at *Furusato*, in Shibuya, where you watch traditional Japanese dances and dine on traditional fare.

For live music, the newly opened *Blue Note*, 5-13-3 Minami Aoyama, Minato-ku, features international jazz musicians and is particularly popular among the resident foreign business community. *Inkstick*, B1 Casa Grande Miwa Bldg, 7-5-11 Roppongi, has live music on Friday and Saturday nights, while *Mint Bar*, across the hall, is a chic mint green cocktail bar with a large video screen.

Less sophisticated, and packed with Western businessmen, is the *Cavern Club*, 3F Roppongi Hosho Bldg, 7-14-1 Roppongi, which features Beatles' lookalikes (Japanese) in Cuban-heeled boots.

The young international set crowds into *Hot Co-rocket*, B1 Daini Omasa Bldg, 5-18-2 Roppongi, to dance to reggae played by an English band; there is Brazilian music on Sundays. Probably the city's largest live music venue is *Shibaura Inkstick*, down in the developing Tokyo Bay area. *Club*

Quattro, Parco 4, Shibuya, is more centrally located, and also features excellent live bands.

Of Tokyo's many discos, the two in which to be seen are the glamorous *Lexington Queen*, B1 Daisan Goto Bldg, 3-13-14 Roppongi, where the visiting rock stars go, and the *Neo Japanesque*, B2 Roppongi Forum Bldg, 5-16-5 Roppongi, small and sophisticated. For black music, try *Mugen*, 3-8-17 Akasaka.

Shopping

Japan is like an enormous production line, continually producing new goods of higher and higher quality; and Tokyo is the nation's shop window. There are, however, certain goods that it is better not to buy in Japan: canny shoppers buy their antiques and pearls in Hong Kong and Japanese high-tech – laptops, for example – may be cheaper outside Japan. Prices are not low, particularly for imported goods, but the range and quality available is hard to beat. The main shopping areas are Ginza (for luxury goods), Shibuya and Shinjuku. Apart from Ginza, the best places for top-quality goods are the arcades in the Imperial, Okura and New Otani hotels. Most department stores now employ foreign staff to help foreign customers. The foreign customers' liaison office in the Seibu department store in Yurakucho, for example, guarantees to search out any product not in stock. They also have clothes in foreigners' sizes (that is, large), run a catering service and even organize trips to the country.

Department stores Tokyo is the home of Japan's oldest and most prestigious department stores, *Mitsukoshi* and *Takashimaya*, both in Nihonbashi. The most vigorous of the newer stores is *Seibu*, whose Yurakucho branch, in the Mullian Centre, has a particularly fine selection of goods. At the centre of Ginza, opposite the two old standbys *Matsuya* and *Matsuzakaya*, is *Wako*, a store selling high-class luxury fashions. Outside Ginza, *Isetan*, in Shinjuku, is worth

looking at; Shibuya seems to be a battle-ground between the two rivals, *Seibu* and *Tokyu*, each of which have mammoth stores.

Malls There are some shopping malls specifically for foreign tourists, selling tax-free goods from cameras to kimonos: *International Arcade*, 1-7-23 Uchisaiwaicho, Chiyoda-ku ☎ 591 2764; *Japan Tax-free Centre*, 5-8-6 Toranomon, Minato-ku ☎ 432 4341; *Sukiyabashi Shopping Centre*, 5-1 Ginza ☎ 571 8027 or 8028.

Multi-purpose stores *Axis*, 5-17-1 Roppongi, is a complex of stores selling high-quality up-to-the-minute merchandise with design as a theme. Issey Miyake's former fabric designer has a shop here. *Wave*, 6-2-27 Roppongi, is a high-tech music store with a computerized record reference system, recording studio, ticket agency and a small cinema showing foreign art films. There is a new branch of *Wave* in Shibuya. Right next door is *Loft*, 21-1 Udagawacho, Shibuya-ku, another venture of the all-conquering Seibu group. It has six floors of designer objects, from Highway Shooters to household goods and an entire floor of clocks and watches, and is always crammed with shoppers. *Tokyu Hands*, 12-18 Udagawacho, Shibuya-ku, sells every craft and hobby tool you have ever wanted, including the much-coveted Japanese carpentry tools.

Books You may not find the book you are looking for in a Tokyo bookshop, but you *will* find an interesting and rather idiosyncratic selection, including plenty of books on Japan. The main places for books in English are *Kinokuniya*, 6th Fl, 3-17-7 Shinjuku; *Maruzen*, 3rd Fl, 2-3-10 Nihonbashi, Chuo-ku; and *Iena*, 3rd Fl, 5-6-1 Ginza. The Okura, Imperial and New Otani hotels also have good bookshops. Jimbocho is the area to scour for secondhand books, and you may also find woodblock prints and old maps here. *Sanseido*, 1-1 Jimbocho, has a fine collection of Victorian art and travel books.

Cameras *Yodobashi Camera*, 1-11-1 Nishi Shinjuku, is the world's largest camera shop, with huge discounts and a tax-free section. *Camera no Sakuraya*, 3-17-2 Shinjuku, is the other big camera shop.

Clothes Japan has become something of a fashion mecca, and there is a vast selection of stylish and high quality clothes, at prices ranging from economical to outrageous. Size is a difficulty. Sleeves and trouser legs are often too short, and shoes are almost always tiny. Do not buy anything without trying it on; a packaged shirt, even one with an Western brand name, is likely to be short in the sleeve. Most of the designer fashions are to be found in Shibuya. Issey Miyake, Comme des Garçons and other top designers are infinitely cheaper here than outside Japan. Their clothes are available in department stores such as Seibu and they also have boutiques, both men's and women's, in *Parco*, 15-1 Udagawacho, Shibuya-ku, a fashion complex of four buildings useful for one-stop shopping. *From 1st*, 5-3-10 Minami Aoyama, Minato-ku, rather more exclusive in atmosphere, also houses designer boutiques. *Wako*, in Ginza, is the place to window shop for classic fashions; only the very wealthy actually buy anything here. *Seed*, 21-1 Udagawacho, Shibuya, has nine floors of top-quality fashion.

Electronic goods For electronic goods, there are more bargains to be found in Akihabara than in the tourist-oriented tax-free shops. Prices here can be as much as 40% below list. *Rajio Kaikan*, 1-15-16 Soto-Kanda, Chiyoda-ku, is a conglomeration of shops selling audio, video and electrical goods. This is one place in Japan where the shopkeepers will bargain. To ensure compatibility, buy only the export model of sophisticated equipment; you can also buy adaptors suitable for each country. Although prices may turn out to be no cheaper than at home, the range of electronic toys in Japan is much wider. To play with the latest audio and video equipment and computers, drop into the *Sony Showroom*, 3-4F Sony Bldg, 5-3-1 Ginza.

Gifts Side by side with Japan's new technology, the old tradition of fine craftsmanship continues. Ginza is the best area for high-quality arts and crafts. Begin your search in a department store. *Mitsukoshi* and *Takashimaya*, both in Nihonbashi, have excellent selections of kimonos, and you can buy the combs and hair pins to go with them in *Matsuzakaya*, in Ginza. For antiques, try the basement of Takashimaya or the *Oriental Bazaar*, 5-9-13 Jingumae, Shibuya-ku. *Kurofune*, 7-7-4 Roppongi, is highly recommended by resident Westerners. The owner, John A. Adair Jr, is a knowledgeable and reputable antiques dealer, and the goods, though expensive, are guaranteed to be the real thing. *Takumi*, 8-4-2 Ginza, sells fine ceramics and specializes in Mashiko ware. The finest Japanese handmade paper, used for everything from umbrellas and fans to doors and windows, is in *Haibara*, 2-7-6 Nihonbashi, Chuo-ku. *Heiando*, 3-10-11 Nihonbashi, Chuo-ku, "By appointment to the Imperial Household," has the best traditional lacquerware. Collectors will find moderately-priced woodblock prints at *Matsushita*, 6-3-12 Minami Aoyama, Shibuya-ku. For pearls, Tokyo's most famous shop is *Mikimoto*, 4-5-5 Ginza, Chuo-ku. Westerners in the know buy their pearls from *Wally Yonamine Co. Inc.*, 4-11-8 Roppongi – expensive, but beautiful and top-quality, and irregular as well as round pearls.

Markets Monthly markets are held in the grounds of some shrines and temples on certain Sundays. You will find plenty of antiques, ceramics and old kimonos, occasionally at bargain prices. There is a market in *Togo Shrine* in Harajuku on the first and fourth Sunday of each month, and at *Nogi Shrine*, near Roppongi, on the second.

Sightseeing

Tokyo is not the best place in Japan for sightseeing. If you have a few hours to spare, it is worth forsaking the city and heading out to Kamakura, Nikko or, for a couple of days, to Kyoto. However, Tokyo does have the finest museums in Japan. Besides the national museums, concentrated in Ueno Park, there are fine private galleries; department stores, too, often have superb exhibitions. For those with limited time, sights not to be missed include Asakusa Kannon Temple in old Edo, Meiji Shrine, the National Museum and the Imperial Palace, with its East Garden. Of the galleries, the Idemitsu has a particularly interesting collection. Most museums and galleries have changing exhibitions and are closed on Mondays. For up-to-date information, consult the local press.

Asakusa Kannon Temple Asakusa Kannon is at the heart of the bustling downtown district of Asakusa. The oldest temple in Tokyo, it was first built in the 7thC to house an image of Kannon, the Buddhist goddess of mercy, which, the story goes, two brothers found in their fishing net. The temple is enormous, with a five-storey pagoda and a huge red lantern, 4 metres tall, a symbol of Asakusa. The streets around the temple, full of tiny stalls, are always thronged with people. *2-3-1 Asakusa, Taito-ku.*

Fukagawa Edo Museum One of Tokyo's newest museums recreates a whole section of Edo (old Tokyo). You can wander the narrow earthen streets or step up into the old wooden houses. *1-3-28 Shirakawa, Koto-ku. Open daily 10–5.*

Goto Art Museum The famous thousand-year-old Genji Monogatari scrolls are displayed for one week in May in this lovely museum set in a hillside garden. For the rest of the year there is a fine collection of Japanese and Chinese paintings, calligraphy and ceramics. *3-9-25 Kaminoge, Setagaya-ku. Open Tue–Sun, 9.30–4.30.*

Hamarikyu Garden Once the summer villa of the shoguns stood here, but now only the garden – one of the loveliest in Tokyo – is left. This one-time playground of the aristocracy features a tidal pond spanned by three bridges, moon-viewing pavilions and tea houses. *Hamarikyu teien, Chuo-ku. Open Tue–Sun, 9–4.30.*

Idemitsu Gallery Idemitsu, one of Japan's oil kings, used his fortune to amass a wonderful collection of ceramics, paintings, calligraphy and bronzes, both Japanese and Chinese. His particular passion was the works of the 17thC Zen monk Sengai, and the gallery owns nearly all of them. There is a tranquil lounge with a tea dispenser, where you can sit and gaze over the Imperial Palace, *9F International Bldg, 3-1-1 Marunouchi, Chiyoda-ku. Open Tue–Sun, 10–5.*

Imperial Palace There is very little to see at the Imperial Palace – top attraction though it is of every itinerary. The official residence of the Emperor, the Palace itself is open only twice a year, on New Year's Day and the Emperor's birthday. Having been rebuilt in ferroconcrete in 1968, it is not, in any case, very impressive. The Imperial Palace East Garden is a spacious and peaceful park with landscaped lawns and flowers. *Chiyoda, Chiyoda-ku. Garden open 9–3; closed Mon and Fri.*

Japan Folkcrafts Museum This fine museum just outside Shibuya houses the collection of well-known folk art patron and author Yanagi Soetsu. There is a changing display of furniture, ceramics and textiles, of outstandingly high quality. The museum itself is a beautiful old wooden house, brought piece by piece from the country and reconstructed here. For craft enthusiasts, this is a must. *4-3-33 Komaba, Meguro-ku. Open Mar–Dec, Tue–Sun, 10–5.*

Koishikawa Korakuen Garden Designed by Tokugawa Yorifusa in the Edo period, Korakuen is a large and beautiful Japanese garden, with winding streams, arching bridges and a lake full of carp. *1-6-4 Koraku, Bunkyo-ku. Open Tue–Sun, 9–4.30.*

Meiji Shrine Set in wooded parkland among trees, streams and flowers, Meiji Shrine provides a breath of fresh air and tranquillity in the bustle of the city. It is always full of pilgrims and visitors, particularly in June, when its famed irises bloom. It enshrines the Emperor Meiji (1868–1912). *1-1 Kamizonocho, Yoyogi, Shibuya-ku.*

Nezu Art Museum Set in a beautiful garden with a stream and tea pavilions, the Nezu has an outstanding collection of Japanese paintings and also lacquerware, ceramics and scrolls. *6-5-36 Minami Aoyama, Minato-ku Open Tue–Sun, 9.30–4.30.*

Ota Memorial Museum of Art Just off the main Harajuku thoroughfare, the Ota Museum is a quiet Japanese house, with two floors of woodblock prints, and a restaurant in the basement. *1-10-10 Jingumae, Shibuya-ku. Open 10.30–5.30; closed Mon and from the 25th of each month.*

Riccar Art Museum This tiny museum houses one of the best collections of woodblocks in Japan, which it displays in changing exhibitions. *7F Riccar Bldg, 2-3-6 Ginza. Open Tue–Sun, 11–6.*

Rikugien Garden A beautifully landscaped garden, Rikugien was laid out in the 17th century around a central lake. With its tea house and miniature mountain, it was a favourite retreat for the Edo aristocracy. *6 Komagome, Bunkyo-ku. Open Tue–Sun, 9–4.30.*

Sumo Museum, For Sumo enthusiasts. *1-3-28 Yokoami, Sumida-ku. Open Mon–Fri, 9.30–4.30.*

Tokyo National Museum The largest museum in Japan, the National Museum houses the best collection of Japanese art in the world. Only a small part of the collection is on display at any one time, so it is worth visiting several times. There are also excellent temporary exhibitions. *13-9 Ueno Koen, Taito-ku. Open Tue–Sun, 9–4.30.*

Tokyo National Museum of Modern Art This museum houses an excellent collection of contemporary Japanese art from the Meiji period onwards. Nearby is the Museum's *Crafts Gallery*, with some fine examples of modern ceramics and textiles, attractively displayed. *3 Kitanomaru Koen, Chiyoda-ku. Open Tue–Sun, 10–5.*

Zojoji Temple Originally built in the 14th century, Zojoji was a Tokugawa family temple, strategically located to protect Edo Castle from dangerous forces, both physical and spiritual. Of the Edo period building, only the main gate remains. *4-7-35 Shiba Koen, Minato-ku.*

Guided tours

The three major companies offering sightseeing tours of Tokyo with English-speaking guides are the *Japan Travel Bureau* ☎ 276 7777, *Fujita Travel Service* ☎ 573 1417 and *Japan Gray Line* ☎ 433 5745 or 436 6881. The half- and full-day tours, covering the major sights, are worth taking only if you are pressed for time. Better value are the nightlife tours (see *Entertainment*). There are also special tours focusing on arts or crafts. Of particular interest are JTB's three full-day "Industrial Tokyo" tours, which take you to factories, computer laboratories and the JAL maintenance base at Haneda.

Out of town

Seasoned Tokyo-dwellers do not travel at the weekend, when the roads are blocked for miles around with traffic, barely moving. If you must travel, take the train; you may have to stand, but you can be certain of arriving in reasonable time.

Japanese like to repeat the old saying, "Don't say *kekko* until you've seen Nikko." *Kekko* means "splendid," and *Nikko*, 120kms/75 miles north of the capital and 2hrs by train, is truly spectacular. Visitors go to see the *Toshogu Shrine*, built by the Tokugawa shoguns as their mausoleum; but Nikko's mountain setting, with lakes (including the beautiful *Chuzenji*), waterfalls and forests is equally magnificent. Nearer at hand is *Kamakura*, tucked between the mountains and sea, 45kms/30 miles and exactly 1hr on the Yokosuka line from Tokyo station. For a few years during the 13thC, Kamakura was the capital of Japan, and it still has a certain aristocratic air. Many artists and intellectuals live in Kamakura's pleasant forested hills, among the temples. Avoid the most popular sights: the huge bronze Buddha and Hachiman Shrine. Instead, get off the train one stop before Kamakura, at Kita Kamakura, and wander through the silent Buddhist temples out into the hills. Beyond Kamakura to the southwest is *Hakone*, just over 100kms/65 miles from Tokyo, accessible by Bullet Train and the most popular resort area for Tokyoites. The combination of mountains, volcanoes, forests and crater lakes is spectacular. After hiking, riding or boating, you can retreat to one of the hot spring hotels or *ryokan* and immerse yourself in healing sulphuric water. Hakone also boasts the *Open-air Museum*, a fine collection of modern Western and Japanese sculpture. The climbing season for *Mount Fuji*, 100kms/65 miles southwest of Tokyo, is July and August. Less arduously, you can visit *Fuji Five Lakes*, which offers good hiking through beautiful countryside. Much closer to the metropolis is *Tokyo Disneyland*, 35–50mins by bus from Tokyo station.

Spectator sports

Baseball is the game closest to the hearts of most young sport-minded businessmen, with rugby just behind. Highlight of the baseball year is not pro baseball but the annual high school tournament in Osaka. It dominates television, and the whole country talks about very little else throughout July and August. Volleyball also has a large following;

it is not so long since the Japanese volleyball team was the world's best. Sumo is a bit of an old men's (or old women's) sport, though many resident Westerners become great enthusiasts. Golf is very much a rich man's sport in Japan, and most Japanese restrict themselves to watching it on television.

Baseball Tokyo is the home of five pro baseball teams. The most popular Tokyo team is the Yomiuri Giants, one of the two strongest Central League teams. Tokyo's other Central League team, the Yakult Swallows, are making their way up the league. The Lotte Orions, based in Kawasaki, and the Seibu Lions, based just outside Tokyo in Saitama, are two successful teams in the Pacific League. The Giants' home field, shared with Pacific League team Nippon Ham Fighters, is the *Tokyo Dome*, 1-3-61, Korakuen, Bunkyo-ku ☎ 811 2111. The Yakult Swallows are based in the *Jingu Stadium*, Kasumigaokacho, Shinjuku-ku ☎ 401 0312. Tickets for games can be bought on the day or on the preceding Tuesday at the stadium or any Tokyo ticket office. The baseball season is from April to October, with the final game in mid-October. One of the major league American teams visits Japan about once a year and plays a series with a Japanese all-star team; five or six of these games are held in Tokyo. For daily baseball schedules, check the English-language press.

Rugby The top teams are those of the three famous universities, Keio, Waseda and Meiji. The rugby season is very short. The final always takes place in Tokyo, in December or January, at the *National Stadium*, 10 Kasumigaokacho, Shinjuku-ku ☎ 469 6081.

Sumo is Japan's *kokugi* or national skill, rather than a mere sport. The *yokozuna*, grand champions, are national heroes. There are sumo tournaments in January, May and September, at the *New Kokugikan*, 1-20 Yokoami, Sumida-ku

☎ 623 5111. Each tournament lasts 15 days and starts on the second Sunday of the month. You will need to reserve well in advance for a good seat. There are usually balcony and bench seats available on the day of the match, or you can stand at the back. Go early for a better seat; most fans arrive late in the day for the most spectacular bouts.

Keeping fit

In Japan, sporting activity is not simply a matter of keeping fit. Golf, for example, is very much tied up with status. Membership of top golf courses such as the Kawana Hotel Golf Course, Japan's most famous, is restricted to top people; others simply cannot enter. Hence, as an indication of your host company's – and your – importance, you may find yourself, golfer or non-golfer, being whisked off for a compulsory Sunday game. The most valued foreign clients may experience the ultimate sporting excursion, a ride on a private luxury yacht. The possibilities open to those left to their own devices are somewhat more limited.

Golf For inveterate golfers with large expense accounts, *Japan Gray Line* ☎ 433 4801 offers a golf tour to one of Japan's finest private courses, the *Fuji Ace Golf Club* ☎ 503 7931 on the slopes of Mount Fuji, normally open only to members and their guests. There is a pick-up service from major hotels.

Fitness centres The popular *Clark Hatch Physical Fitness Centre*, 2-1-3 Azabudai, Minato-ku ☎ 584 4092, is oriented towards the visiting foreign executive. It has reciprocal membership arrangements with all other Clark Hatch Clubs. American-run, it has a fully equipped gym and sauna; facilities are open to men only. Training gear and towels are supplied. The women's equivalent of Clark Hatch is the *Sweden Health Centre*, 5F Sweden Centre, 6-11-9 Roppongi ☎ 404 9739, which is, in fact, affiliated with Clark Hatch. There is a gym and sauna, plus dance

and exercise classes. Facilities are open to non-members Jun–Sep on payment of a sizable monthly fee. There are facilities for visiting executives at the two *Do Sports Plazas*, in Harumi, 5-6-41 Toyosu, Koto-ku ☎ 531 8221, and Shinjuku, Sumitomo Bldg Annex, 2-6-1 Nishi Shinjuku ☎ 344 1971. These large sports centres have a gym, jogging track, pool, squash courts and sauna.

Jogging The best and most popular jogging course takes you around the moats of the *Imperial Palace* and covers about 5kms/3 miles. The *Yoyogi Park* course, about half the length of the Palace course, goes around NHK Television Centre and Yoyogi Stadium. Several of the larger hotels, such as the New Otani and the Tokyo Prince, issue jogging maps.

Massage The best massage in town is at the Capitol Tokyu Hotel. At *Paru Onsen*, 2F Okazaki Bldg, 2-14-13 Shibuya ☎ 409 4882, you can have a massage or *shiatsu* as well as enjoying the jacuzzi.

Skiing There are overnight buses to the nearest ski slopes and some ski areas can be reached in about 90mins by train. Contact the following travel agencies for schedules: *Bell Tour* ☎ 260 6181; *Howa Travel Service* ☎ 342 3271; *Taiyo Recreation Centre* ☎ 295 0041.

Squash Several expatriate groups, such as the American Club and the British Council, have squash clubs. The *Do Sports Plazas* (see *Fitness centres*) have public courts.

Swimming Public pools are extremely crowded. There are pools in the two *Do Sports Plazas* and in other sports centres. The pools in the following hotels are open, at a fee, to non- residents: Capitol Tokyu, Century Hyatt, Holiday Inn, Keio Plaza, Miyako, New Otani, Okura, Shinagawa Prince, Tokyo Prince. The seaside swimming season is from June to August, and during this period the beaches are packed. At other times you will have the beach to yourself. There are fine beaches on the Boso

and Izu peninsulas, and even the beaches of Kamakura, only 1hr from Tokyo by train, are relatively clean.
Tennis There is little chance of a game of tennis in Japan. Ever since Emperor Akihito met his future wife on a tennis court, there has been a tennis boom in Japan, and courts are booked up months in advance.

Local resources
Business services
The business service centres at the Imperial and Okura hotels are undoubtedly the best in town and frequently used by non-residents. By far the most useful of the commercial agencies is *Oak Associates* ☎ 354 9502. Run by Charlotte Kennedy Takahashi, a long-time Japan resident. Oak also organize useful early morning seminars for business people. Another excellent agency is *Jardine Business Centre*, ABS Bldg 2-4-16 Kudan Mihami, Chiyoda-ku ☎ 239 2811. ISS ☎ 265 7101 and *Manpower Japan* ☎ 582 1761 are large organizations with branches throughout Japan. Other companies used by the local business community include *Alpha Services* ☎ 230 0090, *Best International* ☎ 423 4800, *Chescom International Service* ☎ 341 1111, *Japan Convention Service* ☎ 508 1221, *Kao Co Ltd* ☎ 564 3927, *Summit Service* ☎ 499 0245 and *Tory's Office* ☎ 408 9080.
Photocopying and printing If your hotel will not photocopy for you, go to a camera shop, department store or stationer's, all of whom often have photocopying machines; or call *Fuji Xerox Co* ☎ 585 3211. The *Okura Executive Service Centre* ☎ 586 7400 can print your business cards in less than 24hrs. *Nagashima International PR Office* ☎ 504 1111 also prints business cards. For general printing go to *T&T* ☎ 586 3271 or *Hagiwara Printing Co Ltd* ☎ 811 4272.
Interpreters Contact *Oak Associates* (see above) and ask for a personal recommendation. Failing that, try ISS, Japan Convention Service, or *Simul Int'l Inc* ☎ 586 8911. These companies also offer translation services.
Secretarial Use *Temporary Centre Corporation* ☎ 508 1431 or *Temp staff* ☎ 405 5507.
Translation The *Japan Translation Federation* ☎ 452 9705 will advise on translators for specific needs.
Miscellaneous For catering, Western businessmen go to *André Lecomte* ☎ 475 1770, who is both better and cheaper than hotel caterers; he will also find premises for your function. Chef *André Pachon* ☎ 404 0384 also does catering. The best tailor to go to is *Ricky Sarani* ☎ 587 0648, who will make up a dinner jacket (do not hire one) and do emergency repairs.

Communications
Long-distance delivery Federal Express ☎ 201 4331, DHL *Japan Inc* ☎ 454 0501, *Nippon Express Co Ltd* ☎ 574 1211, *Overseas Courier Service* ☎ 453 8311, *World Courier (Japan)* ☎ 508 9281.
Local delivery Business Cuban ☎ 476 5671, *City Service* ☎ 562 5665.
Post offices The main post office, Tokyo Station Plaza, Chiyoda-ku ☎ 284 9527, is open 24hrs for express service. Normal opening hours are Mon–Fri 9–7; Sat 9–5. Use *Tokyo International Post Office*, 2-3-3 Otemachi ☎ 241 4891, for sending international parcels or registered letters.
Telex and fax All major hotels provide telex and fax facilities. Otherwise go to KDD, International Telegraph Office, 1-8-1 Otemachi, Chiyoda-ku ☎ 270 5111, or one of the business service agencies (see above).

Conference/exhibition centres
Trade fairs and exhibitions are organized by the *Japan Convention Bureau*. The main location for international trade fairs is *Tokyo International Trade Fair Grounds*, 5-3-53 Harumi, Chuo-ku

☎ 533 5311. Fairs are also held at the *Convention Centre Tokyo*, Sunshine City ☎ 264 3234, *Tokyo Ryutsu Centre*, 1-1-1 Heiwajima, Ota-ku ☎ 767 2162, and the *Tokyo Trade Centre*, 3F World Trade Centre Bldg Annex, Hamamatsucho ☎ 435 5394. Many conferences and smaller exhibitions tend to be held in the major hotels.

Emergencies

Bureaux de change Currency desks at the major hotels are open seven days a week, from early in the morning until late at night.
Hospitals Major hotels have lists of hospitals with English-speaking staff and some have medical clinics. The following hospitals and clinics have a 24hr emergency service: *Japan Red Cross Hospital* (Nisseki Iryo Centre), 4-1-22 Hiro, Shibuya-ku ☎ 400 1311; *Tokyo Medical and Surgical Clinic*, 2F 32 Mori Bldg, 3-4-30 Shiba Koen, Minato-ku ☎ 436 3028. There are English-speaking staff at *St Luke's International Hospital* (Seiroka Byoin), 1-10 Akashicho, Chuo-ku ☎ 541 5151; *St Mary's International Catholic Hospital* (Seibo Byoin), 2-5-1 Naka-Ochiai, Shinjuku-ku ☎ 951 1111, *Tokyo Adventist Hospital*, 3-17-3 Amanuma, Suginami-ku ☎ 392 6151; *Ishikawa Clinic*, 2F Azabu Sakurada Heights, 3-2-7 Nishi Azabu, Minato-ku ☎ 401 6340; and the *International Clinic*, 1-5-9 Azabudai, Minato-ku ☎ 582 2646. English is spoken at *Besford Dental Office*, 2F 32 Mori Bldg, 3-4-30 Shiba Koen, Minato-ku ☎ 431 4225.
Pharmacies Hospitals supply drugs. There are no 24hr pharmacies. The *American Pharmacy*, Hibiya Park Bldg, 1-8-1 Yurakucho, Chiyoda-ku ☎ 271 4034, stocks Western (mainly American) drugs, cosmetics, dental care products, contraceptives and health foods; if you can't find it here, it is probably not available in Japan.
Police In an emergency, go to the nearest *koban*, neighbourhood police box, or dial 110.

Government offices

For information, advice and statistics, the best offices to approach are *JETRO (Japan External Trade Organisation)*, 2-2-5 Toranomon, Minato-ku ☎ 582 5511, representing Japan's exporting manufacturers, which publishes a useful series of books and pamphlets on the Japanese market, and *MITI (Ministry of International Trade and Industry)*, 1-3-1 Kasumigaseki, Chiyoda-ku ☎ 501 1511, a monolithic body, but a good source of statistics.

Information sources

Business information The *US Chamber of Commerce*, 7F No. 2 Fukide Bldg, 4-1-21 Toranomon, Minato-ku ☎ 433 5381, headed by William E. Franklin, Executive Vice President of Weyerhauser, is immensely effective and powerful, particularly in the area of electronics and telecommunications. They will be willing to provide a list of their members – among whom you will find useful contacts – to inquirers of any nationality. Less powerful (though often more useful than the embassies) are the other chambers of commerce: *Australian*, Nihon Bldg, 2-6-2 Otemachi, Chiyoda-ku ☎ 201 7861; *Belgian-Luxembourg*, Maison Sunshine Suite, 3-1-4 Higashi Ikebukuro, Toshima-ku ☎ 985 1655; *British*, Kowa No. 16 Bldg, 1-9-20 Akasaka, Minato-ku ☎ 505 1734; *Canadian*, Homat Avou 101, 5-15-2 Higashi Gotanda, Shinagawa-ku ☎ 447 9767; *French*, French Bank Bldg, 1-1-2 Akasaka, Minato-ku ☎ 587 0061; *German*, Akasaka Tokyu Bldg, 2-14-3 Nagatacho, Chiyoda-ku ☎ 581 9881; *Netherlands*, Akasaka Q Bldg, 7-9-5 Akasaka, Minato-ku ☎ 586 3701; *Swiss*, c/o Sulzer Brothers (Japan) Ltd, 23F Asahi Tokai Bldg, 2-6-1 Otamachi, Chiyoda-ku ☎ 246 2715.

The *Japan Chamber of Commerce*, 3-2-1 Marunouchi, Chiyoda-ku ☎ 283 7867, and the *Tokyo Chamber of Commerce and Industry*, Tosho Bldg, 3-2-2 Marunouchi, Chiyoda-ku

☎ 283 7500, will also be able to help.

Local media International newspapers are widely available in Tokyo and are more informative than the local English-language ones. Of the latter, the conservative *Japan Times*, run by the Ministry of Foreign Affairs, is the weightiest. The *Asahi Evening News* is the most useful for business information. The monthly *Tokyo Journal* contains articles of local interest and listings. Magazines of relevance to business people include *Tokyo Business Today*, *Japan Economic Journal*, *Japan Foreign Trade Journal*, *Oriental Economist* and *Quarterly Forecast of Japan's Economy*. And, of course, everyone reads the *Far East Economic Review*. The *Kyodo News Service*, the Japanese Reuters, transmits a continuous update of current events, received by the business service centres of major hotels. The cable channels KTYO (radio) and JCTV (television) are broadcast to hotels in English, and there are several satellite channels. JCTV, mainly a news service, shows live news from CNN, plus local news, features and documentaries related to business in Japan.

Tourist information Make your first stop the *Tourist Information Centre* (TIC), 1-6-6 Yurakucho, Chiyoda-ku ☎ 502 1461, which has knowledgeable English-speaking staff and provides free maps, leaflets and information on current cultural events. For travel assistance, ☎ 502 1461 from anywhere in Tokyo. For recorded information on current happenings, ☎ 503 2911.

For general information, contact the *Japan National Tourist Organisation* (*JNTO*), Tokyo Kotsu Kaikan Bldg, 2-10-1 Yurakucho, Chiyoda-ku ☎ 216 1901. The *Japan Travel Bureau* (*JTB*), Foreign Tourist Dept, 3F Nittetsu-Nihonbashi Bldg, 1-13-1 Nihonbashi, Chuo-ku ☎ 276 7771 is also helpful. In addition to *Tokyo Journal*, TIC's *Tour Companion* and *Tokyo Weekender* (produced by the local Western community) are useful guides to what's on. There are also two excellent guidebooks to Tokyo, *Tokyo Access* and *Tokyo City Guide*. For dining out, Rick Kennedy's *Good Tokyo Restaurants* is invaluable.

Thank-yous

The most prestigious gifts are those gift-wrapped from *Takashimaya* in Nihonbashi ☎ 211 4111. Another good place to go for advice on and purchase of gifts is the *Foreign Customer Liaison Office* at *Seibu*, in Yurakucho. You can pay here by credit card, and the foreign staff are experienced and helpful. Failing that, the concierge at your hotel will be able to advise. Gifts are not essential when meeting someone for the first time. The time to give gifts is after you have established a business and personal relationship. The best gifts are top-of-the-line, country-specific specialities, unobtainable in Japan or in international duty-free shops. Best of all is an extremely good wine; top quality Belgian or Swiss chocolates might come second. Gifts should always be extremely expensive and carry a well-known brand-name.

FUKUOKA
City code ☎ 092

Fukuoka is the capital of the large southern island of Kyushu and also its political, economic, cultural and communications centre. Far removed from the influences of Tokyo, it is a flourishing modern city in its own right, with a population of 1.2m and a delightful semitropical climate. It is primarily a business city and a port. The major corporation based in Fukuoka is Nishitetsu, almost a ruling dynasty, which runs a private railway, the buses, a department store and Fukuoka's most prestigious hotel. Japan's major companies and banks are all represented here, and the city's main products are electrical appliances, tools, textiles and foodstuffs. There are American, Chinese and Korean consulates in the city. Fukuoka's proximity to Asia led it to become a leading trading port in ancient times and also a major route through which Chinese culture filtered into Japan, particularly during the Nara and Heian periods (710–1192).

Arriving
From Tokyo or the north it is best to fly to Fukuoka. From Osaka the train is as convenient unless you are simply changing planes at Itami. The journey by air takes 1hr 30mins from Tokyo and 1hr from Osaka. Fukuoka's airport is conveniently near the city centre.

Fukuoka airport
The main air gateway to Kyushu, Fukuoka airport consists of an international terminal and two domestic terminals, 5mins walk apart. International traffic is mainly with Korea, but there are services from other parts of mainland Asia and the South Pacific. The international terminal has two restaurants (including Nishitetsu's Grand Chef), a VIP lounge, small shops selling a limited range of goods and duty-frees, and a bank open for plane arrivals. Of the two domestic terminals, Terminal 1 handles traffic to and from Osaka, Nagoya and Sapporo, while Terminal 2 is for Tokyo (Narita) and Okinawa. Facilities include several restaurants landside open 6.30am–8.15pm, a VIP lounge, a few shops, including a branch of Iwataya department store, with a small range of souvenirs and banks open when a plane arrives. Airport information ☎ 621 6059.

City link The airport is only a 10–20min drive from the city centre and even the executive with a modest per diem allowance should take a cab into town. But there are alternatives.
Car rental Kyushu roads are less crowded than further east, but the roadsigns are just as foreign. A car might (just) be worthwhile considering if you have business outside Fukuoka. Nippon Rentacar, the main chain operating in Fukuoka, has an office at the airport.
Bus Services depart every 5mins for the bus terminal at Hakata station, and for Tenjin.

Railway stations
Fukuoka is the last stop to the west on the Bullet Train line. The journey takes 6hrs from Tokyo, and is not much cheaper than by plane. Travellers coming from Osaka and points west usually make the journey by train.
Hakata station The Bullet Train station is a large modern building surrounded by hotels. A department store, airline offices and the Hakata post office are all located here, as well as termini for the buses and subway. Inquiries ☎ 471 8111.

Getting around
Fukuoka is laid out more or less in a grid, which makes it fairly easy to

find your way around. The subway connects the city's two transport centres, Hakata station and Fukuoka station, where you can change onto the bus, private railway (Nishitetsu, of course) or subway going east. However, Fukuoka is not a large town, nor is it particularly congested. The most convenient ways to get around are usually on foot or by taxi.

Taxis Fukuoka taxi drivers have the friendly, open nature of Kyushu people and, more importantly, seem to know the major restaurants, hotels and offices.

Driving Driving in Fukuoka is easier than in most other Japanese cities, and the roads get congested only during rush hours. Nippon Rentacar ☎ 622 1885 has offices in the city.

Walking Distances in the central Tenjin-Nakasu area are not great, and even the raunchiest parts of Nakasu are generally safe.

Bus The *Nishitetsu Bus Company* has terminals at Hakata station and Fukuoka station. If you have plenty of time and a good map of Fukuoka to follow your route, travelling by bus is more interesting than the subway.

Subway Fukuoka's subway system is clean, smooth, very modern, and – unusually for Japan – not at all crowded. All signs are in English as well as Japanese. From Muromi in the west the line runs into the city past Ohori Park, to Tenjin and Nakasu, and then splits northeast to Kyushu University and southeast down to Hakata station. The subway system is gradually being extended.

Train The train is useful for journeys to the suburbs and out to Kitakyushu. JR local trains depart from Hakata station and head up and down the coast and inland towards Nagasaki; for Kitakyushu, it is best to take the Bullet Train. The Nishitetsu line begins at Fukuoka station, in Tenjin, and follows the JR line through Dazaifu and out to the south.

Area by area

Present-day Fukuoka is divided into two by the Naka River. Hakata, the older, eastern part of the town, was the original port and commercial centre. The castle town of Fukuoka grew up to the west of Hakata in the 17th century, and the two towns amalgamated in 1889. Many businesses are still based in Hakata, but Tenjin, the centre of old Fukuoka, is fast becoming the main business area. The newest area to be developed is the waterfront, about 20mins from the centre of town.

Hakata The oldest part of Fukuoka, Hakata includes the port, the Bullet Train station and districts to the east. Much of the commercial and trading activity of the city takes place here, and the chamber of commerce and prefectural administrative offices are located in this area.

Tenjin An area of wide streets and modern buildings, Tenjin has grown into the centre of Fukuoka. It is the largest shopping and business centre in Kyushu. Banks, business services, the City Hall and other public offices are here, along with major department stores, the new Solaria and IMS buildings, a large underground shopping arcade, bus and train terminals and the majestic Nishitetsu Grand Hotel.

Nakasu This island in the Naka River is virtually deserted by day. In the evening, the buildings looming over the maze of streets are bright with neon, and each turns out to be a warren of tiny bars, cabarets, "snacks" and amusement spots.

The suburbs

Fukuoka is a small city, and the residential suburbs are not far from the city centre. The oldest families live in Daimyo, in what were the samurai areas around the castle. Other wealthy neighbourhoods are out to the west beyond the castle, and the districts of Kiyokawa and Takasago, to the south of Tenjin. The old merchant quarters in Hakata and to the east are rather run-down.

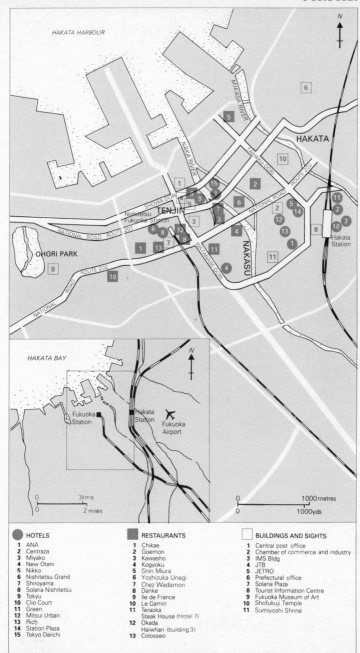

● HOTELS

1 ANA
2 Centraza
3 Miyako
4 New Otani
5 Nikko
6 Nishitetsu Grand
7 Shiroyama
8 Solaria Nishitetsu
9 Tokyu
10 Clio Court
11 Green
12 Mitsui Urban
13 Rich
14 Station Plaza
15 Tokyo Daiichi

■ RESTAURANTS

1 Chikae
2 Goemon
3 Kawasho
4 Kogyoku
5 Shin Miura
6 Yoshizuka Unagi
7 Chez Wadamon
8 Danke
9 Ile de France
10 Le Gamin
11 Teraoka
   Steak House (Hotel 7)
12 Okada
   Haiwhan (building 3)
13 Colosseo

□ BUILDINGS AND SIGHTS

1 Central post office
2 Chamber of commerce and industry
3 IMS Bldg
4 JTB
5 JETRO
6 Prefectural office
7 Solaria Plaza
8 Tourist Information Centre
9 Fukuoka Museum of Art
10 Shofukuji Temple
11 Sumiyoshi Shrine

Hotels

At the top end of the scale among Fukuoka's hotels, the well-known Nishitetsu Grand has age and status, while the Nikko and the New Otani offer many of the conveniences of a modern luxury hotel. At the moment, the only hotel to offer a business service centre is the Nikko; but as Fukuoka continues to grow, many new hotels are planned. There will be a Hyatt on the waterfront by 1991 or 1992, and there is talk of a new Prince and a new Tokyu.

ANA Y///
3-3-3 Hakata-ekimae, Hakata-ku, 812
☎ *471 7111* ℡ *722288 fax 472 7707*
● *AE DC MC V* ● *350 rooms, 6 suites, 4 restaurants, 1 bar, 1 coffee shop*
One of Fukuoka's older hotels, the ANA has a comfortably faded air. It is immensely popular, and the large, slightly dingy lobby is always crowded. The rooms, all with minibar, have views over the Japanese garden, and are spacious and homely. Concierge, shops ● health club with pool, sauna, training gym, jogging track ● 11 meeting rooms (capacity up to 700).

Centraza Y/
4-23 Chuogai, Hakata-ku, 812
☎ *461 0111* ℡ *724211 fax 461 0171*
● *AE DC MC V* ● *200 rooms, 1 suite, 1 restaurant, 1 bar, 2 coffee shops*
The best of the new hotels behind the station, the Centraza offers modern comfortable accommodation at a reasonable price. The two-floor restaurant arcade includes a Chinese restaurant and a sushi bar. Pool, men's sauna ● 9 meeting rooms (capacity up to 500).

Miyako Y/
2-1-1 Hakata-eki Higashi, Hakata-ku, 812 ☎ *441 3111* ℡ *724585 fax 481 1306* ● *AE DC MC V* ●
260 rooms, 9 suites, 2 restaurants, 2 bars, 2 coffee shops
Built in 1972, the squat, cube-like Miyako has an air of solid respectability. Of the hotels behind the station, this is the choice of most visiting foreign executives. The building has some interesting architectural features, such as long thin bedroom windows, which,

though elegant, unfortunately let in very little light. The service is brisk and efficient. Shopping arcade ● 8 meeting rooms (capacity up to 500).

New Otani Y///
1-1-2 Watanabe-dori, Chuo-ku, 810
☎ *714 1111* ℡ *726567 fax 715 5658*
● *AE DC MC V* ● *415 rooms, 8 suites, 6 restaurants, 1 bar, 1 coffee shop*
The New Otani combines the facilities of a modern international hotel with a certain Japanese elegance. The lobby is large and impressive, while the rooms are tastefully furnished, with a discreetly concealed minibar and wide windows overlooking the city. The rooms on the executive floor are particularly spacious. There is a tea-ceremony room, and the hotel's Chinese restaurant has a good reputation locally. Concierge, two-floor shopping plaza including art gallery, beauty salon ● pool, massage room ● 12 meeting rooms (capacity up to 3,000).

Nikko Y////
2-18-25 Hakata-ekimae, Hakata-ku, 812 ☎ *482 1111* ℡ *722722 fax 482 1127* ● *AE DC MC V* ●
352 rooms, 8 suites, 6 restaurants, 1 bar, 1 coffee shop
The gleaming new Nikko (opened July 1989) is the first Fukuoka hotel to offer all the facilities of an international hotel. Located right at the station, it is an imposing building full of pale marble, with sizeable rooms tastefully decorated in pastel greys. There is a ladies' floor, a nonsmoking wing and two executive floors with suites which look onto a

Japanese garden. *Les Celebrites* is a useful French restaurant and *Kawasho* (see *Restaurants*) is a branch of Kyushu's most famous sushi shop, while *Vol de Nuit* (see *Bars*) is a sophisticated meeting place for local and visiting buisness people. 24hr room service, concierge, theatre and travel booking services, hairdresser, arcade of shops • fitness centre with gym, pool and sauna • business service centre with limited facilities, 8 meeting rooms (capacity up to 1,500).

Nishitetsu Grand *Y////*
2-6-60 Daimyo, Chuo-ku, 810
☎ *771 7171* ℡ *723351 fax 751 8224*
• *AE DC MC V* • *298 rooms, 3 suites, 4 restaurants, 1 bar, 1 coffee shop*
This is the best address in Fukuoka. Owned by Nishitetsu, the private railway giant, the Nishitetsu is Fukuoka's most famous and most traditional hotel. Its vast lobby is a suitably imposing place to meet one's business contacts. The bedrooms, though recently refurbished and all with minibar, have an endearingly old-fashioned air. The location is ideal, at the prosperous Daimyo side of the Tenjin business district. Frequent visitors can join the NGH Club, whose special facilities include discounts, fast check-in and check-out and free parking for members. Express check-out, concierge, restaurant and travel reservations, shops, hairdresser • pool • 11 meeting rooms (capacity up to 1,200), international conference hall.

Shiroyama *Y/*
5-3-4 Nakasu, Hakata-ku, 810
☎ *281 2211* ℡ *723219 fax 271 6711*
• *AE DC MC V* • *140 rooms, 4 suites, 4 restaurants, 2 coffee shops*
Situated in the entertainment area of Nakasu, within striking distance of Tenjin, the Shiroyama ("White Mountain") is popular with young Japanese businessmen. Offering views of the river, the elegant all-white rooms, recently refurbished, are equipped with minibar and an extra-large desk. The Steak House (see

Restaurants) is one of Fukuoka's most popular restaurants for business dining. Men's sauna • 3 meeting rooms (capacity up to 350).

Solaria Nishitetsu *Y/*
2-2-43 Tenjin, Chuo-ku, 810
☎ *761 1155* ℡ *722777 fax 781 1211*
• *AE DC MC V* • *169 rooms, 4 suites, 3 restaurants, 1 coffee shop, 1 bar*
The new Solaria (opened May 1989) is Nishitetsu's second hotel and sits atop the Solaria Plaza. Like the Plaza, it is fashionable and modern and designed with young Japanese in mind. The rooms are a good size and comfortably furnished and the location – right in the heart of Tenjin shopping and business district – is unbeatable. Hairdresser, flower shop • 10 meeting rooms (capacity up to 1,000).

Tokyu *Y/*
1-16-1 Tenjin, Chuo-ku, 810
☎ *781 7111* ℡ *723295 fax 781 7198*
• *263 rooms, 3 suites, 3 restaurants, 1 bar, 1 coffee shop*
If you are looking for a base for a few days' working visit, the Tokyu is a good place on balance. On the one hand it lacks prestige and status, the lobby area is distinctly shabby, and the young girls who run it are rather slow and inefficient. But the rooms are spacious and attractively furnished with a Japanese flavour. The location, too, is excellent, mid-way between Nakasu and Tenjin. Beauty salon, pharmacy, travel agent • 6 meeting rooms (capacity up to 300).

OTHER HOTELS
Clio Court *Y/* *5-3 Hakata-eki Chuogai, Hakata-ku* ☎ *472 1111* ℡ *722312 fax 474 3222* • *AE DC MC V*. One of the new hotels just behind Hakata station, the glitzy Clio Court features an arcade full of boutiques and a revolving restaurant.
Green I & II *Y* *4-4 Hakata-eki Chuogai, Hakata-ku* ☎ *451 4111 fax 451 4508* • *AE DC MC V*. A large business hotel with two buildings, just behind the station.

Mitsui Urban *Y*/ *2-8-15 Hakata-ekimae, Hakata-ku* ☎ *451 5111* TX *725222 fax 451 5105* • AE DC MC V. A modest, pleasant hotel, halfway between Hakata station and Nakasu.

Rich *Y*/ *3-27-15 Hakata-ekimae, Hakata-ku* ☎ *451 7811* TX *725291 fax 482 0308* • AE DC MC V. Directly opposite the Mitsui Urban and slightly more upmarket.

Station Plaza *Y*/ *2-1-1 Hakata-ekimae, Hakata-ku* ☎ *431 1211* TX *723536 fax 431 8015*. Opposite Hakata station and well used by Japanese business travellers.

Tokyo Daiichi *Y*/ *5-2-18 Nakasu, Hakata-ku* ☎ *281 3311* TX *726342 fax 281 3938* • AE DC MC V. In the heart of Nakasu, close to bars and restaurants, and within walking distance of Tenjin.

Restaurants

Fukuoka businessmen, particularly the older ones, tend to prefer their own fine Fukuoka cuisine; when they patronize the fancy French restaurants it is mainly to impress important guests. The seafood in Fukuoka is outstanding. This is the place for *fugu* (blowfish), a potentially poisonous winter fish, regarded as a great delicacy. It can only be prepared by licensed chefs but, if properly done, it will endanger only your bank balance. It may be served raw, grilled, in a casserole, mixed with rice or as part of a *kaiseki* meal, and is in season from November to March. In the summer, Fukuoka's eel is a revelation. Tokyo fashions filter slowly through, and even down here you will find knowledgeable young businessmen sampling *nouvelle cuisine*.

JAPANESE
Chikae *Y*/
2-2-17 Daimyo, Chuo-ku ☎ *721 4624* • *reservations essential*
For business entertaining, Chikae is undoubtedly the place – and business entertaining Fukuoka-style, means eating drinking and making merry. Chikae is a vast Valhalla of a place, with a pool in the middle where the chefs net fish, then transform them into sashimi with much aplomb and present them, tails still twitching, on your table. There is plenty of drama, spectacle, noise and raucous laughter here – as well as good food.

Goemon *Y*
14-27 Kamikawabata, Hakata-ku ☎ *291 0593*
At Goemon they do magical things with tofu, the white bean curd which has recently become a part of Western healthy eating. This is a modest, unpretentious little restaurant, with a charmingly rustic air. Upstairs there are tatami rooms for formal entertaining. Your Japanese colleagues may bring you here, but you will also be welcome on your own. There is a new branch of Goemon in a beautiful country setting, a 30mins drive from Fukuoka: Goeman Sawara Sanso, 2030-1 Aza-Kamihirose, Oaza-nishi, Sawara-ku ☎ *804 0459*.

Kawasho *Y*//
5-13 Nishi Nakasu, Chuo-ku ☎ *761 0269* • *closed 2nd and 4th Sun of month* • AE DC V • *reservations essential*
The flower arrangements, paintings and even the designs on the curtains change to suit the seasons in this lovely old Japanese house. There is a lively tempura counter downstairs and quiet tatami rooms upstairs, each opening onto its own tiny garden with rocks and a pool. Tataki Takehiko, owner and master chef, has been serving fine *kaiseki*, tempura and sashimi here since 1945; he now has 12 young *sous*-chefs working under him. This is one of Fukuoka's most famous restaurants, and Japanese

executives reserve well in advance to entertain here. There is a branch of Kawasho in the Nikko Hotel.

Kogyoku [Y]
3-3-9 Haruyoshi, Chuo-ku
☎ *712 5666/751 7447*
Kogyoku is Fukuoka's classiest sushi shop. For an informal meal you can sit downstairs at the counter and point out the fish you want from the glass cabinets. If you come with Japanese colleagues, you will probably be seated upstairs in one of the beautiful private rooms overlooking the river, where your sushi will be accompanied by *kaiseki*.

Shin Miura [Y]/
21-12 Sekijomachi, Hakata-ku
☎ *291 0821 • closed 1st and 3rd Sun of month • reservations only*
Shin Miura, housed in a hundred-year-old samurai mansion down by the harbour, is one of Fukuoka's top restaurants. You will enjoy the attentions of charming kimono-clad ladies, who will prepare the Fukuoka speciality, *mizutaki*, a flavourful stew of chicken and vegetables, cooked at your table.

Yoshizuka Unagi [Y]
2-8-27 Nakasu, Chuo-ku ☎ *271 0700*
• *closed Mon*
Yoshizuka, a small and unpretentious restaurant facing the river, quite simply serves the best eel in Fukuoka. Locals regard it as the best eel in the world, and Yoshizuka is patronized by local gourmets and well-informed visitors. More formal business entertaining takes place upstairs in the tatami rooms. The menu ranges from plain eel with a liberal coating of rich sauce (the exact ingredients are a well-kept secret) to eel *kaiseki*-style.

NON-JAPANESE
Chez Wadamon [Y]/
5-15 Nishi Nakasu, Chuo-ku
☎ *761 2000 • AE DC MC V*
Wadamon is where Fukuoka's top executives wine and dine their clients and is a suitable place for the Western visitor to return hospitality. The cuisine is French with steak – Nagasaki beef – the speciality. The basement rooms are a Japanese evocation of Europe – richly atmospheric, with heavy beams, lamps hung with netting, luxuriant potted plants and ornate china. There are branches of Wadamon in Tokyo's Ginza and Roppongi.

Danke [Y]/
4-9-18 Watanabe-dori, Chuo-ku
☎ *711 0039 • AE DC MC V*
Danke is a favourite of the business community. There are two rooms, suitable for entertaining small groups, with wood-panelled walls, starched white tablecloths and a single rose on each table. Danke is linked to a sake manufacturer and boasts an unusually wide range of sake and French wines at economical prices.

Ile de France [Y]/
1-15-25 Tenjin, Chuo-ku ☎ *721 6985*
• *closed Sun • AE DC MC V*
While the older generation continues to patronize Wadamon and Danke for business entertaining, younger Japanese businessmen are choosing restaurants where the emphasis is on authentic French cuisine rather than the grandeur of the surroundings. Ile de France is like a cosy French bistro, with huge vases of flowers, art nouveau stained glass and antique brass lampstands. Chef Yoichiro Fuchigami spent eight years in Provence, studying under the renowned Roger Vergé, and his cooking is light and delicate, suitable to the Japanese palate. The clientele is young, sophisticated, knowledgeable and gourmet.

Le Gamin [Y]/
104 Chatlet Succes, 2-4-5 Akasaka, Chuo-ku ☎ *761 2721 • closed 3rd Tue of month • AE DC MC V*
Both Japanese and Western businessmen are much in evidence at this elegant French restaurant. Young chef Shinji Ebata studied in France,

and was at London's prestigious Le Gavroche for three years. His cuisine is a blend of *nouvelle* and traditional French, with plenty of local seafood. The wine list is one of the best in Fukuoka.

OTHER RESTAURANTS

If you are here in the winter, *Teraoka*, 5-24-28 Watanabe-dori, Chuo-ku ☎ 731 2480, is the place to become acquainted with Fukuoka's most notorious delicacy, fugu. Young Japanese businessmen are to be found in quantity at the *Shiroyama Hotel*'s *Steak House*, dining on the famous teppanyaki. *Okada*, B1 Matsushita Watanabe Bldg, 4-10-10 Watanabe-dori, Chuo-ku ☎ 713 0290, is also famous for its teppanyaki. For casual meals, the 12th to 14th floors of the *IMS Bldg* are well worth investigating. The restaurants here are stylish and inexpensive, and range from shabu shabu to pasta. *Haiwhan*, on 14F, is a branch of the well-known chain serving Chinese sea-food dishes, and is grand enough for business entertaining. For Italian food, *Colosseo*, 6F Bourg-Milieu Bldg, 1-12-66 Daimyo, Chuo-ku ☎ 712 6234, a branch of the Osaka Colosseo, is a good choice.

Bars

Nakasu and Tenjin are the nightlife areas, not just for Fukuoka, but for the whole of Kyushu. Japanese businessmen like to patronize their locals – two or three bars where they are known and have their labelled bottle of whisky set aside for them – and your Japanese colleagues will no doubt introduce you to theirs.

Of the hotel bars, the smartest is predictably the *Sky Bar* in the Nishitetsu Grand. *Vol de Nuit* in the Nikko is also well used by business travellers, as are the bars in the New Otani and the Tokyu. The *Sky Bar* in the Fukuoka View Hotel, 1-10-1 Kiyokawa, facing the New Otani, is a favourite gathering place for the Japanese business community.

Bosporus Papa, 2F Tokan Daiichi Bldg, Watanabe-dori, not far from the New Otani, is worth a visit for the spectacular decor and sophisticated atmosphere. There is live jazz throughout the evening. *Brasserie Nirin Club*, 5-16 Nakasu, is like an English gentleman's club and popular with the loal business community, while *Wine House Fujita*, 4-1-6 Nakasu, has a good selection of wines and Western food. The hangout for the local foreign community is *Cottonfields*, 1F Egawa Bldg, 2-8-34 Nakasu.

Entertainment

Despite its distance from Uyoto and Tokyo, Fukuoka has plenty of culture and cultural facilities, both contemporary and traditional. Besides regular visits by theatre companies and musicians, both international and Japanese, there are also many lively traditional festivals. The major festival is the Hakata Gion-Yamagasa, in July. Current cultural events are listed in the *Kyushu Journal* and *Rainbow*, and tickets are obtainable through your hotel or from ticket agencies in major department stores. *Theatre, ballet and music* The main venue for performances by visiting theatre and ballet companies and musicians is *Fukuoka Civic Hall*, 1-8-1 Tenjin, Chuo-ku ☎ 711 4111. *Cinema* There are several cinemas in Fukuoka that show English-language movies. German films are shown once a month at the *Sawara Shimin Centre*, 2-2-1 Momochi, Sawara-ku ☎ 831 2321. *Nightclubs* Locals boast that Nakasu is the raunchiest bar area in the country, and the foreign businessman is usually unable to avoid being taken on a tour of its nightclubs and bars. More upmarket – and not to be missed – is the *Versailles Palace*, Maria St, 1-8-6 Maizuru, Chuo-ku ☎ 731 5488. Modelled on Versailles, the fabulous interior cost a fortune, and features ceiling murals, huge chandeliers, sweeping staircases and golden cherubs, amongst which the disco dancers gyrate.

Shopping

Tenjin, with its underground arcades, is the shopping centre of Fukuoka. A wide range of high-quality goods is available, at prices somewhat lower than in Tokyo or Osaka. Look for fine local silks and for porcelain from nearby Arita (a milky-white porcelain with red designs) and Imari (porcelain painted in intricate multicoloured designs). Japanese visitors to Fukuoka buy the famous Hakata dolls.

Books There is a good selection of English-language books in *Kinokuniya*, 6F Tenjin Core Bldg, Tenjin. The *Kyushu Journal* and the SISAC *Kyushu Guide* are available here.

Department stores *Iwataya*, in Tenjin, is considered to be the best department store, although the venerable *Tamaya*, in Nakasu, is still very popular.

Electronic Goods A recent addition to the Fukuoka shopping scene is Utek Plaza, 4-9-25 Watanabe-dori, Chuo-ku, several floors packed with tiny shops selling electronic goods at discount prices. There are also tax-free goods here.

Gifts For old Imari and Arita porcelain look in the department stores and antique shops around Tenjin. *Kukkodo*, Shintencho arcade, Hakata-ku, has been selling traditional Japanese paper for generations. *Hakusen*, Hakata Station Bldg, 1-1 Chuogai, Hakata-eki, stocks a wide range of Hakata dolls.

Multi-purpose shops Solaria Plaza, 2-2-43 Tenjin, Chuo-ku, in central Tenjin, consists of six floors of fashion (including *Emporio Armani* and *Junior Gaultier*), a gym and sports studio, a cinema and a floor of restaurants, all topped with the Solaria Nishitetsu Hotel. The *IMS Bldg*, 1-7-11 Tenjin, Chuo-ku, just across the road, describes itself as a communication centre. It is new, gleaming, shiny and gold-plated, built around a central well with huge mobiles and transparent lifts, and is full of information centres such as

Rainbow Plaza and *Magazine House*, a lounge with an excellent selection of magazines to be read on the premises. There is also a Nissan showroom, a music centre and variety of interesting shops.

Sightseeing

Fukuoka is basically a business city, with little to see. However, there are many interesting sights just outside the city. If you have a weekend to spare, you can explore Kyushu from Fukuoka, or move on to Nagasaki or Kumamoto.

Fukuoka Museum of Art This is one of the largest and best equipped art museums in the country, with a fine collection of paintings and sculpture, including items that belonged to the ruling Kuroda family, and tea-ceremony utensils. The museum hosts important visiting exhibitions which change regularly. *1-6 Ohori Park, Chuo-ku ☎ 714 6057. Open Tue–Sun, 9.30–5.*

Ohori Park Only the gate and a watch tower remain of Fukuoka Castle, built by Lord Kuroda in 1601. The grounds and outer moat now form a large park, with a lake and three small islands linked by bridges. *Chuo-ku.*

Shofukuji Temple This Zen Buddhist temple was founded in 1195, which makes it the oldest in the country. Its founder, Eisai, also introduced tea to Japan from China. *Okunodo, Gokushomachi, Hakata-ku.*

Sumiyoshi Shrine Surrounded by cedars and camphor trees, on a hill in the centre of the city, overlooking the Naka River, Sumiyoshi Shrine is one of Kyushu's oldest, dedicated to the guardian god of sailors. The present buildings date from 1623. *Sumiyoshi, Hakata-ku.*

Guided tours

You can take a sightseeing bus tour, with a (non-stop) commentary in Japanese, around Fukuoka; for enquiries and reservations ☎ 713 5111/2961. There are also guided bus tours of Kyushu.

Out of town

Much of Kyushu is easily accessible from Fukuoka for a weekend trip. *Nagasaki*, with its Meiji period buildings is 2hrs 15mins by limited express. *Kumamoto*'s fine old castle, and *Beppu*, which is noted for its magnificent hot springs, are not much farther. Nearer at hand is *Dazaifu*, 14kms/9 miles south of Fukuoka, for centuries the cultural centre and capital of Kyushu. Consecrated to the god of learning, the *Dazaifu-Temmangu Shrine* is surrounded by plum trees, and is much visited by children who pray for success in examinations. Near the shrine is the fine old *Kanzeonji Temple*. *Karatsu*, just along the coast from Fukuoka, is a coastal resort with a 17thC castle; some of Japan's most beautiful pottery is still being produced here. A little farther are *Imari* and *Arita*, where, according to tradition, translucent porcelain was first made. You can study ancient Arita ware in the museum, or perhaps pick up a bargain in the annual sales, held in Imari in early April and Arita in early May.

Spectator sports

Besides the national sport of sumo wrestling, there are sporting events in Hakata Bay, such as yacht races and windsurfing competitions, which excite local interest. For details see *Rainbow* or *Kyushu Journal*. In the near future, baseball should become an important Fukuoka event, as the city now (as from August 1988) has its own team, the Daiei Hawks.
Sumo One of the six annual national sumo tournaments is held in Fukuoka in mid-November, at the *International Centre*, 2-2 Chikko-Honmachi, Hakata-ku ☎ 272 1111. There are also amateur sumo matches in *Sumiyoshi Shrine* in early October.

Keeping fit

Golf For those on sizeable expense accounts, there are excellent golf courses in Kyushu. One of the most famous is *Koga*, near Fukuoka

☎ 943 2261. If not invited by colleagues, you can arrange an introduction through your hotel.
Fitness centres There is a health centre in the ANA Hotel and several gyms in the city. *Fukuoka Weight Training Gym*, 3-21-21 Nagazumi, Minani-ku ☎ 552 4918, is open to non-members and relatively inexpensive. There is also a gym in the *Solario Plaza*, 2-2-43 Tenjin, ☎ 733 7575.
Jogging Ohori Park is popular with early morning joggers.
Sauna One of the most popular is *Healthspot 24* in the Centraza Hotel.
Swimming It is best to use the hotel pools if you wish to swim in the city; the Nishitetsu Grand and New Otani have pools. There are several beautiful and clean beaches easily accessible from Fukuoka. *Momoji Matsubara* is 30mins by car or 1hr by ferry, while *Niji-no-Matsubara* is near Karatsu.

Local resources
Business services

The Nikko has a business service centre. Of the commercial companies providing a reasonably wide range of business services, the best are *Manpower Japan* ☎ 741 9531 and *Aso Temporary Centre* ☎ 731 1800.
Photocopying All hotels provide photocopying services. There are also machines in department stores and camera shops.
Secretarial For secretarial services, try *Temporary Centre Corporation* ☎ 711 1600.
Translation For translation and interpretation, try *Manpower Japan* or *King's Language Services* ☎ 714 4043.

Communications

International couriers The nearest international courier is in Kitakyushu. *DHL* ☎ *(093) 581 2129.*
Post office The Hakata post office, 8-1 Hakata-eki Chuogai, Hakata-ku ☎ 431 6381, is at Hakata station.
Telex and fax All hotels provide telex and fax service. In case of difficulty, contact *KDD* ☎ 474 3352.

Conference/exhibition centres
The nearest exhibition centre is the *West Japan General Exhibition Centre* in Kitakyushu (see Kitakyushu).

Emergencies
Bureaux de change The bureaux de change in the major hotels are open seven days a week, from early until late.

Hospitals In an emergency, call the *Prefectural Emergency Hospital Information Centre* ☎ 471 0099 or the *Municipal Medical Centre for Emergency Services*, Yakuin 2-chome, Chuo-ku ☎ 741 1099. Consult the *Kyushu Journal* or *Rainbow Plaza* for lists of English-speaking hospitals, doctors and dentists.

Pharmacies Prescription drugs are supplied by hospitals.

Police Fukuoka Prefectural Police Headquarters, Higashi Koen, Hakata-ku ☎ 641 4141.

Government offices
For enquiries about local government departments and services, contact *Fukuoka City Hall*, 1-8-1 Tenjin, Chuo-ku ☎ 711 4111, or *Fukuoka Prefectural Office*, 7-7 Higashi Koen, Hakata-ku ☎ 651 1111. For statistics and information, try the *Fukuoka Department of Commerce and Industry, Tourism Section*, 7-7 Higashi Koen, Hakata-ku ☎ 641 3880.

Information sources
Business information The *Fukuoka Chamber of Commerce*, 2-9-28 Hakata-ekimae, Hakata-ku ☎ 441 1111.

Local media The *Kyushu Journal* is compiled by resident Westerners and is full of useful information and listings. *Rainbow*, published by Rainbow Plaza, has up-to-date information; *SISAC Kyushu Guide* includes restaurant information.

Tourist Information The *Tourist Information Centre* (TIC), 2-1 Hakata-eki Chuogai, Hakata-ku ☎ 473 6696, in Hakata station, is a useful source of maps, literature and information. You can also call the *Japan Travel Phone* collect; ☎ 0120 444 800. The most helpful local travel agent is the *JTB*, Tenjin 1-chome, Chuo-ku ☎ 752 0700. *Fukuoka International Association*, Rainbow Plaza, 8F IMS Bldg, 1-7-11 Tenjin, Chuo-ku ☎ 733 2220 publishes a free monthly newsletter, *Rainbow*, and runs a library and information centre in the IMS building; they are ready to deal with enquiries on any subject, in English. *SISAC Corps*, 801 3-9-10 Tenjin, Chuo-ku ☎ 716 1887, also has an information centre.

Thank-yous
Buy your thank-you gifts in *Iwataya* ☎ 721 1111.

HIROSHIMA

City code ☎ 082

Founded in 1593, Hiroshima was totally destroyed on August 6 1945 by the world's first atomic bomb. In spite of predictions that the area would be unusable for decades, the reconstruction of the city has been rapid and complete. Mazda, Japan's third largest car manufacturer, dominates the scene, along with Ford, with whom it has close links. Many industries are based around the harbour, where Mitsubishi is developing giant sea bed oil rigs. Kirin Beer has its main breweries in Hiroshima, and there are offices of most major Japanese companies.

Arriving

Flying is certainly the quickest way to arrive from Tokyo; the journey takes 90mins, compared with 4hrs 30mins by Bullet Train. From Osaka the Bullet Train takes only 1hr 40mins.

Hiroshima airport

This small airport handles domestic flights only. Facilities include several restaurants, coffee shops and bars on landside only (open 7–7), a VIP lounge and shops selling local delicacies; no banks. Inquiries ☎ 295 5555.
City link The best way to get into the city centre is by taxi (journey time 20mins, 40mins in rush hours).
Car rental Mazda, Toyota, Nissan and Nippon have desks at the airport.
Bus The express bus leaves every 5mins for the station via the ANA Hotel and the city centre, 7.45am–9.30pm.

Hiroshima station

Local JR lines, as well as the Bullet Train, stop at this modern and well-organized station. The complex includes a hotel and department store, and there are taxi ranks and connections with buses and streetcars. Inquiries ☎ 261 1877.

Getting around

It is usually best to travel by cab, but the city centre is compact and walking is a practical way of getting around.
Taxis Cabs wait at stations and hotels or stop if hailed.
Driving If you are going outside the city centre, to the Mazda works or the port for example, you may find it convenient to drive. The main rental

firms have offices in the city.
Streetcar If you have plenty of time, it is not difficult to use the streetcar. The TIC map has the seven streetcar lines marked on it.
Bus More difficult to use than the streetcar, though the network is comprehensive.
Train JR lines skirt the city and travel out in all directions to the suburbs.

Area by area

Although the downtown area is small, Hiroshima is a large, modern city sprawling across the delta of the Ota River. Its long, broad streets are split by six main rivers running to the waterfront. Industries are based to the south, in the direction of the port.

Hachobori is the centre of the city; the major department stores and many offices are here. The business area stretches along the main road to Kamiyacho, where several banks, including the Bank of Hiroshima, are clustered, and down Hondori, lined with insurance companies. Hondori and Namikidori are the main shopping and restaurant areas. To the west of Hondori, on the other side of the river, is the Peace Park (Heiwa Koen). East of Hachobori, across Chuo-dori, are Nagarekawa and Yagenbori, a maze of tiny streets full of restaurants and bars. Across the river and east of the main city centre is the station area, at present rather sleazy and reputedly the haunt of the *yakuza* (Japanese Mafia).
The suburbs The smartest are those to the north in Ushita, Higashi-ku, and to the west, in Itsukaichi.

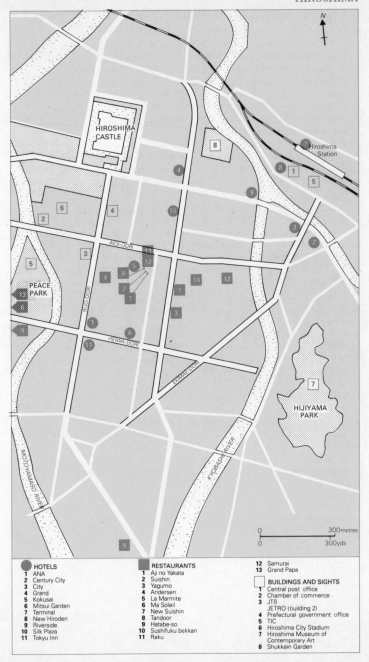

N

HIROSHIMA CASTLE

PEACE PARK

HIJIYAMA PARK

MOTOYAMASO RIVER

KYOBASHI RIVER

Hiroshima Station

AIOI-DORI

RIJO-DORI

HEIWA-DORI

EKIMAE-DORI

0   300 metres
0   300 yds

HOTELS
1 ANA
2 Century City
3 City
4 Grand
5 Kokusai
6 Mitsui Garden
7 Terminal
8 New Hiroden
9 Riverside
10 Silk Plaza
11 Tokyu Inn

RESTAURANTS
1 Aji no Yakata
2 Suishin
3 Yagumo
4 Andersen
5 La Marmite
6 Ma Soleil
7 New Suishin
8 Tandoor
9 Hatabe-so
10 Sushifuku bekkan
11 Raku

12 Samurai
13 Grand Papa

BUILDINGS AND SIGHTS
1 Central post office
2 Chamber of commerce
3 JTB
  JETRO (building 2)
4 Prefectural government office
5 TIC
6 Hiroshima City Stadium
7 Hiroshima Museum of
  Contemporary Art
8 Shukkein Garden

Hotels

New hotels are springing up in Hiroshima, but the Grand – with the weight of tradition behind it – is still considered the best. The modern ANA comes a close second. The new Terminal is also highly rated, and is the first hotel in Hiroshima to have a business service centre.

ANA *Y*||

7-20 Nakamachi, Naka-ku, 730
☎ 241 1111 ⛶ 652751 fax 241 9123
● AE DC MC V ● 427 rooms, 4 suites, 4 restaurants, 2 bars, 2 coffee shops/tea lounges

The ANA near the Peace Park, is a modern luxury hotel. The vast glittering lobby, hung with chandeliers formed of thousands of glass birds, looks out onto a waterfall and rock garden. The bedrooms are less spectacular, but spacious; all have a minibar, and those on the top floors have views across to the Inland Sea. The Vega Bar (see *Bars*) is a gathering place for local and visiting executives. Concierge, hairdresser ● gym, pool, sauna ● 10 meeting rooms (capacity up to 1,000).

Century City *Y*

1-1-25 Matobacho, Minami-ku, 732
☎ 263 3111 ⛶ 653723 fax 263 7601
● AE DC MC V ● 73 rooms, 3 suites, 3 restaurants, 1 bar/coffee shop

The Century City, directly opposite Hiroshima station, deserves discovery by Western business travellers. The rooms are vast, comfortable and tastefully furnished, with minibar and views over the river to the hills. The staff are friendly and helpful. 4 meeting rooms (capacity up to 300).

City *Y*|

1-4 Kyobashicho, Minami-ku, 732
☎ 263 5111 ⛶ 652844 fax 262 2403
● AE DC MC V ● 160 rooms, 3 suites, 3 restaurants, 1 bar, 1 coffee shop

The City is directly opposite the station and has a small but regular clientele of Western business travellers. The rooms are large for Japan and pleasantly furnished, with views over the city to the hills and a desk big enough to work on. International calls via hotel switchboard ● 4 meeting rooms (capacity up to 180).

Grand *Y*|

4-4 Kami-Hachobori, Naka-ku, 730
☎ 227 1313 ⛶ 652666 fax 227 6462
● AE DC MC V ● 368 rooms, 6 suites, 6 restaurants, 1 bar, 1 coffee shop

Secure in its position as Hiroshima's best address, the Grand has an air of quiet dignity. It is located in one of the smarter areas of town, away from the noise and bustle of the city centre. The gracious lobby, looking out onto a waterfall, is normally full of business guests and their clients. The bedrooms are spacious and tastefully furnished. The Abeille Bar (see *Bars*) is a popular gathering place for local executives. Concierge, travel and theatre bookings, shops, hairdresser, shuttle bus service ● 14 meeting rooms (capacity up to 1300).

Kokusai *Y*|

3-13 Tatemachi, Naka-ku, 730
☎ 248 2323 ⛶ 652744 fax 248 2622
● AE DC MC V ● 79 rooms, 3 restaurants, 1 bar

The Kokusai ('International''), with its top-heavy restaurant tower, is a landmark in the middle of the main shopping area. Its bars, restaurants and meeting rooms are always packed with local and visiting businessmen. Kazuo Fujita, the manager of the (rapidly) revolving Sky Lounge restaurant, spent eight years in England and is friendly and willing to help with contacts. The rooms, sadly, have seen better days. 5 meeting rooms (capacity up to 500).

Mitsui Garden *Y*|

9-12 Nakamachi, Naka-ku, 730
☎ 240 1131 ⛶ 652240 fax 242 3001
● 275 rooms, 2 suites, 1 restaurant, 1 bar, 1 coffee shop

Primarily a business hotel, the Mitsui Garden opened in July 1989. The rooms are small but pleasant and still new, gleaming and shiny. There are executive rooms on the 24th floor and 2 nonsmoking floors are planned. No room service except on executive floor, limited hotel parking • 3 meeting rooms (capacity up to 200).

Terminal *Y*/
1-5 Matsubaracho, Minami-ku, 732
☎ *262 1111* [TX] *653717 fax 262 4050*
• *438 rooms, 2 suites, 4 restaurants, 2 bars, 2 coffee shops/tea lounges*
The Terminal is a pleasant, relatively new hotel (opened July 1987), located right at the station, on the Bullet Train side of the tracks. The rooms are spacious and light, well furnished, with desks big enough to work on, and all but the singles have a minibar. The hotel's restaurants and bars are well patronized by the local community and those on the top floor have excellent views across the city. Travel agent, arcade of shops, hairdresser • 50% discount for hotel

guests at the neighbouring Health Spa, which has a gym, pool, sauna and massage parlour • business service centre with limited facilities, 13 meeting rooms (capacity up to 1,300).

OTHER HOTELS
New Hiroden *Y*/ *14-9 Osugacho, Minami-ku, 732* ☎ *263 3456* [TX] *653884 fax 263 3784* • *AE DC MC V*. Near the station, with friendly staff and basic but adequate rooms.
Riverside *Y*/ *7-14 Kaminoboricho, Naka-ku, 730* ☎ *228 1251* [TX] *652554 fax 228 1250* • *AE DC MC V*. Across the river from the station, its spacious rooms overlook the river.
Silk Plaza *Y*/ *14-1 Hachobori, Naka-ku, 730* ☎ *227 8111* [TX] *653753 fax 227 8110* • *AE DC MC V*. Close to the main Hachobori business area, with plenty of character and lively and helpful staff.
Tokyu Inn *Y*/ *3-17 Komachi, Naka-ku, 730* ☎ *244 0109* [TX] *653841 fax 245 4467* • *AE DC MC V*. Good value; big, attractive rooms.

Restaurants

For business entertaining, the classy restaurants in the ANA and the Grand are the usual choices. If you have an evening to yourself, try the mid-range restaurants on the 10th floor of Sogo or wander into any of the establishments in the backstreets which display a red lantern outside. Hiroshima is famous for its oysters – in season from November to February – and for its sake; ask for *jizake*, "local" *sake*, rather than one of the nationwide brands.

JAPANESE *Y*/
Aji no Yakata
1-3 Shintenchi, Naka-ku ☎ *247 1129*
• *AE DC MC V*
Aji no Yakata is a five-floor restaurant complex in the Nagarekawa bar area. The first three floors specialize in sushi, with fresh fish straight from the Inland Sea, while on the top two floors customers gather around gleaming steel counters to enjoy steak cooked teppanyaki-style. Ford and Mazda's foreign employees are frequently to be found here, dining with Japanese colleagues.

Suishin *Y*/
6-7 Tatemachi, Naka-ku ☎ *247 4411*
• *closed Wed* • *DC MC V*
This Hiroshima institution has been serving sushi and sashimi, made with fish fresh from the Inland Sea, since the 1950s. Suishin is the place for globefish, stingfish, rock cod and flat fish, as well as oysters and eel. *Kamameshi* – individual rice casseroles – are the house speciality. The downstairs rooms, furnished with tables, are lively; the top three floors of tatami rooms are reserved for business entertaining.

Yagumo *Y*|
1-23 Mikawacho, Naka-ku
☎ *244 1551* • *AE DC MC V*
Heavy cast-iron kettles hang from the
polished wooden beams of this
enormous reconstructed farmhouse.
The waitresses, in hand-woven cotton
kimonos, serve local specialities like
susugi-nabe, the Hiroshima equivalent
of shabu shabu, to a clientele of
Japanese executives and, often, their
Western guests.

NON-JAPANESE
Andersen *Y*|
7-1 Hondori, Naka-ku ☎ *247 2403* •
closed 3rd Tue of month • *AE DC MC V*
Andersen is a little corner of Europe
in the middle of Hiroshima. Mr
Tataki, the founder, has his chefs
trained in Denmark, and sends there
for ingredients; visiting Danes say
that the pastries in the shop
downstairs are better than the ones
back home. Upstairs, on the opposite
side of the stairwell from the
inexpensive café, there is a fine
restaurant serving *nouvelle cuisine* and
Byakuya, a grand Chinese restaurant.

La Marmite *Y*||
1F U Bldg, 3-11-7 Sendamachi,
Naka-ku ☎ *241 0043* • *closed Tue* •
DC V
La Marmite is a small, intimate and
immensely classy French restaurant a
little way from the centre of town, to
the south of the city. Resident
Westerners make pilgrimages down
here to enjoy Chef Ogawa's masterly
cuisine, light, delicate and impeccably
sauced. In the winter the speciality is
game – wild duck, venison, quail,
pigeon and rabbit. This is a highly
suitable place to return your Japanese
hosts' hospitality.

Ma Soleil *Y*
6-16 Dobashi, Naka-ku ☎ *292 8013* •
closed Mon • *DC V*
Ma Soleil, on the far side of the Peace
Park, is the kind of place that regular
customers hope will remain
undiscovered. From the moment that
the master, genial Mr Motomura,

welcomes you at the door, you know
you are somewhere special. Small and
unpretentious, Ma Soleil feels like a
French bistro. The food, however, is
far from ordinary – delicate and
precise and, at the price, quite
exceptional value. It is worth a trip to
Hiroshima simply to eat here.

New Suishin *Y*||
6-7 Tatemachi, Naka-ku ☎ *248 2935*
• *closed Wed* • *DC MC*
This smart restaurant is in the
basement of Suishin (see earlier).
Each table in the elegant dining room
sports a single rose in a cut-glass
vase, and the service is equally
stylish. Chef Tanaka Tsuneshi's
cuisine is traditional French, with a
Japanese flair.

Tandoor *Y*
3F G House Bldg, 5-7 Tatemachi,
Naka-ku ☎ *247 5622* • *MC V*
The popular Tandoor is Hiroshima's
first authentic Indian restaurant. The
chefs are Indian, brought over by the
owners from a Delhi hotel. Their
North Indian cuisine – featuring *nan*
(unleavened bread), tandoori meats
and meat and vegetarian curries – is
relatively mild, to suit Japanese
palates. Potted palms, large revolving
fans and Indian background music
complete the ambience.

OTHER RESTAURANTS
At *Hatabe-so*, 8-40 Funairicho,
Naka-ku ☎ 231 2018, you dine in a
beautiful old wooden house with a
lantern-lit verandah overlooking a
lake. This is one of Hiroshima's most
venerable *ryotei* and the cuisine, like
the surroundings, is exquisite.
Sushifuku bekkan, 1F Sakura Bldg,
1-15 Horikawacho, Naka-ku ☎ 241
6188, is a branch of Aji no Yakata
(see above). Besides sushi, full course
Japanese dinners are also available,
served in a traditional tatami-matted
environment. Shabu shabu is the
speciality at the new *Raku*, B1
Yushin Bldg, Tatemachi ☎ 247 1600.
For *yakitori*, with plenty of noise,
shouting and smoky atmosphere, the

two branches of *Samurai* (1-6 Tatemachi, Naka-ku ☎ 241 8910 and 11-20 Kaneyamacho, Naka-ku ☎ 247 5630) are popular. There is good French food at economical prices at *Grand Papa*, B1 Dia Palace, 2-18 Dobashi, Naka-ku ☎ 295 0709.

Bars and cafés

Estimates of the number of bars in Nagarekawa and Yagenbori vary, from 3,000 upwards; but it is generally agreed that Hiroshima has more per head than any other city in Japan. The most fashionable bars are undoubtedly those in the hotels.

Of the hotel bars, most visiting executives choose either the elegant *Abeille* in the Grand or the *Vega* at the top of the ANA, where you sip your cocktail while taking in a magnificent view of the city. The ANA's *Stardust*, which features live piano music, is also popular. Of the city bars, *Wine Bar*, 3F Zakuro Bldg, 1-15 Horikawacho, Naka-ku is well used by Ford and Mitsubishi executives, both Japanese and American. There is an enormous wine list and the chef grills steaks behind the counter in the centre of the room. *Wine-ya*, 3F Kuwamoto Bldg, Horikawacho is a paradise for wine connoiseurs. It stocks 300 different wines and there is a wine tasting on the 16th of each month. *Hiroshima Taishikan*, 5-5 Furueshinmachi, Nishi-ku, on the other hand, is dedicated to sake and a good place to explore the intricacies of the Japanese national drink. There are 14 varieties available here, from all over Japan, and the owner, Mr Oki, is on hand to advise.

Coffee lovers should not fail to visit the *Café de Yoshiuki*, 2F Fukuro Amber, 6-1 Fukuromachi just behind Andersens. The café serves nothing but coffee and cheesecake, including coffee made with aged and exceptional beans (hence the nickname "Old Beans Coffee Shop") and one coffee which takes nine hours to filter, and has been rated one of the best coffee shops in Japan.

Entertainment

The best source of current information on what's on is *Hiroshima Signpost*. Make reservations through your hotel or at Play Guide agencies. ***Theatre and music*** Visiting international and Japanese theatre troupes, musicians and orchestras regularly perform in Hiroshima. The main venues are *Yubin Chokin Hall* ☎ 222 2525, *Kosei Nenkin Kaikan* ☎ 243 8881 and *Kenmin Bunka Centre* ☎ 245 2311, Kamiyacho, Naka-ku. There are also concerts and theatre performances in the Museum Studio in the basement of the new Museum of Contemporary Art. ***Nightclubs*** At night the entire male population of Hiroshima seems to crowd into the narrow neon-lit streets of Nagarekawa and Yagenbori. If your taste runs to lovely hostesses and a live *karaoke* band, *Club Tap*, 11-20 Kanayamacho, Naka-ku ☎ 243 5525, on Yagenbori, is one of Hiroshima's best venues. For dancing, *Urbis*, 3F Namiki Bldg, Fukuromachi, Naka-ku, a sophisticated disco, is the place to go. *Deck Shoes*, on Nagarekawa, is favoured by the resident Western community.

Shopping

The main shopping area is *Hondori's* network of paved pedestrian streets and covered arcades. Here you will find many elegant shops and small speciality stores. The fashionable young wander up and down *Namikidori*, dropping into its boutiques, jewellers and cafés. Of the department stores, *Sogo*, at Kamiyacho, is the largest, with the greatest variety of merchandise, while *Fukuya*, at Hachobori, is the oldest, and stocks Paris fashions and other high-class goods. Next door to Fukuya is a branch of *Mitsukoshi*. Local products include writing brushes, clogs, sake and traditional musical instruments.

Sightseeing

The Peace Memorial Park and its museum, sobering reminders of

Hiroshima's destruction, draw millions of visitors each year. But there are more cheerful sights both in and not far from the city.

Hiroshima Castle The castle is a 1958 reconstruction of the original built by Terumoto Mori in 1589; it houses a historical museum. *21-1 Motomachi, Naka-ku. Open Apr–Sep, 9–5.30; Oct–Mar, 9–4.30.*

Hiroshima Museum of Contemporary Art An exciting modern building designed by Kisho Kurakawa, this is Hiroshima's newest museum and the first in Japan to be devoted to contemporary art. *Hijiyama Park, Hijiyama Hill. Open 10–5; summer only, 10–7.*

Miyajima Only 30mins from Hiroshima station, *Miyajima* is one of Japan's most celebrated beauty spots. On this sacred island is the magnificent *Itsukushima Shrine*, with apparently floating in the sea, its famous red *torii* gateway.

Peace Park North across the river from the Peace Park (Heiwa Koen) is the skeletal A-bomb Dome, the ruin of the chamber of industry and commerce which was at the epicentre of the explosion. Within the Park, the *Peace Memorial Museum* has a collection of photographs and exhibits of the destruction, while at the *Peace Memorial Hall*, you can see a 30min film documenting the horrors of the bombing. *1-3 Nakajimacho, Naka-ku. Open 9–4.30.*

Shukkeien Garden The ruling Asano lords had their villa here, and the landscaped garden, laid out by tea-ceremony master Munetsutsu Ueda in 1620, was intended to evoke the gardens of Kyoto. It was reconstructed after the war. *2-11 Kaminoborimachi, Naka-ku. Open Apr–Sep, 9–6; Oct–Mar, 9–5.*

Guided tours

The *Hiroshima Bus Company* ☎ 261 7104 runs half-day tours of the city, with Japanese commentary only, and full-day tours which include Miyajima. You can also hire a sightseeing taxi with a taped English commentary; contact the *Association of Independent Taxi Drivers* ☎ 283 2311. There are cruises of Hiroshima Bay and day cruises in the Inland Sea, arranged by *Seto Inland Sea Lines* ☎ 255 3344. You can even take a short flight over Hiroshima; contact *Hiroshima airport* ☎ 295 5555. There are industrial tours of, for example, the Mazda plant, the Kirin brewery and the Hiroshima Mint (the only one outside Tokyo and Osaka); inquire at your hotel or the *TIC*.

Spectator sports

Baseball The only sport you need to know about in Hiroshima is baseball. The whole city is fiercely proud of their team, the Hiroshima Toyo Carp, Hiroshima Shimin Kyujo, 5-25 Motomachi, Naka-ku ☎ 223 2141. This is the only team in Japan sponsored, not by a major company, but by local government. The Carp broke into the Central League in 1975, and have been national champions several times since. Home games take place at the *Hiroshima City Stadium*, Kamiyacho, Naka-ku.

Keeping fit

Of the hotels, only the ANA has good sports facilities.

Golf There are several comparatively cheap golf courses within an hour's drive of Hiroshima. Inquire at your hotel for details.

Jogging You can jog around the Peace Park or the castle or along one of Hiroshima's many rivers.

Swimming The pool in the ANA is probably the least crowded. If you want to use a public pool go early. These include *Chuo Pool*, 4-41 Motomachi, Naka-ku ☎ 228 0811; *Yoshijima Indoor Pool*; 5-1-53 Konan, Naka-ku ☎ 249 2231; *Prefectural Indoor Pool*, Motomachi, Naka-ku ☎ 221 7071. For sea bathing head north to the beaches on the Japan Sea.

Tennis There is little chance of getting a court but try the *Hiroshima Chuo Tennis Court*, 2-15 Motomachi, Naka-ku ☎ 221 1463.

Local resources

Business services

Compared to other major Japanese industrial cities, Hiroshima is not well equipped with services for foreign business travellers. Of the Hiroshima hotels, only the Terminal has a business centre but major hotels will arrange services such as photocopying, printing, secretarial and translation. Otherwise contact *Manpower Japan* ☎ 223 1100, which provides a wide range of business services.

Communications

International couriers DHL ☎ 295 6140, UPS *Yamato Express* ☎ 242 8701.

Post office The main post office at Hiroshima station ☎ 245 5318, is open 24hrs for express mail.

Telex and fax Most hotels provide telex and fax facilities. If yours does not, contact KDD *Telecom Hiroshima* ☎ 241 2411.

Conference/exhibition centres

The main conference centre is the new *International Conference Centre* in the Peace Park. Conferences also take place at the ANA and Grand hotels and at the *Yubin Chokin Hall, Kosei Nenkin Kaikan* and *Sun Plaza*.

Emergencies

Hospitals In an emergency, call the *Hiroshima Medical Association* ☎ 232 7321. Hiroshima's two main hospitals are the *Municipal Hospital* ☎ 221 2291 and *Funairi Hospital* ☎ 232 6195.

Pharmacies Prescription medicines are supplied by hospitals. There are no 24hr pharmacies.

Police The prefectural police station is at Kamiyacho, Naka-ku ☎ 221 7201.

Government offices

For inquiries about local government departments and services, contact *Hiroshima City Office*, 1-6-34 Kokutaijimachi, Naka-ku ☎ 245 2111.

Information sources

Business information Close to the A-Bomb Dome, the *Hiroshima Chamber of Commerce and Industry*, 5-44 Motomachi, Naka-ku, 730 ☎ 222 6610 is the biggest of 10 local chambers. *JETRO* is housed in the same building.

Local media The most useful English-language newspaper is the *Mainichi Daily News*, published in Osaka. The *Hiroshima Signpost*, produced and published by the local Western community, is full of lively articles and reviews and listings.

Tourist information There is a branch of the *Tourist Information Centre* (TIC) in the station ☎ 261 1877 and in the Peace Park Rest House, 1-1 Nakajimacho, Naka-ku ☎ 247 6738. They will provide maps, information and a free copy of the useful *Tourist's Handbook*. For more detailed information, consult the *Hiroshima City Office, Tourism Section*, 1-6-34 Kokutaijimachi, Naka-ku ☎ 245 2111. The *JTB* in Hiroshima station ☎ 262 5588 is also helpful.

Thank-yous

Buy your gifts from *Fukuya* ☎ 246 6111 or *Mitsukoshi* ☎ 244 3111, who will arrange delivery. One of their gift-wrapped packs of brand-name Western foods would be an acceptable present for your Japanese host.

KITAKYUSHU

City code ☎ 093

Kitakyushu, on the island of Kyushu, is a gigantic industrial city, formed in 1963 by the merger of five formerly independent towns – Kokura, Yahata, Wakamatsu, Moji and Tobata. The area around it, now known as the Kitakyushu Industrial Complex, has been Japan's major centre of iron and steel production for centuries. It is the home of the world's largest steel company, the Nippon Steel Corporation. Although heavy industries make up 45% of Kitakyushu's total production, the recent trend is towards diversification, and the city's products now include industrial robots, integrated circuits and related products, carbon fibre, nuclear reactor parts and oil drilling equipment. Kitakyushu is also an important port, with the only piers for containerized cargo in western Japan.

Arriving

Travellers from Tokyo can either take the Bullet Train to Kitakyushu, a journey of 5hrs 40mins, or fly to Fukuoka and then make the 20min Bullet Train trip to Kokura.

Kokura station

Although quite small, with a faintly rustic air, Kokura station incorporates a shopping arcade. The monorail and streetcar system are within a few minutes' walk.

Getting around

If you are doing business in Kitakyushu, you will probably be collected and driven around by your host company. If left to your own devices, you will have to rely on the trains to get from one part of Kitakyushu to another. Kokura itself is very small, and you can walk or get around by taxi.

Driving With the aid of a good map, driving is a feasible way of getting around Kitakyushu. Good highways link the five towns, and there is a branch of Nippon Rentacar in each.

Train There are two major JR lines in Kitakyushu. One travels east and west from Kokura, effectively linking Kitakyushu's five towns, while the Nippo line heads along the coast to the south. There are regular departures between 5am and midnight.

Monorail Kitakyushu boasts the first monorail system in Japan to be used for mass urban transit. The first line to be completed, the Kokura line, links Kokura station with Moritsune in the southern suburbs.

Area by area

Kokura, the old castle town, is the commercial and cultural centre of the area. It is a charming little town, full of old buildings and a rambling market with stalls full of live fish, squeezed between modern streets lined with office blocks, with the space age monorail arching over all.

Moji Once a small fishing village, Moji is now one of Kyushu's most important commercial ports. It is the nearest point in Kyushu to the main island of Honshu, to which it is linked by a suspension bridge (at 760 metres/2,500 ft, the second longest in Japan) and by a railway tunnel.

Tobata is mainly industrial, with fish-processing plants, a Nippon Steel plant and the Shin Kokura power station. Kyushu Institute of Technology is also in Tobata.

Yahata The Yahata district is a centre of chemical engineering and heavy industry. Nippon Steel is based here, as is the Mitsubishi chemical plant. Kurosaki, in West Yahata, is a busy shopping area. The new Prince hotel is located here.

Wakamatsu has a large shipping centre, with coal shipping installations, engineering works and shipyards. The Hibikinada Industrial Park is here.

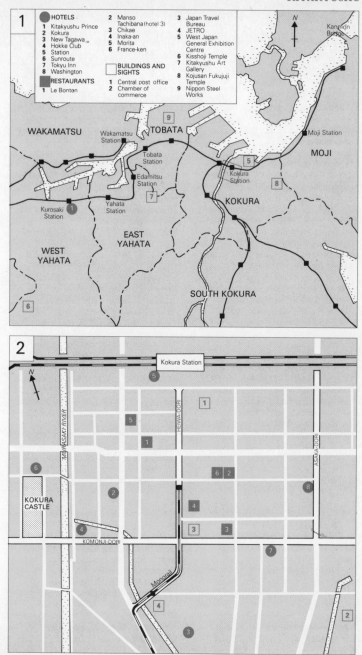

1

HOTELS
1 Kitakyushu Prince
2 Kokura
3 New Tagawa
4 Hokke Club
5 Station
6 Sunroute
7 Tokyu Inn
8 Washington

RESTAURANTS
1 Le Bonton

2 Manso
  Tachibana (hotel 3)
3 Chikae
4 Inaka-an
5 Morita
6 France-ken

**BUILDINGS AND
SIGHTS**
1 Central post office
2 Chamber of
  commerce

3 Japan Travel
  Bureau
4 JETRO
5 West Japan
  General Exhibition
  Centre
6 Kisshoji Temple
7 Kitakyushu Art
  Gallery
8 Kojusan Fukujuji
  Temple
9 Nippon Steel
  Works

N

Kanmon Bridge

WAKAMATSU

Wakamatsu
Station

TOBATA

Moji Station

MOJI

Tobata
Station

Edamitsu
Station

Kokura
Station

KOKURA

Kurosaki
Station

Yahata
Station

EAST
YAHATA

WEST
YAHATA

SOUTH KOKURA

2

Kokura Station

N

MURASAKI RIVER

HEIWA-DORI

ASANO-DORI

KOKURA
CASTLE

KOMONJI-DORI

Monorail

Hotels

Most Western visitors to Kitakyushu stay in Kokura, at the New Tagawa or the Kokura. There are also several reliable chain hotels and a huge new Prince at Kurosaki in Yahata.

Kitakyushu Prince *Y/||*
*3-1 Higashi Magarimachi, Yahata
Nishi-ku, 806 ☎ 631 1111 ⓉⓍ 712377
fax 631 1148 • 217 rooms, 3 suites,
3 restaurants, 1 bar, 3 tea lounges/coffee
shops*
The new Kitakyushu Prince opened in April 1989 and is located, rather inexplicably, in Kurosaki. Despite the fact that this area is almost totally industrial, the Prince is something of a resort hotel, with an athletics arena, 23 tennis courts and avenues of luxury shops. The rooms are expensive and disappointingly small, though, for those whose taste runs to it, there is an excellent view over the industrial landscape of Yahata. No room service, limited concierge services • athletics arena, pool, indoor and outdoor tennis courts • 5 meeting rooms (capacity up to 1,000).

Kokura *Y*
*3-10 Senbamachi, Kokura Kita-ku, 802
☎ 531 1151 ⓉⓍ 712757 fax 551 0971
• AE DC MC V • 96 rooms, 5 suites,
2 restaurants, 1 bar, 2 coffee shops*
The Kokura is a large modern international-style hotel, with helpful English-speaking staff. The rooms are big and attractively furnished. Concierge, small shopping arcade • 12 meeting rooms (capacity up to 500).

New Tagawa *Y/|*
*3-46 Furusenbacho, Kokura Kita-ku,
802 ☎ 521 3831 ⓉⓍ 712371
fax 521 0128 • AE DC MC V •
113 rooms, 2 suites, 2 restaurants,
1 bar, 1 coffee shop*
The New Tagawa used to be a *ryokan*, and the hotel buildings are dotted around a large and beautiful Japanese garden. Besides the modern hotel building, with its large and comfortable rooms overlooking the garden, there are small traditional

wooden Japanese houses where you can stay or simply come and dine (see *Restaurants*). International calls via hotel switchboard • 7 meeting rooms (capacity up to 400).

OTHER HOTELS

Hokke Club *Y/* *1-1-15 Bashaku,
Kokura Kita-ku, 802 ☎ 531 5531
fax 522 5902.* A very pleasant business hotel, with views across the river to the castle.
Station *Y/* *1-1-1 Asano, Kokura
Kita-ku, 802 ☎ 521 5031
fax 521 5716 • AE DC V.* By Kokura station.
Sunroute *Y/* *1-2-16 Muromachi,
Kokura Kita-ku, 802 ☎ 561 3311
ⓉⓍ 712607 fax 571 0973 • AE DC
MC V.* Beside Kokura Castle.
Tokyu Inn *Y/* *8-5 Konyacho,
Kokura Kita-ku, 802 ☎ 521 0109
ⓉⓍ 712690 fax 521 4588 • AE DC
MC V.* One of the best business hotels.
Washington *Y/* *1-9-8 Kajimachi,
Kokura Kita-ku, 802 ☎ 531 3111
fax 511 0170 • AE DC MC V.* Another good business hotel.

Restaurants

There are plenty of restaurants catering to a business clientele, and the city is renowned for fish, seafood and chicken dishes.

Le Bonton *Y/*
*1-4-12 Uomachi, Kokura Kita-ku
☎ 521 0035 • AE DC V*
Le Bonton has been serving superbly fresh seafood and Matsuzaka beef to a largely business clientele since 1953. Downstairs is a teppanyaki bar. On the first floor, both cuisine and ambience are French.

Manso *Y/*
*1-4-14 Kajimachi, Kokura Kita-ku
☎ 521 8466 • closed 1st and 3rd Sun*

of month • *AE DC V*

Manso is the place for fish of the season – *fugu* in winter, turbot in spring. Owner Hiroshi Noda and his assistants grill it, fry it, simmer it, or simply cut it into perfect rectangular slices and serve it raw. Company directors and industrial magnates entertain their clients in Manso's tatami rooms.

Tachibana Y|

New Tagawa Hotel, 3-46 Furusenbacho, Kokura Kita-ku ☎ *521 3831* • *AE DC MC V*
In the tiny Japanese houses set in the New Tagawa's beautiful landscaped gardens, kimono-clad ladies serve a delicate meal of *kaiseki*. The small rooms on the second floor of the main restaurant are suitable for formal entertaining, and the best place in Kitakyushu to entertain your Japanese hosts.

OTHER RESTAURANTS

Visitors from out of town are often entertained at the Kokura branch of *Chikae*, 1-4-26 Sakaimachi, Kokura Kita-ku ☎ 541 0791. Like the newer Fukuoka *Chikae* (see *Fukuoka, Restaurants*), it features live seafood, caught and sliced up with much drama right before your eyes. For eel, the best place in town is *Inaka-an*, 1-1-14 Kajimachi, Kokura Kita-ku, ☎ 551 0851, where the eel may be served steamed as well as grilled. There is excellent sushi to be had at *Morita*, 2F Inkspot Bldg, 2-5-17 Uomachi, Kokura Kita-ku ☎ 531 1058. For Western food, *France-ken*, 1-4-12 Kajimachi, Kokura Kita-ku ☎ 531 0618, is highly recommended by local gourmets.

Relaxation

Entertainment Kitakyushu has a lively folk tradition and many festivals. The Kokura Gion Festival in mid-July is one of Japan's most celebrated. There are also several cinemas showing English-language movies: for details, see listings in the *Kyushu Post*. There is plenty more entertainment to be had in Fukuoka, which is only 20mins away by Bullet Train.

Shopping The main shopping areas are Kokura and Kurosaki, in West Yahata. Kitakyushu's best department stores are *Izutsuya* and *Tamaya*, in Kokura, and *Sogo*, in Kurosaki.

Sightseeing Worth visiting in or near the city are the *Kisshoji Temple*, the *Kojusan Fukujuji Temple*, *Kokura Castle* and *Kitakyushu Art Gallery*. Not far beyond the smokestacks is beautiful mountainous countryside. A few hours away are the mountainous *Kunisaki Peninsula*, full of old temples and stone Buddhas; *Beppu*, a famous hot-spring resort; and *Mount Aso*, a spectacular volcano.

Golf Moji Golf Course is one of Japan's oldest and best; you will need an introduction.

Fitness centre The newly-opened *Orio Sports Centre* ☎ 691 0812 has a gym and pool and facilities for basketball and volleyball.

Hiking The nearest hiking area is *Hiraodai*.

Swimming Along the north shore of Wakamatsu is a long stretch of beautiful beaches. *Waita* is the most popular swimming beach; there are, however, many quieter, cleaner beaches nearby.

Local resources
Business services

There is no provision for business services, nor for translators or interpreters. You will have to rely on your hotel or business associates to provide these.

Communications

International couriers DHL ☎ 581 2129.

Post office The main post office is at 3-8-1 Kyomachi, Kokura Kita-ku ☎ 541 3545.

Telex and fax If your hotel does not have telex and fax facilities, the nearest *DHH* ☎ (092) 474 3352 is in Fukuoka.

Conference/exhibition centres

West Japan General Exhibition Centre ☎ 511 6848, *Commercial and Industrial Trade Centre* ☎ 541 1969.

Emergencies

Hospital *Kitakyushu Municipal Hospital*, 2-1-1 Bashaku, Kokura Kita-ku ☎ 541 1831.

Police The central municipal police station is at 5-1 Journai, Kokura Kita-ku ☎ 561 7171.

Government offices

For inquiries about local government offices and services, contact the *Economic Bureau*, Kitakyushu City, 1-1 Journai, Kokura Kita-ku, 803 ☎ 582 2062. The *Fukuoka Prefectural Office* is also willing to provide information.

Information sources

Business information The nearest chamber of commerce is to be found in Fukuoka.

Local media The *Kyushu Post*, produced by resident Westerners, is a useful source of information and listings.

Tourist information *JTB*, JTB Bldg, 1-1-1 Sakaimachi, Kokura Kita-ku ☎ 551 5121. You can also use the *Japan Travel Phone*: ☎ 0120 444 800. The *Fukuoka City International Exchange Centre* ☎ (092) 733 2220 is helpful.

Thank-yous

The major department stores are the appropriate places to buy gifts (see *Shopping*.

KOBE

Kobe is Japan's busiest port, with the largest container capacity in the world. Its industries and commerce are mainly related to the port, and include shipbuilding and iron and steel production. Kobe was one of the first ports to be opened to trade with the West, in 1868. Many Westerners settled here and set up businesses, and a flourishing foreign community grew up. Kobe still has a very international flavour, with a greater density of foreigners than Tokyo, including a large Indian community. Squeezed between the mountains and the sea, Kobe can expand only into the sea. The city's first man-made island, Port Island, opened in the harbour in 1981. Rokko Island, the world's largest artificial island, was completed in 1989. Facilities are now under construction and will include residential and industrial areas, cultural facilities and a long beach.

Arriving

From 1993 visitors will be able to fly to Osaka's new international airport (Kansai) then take a boat straight across Osaka Bay to Kobe. Until then, the closest airport is Itami (see Osaka). The limousine bus departs from the airport for Sannomiya station every 15mins between 7am and 9.15pm; journey time is at least 40mins.

Railway stations

Shin Kobe station Before boarding the Hikari Bullet Train, check that it stops at Shin Kobe; some pass straight through. There is a subway link down to Sannomiya station.
Sannomiya station, at the centre of one of Kobe's liveliest shopping areas, houses the terminals for the JR, Hankyu and Hanshin lines from Osaka and Kyoto. The monorail to Port Island starts from here.

Getting around

Kobe is a long, narrow city, with the train lines running east–west through it. North–south transportation is more difficult, but distances in this direction are quite short; walk or take a taxi.
Taxis You should have no trouble hailing a taxi on the street; if you do, stations and hotels are good places to pick one up.
Driving The main car rental firms

have offices in the city, but driving is really more trouble than it is worth.
Subway Kobe's subway system, which opened in 1985, runs from Shin Kobe station west along the city.
Monorail The driverless Port Liner leaves Sannomiya every 6mins from 5.20am to 11.44pm and takes a circular route around Port Island. Station names and announcements are in English as well as Japanese.
Train The JR, Hankyu and Hanshin lines connect Rokko and Sannomiya in eastern Kobe with Kobe station in the west. Check that you are boarding a local train, not a non-stop express.

Area by area

The bustling station area of Sannomiya is the heart of Kobe. To the south, running straight down to the port, and lined with trees, is Flower Road. Many hotels and offices and the City Hall are located on this broad boulevard, and the Trade Centre Building is just off it. The main business area extends east, between the railway tracks and the sea, from Flower Road as far as Kobe station, with most businesses concentrated on Sakaemachi-dori. Over the bridge is Port Island, a futuristic complex of skyscrapers which includes a convention centre, exhibition hall and the Portopia

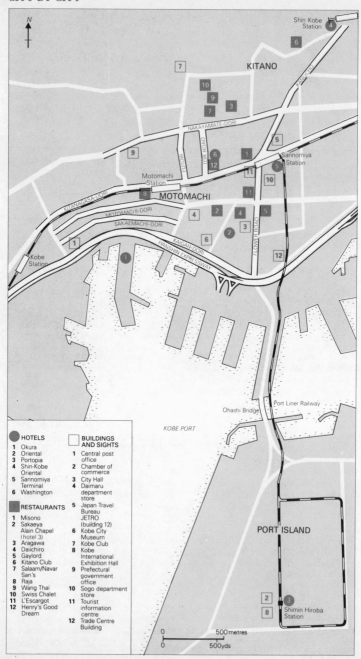

KITANO

NAKAYAMATE-DORI

Shin Kobe Station

Sannomiya Station

Motomachi Station

MOTOMACHI

KITANAGASA-DORI

MOTOMACHI-DORI

SAKAEMACHI-DORI

KAIGAN-DORI

HANSHIN EXPRESSWAY

Kobe Station

Ohashi Bridge

Port Liner Railway

KOBE PORT

PORT ISLAND

Shimin Hiroba Station

HOTELS
1 Okura
2 Oriental
3 Portopia
4 Shin-Kobe Oriental
5 Sannomiya Terminal
6 Washington

RESTAURANTS
1 Misono
2 Sakaeya Alain Chapel (hotel 3)
3 Aragawa
4 Daichiro
5 Gaylord
6 Kitano Club
7 Salaam/Navar San's
8 Raja
9 Wang Thai
10 Swiss Chalet
11 L'Escargot
12 Henry's Good Dream

BUILDINGS AND SIGHTS
1 Central post office
2 Chamber of commerce
3 City Hall
4 Daimaru department store
5 Japan Travel Bureau JETRO (building 12)
6 Kobe City Museum
7 Kobe Club
8 Kobe International Exhibition Hall
9 Prefectural government office
10 Sogo department store
11 Tourist information centre
12 Trade Centre Building

0   500 metres
0   500 yds

Hotel. Projecting into the bay to the east is Rokko island and to the west the Meriken area, slated to be the passenger terminal for boats serving Kansai International airport; the new Okura Hotel is here. To the north of Sannomiya, stretching up the hill, is Kitano, the classiest area of town and an exclusive residential district. Here you will find embassies, consulates, nightclubs, restaurants and streets full of old Western-style houses built by early foreign settlers. West of Sannomiya is Motomachi, a smart shopping area. South of here is Kobe's sizeable Chinatown, Nankinmachi.

The suburbs Two of the most exclusive suburbs – where old Japanese families and long-term Western residents have their homes – are Nishinomiya and Ashiya, between Kobe and Osaka. Mikage, between Ashiya and Rokko, is full of up-and-coming young executives, while those who can afford it live on the cool slopes of Mount Rokko, or west of Kobe, near the beaches at Suma.

Hotels

Spurred by the hundredth anniversary of Kobe City in 1989, hotel building is booming. While many people still swear by the grand old Oriental, the brand new Okura offers not only the prestige of its name but also up-to-the-minute facilities. The Portopia is also popular. There are more hotels in the planning stage. Work is due to begin on a New Otani in the developing Kobe station area and there is talk of a new Ramada on Rokko Island.

Okura ¥///

Meriken Koen, 2-1 Hatobacho, Chuo-ku, 650 ☎ *333 0111* ⊤ₓ *5622123 fax 333 6673*
● *AE DC MC V* ● *472 rooms, 17 suites, 5 restaurants, 2 bars, 1 coffee shop*
A grand new building rising above Meriken Park, where the boats serving Kansai International airport will dock, the Okura is a classy hotel modelled after the Tokyo Okura. The style is dignified and the decor distinctive. The rooms, designed by David Hicks, designer to the British Royal Family, feature thick checked quilts and marble bathtubs and are both stylish and homely. The business service centre is exceptionally large and well-equipped. The main bar (see *Bars*) is a natural gathering place for travelling executives, while the Emerald Restaurant (see *Restaurants*) offers the Okura's superb French cuisine together with breathtaking views across Osaka Bay and over the city to the mountains close behind. Express checkout, concierge, booking services, travel agent, shops, hotel bus to Sannomiya station ● health club with gym, pools and tennis courts ● business service centre with extensive facilities, 15 meeting rooms (capacity up to 2,500).

Oriental ¥///

25 Kyomachi, Chuo-ku, 650 ☎ *331 8111* ⊤ₓ *5622327 fax 391 8708* ● *AE DC MC V* ● *188 rooms, 2 suites, 5 restaurants, 1 bar, 3 coffee shops*
The first Westerners to come to Kobe stayed at the Oriental Hotel. It is still Kobe's most prestigious, although the old buildings have long since been replaced by modern ones, dating from 1966. The spacious and dignified lobby is a meeting place for the local Japanese community, and many visiting Western executives stay here. Service is impeccable, but the bedrooms, all with minibar, are showing signs of age, and are rather cramped and dark. Concierge, arcade of shops ● secretarial services, 10 meeting rooms (capacity up to 300).

Portopia *Y*//

6-10-1, Minatojima, Nakamachi,
Chuo-ku, 650 ☎ 302 1111
ⓉⓍ 5622112 fax 302 6877 • AE
DC MC V • 763 rooms, 15 suites, 13
restaurants, 1 bar, 2 coffee shops
The elegant oval-shaped Portopia,
opened in 1981, beside the
international conference centre on
Port Island. A large proportion of its
clientele are businessmen, both
Western and Japanese. The striking
circular lounge, with chandeliers and
a waterfall, is ringed with shops,
including an art gallery and branches
of Sogo and Mitsukoshi, and there
are spectacular views over Kobe and
the Inland Sea from the spacious
bedrooms, all with minibar. The
rooms in the new annex all have
balconies. The three-star Alain
Chapel restaurant (see *Restaurants*) is
one the city's top places for business
dining. Pool, gym, tennis courts,
jogging track, sauna • secretarial
services, 31 meeting rooms (capacity
up to 1,500).

Shin Kobe Oriental *Y*////

1-chome Kitanocho, Chuo-ku, 650
☎ 291 1121 ⓉⓍ 562284 fax 291 1154

• AE DC MC V • 589 rooms, 11 suites,
6 restaurants, 1 bar, 3 coffee shops
Located right at Shin Kobe station,
the Shin Kobe Oriental (no relation
to the dignified older Oriental) is a
glossy new hotel, all pale marble,
chandeliers, soft music and
transparent lifts. Oriented largely
towards weekend guests, it also has
good business facilities. There are two
executive floors with a lounge and a
small business service centre.
Concierge and booking services,
arcade of shops • fitness centre with
gym, pool, sauna • business service
centre with limited facilities, 24
meeting rooms (capacity up to 2,500).

OTHER HOTELS

Sannomiya Terminal *Y*// 8-chome
Kumoi-dori 1-2, Chuo-ku, 651 ☎ 291
0001 ⓉⓍ 5622131 fax 291 0020 • AE
DC MC V. A typical station hotel, the
Sannomiya Terminal has unusually
attractive bedrooms with a view of
the Kobe hills.
Washington *Y*/ 2-11-5
Shimayamate-dori, Chuo-ku, 650
☎ 331 6111 fax 331 6651 • AE DC
MC V. In the main shopping area
north of Sannomiya station.

Restaurants

Japanese businessmen visiting Kobe are always glad of the chance to
indulge their taste for foreign food. Kobe's French, Indian and Chinese
restaurants are more famous than its Japanese ones. Kobe beef – the cows
are fed on beer and massaged daily – is the tenderest in the world.

JAPANESE
Misono *Y*//

1-6-7 Kitanagasa-dori, Chuo-ku
☎ 331 2890 • AE DC MC V
The teppanyaki style of cooking was
invented in 1945 by Shigeji Fujioka,
the founder of Misono, and this large
and impressive restaurant complex
still serves only teppanyaki. Each
table is topped with a steel hotplate
where the chefs fry up succulent
slices of prime Kobe beef. The
clientele has included presidents and
prime ministers, as well as luminaries
of the business world.

Sakaeya *Y*/

2-2-7 Sannomiyacho, Chuo-ku
☎ 331 5772 • closed Wed • DC V
Kobe's best tempura is to be found in
this tiny rambling house near
Motomachi station. On the ground
floor is a counter with space for just
10, where the chef cooks fresh
tempura before the customers' eyes.
A steep staircase winds past a little
stone lantern and wicker fence to the
tatami rooms, where Japanese
businessmen gather to feast, often
bringing with them their Western
colleagues.

NON-JAPANESE

Alain Chapel [Y]//

*31F Portopia Hotel, 6-10-1
Minatojima, Nakamachi, Chuo-ku
☎ 302 1111 • AE DC MC V*

For French food, the Alain Chapel is undoubtedly the place. Perched high above the city with views over the Inland Sea, it is one of Kobe's most prestigious restaurants and the scene of much business entertaining. It features the *nouvelle cuisine* of Michelin three-star chef Alain Chapel, who comes twice a year from Lyons to oversee the planning of the menu. The wine list is extensive.

Aragawa [Y]/////

*2-15-18 Nakayamate, Chuo-ku
☎ 221 8547 or 231 3315 • AE DC V
• reservations essential*

Aragawa is a small and exclusive restaurant in Kitano, specializing in charcoal-grilled steaks of the famous Kobe beef. The red-carpeted rooms are very Western in atmosphere, with heavy wooden beams, wood and brick walls and candles on the white tablecloths. This is where top Western executives entertain their Japanese counterparts.

Daiichiro [Y]/

94 Edomachi, Chuo-ku ☎ 331 0031

For a Chinese restaurant, Daiichiro is unusually restrained in decor. It is the fine Peking cuisine that draws Japanese businessmen in droves. Daiichiro's speciality is hors d'oeuvres, and the seafood, straight from the sea, is particularly fine.

Gaylord [Y]

B1 Meiji Seimei Bldg, 8-3-7 Isogami-dori, Chuo-ku ☎ 251 4359 • AE V

A little corner of the Raj in Japan, Gaylord is probably Japan's oldest Indian restaurant. Chefs and waiters are all Indian, and the food is authentic Punjabi. The setting is richly Indian, from the carved wooden ceiling and tables, to the red flock wallpaper and Indian music; the clientele is sophisticated and cosmopolitan.

Kitano Club [Y]//

*1-5-7 Kitanocho, Chuo-ku ☎ 222 5123
• AE DC MC V*

Set high on the hill in the smartest part of town, with a spectacular view over Kobe, the Kitano Club has long been the place where the sophisticated and wealthy gather. The cuisine is French, but it is the ambience that attracts – the marble pillars, red carpet, heavy draperies and soft piano music. The complex also includes a nightclub (see *Entertainment*).

Salaam [Y]

*1F Ijin Plaza Bldg, 2-12-21
Yamamoto-dori, Chuo-ku ☎ 222 1780
• closed Mon • AE V*

The creation of Polish expatriate Victor Navarsky, Salaam is Japan's first Middle Eastern restaurant. The decor is straight out of the Arabian Nights, all ornate brass lampstands, hookah hookah, Turkish coffee pots and inlaid woodwork. The cuisine, equally rich and exotic, ranges from mezze, all freshly prepared, to kebabs, tagine and couscous, including plenty of vegetarian dishes. Located in stylish Kitano, Salaam is a good place to dine alone or to take Japanese colleagues for a relaxed meal.

OTHER RESTAURANTS

Kobe is a cosmopolitan city and one of its prime attractions is the vast number of restaurants devoted to cuisine from all over the world. The most famous is *Gaylord* (see entry), but nowadays it has many competitors; many prefer the fine Indian cuisine at *Raja*, B1 Sanotatsu Bldg, Sakaemachi 2-chome ☎ 332 5253. Kobe also boasts fine Thai restaurants, of which the oldest and best is *Wang Thai*, 2F President Arcade, 2-14-22 Yamamoto-dori, Chuo-ku ☎ 222 2507, where chef Si Wa Sessuwan, from Bangkok, cooks up authentically fiery dishes. There is a good value lunchtime buffet from the 1st to the 10th of each month. Just across the road (Ijinkan-dori, in

Kitano, Kobe's main restaurant district) is *Swiss Chalet*, 3-2-4 Kitanocho, Chuo-ku ☎ 221 4343, popular not only for its fondues and fine Swiss food, but for its Swiss maid waitresses, cuckoo clocks and alpen horns. Around the corner is *Salaam* (see entry) and, directly below it, *Navar-san's*, another outlet of the eponymous Victor Navarsky and the only restaurant in Kobe to serve an authentic New York Sunday brunch, much appreciated by the local New York expatriates. As for French food, while *Alain Chapel* is justly celebrated, closely followed by the Okura's *Emerald* restaurant, there is also a plethora of humbler establishments serving homely French cuisine at more economical prices – *L'Escargot*, 1-5-4 Sannomiyacho, Chuo-ku ☎ 331 5034, for example, or *Henry's Good Dream* on Tor Road ☎ 333 7688.

Clubs

The *Kobe Club* is affilated to the Tokyo American Club and American Clubs worldwide and has reciprocal arrangements. It has an excellent restaurant.

Bars

An evening out with Japanese colleagues is likely to begin with a visit to one of the thousands of tiny bars in the streets behind Sannomiya station, before moving on to dinner or one of Kitano's smart cabarets.

Of the hotel bars, the most frequented by visiting executives are the Oriental's Cellar Bar, the Okura's Emerald Bar and the Sky Lounge at the Portopia, which has the best view in Kobe. There are also plenty of sophisticated drinking spots, such as the immensely elegant *Le Club*, 1F Fix 213 Bldg, 2-13-14 Yamamoto-dori, Chuo-ku, on Ijinkan-dori, and *Prego*, B1 Rirans Gate, 2-4-24 Yamamoto-dori, Chuo-ku, featuring an ineffably sleek interior designed by the celebrated Sugimoto Takashi. For the resident Western community, there are only two places to go in

Kobe. Both are owned by American Marty Kuehnert, something of a celebrity himself in Japan. *The Attic*, Ijinkan Club Bldg, 4-1-12 Kitanocho, Chuo-ku, is like a corner of Los Angeles, with plenty of Budweiser, plus the Atticburger, the best burger in Kobe. *Attic Junior*, B1 Fix 213 Bldg, directly under Le Club, is actually not an attic but a basement and a temple to baseball. This is where American major league players drink when they are in town, and no baseball devotee should pass up the chance of meeting them. For non baseball fans there is a sophisticated selection of bourbons, wines and beers and a cosmopolitan clientele.

Entertainment

For entertainment, Kobe dwellers tend to go to Osaka, a mere 20mins by train. Like most Japanese cities, Kobe is stronger on nightlife than culture. For information see *Kansai Time Out* and the Monday edition of the *Mainichi Daily News*.
Ticket Agencies Theatre and concert tickets for Osaka as well as Kobe can be bought through your hotel or at Play Guide ticket agencies in major department stores.
Theatre, cinema and music There is a much wider choice in Osaka, although Kobe has its share of films, concerts and Japanese and Western theatre. Concerts and theatre often take place at the *Kobe Cultural Hall* ☎ 351 3535.
Nightclubs For nightlife, head for the area north of Sannomiya station. The bars near the station are fairly sleazy, but up on the hill in Kitano you will find some of western Japan's most sophisticated nightclubs. The *Kitano Club*, 1-5-7 Kitanocho, Chuo-ku ☎ 222 5123 (see *Restaurants*) is undoubtedly Kobe's best. Both Japanese and Westerners enjoy the classy atmosphere and live music at the *Casablanca Club*, 3-1-6 Kitanocho, Chuo-ku ☎ 241 0200. Local Westerners as well as fashionable Japanese can be found at *Shekinah*, 8F Palais Kitanozaka Bldg,

4-7-11 Kanocho, Chuo-ku
☎ 332 0666, and at another of
Kobe's most popular discos, the
Vivi en Lee, Washington Hotel,
2-11-5 Shimayamate-dori,
Chuo-ku ☎ 331 6111.

Shopping
Motomachi, with its covered arcades,
is the place to go for fashions and
quality goods. Among the boutiques
there are shops selling cameras,
electronic and tax-free goods,
handicrafts and fine arts. *Toho Sanoya
Honten*, 6-7-3 Motomachi, is a famous
old ceramics shop. Sannomiya is a
maze of shops, stretching along
Centre-gai arcade, with, under it,
Santica Town, a vast network of
shops, restaurants and tiny bars. Of
Kobe's four department stores, the
most popular is *Sogo*, at Sannomiya,
and *Daimaru*, at Motomachi. North
from Daimaru is Tor Road, lined
with restaurants and antique shops.
The smart Kitano area has boutiques
full of high-class fashions and shops
selling luxury goods such as pearls.

Sightseeing
Kobe is beautifully situated between
the mountains and the sea, but it has
few sights.
Kitano Kobe's main historic area is
where the early foreign settlers lived,
and streets full of their splendid old
houses – including some wonderful
examples of eccentric architecture –
have been carefully preserved, if
rather commercialized, Japanese-style.
Many of the houses can be visited.
Kobe City Museum This exceptionally
fine municipal museum houses the
Namban Art Collection, a fascinating
collection of 16th–19thC paintings of
Kobe's exotic foreign residents by
Japanese artists. *24 Kyomachi,
Chuo-ku. Open Tue–Sun, 10–4.30.*
Minatogawa Shrine The most
famous of Kobe's shrines,
Minatogawa is just north of Kobe
station and is dedicated to the 14thC
hero Masashige Kusunoki.
Nada Inveterate sake drinkers will
want to make a pilgrimage to Nada,

just 10kms/6 miles from Sannomiya.
You can walk around the fine old
breweries with their black wooden
walls, or visit one of the museums
run by the three major brewers,
Hakatsuru, Kikumasamune and
Sawanotsuru. *Kikumasamune
Memorial Museum, Nozaki Nishimachi
1-chome, Higashi Nada-ku
☎ 851 2275. Open Jan–Mar,
Mon–Fri, 8.30–5; reservations
essential ☎ 882 6333 (Sawanotsuru).*

Out of town
The mountain range visible behind
Kobe is the Rokko range, of which
the highest peak is *Mount Rokko*.
There is a cable car to the top, from
which you can enjoy views across the
city and the Inland Sea to Shikoku
Island. On the other side of the peak
is Japan's longest ropeway to *Arima
Spa*, which can also be reached by
bus direct from Sannomiya. Arima is
a famous hot spring resort, the oldest
in Japan, nestling in a gorge among
cherry and maple trees. Half an hour
west of Kobe is the town of *Himeji*,
with its castle, the *White Heron*,
considered one of the most beautiful
in Japan. Well off the tourist track is
Awaji Island, a short boat ride from
Kobe; there are no sights here, but
plenty of countryside. A new bridge
links Awaji with *Shikoku*, a lovely
island full of spectacular mountains,
hot springs and terraced rice paddies.

Spectator sports
There is very little sport in Kobe
itself but a wide choice in Osaka.
Baseball The Orix Braves are the
Kobe home team, based at the
*Nishinomiya Stadium. Koshien
Stadium*, home of the popular Osaka-
based Hanshin Tigers (see *Osaka*) is
in Nishinomiya, a Kobe suburb:
Naruocho, Nishinomiya ☎ (0798) 47
1041.

Keeping fit
Public facilities are unusually well
developed, thanks to the presence of
a large international community, and
there are outdoor facilities on the top

of Mount Rokko. There is plenty of information about sporting activities in *Kansai Time Out*. There are also health clubs in the Okura, Portopia and Shin Kobe Oriental (see *Hotels*).
Golf Japan's oldest golf course, with 18 holes, constructed in 1903 by Englishman Arthur Groom, is on the summit of *Mount Rokko*.
Fitness centres YMCA *Fitness Centre*, 2-7-15 Kanocho, Chuo-ku ☎ 241 7201, and *Mac Sports Club*, 7-8-31 Motoyama Minami-machi, Higashi Nada-ku ☎ 452 1801, are open to non-members for the day; they offer facilities such as weight training, swimming, sauna, gym, tennis courts and jogging track.
Hiking There are good hiking trails around Kobe's mountain ranges, particularly on *Mount Futatabi*. The popular tracks tend to be crowded.
Jogging The *Kobe Hash Harriers* meet once a week to run.
Skiing The nearest ski slope is *Mount Rokko Jinko Skiing Area*, Nada-ku ☎ 891 0366. This is a very popular slope, and it is best to ski in the middle of the week. Farther afield, there are ski slopes on *Mount Kannabe* and a new slope on *Mount Hyonosen*. *Taiyo Recreation Centre* ☎ (06) 353 5338 and *Big Tour Osaka Centre* ☎ (06) 363 0451 organize bus trips from Kobe to various ski slopes.
Swimming There are pools in the health clubs. The public pools are cheap but always very crowded: *Hyogo Prefectural Sports Centre Pool*, 1 Hasuike, Nagata-ku ☎ 631 1071. Kobe's *Suma Beach* is popular with young surfers, while *Maiko* and *Shioya* are quieter and cleaner.

Local resources
Business services

The best business service centre in Kobe is in the Okura; the Portopia and the Shin Kobe Oriental also have centres (see *Hotels*). Otherwise use the local branch of the national companies: *Manpower Japan* ☎ 291 8800, *Kao Co* ☎ 252 1150 and *Temporary Centre Corporation* ☎ 291 0121.

Photocopying and printing Your hotel will arrange photocopying for you. For large quantities, contact XEROX *System Centre* ☎ 251 1701 or *Nice Print* ☎ 332 6918, which also print namecards. For general printing, use *Daishin Printing Co Ltd* ☎ 302 2700.

Communications
International couriers None operate from Kobe. Use the Osaka couriers.
Post Office The main post office is at 6-2-1 Sakaemachi-dori, Chuo-ku ☎ 351 7011.
Telex and fax Most hotels have telex and fax facilities. If necessary, use KDD ☎ 331 0420.

Conference/exhibition centres

Kobe is second only to Tokyo in the number of international conferences it hosts – more than 450 conferences, trade fairs and exhibitions take place annually. There are a total of 52 conference sites in Kobe. The main conference centre is the *Kobe International Conference Hall*, 6-9-1 Minatojima Nakamachi, Chuo-ku ☎ 302 5200 (on Port Island). Other important centres are *Kobe Port Terminal Hall*, 4-5 Shinkocho, Chuo-ku ☎ 391 7638; *Kobe Trade Promotion Centre*, Minatojima 6-chome, Chuo-ku ☎ 302 1035; and *Sanbo Hall* 5-1-32 Hamabe-dori, Chuo-ku ☎ 251 3551.

Emergencies

Hospitals The following hospitals have 24hr casualty departments: *Kobe Adventist Hospital*, 8-4-1 Arinodai, Kita-ku ☎ 981 0161; *Kobe Kaisei Hospital*, 3-11-15 Shinohara-Kitamachi, Nada-ku ☎ 871 5201; *Kobe Central Municipal Hospital*, 4-6 Minatojima-Nakamachi, Chuo-ku ☎ 302 4321 (on Port Island). For dental treatment contact *Dr Thomas Ward*, Oriental Dental Clinic, Oriental Ika-Shika Bldg, 3-4-7 Nakayamate-dori, Chuo-ku ☎ 321 2717.
Pharmacies Prescription drugs are supplied by hospitals and doctors.

For over-the-counter medicines, most pharmacies are open from 10am–8pm. Go to *Shinyaku-do*, Santica Town, 1-1 Sannomiyacho, Chuo-ku ☎ 391 1778. *Police* Ikuta police station ☎ 331 0044.

Government offices

For inquiries, contact *Kobe City Hall*, 6-5 Kanocho, Chuo-ku ☎ 331 8181, or *Hyogo Prefectural Office*, 5-10 Shimoyamate-dori, Chuo-ku ☎ 341 7711.

Information sources

Business information Kobe Chamber of Commerce, 6-1 Nakamachi Minatojima ☎ 303 1000. You will probably find the foreign chambers of commerce in Osaka more helpful. The JETRO office is at 5-1-14 Hamabe-dori, Chuo-ku ☎ 231 3081.
Local media Mainichi Daily News, printed in Osaka, carries information about current events in the Kansai area. The excellent monthly *Kansai Time Out* has articles about Kansai as well as comprehensive listings of current entertainment and sporting events.

Tourist information There is a small *Tourist Information Office*, 2F Kobe Kotsu Centre Bldg, JNR Sannomiya station, west exit ☎ 392 0020. At the station there is a helpful branch of the *JTB* ☎ 231 4118. Also try *Kobe International Tourist Association*, 6th Fl, International Conference Centre, Port Island ☎ 303 1010. *Community House and Information Centre* (CHIC), 4-6-15 Ikutacho, Chuo-ku ☎ 242 1043, is run by members of Kobe's foreign community to provide helpful information and support, primarily for Western residents, but also for visiting Westerners. Their publication *Living in Kobe* is full of invaluable information.

Thank-yous

The top department stores are the most suitable place to buy gifts, and they will arrange delivery: *Daimaru* ☎ 331 8121; *Hankyu* ☎ 321 3521; *Sogo* ☎ 221 4181. To send flowers within Japan or abroad, contact *Shinko Flower Shop*, 3-1-19 Shimoyamate-dori, Chuo-ku ☎ 331 9221.

KYOTO

City code ☎ 075

At first sight Kyoto looks like any other Japanese city, all concrete office blocks and traffic-filled streets. Behind this aggressively modern façade, however, lies the Kyoto that most visitors come to see: the ancient capital of Japan and still its cultural centre, a city studded with hundreds of temples, shrines, palaces and gardens, as well as charming little backstreets lined with old wooden houses. If you have time to spare, this is the ideal place to relax for a weekend and discover traditional Japan.

Kyoto was the capital of Japan and the home of the Imperial family from 794 until 1868; the emperors are still enthroned here in the Imperial Palace. Even when the centre of power moved to Tokyo, Kyoto remained the home of traditional culture and the arts. It is also an important industrial city, producing electrical appliances and precision machines, and the centre of biotechnological research in the Kansai area.

Arriving

The closest airport to Kyoto is Itami (see *Osaka*) from where there is a limousine bus service into the city every 20mins during the day, taking 60–90mins. From Tokyo the Bullet Train takes 2hrs 40mins and is quicker and simpler than flying. From Osaka it takes only 16mins.

Railway stations

The Bullet Train arrives in Kyoto station, which is rather far from the city centre. If you are coming from Osaka or Kobe, it is more convenient – and cheaper – to take the Hankyu line to Kawaramachi. From Osaka you can also take the Keihan line to Sanjo Keihan in the city centre.
Kyoto station The Bullet Train and all JR trains, including those to and

from Osaka and Kobe to the west, Nara to the south and Nagoya to the east, all stop at Kyoto station, convenient for the subway and buses. The station building itself is quite small, with a department store above it and a cluster of hotels, an underground shopping arcade and more department stores around it. Inquiries ☎ 361 5786.
Kawaramachi station The terminus of the Hankyu line, from Osaka, Kawaramachi station is in the basement of Hankyu department store, in the busiest part of the city, near Gion.
Sanjo Keihan station is also in the downtown area, but across the river from Kawaramachi. Change to another train to go on to the Miyako from here. Inquiries ☎ 561 0033.

HOTELS	RESTAURANTS	BUILDINGS AND SIGHTS
1 ANA	1 Gion Suehiro	1 Central post office
2 Brighton	2 Junsei	2 JTB
3 Fujita	3 Kyo Yamato	3 Chamber of commerce and industry
4 Grand	4 Minokichi	4 Kyoto Tower
5 International	5 Mishima Tei	5 Prefectural government office
6 Kyoto	6 Toriyasu	TIC (in Kyoto Tower)
7 Miyako	Yachiyo (hotel 12)	6 Daitokuji Temple
8 Royal	7 Yagenbori	
9 Ryokan Hiiragiya	8 Yoshikawa Tempura	
10 Takaragaike Prince	9 Ashiya	
11 Tawaraya	L'Espoir (hotel 7)	
12 Yachiyo	10 Manyoken	
13 Gimmond	11 Minoko	
14 Holiday Inn	12 Hyotei	
15 New Hankyu	13 Kyorinsen	
16 New Miyako	14 Gonbei	
17 Prince	15 Mikaku	
18 Tokyu	16 Natsuka	
	17 Cipolla	

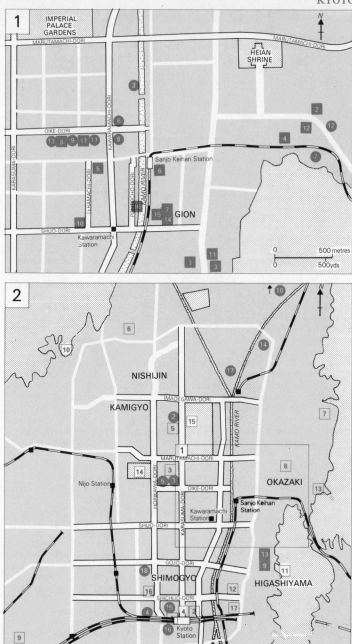

1

IMPERIAL PALACE GARDENS

MARUTAMACHI-DORI

HEIAN SHRINE

MARUTAMACHI-DORI

N

KAWARAMACHI-DORI

KARASUMA-DORI

③

⑥

OIKE-DORI

⑬ ⑧ ⑨ ⑰ ⑪

⑧

②

⑫ ⑫

④

⑦

KAMO RIVER

Sanjo Keihan Station

⑤

PONTOCHO-DORI

⑥

TEHAMACHI-DORI

⑮

⑦

GION

⑭

SHIJO-DORI

⑩

Kawaramachi Station

⑪

①

③

0   500 metres

0   500 yds

2

⑩

⑥

⑩

NISHIJIN

⑭

KAMIGYO

⑰

KAMO RIVER

⑦

IMADEGAWA-DORI

②

⑮

⑤

①

HORIKAWA-DORI

MARUTAMACHI-DORI

⑧

⑭

③

OKAZAKI

⑬

Nijo Station

⑤ ✕

OIKE-DORI

KARASUMA-DORI

Sanjo Keihan Station

Kawaramachi Station

SHIJO-DORI

GOJO-DORI

⑬

⑨

⑱

SHIMOGYO

⑪

HIGASHIYAMA

⑯

⑫

SHICHIJO-DORI

⑰

④

⑮

④

②

⑨

⑯

Kyoto Station

Getting around

Kyoto, like Peking, is laid out in a grid following the classical Chinese model, with nine numbered main streets running east-west, and named north-south avenues. This makes it fairly easy to find your way around, and with the aid of a good map you can take on the bus system. If time is of the essence, taxi is the only choice; but allow plenty of time if you are travelling in the morning or evening rush hours.

Taxis Kyoto has more taxis than anywhere else in Japan, including Tokyo, and you can find one anywhere, at any time of day or night – though like all Japanese taxi drivers, Kyoto drivers sometimes get lost. Of the many taxi companies, light green *Taxis* ☎ 681 3727 and black *MK Company* taxis ☎ 721 4141 are said to be the best.

Driving All the main rental chains have offices in Kyoto.

Walking While it is pleasant to walk around the backstreets and between the temples on the east side of the city, you should avoid the main traffic-filled thoroughfares. Distances from one part of the city to another are vast; for example, it would take up to 90mins to walk from the railway station to the Imperial Palace.

Bus If you are visiting Kyoto for pleasure rather than business, the bus is a convenient way of getting around except in rush hours. But you will need a map; the simple one on the back of the TIC map of Kyoto shows main routes and bus numbers. Within the city, the fare is the same to every destination; if you are leaving the city, you will have to take a numbered ticket from the dispenser by the door as you enter and pay the fare for that number, as shown on the chart at the front of the bus. To stop the bus, press the small purple buzzer and, as you get off, put the correct fare into the plastic box beside the driver. Although there is usually a change machine for Y500 coins and Y,1000 notes beside the box, it is best to have plenty of change.

Subway Kyoto's subway is spotlessly clean, safe and rarely crowded. It runs from Takeda via the station straight up the middle of the city to Kitaoji and is a rapid and convenient way of getting between the north and south of the city.

Train There are several railway lines connecting central Kyoto with the suburbs. The Hankyu line, from Osaka, cuts straight across the city to Kawaramachi, while the Keihan line, also from Osaka, becomes a streetcar at Sanjo and trundles past the Miyako and out towards Otsu. The Keifuku or the JR will take you to Arashiyama, and the JR and Kintetsu lines go down to Nara. To the north of the city, a second Keifuku line goes up towards Mount Hiei and Kurama. In general, the private lines are quicker and cheaper and depart more frequently than the JR. Apart from the streetcar lines, all the railways have different types of train, including non-stop expresses. If you are travelling locally, check that you do not board the express.

Area by area

Kyoto is a remarkably homogeneous city, bounded by hills on three sides. Although the city does have certain distinct areas, Kyotoites orient themselves by street rather than by neighbourhood. The east-west streets of the Kyoto grid are conveniently numbered, from Shichijo, "Seven", down by the station, through Gojo, "Five", and Sanjo, "Three", up to Nijo (as in the castle), "Two".

City centre Bounded by Shijo to the south, Karasuma to the west, Oike-dori to the north and the river to the east, this is an area full of traffic, crowds and modern shops, including the main department stores. Hidden behind the main streets are tiny backstreets of old wooden houses. Running between Kawaramachi and the river is Pontocho, lined with restaurants. To the north of the shopping area is Oike-dori, a wide boulevard running from the Kyoto hotel to Nijo station. This is the main business section of the city. Offices of various companies including airlines, the Kyoto Chamber of Commerce and the City Hall are here.

Kamigyo and the north The northern part of town is mainly residential: row after row of narrow streets lined with wooden houses and tiny corner shops. The bright lights and *pachinko* parlours are limited to the main roads that cut across it. Here you will find the Imperial Palace, many famous temples such as Kinkakuji and Ryoanji, and, to the east, Kyoto University. Nishijin, to the west, is the centre of silk weaving. Farther out into the northern suburbs is Takaragaike, home of the Kyoto International Conference Hall.

Higashiyama and the east Across Shijo Bridge, to the east of Kawaramachi, is Gion, the traditional entertainment area. Its narrow streets are lined with old houses, many of which are restaurants or geisha quarters. To the east of Gion, stretching the length of the city, is Higashiyama, "East Mountain", a tranquil area popular with walkers.

Some of Kyoto's most beautiful temples are here, from Ginkakuji in the north, through Nanzenji, to Kiyomizu. Tucked in near Nanzenji is the Miyako Hotel. In nearby Okazaki is a small cultural centre, with museums and Noh theatres.

Shimogyo and the south The area around Kyoto station and stretching up Karasuma is Kyoto's second main shopping area, rather dusty and traffic-filled, which also includes hotels, temples and the Kyoto National Museum. To the south is Fushimi, home of Fushimi sake (one of Japan's finest) and Kyoto's main industrial centre.

Western Kyoto The western part of Kyoto is a bleak residential area.

The suburbs Because of its hills, Kyoto does not have many suburbs, but they are smarter than the city itself. Many of the older families live around the northern edges, in Kitano and Kinugasa. Ohara and Kurama, to the north, are also full of wealthy families, as is Arashiyama – a popular tourist spot full of rushing streams and wooded hills – to the west.

Hotels

Kyoto's hotels, like the city, have a certain mellow charm. Of the Western-style hotels, the choice ranges from the legendary Miyako to modern luxury hotels like the ANA and the Takaragaike Prince. For the ultimate Japanese hospitality, Kyoto's *ryokan* (see *Planning and Reference: Hotels*) are the best in the country.

ANA [Y]//
Nijo-jo-mae, Horikawa-dori, Nakagyo-ku, 604 ☎ *231 1155*
[TX] *5423181 fax 231 5333* • *AE DC MC V* • *294 rooms, 9 suites, 5 restaurants, 1 bar, 1 coffee shop*
Opened in 1986, the ANA is the first to provide a wide range of modern facilities, such as business services. It is well up to ANA standards, with a luxurious lobby area looking out onto a waterfall and Japanese garden. The rooms are a good size, decorated in cool greens or dusty pinks, each with a minibar and large leather-topped

desk. The staff are helpful and eager to please. Concierge, travel desk, arcade of shops • sauna, pool, massage, jogging, special arrangements with nearby tennis and golf clubs • secretarial services, 10 meeting rooms (capacity up to 1,500).

Brighton [Y]//
Nakadachiuri, Shinmachi-dori, Kamigyo-ku, 602 ☎ *441 4411*
[TX] *5422690 fax 431 2360* • *AE DC MC V* • *181 rooms, 2 suites, 5 restaurants, 1 lounge, 1 bar*
The Brighton, named after Brighton,

England, opened in July 1988 and the Mayor of Brighton was invited to the opening. It is a glossy modern hotel, all gleaming marble and glass, with a vast atrium lobby six floors high – rather a surprise among the winding Kyoto backstreets near the old Imperial Palace, where it is located. The rooms are exceptionally spacious, with separate living and sleeping areas, and excellent value. There are executive suites on the sixth floor. Limited concierge service and selection of shops • outdoor pool • business service centre with limited facilities, 4 meeting rooms (capacity up to 500).

Fujita Y///

Kamogawa-Nijo, Nakagyo-ku, 604
☎ *222 1511* Ⓣ *5422571 fax 256 4561*
• *AE DC MC V* • *176 rooms, 4 suites, 4 restaurants, 1 bar, 1 coffee shop*
Situated just north of the city centre, the Fujita has a distinctive style. The main block stretches along the riverside; next to it is a small Japanese house, a replica of Baron Fujita's 1907 villa. The peaceful lobby looks out onto a waterfall and a Japanese garden, with mandarin ducks and black carp. The bedrooms have a Japanese atmosphere, with woodblock prints, large plants and sliding paper windows looking across the river to Higashiyama. Concierge, theatre and travel reservations, arcade of shops • 3 meeting rooms (capacity up to 150).

Grand Y///

Shiokoji, Horikawa, Shimogyo-ku, 600
☎ *341 2311* Ⓣ *5422551 fax 341 3073*
• *Royal Hotel Osaka* • *AE DC MC V* • *546 rooms, 14 suites, 4 restaurants, 2 bars, 1 coffee shop*
The Grand is a vast, solid hotel, offering old-fashioned comforts and service. It is rather far from the action, in a grim section of town, but convenient for the airport bus which departs from here. With the exception of a business service centre, it has every conceivable facility, including conference rooms with

moveable stages and audiovisual equipment. The bedrooms are small and simply furnished, with paper screens over the windows. Concierge, travel booking, arcade of shops • heated indoor pool, sauna (men only) • 23 meeting rooms (capacity up to 800).

International Y/

Nijo-jo, Horikawa-dori, Nakagyo-ku, 604 ☎ *222 1111* Ⓣ *5422158 fax 231 9381* • *Fujita* • *AE DC MC V* • *288 rooms, 12 suites, 1 restaurant, 1 bar, 1 coffee shop*
Opposite Nijo Castle and beside the new ANA, the International has long been popular with both business travellers and tourists. The lobby, built around a Japanese garden, is always crowded and bustling. The rooms have a spectacular view over the castle and are appropriately Japanese in style, with paper doors and windows. Concierge, travel and theatre booking, shops • 5 meeting rooms (capacity up to 100).

Kyoto Y/

Kawaramachi-Oike, Nakagyo-ku, 604 ☎ *211 5111* Ⓣ *5422126 fax 211 4209* • *Nikko* • *AE DC MC V* • *495 rooms, 12 suites, 7 restaurants, 1 bar*
Second only to the Miyako, the Kyoto is a popular, modern hotel with every luxury. It is right in the centre of the city, close to shopping and sightseeing areas. The rooms are small but attractively furnished, and all have a minibar and are soundproofed; the rooms in the newer building are more spacious. Service is brisk and efficient. Concierge, shops, hairdresser • 15 meeting rooms (capacity up to 800).

Miyako Y////

Sanjo Keage, Higashiyama-ku, 605 ☎ *771 7111* Ⓣ *5422132 fax 751 2490* • *445 rooms, 10 suites, 6 restaurants, 2 bars, 2 coffee shops*
Undoubtedly Kyoto's best hotel, the gracious Miyako is where visiting royalty and presidents invariably stay. It has the patina of centuries of

tradition and service, combined with every modern luxury. The elegant bedrooms, all with minibar, are decorated in pale brocades and marble, and have views over shrines, temples and palaces. For the complete Japanese experience, you can stay in one of the tiny traditional wood and paper houses, set on the hillside in the 16-acre landscaped gardens. The tatami rooms, with sliding screens and sunken wooden baths, also have central heating, extra mattresses, shower and television. The new annexe incorporates a fitness centre and a fine French restaurant, L'Espoir (see *Restaurants*). Concierge, travel and theatre bookings, shops, hairdresser, barber, shuttle bus to city centre and Kyoto station, limousine bus to Itami airport • fitness centre (presently members only), with gym, pool, massage, sauna; outdoor pool; concessionary rates at nearby golf course and tennis courts • 20 meetings rooms (capacity up to 2,000).

Royal Y|||
Kawaramachi Sanjo, Nakagyo-ku, 604
☎ *223 1234* TX *5422888 fax 223 1702*
• *AE DC MC V* • *295 rooms, 5 suites, 2 restaurants, 2 bars, 1 coffee shop*
The Royal is probably the best located of all the Kyoto hotels, directly on the main Kawaramachi-dori. The lobby is rather dismal, but the rooms are light and airy, with comfortable furnishings. Ask for one of the newly decorated twin rooms, which look out over the city. Concierge, theatre and travel bookings, shops • 10 meeting rooms (capacity up to 150).

Ryokan Hiiragiya Y|||||
Anegakoji, Fuyacho, Nakagyo-ku, 604
☎ *221 1136* TX *5432045 fax 221 1139*
• *AE DC MC V* • *33 rooms*
Hiiragiya is the most famous and Westernized of Kyoto's *ryokans*. It is a rambling Japanese house, more than 100 years old, with a beautiful garden with mossy stone lantern, maple trees and a stream full of carp. Each of the

spacious rooms has a modern Western-style bathroom. Hiiragiya is efficiently run by its uniformed, English-speaking staff, which gives it the atmosphere almost of a hotel in the guise of a *ryokan*. • 1 banquet hall (capacity up to 30).

Takaragaike Prince Y|||||
Takaragaike, Sakyo-ku, 606
☎ *712 1111* TX *5423261 fax 712 7677*
• *AE DC MC V* • *294 rooms, 28 suites, 4 restaurants, 1 bar*
Set in woodlands in the hills to the north of the city, the Takaragaike Prince is a striking modern building, completely round, designed by distinguished architect Togo Murano. The rooms are vast and tastefully furnished with Nishijin silk on the walls and there is a tea-ceremony house in the beautiful Japanese garden. Sadly, the Prince is fairly inconvenient, unless you are attending one of the many high-level conferences at the adjacent international conference centre. 24hr room service, express check out, concierge, booking services, souvenir shop; hotel bus to Kyoto station 5 times a day • business service centre with limited facilities • 7 meeting rooms (capacity up to 1,800).

Tawaraya Y|||||
Anegakoji-agaru, Fuyacho, Nakagyo-ku, 604 ☎ *211 5566*
TX *5423273 fax 211 2204* • *AE DC V* • *19 rooms*
The Okazaki family have kept an inn here for the last 300 years, making this the oldest *ryokan* in Kyoto. It is also one of the most expensive hotels in Japan. The present building, dating from 1850, is a maze of winding passages and sliding doors opening on to tiny gardens. The rooms are cool, spacious and silent; the only concession to modernity is the bathroom, with its Western toilet.

Yachiyo Y|||
Nanzenji, Sakyo-ku, 606 ☎ *771 4148*
TX *5423238 fax 771 4140* • *AE DC MC V* • *22 rooms, 3 suites, 1 restaurant*

Beyond the wooden entrance hall is a maze of dark corridors and stairways crisscrossing the labyrinthine two-floored Japanese house. The tatami rooms are all different. Most have Japanese-style bathrooms, with a deep sunken wooden bath. Japanese television only, travel and theatre bookings.

OTHER HOTELS

Gimmond *Y*/ *Nishi-iru, Takakura Oike-dori, Nakagyo-ku, 604* ☎ *221 4111* ☒ *5423219 fax 221 8250* • *AE DC MC V*. Functional and friendly, near offices, shops and transport.
Holiday Inn *Y*/ *36 Nishi-Shirakicho, Takano, Sakyo-ku, 606* ☎ *721 3131* ☒ *5422251 fax 781 6178*

• *AE DC MC V*. In northern Kyoto; lots of sports facilities.
New Hankyu *Y*// *Shiokoji-shinmachi, Shimogyo-ku, 600* ☎ *343 5300* ☒ *5423142 fax 343 5324* • *AE DC MC V*. Opposite Kyoto station.
New Miyako *Y*/ *Hachijo-guchi, Minami-ku, 601* ☎ *661 7111* ☒ *5423211 fax 661 7135* • *AE DC MC V*. An enormous modern hotel just behind the station; recently enlarged.
Prince *Y* *43 Matsubaracho, Shimogamo, Sakyo-ku, 606* ☎ *781 4141* ☒ *5422611 fax 781 4150* • *AE DC MC V*. Small, in northern Kyoto.
Tokyu *Y*// *Gojo-sagaru, Horikawa-dori, Shimogyo-ku, 600* ☎ *341 2411* ☒ *5422459 fax 341 2488* • *AE DC MC V*. Just north of the station.

Restaurants

Although Kyoto has its share of fine Western restaurants, it is really the place to master the intricacies of Japanese cuisine. In the backstreets of Pontocho and Gion, you will find plenty of little restaurants selling moderately-priced everyday fare, while for business entertaining, Kyoto's oldest, grandest and most expensive restaurants serve the best *kaiseki* in the country. Some of the finest food in the city is to be found in the temple restaurants, where you can dine on *shojin ryori* – mainly vegetarian – cuisine and try some *tofu* (bean curd) dishes.

JAPANESE

Gion Suehiro *Y*/
570-46 Gionmachi Minamigawa, Higashiyama-ku ☎ *541 1337-9* • *AE DC MC V*
Gion is where the geisha learn their trade, and at Gion Suehiro you will be served and entertained by *maiko*, youthful trainee geisha. Your Japanese colleagues are likely to bring you to this highly popular restaurant, which epitomizes what most Japanese believe to be the Westerner's image of Japan. You will dine on shabu shabu, sukiyaki, *kaiseki* or even snapping turtle, depending on the season.

Junsei *Y*
60 Kusakawacho, Nanzenji, Sakyo-ku ☎ *761 2311* • *AE DC MC V*
Inside the grounds of Nanzenji Temple are many restaurants serving simmered bean curd (*yudofu*) and

other dishes typical of Buddhist cuisine. One of the oldest, most famous and most popular is Junsei. Built in 1834 as a medical school, it consists of 17 rooms spread through a beautiful Japanese garden, complete with the original herb gardens. You can dine cheaply in the vast main dining hall or entertain, as many Japanese executives do, in one of the small private rooms, overlooking the trickling streams, bamboo groves and carp-filled ponds.

Kyo Yamato *Y*////
Minami-mon-mae, Kodaiji, Higashiyama-ku ☎ *525 1555* • *reservations only* • *AE DC MC V*
Kyo Yamato has been looking across the roofs of Kyoto for over a thousand years. It began life as a summer palace for the Imperial family and over the centuries many

great figures from Japanese history have come to admire the view from this rambling old house perched on the mountainside. The cuisine here is Kyo *kaiseki*, the elegant Kyoto version of *kaiseki*, said to be the oldest and best; and, while Kyo Yamato is one of Kyoto's most distinguished *ryotei*, it is also, unusually, welcoming to foreigners. Ask your hotel to provide an introduction for you.

Minokichi Ⓨ///
Dobutsuen-mae-dori, Sanjo-agaru, Sakyo-ku ☎ 771 4185 • AE DC MC V
Minokichi is just down the road from the Miyako Hotel. It first opened its doors in 1716, and its *kaiseki* dishes, served on the finest porcelain, have been famous ever since, though more robust dishes, such as shabu shabu or tempura, have been introduced to suit Western tastes. Top politicians and company directors often entertain in the private tatami rooms.

Mishima Tei Ⓨ//
Sanjo Teramachi, Nakagyo-ku ☎ 221 0003 • AE DC MC V
In the heart of Kyoto, at the end of Teramachi shopping arcade, is a tall wooden house. Mishima Tei opened as a butcher's and meat restaurant in 1873, when meat was still an exotic delicacy, and its sukiyaki, *mizutaki* (with chicken) and *oil yaki* (fried beefsteak) are famous. The house itself is a warren of tiny tatami rooms, with bamboo ceilings and hanging screens. The rooms are often used for formal entertaining.

Toriyasu Ⓨ
Shimbashi-agaru, Nawate-dori, Higashiyama-ku ☎ 561 7203 • *closed Mon* • AE DC MC V
Toriyasu sells chicken – Tamba chicken, the best. Even the little wicker basket that holds your steaming towel is chicken-shaped. You can have chicken skewered on a stick (*yakitori*), simmered in a casserole (*mizutaki*), made into tempura or served in a box.

Yachiyo Ⓨ
Nanzenji, Sakyo-ku ☎ 771 4148 • AE DC MC V
Yachiyo is a famous old *ryokan* (see *Hotels*), but it also has a small tea room and restaurant just inside the gates to Nanzenji Temple, where visitors can dine on simple Kyoto cuisine, served in a beautiful lacquered box.

Yagenbori Ⓨ/
Sueyoshicho Kiritoshi-kado, Gion, Higashiyama-ku ☎ 551 3331 • AE DC V
Yagenbori is many people's favourite restaurant. This charming old wooden building is right in the teahouse district of Gion, along the Shirakawa canal, and is packed full of folk art and ceramics. You can sit at the counter and watch the chefs at work, turning a live fish into sashimi with a few deft knife strokes; or dine more grandly on *kaiseki* in one of the tatami rooms.

Yoshikawa Tempura Ⓨ/
Tominokoji, Oike-sagaru, Nakagyo-ku ☎ 221 5544/0052 • *closed Sun* • AE DC MC V
Of Kyoto's myriad tempura restaurants, Yoshikawa Tempura is undoubtedly the best. You thread your way down a narrow alley beside a tall wicker fence, and slide open a wooden door to enter the tiny restaurant. There is room for just 12 around the polished pine bench, where the young chef creates light-as-air tempura, serving each piping-hot morsel directly onto your plate. For more formal entertaining, there are rooms in the Yoshikawa Ryokan, where you dine on tempura *kaiseki*.

NON-JAPANESE
Ashiya Ⓨ///
4-172-13 Kiyomizu, Higashiyama-ku ☎ 541 7961 • *closed Mon* • AE DC V
Down a side alley on the way to Kiyomizu Temple, Ashiya was started by American Bob Strickland in 1965. It has been one of the smartest Kyoto dining spots ever since, and is a

suitable place to entertain Japanese colleagues. Dinner in the beautifully restored hundred-year-old inn begins with drinks (including genuine American-style martinis) in the upstairs gallery where the works of local artists are displayed. Downstairs, customers dine on the finest Kobe and Omi beefsteak, cooked teppanyaki style.

L'Espoir *Y*////
Miyako Hotel, Sanjo Keage, Higashiyama-ku ☎ *771 7111* ● *AE DC MC V*

Despite its youth (it opened in 1988) L'Espoir is quickly establishing itself as probably the city's top French restaurant. The chef, sommelier and staff all trained at the three-star Baumanière in Provence, and the cuisine is some of the finest in Japan – light and imaginative in the *nouvelle* style, and incorporating some of the fine traditional ingredients (such as yuba) for which Kyoto is famous. As an added extra, diners can enjoy a magnificent view over the city.

Manyoken *Y*///
Fuyacho, Shijo, Shimogyo-ku ☎ *221 1022* ● *closed 2nd and 4th Tue of each month* ● *AE DC MC V*

Manyoken is Kyoto's oldest and most famous Western-style restaurant. Since its opening in 1910, it has served classic French cuisine to generations of customers, including royalty and presidents. The opulent decor, with plush red carpets, curving marble staircases and massive chandeliers, is much admired by the Japanese, as is the formality of the service. There is an extensive list of fine wines.

OTHER RESTAURANTS
Kyoto is a city of endless discoveries. Its backstreets are lined with charming old buildings which turn out to serve exquisite *kaiseki*, often surprisingly cheaply – *Minoko*, 480 Kiyoicho, Gion, Higashiyama-ku ☎ 561 0328, for example; *Hyotei*, 35 Kusakawacho, Nanzenji, Sakyo-ku

☎ 771 4116, set in a beautiful garden; or *Kyorinsen*, Kodaiji, Ninenzaka, Higashiyama-ku ☎ 541 9111. For a more economical meal, the noodle dishes at *Gonbei*, Kiridoshi, Shijo Gion ☎ 561 3350, are famous. For sukiyaki, *Mikaku*, Kawabata-dori, Shijo-agaru, Gion ☎ 525 1129, is both good and accessible. Kyoto also has its share of restaurants serving good Western food at reasonable prices. For French food, *Natsuka*, 2F Shiori Bldg, Shijo-Pontocho-agaru ☎ 255 2105, is worth investigating, while for Italian food, *Cipolla*, Fuyacho Oike, ☎ 221 6334, is popular.

Bars
Kyoto's bar area is Pontocho. Some bars are forbiddingly traditional and very pricey; others are downright sleazy. Never enter a bar that employs a pavement tout. On a hot summer evening, those overlooking the river are pleasantly cool.

Important business decisions continue to be made down in Gion, in Japan's only remaining geisha quarters. Japanese businessmen are well used to the phenomenal cost of a geisha evening; fortunately, it is considered an improper way for foreign business people to entertain their Japanese colleagues.

Of the hotel bars, the most popular among visiting executives are those in the Miyako and the Kyoto. *Rosenthal*, Sanjo-sagaru-nishi, Kawaramachi-dori, Nakagyo-ku, is Kyoto's oldest beerhall and very popular with the city's foreign community, while fashionable Japanese are to be found in *Wine River*, Takoyakushi-higashi, Kawaramachi, Nakagyo-ku. *Samboa*, Teramachi Sanjo-sagaru, Nakagyo-ku, is also popular.

Entertainment
Kyoto has been the cultural centre of Japan for a thousand years, and the entertainment available ranges from the most traditional, such as Noh theatre and geisha parties, to the most modern. At dusk you can see geisha

and trainee geisha (*maiko*) hurrying to work through Gion and Pontocho.

For current information on entertainment, look at the notice board at the TIC, or check the *Kyoto Monthly Guide*, *Kansai Time Out*, *Kaleidoscope Kyoto* or the *Mainichi Daily News*. Most cultural activities in Kyoto take place between October and May. Make reservations through your hotel or at Play Guide ticket agencies in major department stores.

Theatre Kyoto is the home of the ancient, aristocratic and ritualistic *Noh* drama; translations of the most popular Noh plays are available in Maruzen and other bookshops stocking foreign books. Performances, held on Saturdays and Sundays for about 3hrs, usually consist of three Noh plays interspersed with two *kyogen* comic interludes. The main Noh theatres are *Kanze Kaikan*, 44 Okazaki, Enshojicho, Sakyo-ku, *Kongo Noh Gakudo*, Shijo-agaru, Muromachi-dori, Nakagyo-ku, and *Oe Noh Gakudo*, Yanaginobamba Higashi-iru, Oshikoji-dori, Nakagyo-ku. If you are in Kyoto in June, do not miss *Takigi Noh*, "Torchlight Noh", in the spectacular grounds of the Heian shrine.

All the *Kabuki* stars come up from Tokyo in December, and do a series of gala performances at the *Minami-za*, Nakanocho, Shijo Ohashi Higashizume, Higashiyama-ku.

Maiko (apprentice geisha) perform "cherry dances" throughout April at the *Kobu Kaburenjo*, Gion, Higashiyama-ku. You can see geisha dances in spring and autumn at the *Pontocho Kaburenjo*, Sanjo-agaru, Pontocho-dori, Nakagyo-ku. At *Gion Corner*, Hanamikoji Shijo-sagaru, Gion, between March and November, there is a twice-nightly geisha show for tourists that includes traditional arts such as *bunraku*, *kyogen*, tea ceremony and *koto*.

Cinema Plenty of cinemas show foreign films, mainly English-language.

Music The choice of music ranges from traditional Japanese through Western classical to rock at Kyoto's six concert halls.

Nightclubs Nightlife in Kyoto is rather subdued and comes to an end at 11.30. The lights stay on a little longer at the sophisticated *Maharaja Discotheque Saloon*, 2F Fuji Kanko Bldg, 574 Gionmachi Minamigawa, Higashiyama-ku.

Shopping

Kyoto is the place to buy traditional arts and handicrafts, such as Nishijin silk, Kiyomizu porcelain, lacquerware, elegant dolls, screens, fans and bronzes. For expensive but top-quality goods, visit the arcades of the Miyako, Kyoto and International hotels. For window shopping the area around Kawaramachi and the river, between Sanjo and Shijo, is a warren of arcades and little lanes full of interesting shops. Teramachi, a few blocks in from Kawaramachi, is lined with dark old houses, including *Ippodo*, which is the best place to buy tea-ceremony tea, and curio and antique shops. Ninnenzaka and Sannenzaka, on the way to Kiyomizu, are full of little pottery and handicraft shops.

Department stores Kyoto's best department stores are *Takashimaya* and *Hankyu*, both at Shijo Kawaramachi, and *Daimaru*, on Shijo.

Gifts There are many shops selling Kyoto handicrafts in the main shopping street along *Kawaramachi* between Shijo and Oike-dori, and on the two covered arcades parallel to Kawaramachi to the west. For a less commercialized atmosphere, take a leisurely stroll around *Ninnenzaka* and *Sannenzaka*, near Kiyomizu Temple. The tour buses always stop at the *Kyoto Handicraft Centre*, Kumano Jinja Higashi, Sakyo-ku. Here you can watch craftsmen at work and buy their products, including silk, dolls, woodblock prints, lacquerware and pottery. You could also try the *Kyoto Craft Centre*, 275 Gionmachi Kitagawa, Higashiyama-ku, which also features craftsmen at work, and the basement shop in the *Kyoto Museum of Traditional Industry*, Nijo-dori, Okazaki, Sakyo-ku. Kyoto also has some outstanding specialist shops. The most famous doll shop in Japan is *Tanakaya*, Shijo Yanaginobamba, Shimogyo-ku. For fans, go to *Miyawaki Baisen-an*, Tominokoji-nishi, Rokkaku-dori, Nakagyo-ku, and for folk art to *Yamato Mingei-ten*, Takoyakushi-agaru, Kawaramachi, Nakagyo-ku.

Antiques Kyoto is full of antique shops, mainly very expensive. The arcades of the top hotels have goods of an assured quality at high prices, and you can be certain at least of high prices in the little antique shops along *Shinmonzen* and *Furumonzen*, between Sanjo and Shijo, and down *Teramachi*. For pottery and curios, wander the small streets around Kiyomizu Temple.

Markets There are markets at the YWCA *Thrift Shop* on the third Saturday of each month, and at *Toji Temple* on the 21st and *Kitano Shrine* on the 25th of each month. Go early for the best selection.

Sightseeing

It would be a hopeless task to attempt to see all of Kyoto's 1,650 Buddhist temples, 400 Shinto shrines, 60 temple gardens, 3 palaces and half a dozen museums. The best approach is simply to stroll through a chosen area, such as northern Kyoto or Higashiyama, where you will discover tiny temples well off the tourist track, as well as some of the more important ones. You will, however, need to make arrangements in advance to see four of Kyoto's most famous sights – the three palaces (the Old Imperial Palace, Katsura and the Shugakuin) and Saihoji, the Moss Temple. Make sure you do so, through your hotel or any JNTO (tourist office) or JTB office, as soon as you arrive in Kyoto, at the very latest. Most temples and shrines are open from 9 to 5. To avoid other tourists it is best to make an early start.

Daitokuji Temple You could spend half a day simply wandering through the grounds of Daitokuji, a functioning Zen temple in the north of Kyoto. Of its many small sub-temples, four are open to the public. Koto-in and Zuiho-in have classic Zen gardens and fine works of art. *Daitokuji, Kita-ku.*

Ginkakuji Temple The Silver Pavilion was built in 1489 as the retreat of the shogun Yoshimasa Ashikaga. A devotee of the tea ceremony, he had a tiny house constructed for it here, the first in Japan. The garden, designed for moon-viewing, was built by the great Soami. After the shogun's death, the villa became a temple. *Ginkakuji, Sakyo-ku.*

Heian Shrine The most famous of Kyoto's shrines, built in 1895, is a model of the old Imperial Palace. Its grounds are particularly beautiful at cherry blossom time. *Okazaki, Higashiyama-ku.*

Katsura Imperial Villa It is well worth the trouble of getting a pass to see the Katsura Imperial Villa. Built for a brother of the Emperor, and completed in 1624, the magnificent villa took 27 years to build, and is considered one of the pinnacles of Japanese architecture. Tea houses, moon-viewing pavilions and lakes with tiny islands are scattered around the grounds, which were designed by the great Kobori Enshu and are considered the most perfect of all Japanese gardens. *Katsura Rikyu, Nishikyo-ku. Open daily exc Sat pm, Sun and 2nd and 4th Sat of month.*

Kinkakuji Temple The Golden Pavilion, one of Kyoto's most famous and beautiful temples, is completely covered in gold leaf and exquisitely set in a small lake. It was originally built by Yoshimitsu, the third Ashikaga shogun, in 1397. The pavilion was burned to the ground by a mad priest in 1950 and rebuilt exactly as before. *Kinugasa, Kita-ku.*

Kiyomizu Temple This magnificent temple, jutting out of the hillside supported on great wooden pillars, was built in 1633. Spectacular views of the city from its balcony. *Kiyomizu-dera, Higashiyama-ku.*

Kyoto National Museum The ideal place for a rainy day, this is one of Japan's best museums, with a fine collection of paintings, pottery, lacquerware and armour. *527 Chayamachi, Higashiyama-ku. Open Tue–Sun 9–4.30.*

Nanzenji Temple There are 12 sub-temples in this vast complex, noted for the 16thC paintings on its sliding doors and a beautiful garden of white sand and rocks. *Okazaki, Higashiyama-ku.*

Nijo Castle Built in 1603, Nijo Castle was the Kyoto residence of the first great Tokugawa shogun, Ieyasu. While enjoying a lavish lifestyle in this opulent villa, surrounded by priceless works of art, the shogun was ever mindful of security. The "nightingale floors" of the corridors creak under the lightest tread, to warn the guards of any intruders. In Ieyasu's time there were no trees in the magnificent landscaped gardens, for the falling leaves reminded him of death. *Nijo-jo, Nakagyo-ku.*

Nishi Honganji The little-known Nishi Honganji, main temple of the Jodo Shinshu Buddhist sect, was originally built as an imperial palace and is one of Kyoto's finest temples. Ask to be shown the beautiful painted wooden screens and old Noh theatre inside the temple. *Shimogyo-ku.*

Old Imperial Palace The original palace of the emperors, farther to the north west, was razed by fire in 1788, and the present palace dates from 1854. To join a tour (10am and 2pm), arrive 20mins beforehand with your passport. *Kamigyo-ku. Open daily exc Sat pm, Sun and 2nd and 4th Sat of month.*

Ryoanji Temple Arrive very early, before the crowds, to savour the tranquillity of this most famous of Zen gardens. *Ukyo-ku.*

Saihoji Temple You will have to reserve in advance and pay a sizeable fee to enter Saihoji, the Moss Temple. The temple and garden,

with its heart-shaped pond and hundred varieties of moss, were designed in 1339 by Muso Kokushi. *Saihoji, 56 Kamigayacho, Matsuo, Nishikyo-ku ☎ 391 3631.*

Sanjusangendo This popular temple houses 1,001 images of Kannon, the thousand-armed goddess of mercy, clustered around a large image carved in 1254. *Higashiyama-ku.*

Shugakuin Imperial Villa Set in the hills overlooking the city, the Shugakuin has beautiful and extensive gardens dotted with pavilions and tea ceremony rooms. It was built in 1629 as a retirement villa for the Emperor Gomizuno-o. You will have to make an appointment to join a tour. *Sakyo-ku. Open daily exc Sat pm, Sun and 2nd and 4th Sat of month.*

Walking routes
The most satisfying way to get to know Kyoto is to explore small parts of it on foot. You can get detailed walking maps at the Tourist Information Centre.

Higashiyama There is a pleasant walk from Kiyomizu Temple through winding lanes across Maruyama Park to Heian Shrine, taking about 1hr.

The Philosopher's Path Beginning at Ginkakuji, follow the philosopher's footsteps along the canal lined with cherry trees to Nanzenji, a 50min walk.

Kinkakuji and Ryoanji This 40min walk will take you through northern Kyoto's tree-lined backstreets and into two of its most beautiful temples.

Arashiyama Take a circular route around Arashiyama to enjoy its temples, hills and rushing river – a walk of about 80mins.

Ohara Allow half a day to visit this lovely country area. A gentle stroll around the *Jakko-in* and *Sanzen-in temples*, with their sad and romantic history, will take 2hrs.

Guided tours
Half-day bus tours, with English-speaking guides and a pick-up service from main hotels, cover some of Kyoto's major sights; you can also

combine a morning and an afternoon tour. Contact *JTB* ☎ *361 7241*, *Fujita Travel Service* ☎ 222 0121 or *Kinki Nippon Tourist* ☎ 222 1224. There are also tours of the Inaba cloisonné workshops and the Yuzen silk-dyeing centre.

Spectator sports

Rugby The only sport at which Kyoto shines is rugby. Kyoto's *Doshisha University* team is the best team in Japan, and there are annual matches in December and January at the team's home ground, *Hanazono Stadium*.

Keeping fit

There are limited keep-fit and sporting opportunities in Kyoto itself, but more in the nearby countryside and around Lake Biwa. Of the Kyoto hotels, the Holiday Inn has by far the best sporting facilities, most of which are open to non-residents for a fee.
Cycling There is a 10km/6-mile cycling course around Arashiyama and Sagano, starting from Hankyu Arashiyama station. Rent a bicycle at *Cycpick*, Hankyu Arashiyama ☎ 882 1111, or *Keihan Rent-a-cycle*, Togetsukyo Arashiyama ☎ 861 1656.
Fitness centres There is a well-equipped health centre in the Holiday Inn. Of the public health centres, the following are open to non-members or have a nominal membership fee.
Kampo Kyoto, 13 Shurishikicho, Matsugasaki, Sakyo-ku ☎ 721 3111, has a gym and sauna.
Kyoto City Sports, 23 Shironokoshi, Shimotoba, Fushimi-ku ☎ 621 8188, is a vast sports centre with a gym, a 100-metre/110-yd indoor running track, racquetball and tennis courts, swimming pools, a sauna and a hot-spring bath. Kyoto's classiest health centre is *Act One*, 2F Gondolia-Mibu Bldg, 53 Mibuboujyocho, Nakagyo-ku ☎ 841 1596, which offers weight training, a gym, and a personal fitness programme.
Hiking There is good hiking in the mountains that surround Kyoto. The

nearest is *Mount Hiei*, in the northeast, and there are also hiking courses in Biwako Valley. Check *Kansai Time Out* for monthly hikes organized by the *Kansai Ramblers*.
Jogging In the morning there are plenty of joggers along the banks of the Kamo, Takano and Katsura rivers. Kyoto's tree-lined back streets are ideal for joggers, and you can also jog around Nijo Castle.
Skiing The nearest ski slopes are in the mountains to the west of Lake Biwa, at *Biwako Valley* ☎ (06) 343 1271, *Hirasan* ☎ (07759) 60516, and, farther north, at *Hakodateyama* ☎ (0740) 22 2486. Buses bound for the ski areas pick up in Kyoto; contact *Big Tour Osaka Centre* ☎ (06) 363 0451.
Swimming There are indoor pools in the ANA and Grand hotels and in the Holiday Inn. The public pools are, as everywhere, very crowded. For outdoor swimming, go to Lake Biwa, the largest freshwater lake in Japan, or head north to the relatively clean beaches along the Japan Sea coast.
Tennis Try the Holiday Inn, or book well in advance at the *Ohara Green Tennis Club* Uenocho, Ohara, Sakyo-ku ☎ 744 2461 (open to non-members).
Windsurfing Contact *All Kansai Windsurfing* ☎ (0775) 79 0333 or *Biwako Adventure Sports* ☎ (0775) 72 1254 if you want to windsurf on Lake Biwa.

Local resources

Business services

The only formal business service centres are at the ANA, Brighton and Takaragaike Prince; but all the major hotels will make every effort to meet your requirements. Otherwise try the Kyoto branch of *Manpower Japan* ☎ 241 2030.
Photocopying and printing You can arrange photocopying or printing through your hotel. Some department stores, camera shops and stationers have photocopiers.
Secretarial For secretarial assistance, try *Career Staff* ☎ 255 5691.

Communications

International Couriers DHL
☎ 661 7255.
Post office Main office: Kyoto
station, Shimogyo-ku, open 24hrs.
Inquiries ☎ 365 2471.
Telex and fax At major hotels,
Manpower Japan (see above) and KDD
Telecom Kyoto, 338 Tominagacho,
Matsubara-agaru 2-chome,
Kawaramachi-dori, Shimogyo-ku
☎ 341 2733.

Conference/exhibition centres

The *Kyoto International Conference
Hall*, Takaragaike, Sakyo-ku, 606
☎ 791 3111 is one of the largest and
best equipped convention centres in
Asia. Exhibitions and trade fairs are
also held at the *Kyoto Trade Fair
Centre* 21 Nakajima, Horibatacho,
Fushimi-ku ☎ 611 0011.

Emergencies

Bureaux de change At major hotels,
open seven days a week, from early
until late.
Hospitals The following hospitals
provide emergency service at night
and on holidays and weekends; you
will be accepted only if you arrive by
ambulance: *Kyoto First Red Cross
Hospital*, 15-749 Honmachi,
Higashiyama-ku ☎ 561 1121; *Kyoto
Second Red Cross Hospital*,
Marutamachi-sagaru, Kamanza-dori,
Kamigyo-ku ☎ 231 5171; and *Kyoto
Prefectural University of Medicine
Hospital*, Hirokoji, Kawaramachi-
dori, Kamikyo-ku ☎ 251 5111.
There are two American doctors at
the *Japan Baptist Hospital*, 47
Yamanomotocho, Kitashirakawa,
Sakyo-ku ☎ 781 5191. For
emergency dental service, contact
*Kyoto Prefecture Emergency Dental
Clinic*, 33 Gosho Dencho,
Murasakino, Kita-ku ☎ 441 7174;
their south Kyoto clinic is at
Imamachi, Fushimi-ku ☎ 622 3000.
Pharmacies Prescription drugs are
issued only by hospitals. There are no
24hr pharmacies.
Police Kyoto Prefectural Police ☎ 451
9111. In an emergency ☎ 110.

Government offices

For enquiries about local government
departments and services, contact the
Kyoto City Government, Oike
Kawaramachi, Nakagyo-ku
☎ 222 3111.

Information sources

*Business information Kyoto Chamber
of Commerce*, Ebisugawa-agaru,
Karasuma-dori, Nakagyo-ku ☎ 231
0181.
Local media Many international
newspapers are available in Kyoto. Of
the five locally-produced English-
language papers, the *Mainichi Daily
News*, based in Osaka, carries news
and information relevant to Kansai
and is the most useful. The lively
monthly *Kansai Time Out* has articles
on Kyoto and listings of local events.
The locally produced *Kyoto Visitor's
Guide* is also full of useful
information – articles, listings and
shopping and restaurant suggestions.
The only English-language television
is the cable news channel transmitted
to major hotels.
Tourist Information The staff at
the Kyoto *Tourist Information Office*,
Kyoto Tower Bldg, Higashi-
Shiokojicho, Shimogyo-ku
☎ 371 5649, are extremely
efficient, knowledgeable and
friendly and will load you down with
maps, literature and information.
They have a bulletin board of the
week's events. For the Japan Travel
Phone, a TIC service, ☎ 371 5649
within Kyoto, and for the TIC
recorded information service ☎ 361
2911. For enjoyment as well as
information, read *Kyoto, a
Contemplative Guide* and *Old Kyoto, a
Guide to Traditional Shops, Restaurants
and Inns*.

Thank-yous

Uji tea is the standard gift to buy in
Kyoto. Buy it beautifully gift-
wrapped from *Takashimaya* ☎ 221
8811, who will also deliver, or, for
the ultimate in finesse, from *Ippodo*,
Teramachi, Nakagyo-ku ☎ 211 3421,
Japan's best tea shop.

NAGOYA

City code ☎ 052

Japan's fourth largest city and third largest port lies in the middle of the Tokyo-Hiroshima megalopolis and is the only stop on the Hikari Bullet Train between Tokyo and Kyoto. Nagoya is a prosperous commercial and industrial city, with a population of over 2m. Heavy industries – primarily automobile manufacture, plus the production of rolling stock, chemicals and textiles – thrive alongside traditional light industries such as ceramics, for which this area has been famous since the 12thC. Advanced technological plants are now under development, and coastal waters are being reclaimed to meet the need for more industrial land.

Japan's three great historical warlords (see *Sightseeing*) hailed from this area, and the city grew up around their strongholds and around the great castle that Tokugawa Ieyasu built here in 1612 for his son. In the 1930s Nagoya became a centre of the aircraft and munitions industries, and in consequence it became a prime target for US bombers and was completely flattened in World War II. It has since regained its former prosperity and continues to expand and internationalize (the current by-word). In 1989, the one-hundredth anniversary of the city's founding, it hosted the World Design Exposition. Long-term plans include the building of an off-shore international airport in the Bay of Ise and the construction of a superconductive magnetic levitation train line which will link Nagoya to Tokyo in less than an hour.

Arriving

More and more international airlines are establishing offices and landing rights at Nagoya airport. Currently travellers arriving from Hong Kong, Seoul, Manila, Singapore, Vancouver and Sydney, Australia, have the option of flying direct to Nagoya; it is also worthwhile flying from more distant parts of Japan. From Tokyo it is quicker and simpler to take the Bullet Train.

Komaki airport

In terms of importance and size, Komaki is third after Tokyo's Narita and Osaka's Itami airports. The small amount of international traffic that passes through is handled quickly and efficiently, and there are flights to all major Japanese cities. A variety of restaurants, coffee shops and bars are open until 9pm on landside, but facilities are very limited on airside; executive lounge, shops selling local foods and souvenirs, of interest mainly to Japanese travellers, and one bank. Information ☎ (0568) 28 5633.

City link If you have little luggage or are staying near the railway station, the bus is a reasonably fast and convenient way of getting into the city.

Taxi A taxi is more convenient than the bus, but only a little quicker and much more expensive.

Car rental It is difficult to find your way from Komaki to Nagoya, and if you plan to drive in the city, it is better to pick up a car in town. At Komaki there are branches of Japan Rentacar, Nippon and Mazda.

Bus The bus to Meitetsu bus centre, near Nagoya station, departs every 15mins, and takes about 40mins.

Railway stations

The Bullet Train takes just under 2hrs from Tokyo, 45mins from Kyoto and 60mins from Osaka.

Nagoya station The station is enormous and the Bullet Train tracks are inconveniently located on the far side, away from the city centre. The JR lines out to the suburbs depart from here, as does the Kintetsu line and the Meitetsu line (though this is difficult to find). The station area itself is a hive of activity, with five hotels and three department stores nearby. Inquiries ☎ 564 2444.

Getting around

After Nagoya's total destruction in the war, it was rebuilt in a neat grid, with wide boulevards dividing the town into areas. As a result, it is particularly easy to find your way around the central district on foot. Unless you want to go somewhere very out-of-the-way, you will find taxis and the subway system the most convenient modes of transport.

Taxis Taxis are plentiful, and the drivers are fairly efficient at finding their way around. There are always taxis waiting in the ranks at the station and outside the major hotels, but you should have no problem flagging them down on the streets.

Limousines Teisan Auto Company ☎ 911 1351 and *Tokyu Shachi Bus* ☎ 913 1111 offer cars with drivers, a few of whom speak some English.

Driving Although the streets are wide and straight, they tend to be congested, particularly at rush hours, and parking is a problem. If you want to drive, the main car rental chains have branches in the city.

Bus Nagoya has an extensive bus system, best avoided unless you can read Japanese.

Subway Nagoya's subways are fast and comfortable, but extremely crowded during the morning and evening rush hours. A very useful map in English is available from the Tourist Information Centre (TIC). There are four lines, one of which links the station to Fushimi and Sakae, the main interchanges. The station names are marked in English, and platforms are indicated by the destination of the train. If you are making more than five journeys, it is worthwhile buying a one-day pass, valid on buses as well as the subway; buy one at any main subway station.

Train Of the train lines out to the suburbs, the private Kintetsu and Meitetsu lines are cheaper, more frequent and more comfortable than the JR lines.

Area by area

In spite of its modern grid plan, Nagoya is still an old castle town. The former samurais' neighbourhood, now simply the wealthier section of town, lies just outside the castle wall, with the "pleasure quarters" a respectable distance away. Until recently, the station formed the boundary of the main city, but now the urban sprawl beyond is being transformed into an area of offices and hotels.

Fushimi An area of soaring office blocks and wide boulevards, Fushimi is the business centre of this primarily business city. Here, alongside Nagoya's top hotels, the Hilton and the Kanko, you will find branches of the major banks, and offices of local and national corporations. The Nagoya Chamber of Commerce and Industry is to the south.

Sakae Here, too, are offices spreading up and down the wide and green Hisaya-Odori, "Park Way", which runs north-south through the city. But most people come for the shops, restaurants, bars, cabarets and cinemas, and at night Sakae is the place to be.

Nagoya Castle area This is where the samurai families used to live, well removed from the hustle and bustle of the city centre. Among the old houses and smart residences are exclusive *ryotei* and the city and prefectural government buildings.

The suburbs

Many of Nagoya's wealthiest families live in the cool hills along the eastern edge of the city, in the Motoyama-Yamate district, near Nagoya University. This is an area of parks and greenery, including Higashiyama Botanical Gardens. Many people commute into Nagoya from Ichinomiya and Inuyama, smart residential towns a short train ride to the north.

Hotels

While the Castle and the Kanko are the city's grand old hotels, owned by old Nagoya families and favoured by Nagoyans, the new Hilton and the Tokyu provide stiff competition and for both location and facilities undoubtedly have the edge. New international hotels are planned, beginning with a new ANA.

Castle ⓨ‖
3-19 Hinokuchicho, Nishi-ku, 451
☎ *521 2121* ⓉⓍ *4452988 fax 531 3313*
• *AE DC MC V* • *237 rooms, 4 suites, 4 restaurants, 2 bars, 2 coffee shops*
Nagoya's grandest (but not its oldest) hotel stretches along the moat-side, directly opposite Nagoya Castle. The bedrooms, all with minibar, are huge and attractively furnished; all but the single rooms have views of the castle. There are original oil paintings in each room and in the lobby. The top-floor restaurant and bar, with their views of the castle, floodlit at night,

are classy and popular, and Rosen (see *Bars*) is where many executives, both Japanese and Western, meet after work for a civilized drink. Concierge, theatre and travel bookings, shops, beauty salon • health club with gym, pool and sauna • secretarial services, 13 meeting rooms (capacity up to 3,500).

Castle Plaza ⓨ‖
4-3-25 Mei-eki, Nakamura-ku, 450
☎ *582 2121* ⓉⓍ *59678 fax 582 8666*
• *AE DC MC V* • *260 rooms, 2 suites, 4 restaurants, 1 bar*

HOTELS

1 Castle
2 Castle Plaza
3 Hilton
4 International
5 Kanko
6 Miyako
7 Tokyu
8 Daiichi
9 Fuji Park
10 Meitetsu Grand
11 Meitetsu New Grand
12 Sakae Tokyu Inn
13 Terminal

RESTAURANTS

1 Kawabun
2 Koraku
3 Mishima
4 Shoumon
5 Torikyu
6 Hakuakan
7 Hotel Okura /Tohkalin
8 Zambi

9 Hasshokan
10 Yuzen
11 Kase
12 Ibasho
13 Ushijima
14 L'Etoile du Geant
15 Bistro de Chouchou
16 Matenro

BUILDINGS AND SIGHTS

1 Aichi-ken Trade Centre
2 Central post office
3 JETRO
4 JTB
5 Matsuzakaya department store
6 Mitsukoshi department store
7 Chamber of commerce
8 Nagoya International Centre
9 Television Tower
10 TIC
11 Aichi Cultural Centre

NAGOYA CASTLE

Nagoya Station

FUSHIMI-DORI

HONMACHI-DORI

NISHIKI-DORI

While top executives stay at the Castle, the Castle Plaza caters for their junior colleagues. The rooms are neat and reasonably spacious, and there is an excellent range of sporting facilities. Arcade of shops ● health club with pool, jogging tracks, gym and sauna ● 10 meeting rooms (capacity up to 500).

Hilton 〽//
1-3-3 Sakae, Naka-ku ☎ *212 1111* TX
4422121 fax 212 1225 ● *AE DC MC V*
● *427 rooms, 26 suites, 4 restaurants, 2 bars, 2 coffee shops/tea lounges*
The new Hilton (opened March 1989) is Japan's newest Hilton, Nagoya's tallest building and, for travelling executives, undoubtedly the city's best hotel. Located midway between the station and Sakae, in the heart of the Fushimi business district, it is designed specifically with the needs of

the business traveller in mind. The rooms are not only spacious but luxuriously furnished, with thick carpets, duvets and big desks; all rooms are equipped with minibars. The executive floors have magnificent views over the city; privileges include use of the executive lounge, complimentary breakfast and complimentary use of the fitness centre. The business service centre is the best in town. 24hr room service, express checkout, concierge and booking services, arcade of quality shops ● fitness centre with gym, pool, sauna and tennis courts ● business service centre, 10 meeting rooms (capacity up to 1,200).

International 〽//
3-23-3 Nishiki, Naka-ku, 460
☎ *961 3111* TX *4443720*
fax 962 5937 ● *AE DC MC V* ●

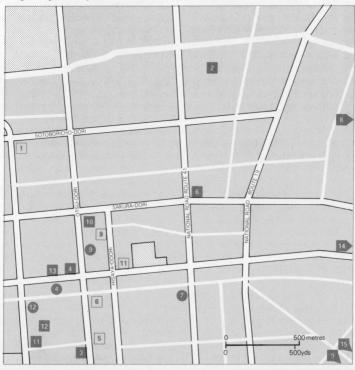

*252 rooms, 8 suites, 3 restaurants,
2 bars, 2 coffee shops*
The International, conveniently
located right in Sakae, has long been
popular with business travellers.
There are several types of single
room, including spacious rooms and
large bright singles decorated in lime
greens and yellows. Avoid the
cheapest singles, which are very dark.
Concierge, travel bookings, shops,
beauty salon • special rates at the
Copin International Sports Club with
gym and sauna • 13 meeting rooms
(capacity up to 500).

Kanko *Y||*
1-19-30 Nishiki, Naka-ku, 460 ☎ *231
7711* ᴛx *4427413 fax 231 7719* • *AE
DC MC V* • *496 rooms, 9 suites, 3
restaurants, 3 bars, 3 coffee shops*
The Kanko is ideally located in the
middle of the Fushimi business area,
equidistant from the station and
Sakae. There has been a Kanko here
since 1936, which makes it the oldest
of the city hotels. The bedrooms all
have huge windows and window seats
and are comfortably furnished. Many
of the guests are foreign, mainly
business travellers. Arcade of shops,
hairdresser • 12 meeting rooms
(capacity up to 1,200).

Miyako *Y||*
4-9-10 Mei-eki, Nakamura-ku, 450
☎ *571 3211* ᴛx *4422086
fax 271 3242* • *398 rooms, 2 suites,
3 restaurants, 1 bar, 2 coffee shops*
The tranquil Miyako, just around the
corner from the station, is popular
with visiting international artists and
musicians as well as businessmen.
The rooms are large, light and
soundproofed, with a big desk, and
the service is up to the Miyako's
usual high standards. Arcade of
shops, beauty salon • 15 meeting
rooms (capacity up to 1,000)

Tokyu *Y||*
4-6-8 Sakae, 460 ☎ *251 2411*
ᴛx *4422046 fax 251 2422* • *AE DC
MC V* • *553 rooms, 15 suites,
3 restaurants, 1 bar, 1 coffee shop*

The biggest Tokyu yet features an
atrium lobby that is literally
breathtaking, with pillars, classical
porticoes, waterfalls, acres of marble
and full-size trees. The Versailles
Ballroom, aglitter with chandeliers,
doubles as a vast convention hall, and
there is also an exceptionally well-
equipped sports centre. The rooms
are altogether more modest, in both
scale and decor, though still a good
size and perfectly serviceable.
Concierge and booking services,
arcade of shops • well-equipped
fitness centre with pool, gym, sauna,
snack bars • secretarial services,
11 meeting rooms (capacity up to
2,000).

OTHER HOTELS
Daiichi *Y|* *3-27-5 Mei-eki,
Nakamura-ku, 450* ☎ *581 4411*
ᴛx *9517269 fax 581 4427* • *AE
DC MC V*. One of the cluster of new
hotels around the station, this is
unusually attractive.
Fuji Park *Y|* *3-15-30 Nishiki,
Naka-ku, 460* ☎ *962 2289*
ᴛx *4444489 fax 951 7269* • *AE
DC MC V*. A small, quiet, pleasant
hotel, in the heart of Sakae.
Meitetsu Grand *Y|* *1-2-4 Mei-
eki, Nakamura-ku, 450* ☎ *582 2211*
ᴛx *4422031 fax 582 2230* • *AE DC MC
V*. On the top floors of a department
store a few minutes' walk from the
station, popular with Japanese
business travellers.
Meitetsu New Grand *Y|* *6-9
Tsubakicho, Nakamura-ku, 453*
☎ *452 5511* ᴛx *4432803 fax 452 5893*
• *AE DC MC V*. The first hotel in the
developing area at the back of Nagoya
station, very close to the Bullet Train
exit.
Sakae Tokyu Inn *Y* *3-1-8 Sakae,
Naka-ku, 460* ☎ *251 0109*
ᴛx *4422550 fax 251 0299* • *AE DC
MC V*. Midway between Fushimi and
Sakae.
Terminal *Y|* *1-2-1 Mei-eki,
Nakamura-ku, 450* ☎ *561 3751*
ᴛx *4457263 fax 581 3236* • *AE
DC MC V*. Right inside the station,
the ageing Terminal is still popular.

Restaurants

Nagoya has plenty of restaurants to cater for its large business community, ranging from exclusive *ryotei* in the suburbs out towards the castle, to the small restaurants lining the streets around Sakae, where you stop off for a quick bite before moving on to a bar. *Cochin*, Nagoya chicken, is considered the best in Japan and is the speciality of several of Nagoya's finest restaurants.

JAPANESE

Kawabun *Y*////
2-12-19 Marunouchi, Naka-ku
☎ *231 1381 • closed Sun*
The somewhat run-down exterior of this venerable *ryotei* – located in a dusty backstreet behind the Hotel Okura Restaurant – belies its true status. Entry to its *tatami* rooms is restricted to the city's leaders and top executives and their guests. If your host does you the honour of bringing you here, you will dine on *kaiseki*, featuring, of course, Nagoya chicken, in the most elegant of surroundings.

Koraku *Y*////
3-3 Chikaramachi, Higashi-ku
☎ *931 3472 • closed Sun*
To enter Koraku you go through a thatched gate, up a winding path of mossy stepping stones, past a tea-house to your left, around a brushwood fence, and arrive at the imposing entrance of this ancient samurai mansion, where you are greeted by ladies in kimonos. If you are not with one of their distinguished regular customers, this is as far as you will get, for Koraku is one of Nagoya's most exclusive *ryotei*. The highly privileged can discover whether the chicken dishes here are truly, as the restaurant claims, the best in Nagoya.

Mishima *Y*/
3-27-4 Sakae, Naka-ku ☎ *242 0828*
At Mishima, the humble sardine becomes a delicacy. Every dish in this elegant restaurant, in a lovely old Japanese house, contains sardines – raw, grilled, simmered, or brought to the table resting on a fragrant leaf of the *ho* tree, on a flaming charcoal brazier.

Shoumon *Y*////
2F No 5 Nishiki Bldg, 3-17-1 Nishiki, Naka-ku ☎ *951 2920 • AE DC MC V*
• reservations recommended
Despite its humble appearance, tucked away in the heart of Sakae, Shoumon is the city's top venue for business dining. This is where top Mitsubishi and Toyota executives are entertained, and the restaurant is always full of faces famous in Japan, from TV stars and kabuki actors to sumo wrestlers and baseball stars. As to the cuisine, it is steak, cooked sumiyaki style, over charcoal; and it is said to be the best steak in Nagoya.

Torikyu *Y*/
1-1-15 Mei-eki Minami, Nakamura-ku
☎ *541 1888 • closed Sun*
Torikyu is a fine and famous restaurant which welcomes all comers. It backs onto the river, and in the old days customers used to arrive by boat. The food here is chicken, raw, grilled, in a casserole, or in *kaiseki*. You may well come here in a party with your Japanese colleagues and take over one of the spacious tatami rooms overlooking the river.

NON-JAPANESE

Hakuakan *Y*/
B1 Yokota Bldg, 2-28-24 Izumi, Higashi-ku ☎ *931 1569 • closed Mon*
• AE DC MC V
At Hakuakan, which means "white house", everything, from the heavy chandeliers to the ornate period furniture and cabinets full of porcelain, is French. Chef Tani trained at Tokyo's prestigious Chez Inno (see *Tokyo Restaurants*), and his classic and *nouvelle* cooking is highly rated by the business community.

Hotel Okura Restaurant $\boxed{Y}$/
25F Tokyo Kaijo Bldg, 2-2-19
Marunouchi, Naka-ku ☎ *201 3201* ●
AE DC MC V
For prestige, this is certainly
Nagoya's top Western restaurant.
Chief executives wine and dine each
other here, and it is an appropriate
place to return hospitality. Chef
Tsuneo Fukuda hails from the Tokyo
Okura, and the menu covers all the
major European cuisines. The wine
list is equally eclectic.

Tohkalin $\boxed{Y}$/
25F Tokyo Kaijo Bldg, 2-2-19
Marunouchi, Naka-ku ☎ *201 3201* ●
AE DC V ● *reservations essential*
Much of Nagoya's business
entertaining takes place within the
private rooms of Tokhalin. Among
other Cantonese delights, chef Ryo
Juno (from Hong Kong) prepares
whole roast piglet (order a week in
advance), braised deer tail and bear
paw.

Zambi $\boxed{Y}$/
7-17 Daikancho, Higashi-ku
☎ *936 4511-3* ● *AE DC MC V*
Zambi is a sophisticated restaurant bar,
dark and atmospheric, with log walls,
potted palms and spotlights, hidden
inside a Japanese house in the suburbs.
Late in the evening Nagoya's
international community gathers here to
drink, talk and snack. Zambi is open
until 2am, and businessmen drop in for
steaks and seafood, plus a liberal dose of
alcohol. There is live piano music as the
night draws on.

OTHER RESTAURANTS
For those who value such
information, *Hasshokan*, 29 Ishizaka,
Yagoto Hirojicho, Showa-ku
☎ 831 1585, is Nagoya's most
famous and venerable *ryotei*. It is set
in a beautiful garden, the china is
priceless and designed by the
celebrated artist Rosanjin, and it was
a favourite of the late Emperor.
Needless to say, it is not open to the
public. For more accessible *kaiseki*,
try *Yuzen*, 10F Annex, 3-5-4 Nishiki

☎ 961 3190, or *Kase*, 3-20-19 Sakae
☎ 251 8494, both in the Sakae area.
For eel, *Ibasho*, 3-13-22 Sakae ☎ 951
1166, is said to be the best. And for
vegetarians and anyone who is curious
about the possibilites of tofu, Nagoya
is blessed with a chain of tofu
restaurants, *Suzu no ya*; ask at your
hotel for the nearest branch. As for
Western food, *Ushijima*, 4F Yaozen
Bldg, Nishiki 3-chome, Naka-ku
☎ 962 3344, is grand and famous for
its steak. *L'Etoile du Geant*, 1-8
Horiwaricho, Chikusa-ku
☎ 762 0077, is a renowned French
restaurant. The favourite of Nagoya's
French community is *Bistro de
Chouchou*, Yamate Ave, 70
Yamazatocho, Showa-ku ☎ 833 9907,
whose chef, Namba-san, spent 10
years in France. For Cantonese
cooking, the newly opened *Matenro*,
17F Nitochi Nagoya Bldg, 2-1-1
Sakae ☎ 204 0058, is worth
investigating.

Bars
A Nagoya night might begin with a
drink in a sober hotel bar, such as the
Castle's *Rosen*, in an atmosphere
more like a gentlemen's club than a
bar. Many high-powered discussions
are concluded and vital decisions
made in the deep leather armchairs
around its well-spaced tables.
Business travellers are also to be
found in the Hilton's *Seasons Bar*, the
Tokyu's *Fontana di Trevi*, and the
Gaslight, 10F Daini Washington
Hotel, 3-12-22 Nishiki, Naka-ku. The
Gaslight is also favoured by young
Japanese businessmen, who meet here
before moving on to the sleazier dives
of Sakae.
   Urubana, 2F Eizen Bldg, Nishiki
3-chome, is a Brazilian bar and the
place to find Nagoya's foreign
community, ranging from American
and Australian expatriates to
businessmen here for only a couple of
days.

Entertainment
Nagoya is the cultural centre of the
area, and visiting performers usually

stop here on their way to Kyoto and Osaka from Tokyo. Many performances take place at the *Aichi Cultural Centre*. The excellent monthly *Nagoya Calendar* will keep you up to date with what's on. Make reservations through your hotel or at Play Guide ticket agencies in major department stores.

Theatre, ballet and opera In any given month your choice of drama and dance at one of Nagoya's seven theatres might range from Ibsen to the Paris Opera to Ennosuke and his kabuki troupe up from Tokyo.

Cinema Most of Nagoya's many foreign films are English or American.

Music There is plenty of choice in Nagoya for everyone, from those who want to hear the *Yomiuri Nikkyo Orchestra* playing Stravinsky to lovers of sitar. The main venue for concerts is the *Aichi Cultural Centre*, Sakae.

Nightclubs Your Japanese colleagues will probably plan a full programme of evening activities for you. In the unlikely event of finding yourself at loose ends in Nagoya, you will meet fellow Westerners at the highly respectable *Playboy Club*, 12F Imaike Bldg, 5-1-5 Imaike Chikusaku; single women will also feel comfortable here. Another popular venue is the *Esquire Club*, No 3 Washington Bldg, 3-19-30 Nishiki, Naka-ku. For those who really want to let their hair down, *Star Eyes*, G House Bldg, 3-4-1 Kikusakacho, Chikusa-ku, is the place.

Shopping

The region around Nagoya is rich in traditions and handicrafts. Look for Seto pottery, handmade paper from Mino, paper lanterns and oiled paper umbrellas from Gifu, lacquerware and woodcarving from Takayama, and cloisonné, intricately tie-dyed fabric (*shibori*) and Noritake china from Nagoya itself. Most of the major shops are clustered around Sakae, where there is an underground warren of shopping arcades. There is a second smaller shopping centre

around and under Nagoya station.

Department stores Nagoya has six department stores, including two branches of *Matsuzakaya* and two of *Mitsukoshi*. *Meitetsu*, above Nagoya Meitetsu station, is associated with the Nagoya-based private railway line and has branches throughout the region.

Electrical goods *Radio Centre Ameyoko Bldg*, 3-30-86 Osu, Naka-ku, is a miniature version of Tokyo's Akihabara, packed with camera and electrical shops; you may pick up some bargains here.

Gifts To get some idea of the exceptionally fine local handcrafts available in Nagoya, begin by looking at the extensive selection in any of the major department stores. Jewellery made of pearls from the nearby Ise peninsula are sold by *K Mikimoto Co*, Chunichi Bldg, 4-1-1 Sakae, Naka-ku. For the best china, go direct to *Noritake Sales Ltd*, 2-1 Shinsakae, Naka-ku, and for cloisonné to *Ando Cloisonné*, 3-27-17 Sakae, Naka-ku. The craft shops in the arcades also have good selections.

Sightseeing

Many of the great battles of Japanese history took place in this region, and Japan's most famous warlords, Oda Nobunaga, Toyotomi Hideyoshi and Tokugawa Ieyasu all came from in or around Nagoya. Most of Nagoya's vestiges of grandeur were destroyed in World War II, but the surrounding area is rich in interest and historical remains.

Atsuta Shrine Atsuta Shrine, to the south of the city, is the home of the Sacred Grass-Mowing Sword (one of the emperor's three pieces of regalia) and one of Japan's three holiest shrines. It was founded in the 3rd century, and the great wooden buildings stand in glades of towering cedars.

Nagoya Castle The high point of most tours of the city is the castle. The present castle, sadly, is a 1959 ferroconcrete copy of Tokugawa Ieyasu's original, built for his son

Yoshinao in 1612, which was destroyed in the war. Even so, it is magnificent, set in beautiful grounds, and it houses a fine collection of art treasures from the old palace. *Open 9.30–4.30.*

Tokugawa Art Museum Built on the site of the Tokugawa mansion, the museum contains a splendid collection of Japanese paintings, ceramics, lacquerware and prints, amassed by the Tokugawa family. *Shindekimachi, Higashi-ku. Open daily Tue–Sun, 10–5.*

Toyota Automobile Museum Opened recently by the Toyota Corporation, this museum has a fine collection of cars from the late 19th century onwards. *Nagakute. Open daily Tue–Sun, 9.30–4.30.*

Guided tours
Half- and full-day tours of the city, covering the major sights, with a commentary in Japanese only, can be booked through the TIC or *Nagoya Yuran Bus* ☎ 561 4036. Be sure to reserve in advance if you want to take the popular *Industrial Tour*, every Friday, which visits factories such as Ando Cloisonné, Arimatsu Shibori (tie-dyeing) and Noritake (china); you can also visit these and other factories privately.

Out of town
Both *Kyoto* and *Nara* are a comfortable day trip from Nagoya, though each is well worth a longer visit. Nagoya is also a convenient base from which to visit *Ise*, the most important shrine in Japan. This has been a holy place for well over a thousand years, although the vast wooden buildings that you see are ceremonially rebuilt every 20 years (the last time was in 1973). If you have half a day to spare, visit *Inuyama*, 30kms/19 miles from Nagoya, and see Japan's oldest surviving castle, built in 1440. Just down the road from Inuyama is *Meiji Mura*, a marvellous collection of buildings from the Meiji era (1868–1912).

Spectator sports
Baseball Nagoya's Chunichi Dragons are a Central League team. Reserve well in advance to see them play on their home ground, *Nagoya Stadium* ☎ 351 5171 (office) or 2222 (tickets). ***Sumo*** The sumo giants do battle at the *Aichi Prefectural Gymnasium*, 1-1 Ninomaru, Naka-ku ☎ 971 2516, in July.

Keeping fit
Golf The *Forest Park* course in Kasugai, 18kms/12 miles north of Nagoya, is open to the public ☎ (056) 153 1551. Towards Ise is the *Shima* course ☎ (059) 947 3256, where you play on a sandy beach under pine trees.

Fitness centres Fitness centres have blossomed in many of the Nagoya hotels; there are excellent facilities in the Castle, Castle Plaza, Hilton and Tokyu. Of the public centres, the *Nagoya Sports Centre*, 1-60 Monzencho, Naka-ku ☎ 321 1591, has a wide range of facilities, including a skating rink, and is open to non-members. *Tsuyuhashi Sports Centre*, 2-14-1 Tsuyuhashi, Nakagawa-ku ☎ 362 4411 and *Nagoya Shampia Sports Centre*, 3-6-27 Shirogane, Showa-ku ☎ 871 4611, are a little farther out; both have heated pools.

Jogging The best area for jogging is around Nagoya Castle and Meijo Park; the longest course here is 4.6kms/3 miles long.

Swimming Outdoor pools are open during July and August only. There are indoor pools in the sports centres. ***Tennis*** There is more chance of a game of tennis in Nagoya than in Tokyo, although the odds are still against it. Try the *Odaka Ryokuchi* courts, Odakacho, Midori-ku ☎ 622 2282, *Obata Ryokuchi* courts, Obata, Moriyama-ku ☎ 791 9492, or the *Shonai Koen* courts, Nazukacho, Nishi-ku ☎ 522 8381.

Local resources
Business services
The Hilton has the best business

service centre in town, and there are also facilities at the Tokyu and Castle hotels. There are branches of *Manpower Japan* ☎ 962 7771 and *Kaken Co* ☎ 571 4131, nationwide companies providing a reasonably-wide range of business services.

Photocopying and printing All major hotels provide photocopying and will arrange for printing services.

Secretarial For secretarial services contact *Career Staff* ☎ 962 2228, *Temporary Centre Corporation* ☎ 586 4525 or *Tempstaff* ☎ 951 2357.

Translation Manpower Japan, International Translation and Printing and *ASI* ☎ 671 0358 will provide translators. For interpreters, the people to contact are *Manpower Japan* or *TS International Co* ☎ 951 2357.

Communications

International couriers DHL ☎ 571 1455.

Post offices The main post office, at Nagoya station ☎ 564 2100, is open 24hrs.

Telex and fax All hotels provide telex and fax services; otherwise go to *KDD Nagoya* ☎ 203 3311.

Conference/exhibition centres

Conferences are generally held either in a hotel or at the *Nagoya International Centre*, 1-47-1 Nagono, Nakamura-ku ☎ 581 5678. The main exhibition halls are *Nagoya Trade and Industry Centre*, 2-6 Fukiage, Chikusa-ku ☎ 735 2111, *Nagoya International Exhibition Hall*, 2-2 Kinjo Futo, Minato-ku ☎ 398 1771, and *Aichi-ken Trade Centre*, 3-1-6 Marunouchi, Naka-ku ☎ 231 6351. For inquiries contact *Nagoya Convention and Visitors' Bureau*, 2-10-19 Sakae, Naka-ku ☎ 201 5733.

Emergencies

Hospitals 170 hospitals and 989 clinics take part in Nagoya's 24hr medical care system. In an emergency ☎ 119 for an ambulance or call the *Medical Care Information Centre* ☎ 263 1133, who will tell you the nearest hospital available.

Pharmacies Hospitals supply prescription drugs.

Police Aichi Prefectural Police Headquarters ☎ 951 1611.

Government offices

For inquiries about local government departments and services, contact *Nagoya City Office*, 3-1-1 San-no-maru, Naka-ku ☎ 961 1111; for information on the prefecture, *Aichi Prefectural Government Office* ☎ 961 2111.

Information sources

Business information The *Nagoya Chamber of Commerce*, 2-10-19 Sakae, Naka-ku ☎ 221 7211 will provide information and help with contacts in relevant trade or manufacturers' associations. *JETRO*, 2-4 Marunouchi, Naka-ku ☎ 211 4517, is also helpful for information, assistance and contacts.

Local media Of the five local English-language newspapers, the *Mainichi Daily News*, based in Osaka, has news and information related to Nagoya and central Japan.

Tourist information The most useful source of information and assistance is the *Nagoya International Centre* 1-47-1 Nagono, Nakamura-ku ☎ 581 5678, staffed largely by resident Westerners, who are available daily to help visitors or telephone callers, from 9am to 8.30pm. They publish the excellent *Nagoya Calendar*. The *TIC*, Nagoya station ☎ 541 4301, will provide maps, information, suggestions and several monthly guides, including *Nagoya Eyes* and *Nagoya Avenues*. To call TIC collect ☎ 0120 222 800. Of the travel agencies, the *JTB*, Matsuzakaya department store, Nagoya station ☎ 563 0041 is the most helpful.

Thank-yous

The most suitable places to buy your thank-you gifts are the most prestigious department stores, *Mitsukoshi* and *Matsuzakaya*, either of which will pack the gift beautifully and deliver it.

OSAKA

Osaka is a huge commercial and industrial city. A quarter of the country's industrial output is produced here, including textiles, iron and steel; the airport and docks handle 40% of total exports. Home to Japan's pharmaceutical industry, it is a leader in the development of up-to-the-minute biotechnology. Osaka was founded by the 16thC warlord Hideyoshi, who, wise to the importance of commerce, made it a city of merchants, forcing them to live here and giving special privileges to the wealthiest. The great business and banking dynasties – Sumitomo, Itochu, Marubeni, Sanwa and Daiwa – all have their roots here. The city is currently being transformed by the 21st Century Plan, an ambitious series of projects which includes Kansai International Airport, a 24hr offshore international airport due to open in 1993, the biggest convention hall in the Kansai area and the development of Technoport Osaka, a business and research complex with high-tech facilities, on reclaimed land in Osaka Bay.

Arriving

Experienced business travellers often prefer to fly direct to Osaka rather than to Tokyo, in spite of Itami's limited landing times, and fly on to Haneda, thus avoiding the long trek in from Tokyo's Narita. From 1993, this alternative will become yet more attractive, with the opening of Kansai International Airport.

Osaka International (Itami) Airport

Japan's second international airport, Itami, handles flights direct from Europe, North America and Asia as well as via Tokyo, with connections to every other major Japanese city. Landing is permitted only between 6am and 9pm. There is a good range of restaurants, coffee shops, bars; some useful shops selling luxury goods, souvenirs; several banks, open until 7.30pm. Airport information ☎ 856 6781.

Nearby hotels Osaka Airport, Nishimachi, Hotarugaike, Toyonaka 560 ☎ 855 4621 ☒ 5286125 fax 655 4620. *Senri Hankyu*, 2-1-1 Higashimachi, Shin Senri, Toyonaka 565 ☎ 872 2211 ☒ 5287103 fax 832 2161; one of the best airport hotels in Japan, 5mins from Itami.

City link There is no rail link between Itami and Osaka. The best way to get into the city is by bus or taxi; some hotels provide a shuttle bus service.

Taxi A taxi direct to your hotel may save a little time, but the cost will be much higher.

Car rental Nippon Rentacar has a branch at the airport.

Bus The limousine bus leaves Itami every 7–8mins between 7am and 9.30pm. The journey takes about 30mins, but allow twice that in rush hour. Buses stop at the major hotels and stations.

Railway stations

Although it is worthwhile flying from Tokyo, Osaka is accessible by train from most major cities.

Shin Osaka station This large modern station, slightly to the north of Osaka, is the Bullet Train station, connected to Umeda and points south by subway (the Midosuji line) and rail.

Osaka station An enormous complex, recently renovated, this station houses department stores, hotels and an underground shopping arcade, as well as the main JR lines to Kyoto and Kobe. It is very close to Umeda, for the Midosuji subway line, and to Hankyu and Hanshin Umeda stations.

Getting around

Although Osaka is almost as congested as Tokyo, the subway is frequent, quick and easy to use and, particularly in rush hours, preferable to taxis.

Taxis Cabs are available throughout the city. Osaka taxi drivers are said to be friendlier than those in Tokyo, but they are just as unlikely to know the way.

Driving The main rental chains all have offices in Osaka, but unless your business takes you outside the central city area, it is better not to drive. Osaka is congested, especially at rush hours, and parking is difficult.

Walking Accurate walking maps are widely available, but distances can be deceptive – Osaka is an enormous city.

Bus Buses are plentiful but difficult to use; bus stops are marked in Japanese only.

Subway Osaka's subways are rapid, efficient, and apparently designed with the Western traveller in mind. Maps of the subway system are widely available, and every station name is given in English as well as Japanese. There are six subway lines, distinguished by colour, which crisscross the city. Services run every 4mins (more frequently in rush hour) between 5.30am and 11.45pm. The most useful, the Midosuji line, links the Umeda station complex with Shin Osaka and the three other main city stations, Shinsaibashi, Namba and Tennoji. If you are making more than seven journeys within the city, it is worth buying a one-day pass, which covers subways and buses and is available in main ticket offices.

Train Of the five private railway lines, the most useful are the Hankyu and Hanshin lines from Umeda, which serve northern Osaka and go on to Kobe. The Hankyu and Keihan lines go to Kyoto, and the Kintetsu line from Namba goes out through Nipponbashi towards Nara. There are stopping, semi-express and express trains, marked as such and identified in different colours on the station timetables. JR lines loop the city and also link Umeda with the port.

Area by area

At present the main business and commercial areas are Kitahama, Yodoyabashi and Hommachi, on Midosuji, a wide boulevard lined with gingko trees which runs down the centre of Osaka, linking north (Kita) and south (Minami). Many companies are buying up office space in Osaka Business Park, the business area near the castle which should be fully operational by 1992. Running from north to south, the main areas are:

Umeda The area around the Osaka Umeda station complex is crowded with skyscrapers and the wide roads are full of traffic. The main concentration of hotels is here, together with office blocks and department stores. There is also a vast underground shopping arcade, nearly 3kms/2 miles long. Umeda has plenty of restaurants, bars and nightclubs, of the smarter, more fashionable variety, as well as more colourful nightlife down the side streets.

Nakanoshima Located over the bridge south of Umeda, this small but green and pleasant island – fancifully known as Osaka's "Ile de la Cité" – contains the Bank of Japan, a leading newspaper (the *Asahi Shimbun*), Osaka's top hotel (the Royal), the International Trade Centre, the Festival Hall, the science faculties of the university and offices of several businesses and international corporations.

Kitahama, Yodoyabashi and Hommachi Straddling Kita and Minami is Osaka's business area, extending from Yodoyabashi (across the bridge from Nakanoshima) down Midosuji to Hommachi, and eastwards into Kitahama. The main concentration of banks and businesses is in Kitahama and Hommachi; these include the head offices of major trading companies such as Marubeni, Sumitomo, Nissho Iwai and C. Itoh. The Osaka Chamber of Commerce

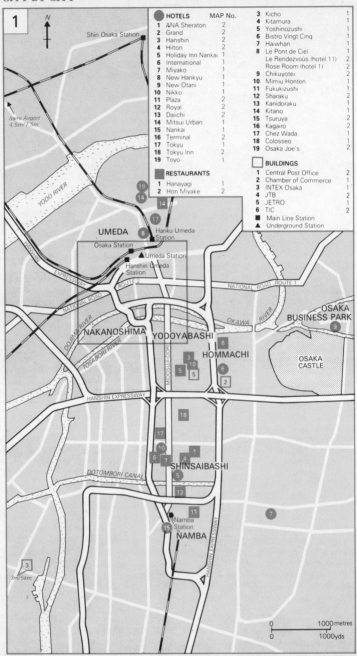

1

Shin Osaka Station

Itami Airport
4.5m/7.5m

	HOTELS	MAP No.
1	ANA Sheraton	2
2	Grand	2
3	Hanshin	2
4	Hilton	2
5	Holiday Inn Nankai	1
6	International	1
7	Miyako	1
8	New Hankyu	1
9	New Otani	1
10	Nikko	1
11	Plaza	2
12	Royal	2
13	Daiichi	1
14	Mitsui Urban	1
15	Nankai	1
16	Terminal	2
17	Tokyu	1
18	Tokyu Inn	2
19	Toyo	1

	RESTAURANTS	
1	Hanayagi	1
2	Hon Miyake	2

3	Kicho	1
4	Kitamura	1
5	Yoshinozushi	1
6	Bistro Vingt Cinq	1
7	Haiwhan	1
8	Le Pont de Ciel	1
	Le Rendezvous (hotel 11)	2
	Rose Room (hotel 1)	2
9	Chikuyotei	2
10	Mimiu Honten	1
11	Fukukizushi	1
12	Sharaku	2
13	Kanidoraku	1
14	Kitano	1
15	Tsuruya	2
16	Kagairo	2
17	Chez Wada	1
18	Colosseo	1
19	Osaka Joe's	2

	BUILDINGS	
1	Central Post Office	2
2	Chamber of Commerce	1
3	INTEX Osaka	1
4	JTB	2
5	JETRO	1
6	TIC	2
■	Main Line Station	
▲	Underground Station	

YODO RIVER

UMEDA — Hanku Umeda Station

Osaka Station
▲ Umeda Station
Hanshin Umeda Station

ROUTE 2

NATIONAL ROAD — ROUTE 1

NATIONAL ROAD

DOJIMA RIVER

NAKANOSHIMA — YODOYABASHI

OKAWA RIVER

OSAKA BUSINESS PARK

TOSABORI RIVER

HOMMACHI

OSAKA CASTLE

HANSHIN EXPRESSWAY

DOTOMBORI CANAL

SHINSAIBASHI

Namba Station

NAMBA

3m/5km

0   1000 metres
0   1000 yds

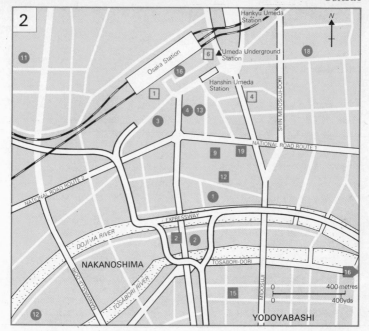

and Industry, the stock exchange, and the Foreign Trade Institute are in this area.

Osaka Castle and Osaka Business Park The main administrative and prefectural offices are to the east of Hommachi, next to Osaka Castle. On the far side of the castle is a cluster of skyscrapers – Osaka Business Park, which is now nearly completed. KDD, Matsushita and Sumitomo and many other large companies have already established offices here.

Shinsaibashi Just south of Hommachi, around the Nikko Hotel, is Shinsaibashi, Osaka's main shopping area. Behind the department stores on Midosuji stretch a network of covered arcades and tiny streets full of restaurants (including some of the finest in Osaka), boutiques and speciality shops. The streets are laid out in a grid, bordered by Midosuji and Dotombori, making it easy to find your way around.

Dotombori Full of neon lights and tiny restaurants, this is the place to

come for Osaka's famed nightlife; it was here that pleasure-seeking Osakans used to bankrupt themselves.

Namba Around Namba station is a maze of lively, cluttered alleys, full of drinking spots, tiny restaurants and "soapland" massage parlours. In the middle of all this you can also find department stores, theatres and a vast underground shopping arcade. Farther south you will find the Shin Sekai pleasure quarters, one of Japan's most famous.

The suburbs

Most Osakans commute to work from the suburbs. There are smart suburbs to the north of the city – Toyanaka, near the airport, and Minoo, farther out – and to the south, Tezukayama, out beyond Namba. Smartest of all are the suburbs between Osaka and Kobe, and in particular Ashiya, where most top executives and members of the foreign business community make their homes.

Hotels

Top companies still put their executives in the Royal or the Plaza, but the plethora of new deluxe international-style hotels, such as the ANA, Hilton and New Otani has given the business traveller a much wider choice.

ANA-Sheraton *Y////*
1-3-1 Dojimahama, Kita-ku, 530
☎ *347 1112* TX *5236884*
fax 348 9208 • *AE DC MC V* •
474 rooms, 26 suites, 5 restaurants,
2 bars, 1 coffee shop
An American-style de luxe hotel, in the commercial area of north Osaka. The lobby may be too lavish for some tastes, but the rooms, all with minibar, are ample and comfortable. The business centre provides secretarial and other services. The Rose Room (see *Restaurants*) is a favourite among foreign businessmen and diplomats. 24hr room service, travel desk, shops, hairdresser, florist, shuttle bus to Osaka station, airport limousine • sauna, pool • business service centre with extensive facilities, 11 meeting rooms (capacity up to 800).

Grand *Y///*
2-3-18 Nakanoshima, Kita-ku, 530
☎ *202 1212* TX *5222301*
fax 227 5054 • *Royal Hotels* •
AE DC MC V • *345 rooms, 13 suites,*
3 restaurants, 1 bar, 1 coffee shop
The Grand was once Osaka's best. Sadly, it is now looking much the worse for wear, although it still has a following among artists and musicians as well as businessmen, undeterred by its cramped rooms and general air of faded grandeur. Good location, next to the Yodoyabashi commercial area. Travel and theatre bookings • 10 meeting rooms (capacity up to 250).

Hanshin *Y/*
2-3-30 Umeda, Kita-ku, 530
☎ *344 1661* TX *5234269*
fax 344 9860 • *Inter Japan* •
AE DC MC V • *243 rooms, 1 restaurant,*
2 bars, 1 coffee shop
The Hanshin occupies the top floors of a large office block close to Osaka station. The rooms are small but attractively furnished in the Japanese mode, with paper screens that slide over the windows. A particularly pleasant mid-range hotel. Shuttle bus to airport • sauna • 5 meeting rooms (capacity up to 200).

Hilton *Y////*
1-8-8 Umeda, Kita-ku, 530
☎ *347 7111* TX *5242201*
fax 347 7001 • *AE DC MC V* •
485 rooms, 42 suites, 4 restaurants,
1 bar, 3 coffee shops/tea lounges
While it may lack history – and thus prestige in Japanese eyes – for comfort, convenience and sheer luxury, the graceful new Hilton is hard to beat. Located by Osaka station, the Hilton is Osaka's only foreign-managed hotel. It is designed specifically to cater for the travelling executive. The rooms are exceptionally spacious, suitable to live and work in. There are three executive floors staffed by friendly and knowledgeable concierges, with separate check in, a private lounge and complimentary breakfast and drinks. The French cuisine at the Seasons is highly rated locally, the Lipo and Windows on the World bars (see *Bars*) are well-used, and there are eight floors of luxury shops and restaurants in the Hilton Plaza next door. 24hr room service, hairdresser, pharmacy • health club with gym and sauna, indoor pool, tennis court • business service centre with extensive facilities, 19 meeting rooms (capacity up to 1,000).

Holiday Inn Nankai *Y///*
2-5-15 Shinsaibashi-suji, Chuo-ku, 542
☎ *213 8281* TX *5222939*
fax 213 8640 • *AE DC MC V* •
228 rooms, 2 suites, 4 restaurants,
2 bars, 1 coffee shop
Probably the only good mid-range hotel in south Osaka, the Holiday Inn

is a safe, if unimaginative, option.
Shops • pool • 2 meeting rooms
(capacity up to 200).

International *Y/*
2-33 Honmachibashi, Chuo-ku, 540
☎ *941 2661* ⊤⊠ *5293415*
fax 941 5362 • AE DC MC V •
391 rooms, 3 suites, 5 restaurants, 1
bar, 1 coffee shop
The International is a large, friendly
business hotel situated in the midst of
offices in the Hommachi business
district. It offers functional,
reasonably-priced accommodation.
Concierge, travel and theatre
bookings • 12 meeting rooms
(capacity up to 1,500).

Miyako *Y///*
6-1-55 Uehommachi, Tennoji-ku, 543
☎ *773 1111* ⊤⊠ *5277555*
fax 773 3322 • Kintetsu •
AE DC MC V • 584 rooms, 24 suites,
4 restaurants, 2 bars, 1 coffee shop
Located slightly off the beaten track,
the Miyako is a glossy de luxe hotel.
Rooms are pleasant and spacious,
particularly those on the executive
floor, which has a private lounge and
secretarial services. 24hr room
service, shops, beauty salon • pool,
gym • business service centre with
limited facilities, 20 meeting rooms
(capacity up to 2,000).

New Hankyu *Y///*
1-1-35 Shibata, Kita-ku, 530
☎ *372 5101* ⊤⊠ *5233245*
fax 374 6885 • AE DC MC V •
1,029 rooms, 6 restaurants, 2 bars,
3 coffee shops/tea lounges
Very much a business hotel,
conveniently located at Umeda
station, the New Hankyu is big and
impersonal, but efficient and much
used by Japanese businessmen. 8
meeting rooms (capacity up to 800).

New Otani *Y/////*
1-4-1, Shiromi, Higashi-ku, 540
☎ *941 1111* ⊤⊠ *5293330*
fax 941 9769 • AE DC MC V •
596 rooms, 14 suites, 6 restaurants,
1 bar, 3 lounges
As one would expect, the New Otani
is a vast luxury hotel with an
expansive atrium lobby, arcades of
expensive shops and spacious rooms
well equipped for both business and
leisure. More unexpectedly, it also
commands the best views in Osaka.
To one side is the castle (floodlit at
night), the castle park and the river,
to the other the skyscrapers of the
Business Park. There are two
executive floors and an exceptionally
large and well-equipped business
centre. 24hr room service, medical
clinic, arcade of luxury shops,
hairdresser, gift shop, chemist •
fitness club with gym, sauna, tennis
courts, indoor and outdoor pools •
business service centre with extensive
facilities, 19 meeting rooms (capacity
up to 4000).

Nikko *Y////*
1-3-3 Nishi Shinsaibashi, Chuo-ku, 542
☎ *244 1111* ⊤⊠ *5227575*
fax 245 2432 • AE DC MC V •
647 rooms, 8 suites, 4 restaurants,
2 bars, 3 coffee shops/tea lounges
Towering above the business and
entertainment area of Shinsaibashi,
the Nikko, a gleaming white, modern
luxury hotel, is undoubtedly the best
in south Osaka. Foreign staff help
with guest relations, and there are
romantic rooms designed by Hanae
Mori, the Japanese fashion and
interior designer, as well as executive
suites with a more masculine decor.
Les Célébrités (French) and Benkay
(Japanese) are useful restaurants. The
Samba Club (see *Entertainment*) is one
of Osaka's most sophisticated discos.
24hr room service, concierge and
travel desk, arcade of shops, JAL
office • secretarial services, 17
meeting rooms (capacity up to 1,000).

Plaza *Y////*
2-2-49 Oyodo Minami, Kita-ku, 531
☎ *453 1111* ⊤⊠ *5245557*
fax 454 0169 • AE DC MC V •
526 rooms, 14 suites, 6 restaurants,
5 bars, 1 coffee shop
A deluxe hotel with a relaxed,
understated style, the Plaza is many

business travellers' favourite and is famous for the quality of its service. The rooms are spacious, and there are extra-large corner rooms in the executive suites. Le Rendezvous, (see *Restaurants*) renowned for its French cuisine "après la cuisine" of Louis Outhier is generally rated Osaka's top French restaurant and is an automatic choice for business dining. 24hr room service, travel desk, arcade of shops, hairdresser, shuttle bus to Osaka station • outdoor pool • secretarial services, 20 meeting rooms (capacity up to 1,500).

Royal *Y*////
5-3-68, Nakanoshima, Kita-ku, 530
☎ *448 1121* ⊤ₓ *5245407*
fax 448 4414 • *AE DC MC V* •
1,149 rooms, 51 suites, 3 bars, 13 restaurants, 5 coffee shops/tea lounges
The Royal is considered by many to be Osaka's best hotel and is certainly its most prestigious. It is enormous, with a spectacularly imposing lobby, overlooking a Japanese garden. The bedrooms, all soundproofed and air-conditioned, are restrained and businesslike. The Royal Tower rooms on the top three floors of the executive tower offer more space and luxury. In the basement are branches of two famous Japanese restaurants, Kitcho and Nadaman (see *Restaurants*) and also branches of luxury and department stores. The Cellar and Leach Bars (see *Bars*) are favourite gathering places. Travel desk, hotel bus to Yodoyabashi subway station • indoor pool, sauna •

business service centre with extensive facilities, 58 meeting rooms (capacity up to 6,000).

OTHER HOTELS
Daiichi *Y*// *1-9-20 Umeda, Kita-ku, 530* ☎ *341 4411* ⊤ₓ *5234423 fax 341 4930* • *AE DC MC V*.
Distinctive round orange skyscraper very near Osaka station.
Mitsui Urban *Y*/ *3-18-8 Toyosaki, Kita-ku, 531* ☎ *374 1111* ⊤ₓ *5233701 fax 374 1085* • *AE DC MC V*. Close to Nakatsu station (convenient for Umeda) and particularly pleasant for the price.
Nankai *Y*/ *1-17-11 Namba Naka, Naniwa-ku, 556* ☎ *649 1521 fax 632 5061* • *AE DC MC V*.
Budget hotel in south Osaka, close to Namba station.
Terminal *Y*// *3-1-1 Umeda, Kita-ku, 530* ☎ *344 1235* ⊤ₓ *5233738 fax 344 1130* • *AE DC MC V*. Above Osaka station.
Tokyu *Y*/ *7-20 Chayamachi, Kita-ku, 530* ☎ *373 2411* ⊤ₓ *5236751 fax 376 0343* • *AE DC MC V*. The best of the hotels to the north of Osaka station, and has an outdoor pool.
Tokyu Inn *Y*/ *2-1 Doyamacho, Kita-ku, 530* ☎ *315 0109 fax 315 6019* • *AE DC MC V*.
Modestly priced, but a long walk from Umeda station.
Toyo *Y*// *3-16-19 Toyosaki, Kita-ku, 531* ☎ *372 8181* ⊤ₓ *5233886 fax 372 8101* • *AE DC MC V*.
Superior business hotel above Nakatsu subway station.

Restaurants

While Kyotoites are said to spend all their money on kimonos, Osakans traditionally bankrupt themselves for food, making Osaka the home of fine dining (the most ruinously expensive restaurant in Japan, Kitcho, is in Osaka). Much expense-account dining takes place in the smart restaurants of Kita, but for a meal after work with colleagues, Japanese executives are likely to head for the noisy little eateries along Dotombori.

JAPANESE
Hanayagi *Y*/
1-14-14 Higashi Shinsaibashi, Chuo-ku
☎ *271 8028* • *closed Tue* • *AE DC V*

Despite its modest exterior, Hanayagi has a reputation as being one of the best tempura restaurants in Kansai. Only 12 at a time can fit along the unpolished wooden counter, but turnover is rapid and it is worth the wait.

Hon Miyake [Y]|
10F Asahi Bldg, 3-2-4 Nakanoshima, Kita-ku ☎ *231 3188 • closed Sun*
In the middle of the Nakanoshima commercial area, on the 10th floor of an office block, is a little old Japanese restaurant, founded 80 years ago. You follow a cobbled path past a small garden with bamboos and a stone basin, to a tiny Japanese house, where an elderly kimono-clad lady serves up the finest sukiyaki, shabu shabu and *butteryaki* (beef sautéed in butter). Hon Miyake is one of Osaka's more famous restaurants, and a popular choice for business entertaining.

Kitcho
2-6-7 Koraibashi, Chuo-ku ☎ *231 1937 • closed Sun*
Kitcho is considered Japan's best restaurant. You will not get in except by personal invitation; regard it as a mark of the highest esteem to be brought here. You will dine on the finest *kaiseki* cuisine in an atmosphere impeccably Japanese, served with the utmost finesse by kimono-clad ladies. No bill will be presented, but you may be sure that the meal will make a sizable dent in your host's account. There are more accessible branches of Kitcho in several top hotels.

Kitamura [Y]|
1-16-27 Higashi Shinsaibashi, Chuo-ku ☎ *245 4129 • closed Sun • AE DC MC V • reservations essential*
This venerable sukiyaki restaurant was founded in 1881, and still occupies the same large and beautiful old Japanese house in a small alley just off Midosuji in Shinsaibashi. The ambience is intensely Japanese, quiet and refined, with a tiny garden containing bamboos and a stone basin, and austere tatami rooms. The owner, Mr Kitamura, welcomes Western guests, whether they are alone or with Japanese colleagues.

A popular choice among Japanese for business entertaining.

Yoshinozushi [Y]|
3-4-14 Awajimachi, Chuo-ku ☎ *231 7181 • closed Sun and 2nd and 3rd Sat of month • AE DC V*
Centuries ago, when Tokyo was still the tiny fishing village of Edo, Osaka was a thriving port, whose plump merchants tucked into Osaka sushi. Nowadays the average Osaka sushi bar serves Edomae, Tokyo-style sushi. Yoshinozushi, in the heart of the business district of Hommachi, is a sort of shrine to Osaka sushi. Here you can admire Mr Oyama's collection of wooden pressing boxes and watch the chefs press rice and fish into multi-coloured cubes. The rooms upstairs are reserved for business entertaining.

NON-JAPANESE
Bistro Vingt Cinq [Y]||
1-9-31 Nishi Shinsaibashi, Chuo-ku ☎ *245 6223 • closed 3rd Sun of month • AE DC MC V*
Chef Hara Yoshikata's *nouvelle cuisine* is outstanding, and Westerners, including the local French, are much in evidence at this smart and fashionable bistro, just around the corner from the Nikko Hotel. The room, decorated in classical style, is small, but tables are widely spaced and the atmosphere is intimate. In the evening the clientele consists largely of businessmen, both Japanese and Western. A respectable wine list of mainly French wines.

Haiwhan [Y]|||
11F Midosuji Bldg, 1-4-4 Nishi Shinsaibashi, Chuo-ku ☎ *281 0080 • AE DC MC V • reservations for private rooms*
Almost next to the Nikko Hotel, this celebrated Cantonese seafood restaurant is popular among Japanese businessmen, who use the many small private rooms for entertaining. The decor is extravagantly ornate, with carved wooden tables, luxuriant foliage, stone lions and copper and

bronze screens. A huge tank of fish occupies the centre of the room. Live prawns are the speciality. Less expensive set-menu meals are available.

Le Pont de Ciel   [Y]///
30F Ohbayashi Bldg, 4-33 Kitahama Higashi, Chuo-ku ☎ *947 0888* • *AE DC MC V*
Le Pont de Ciel is in one of Osaka's most spectacular locations, 30 floors above the city, looking out across the greenery of Nakanoshima's parks to the skyscrapers of Osaka and the mountains in the distance. The Ohbayashi Building houses the French consulate, Banque National de Paris and several French companies and, as one would expect from such demanding company, the cuisine, under young chef Frederick Médigue, is some of the best in the city. Le Pont de Ciel is one of Osaka's top venues for business entertaining.

Le Rendezvous   [Y]///
23F Plaza Hotel, 2-2-49 Oyodo Minami, Kita-ku ☎ *453 1111* • *AE DC MC V*
For most Osakans there is no question as to which is Osaka's best French restaurant. Le Rendezvous has been providing the city with impeccable cuisine for the last 20 years, under the direction of such luminaries as Paul Bocuse and Louis Outhier. The style – weighty and dignified – the impressive wine list, the unobtrusive service and the cuisine, undoubtedly some of the best in Asia, all combine to ensure that this venerable institution remains Osaka's premier venue for top level business entertaining.

Rose Room   [Y]////
ANA-Sheraton Hotel, 1-3-1 Dojimahama, Kita-ku ☎ *347 1112* • *AE DC MC V* • *reservations essential*
This elegant hotel restaurant is one of Osaka's best. Chef Yokota Tomoyoshi was apprenticed at the Grillon in Paris and has won three stars in

Gourmand, the Japanese equivalent of the *Michelin Guide*, for his classic and light French cuisine. He likes to meet the guests and recommend particular wines from the extensive list. The spacious dining room with rose motif decor is suitable for business entertaining; your fellow guests will include top level foreign and Japanese executives and diplomats.

OTHER RESTAURANTS
Japanese Osakans boast that they are down-to-earth folk, interested in quantity and quality when it comes to food and, unlike Tokyoites, not impressed by high prices or grand surroundings. To prove the point, the city is full of restaurants where food comes first and the environment is raucous, noisy and not at all conducive to business discussions. The home of Osaka eel, lighter and more delicate than the Tokyo variety, is *Chikuyotei*, 1-1-43 Sonezakishinchi, Kita-ku ☎ 341 1869; while for udonsuki, wide flat udon noodles served hotpot-style, *Mimiu Honten*, 4-6-18 Hirano-machi, Chuo-ku ☎ 231 5770, is the place. For sushi (Edomae – the familiar Tokyo variety – as opposed to Osaka sushi), many Osakans swear by *Fukukizushi*, 1-9-6 Nipponbashi, Chuo-ku ☎ 632 0865, where Yamamoto Kanji carries on the traditions begun by his family 80 years ago. *Sharaku*, 1F Sankyo Bldg, 1-2 Dojima, Kita-ku ☎ 344 4252, around the corner from the ANA-Sheraton, is also popular and good quality. The attraction at *Kanidoraku*, 1-16-18 Dotombori, Minami-ku ☎ 211 8975, is crab, as signalled by the gigantic mechanical crab waving its claws above the door. And for teppanyaki, heavily augmented with garlic, the place where visiting Westerners congregate is *Kitano*, 1-5 Tsurunocho, Kita-ku ☎ 372 0889. At the other end of the scale, Osaka boasts many of the country's oldest and most exclusive *ryotei*. Regard it as a very great privilege and compliment if you are invited to *Tsuruya*, 4-4-6 Imabashi, Chuo-ku ☎ 231 0456, or

Kagairo 1-1-14 Kitahama, Chuo-ku
☎ 231 7214.
Non-Japanese For expense account
dining, most Japanese business people
choose one of the city's smart French
restaurants; the four given full entries
are generally considered to be the
cream. The *Chambord* at the Royal,
Les Célébrités at the Nikko and the
Seasons at the Hilton are also much
admired as is *Chez Wada*, 16
Yahatacho, Chuo-ku ☎ 212 1780.
For serious eating, resident
Westerners gather at *Colosseo*, B1
Norin Kaikan, 3-2-6 Minami Semba,
Minami-ku ☎ 252 2042, where the
Italian chef prepares authentic pasta.
At *Osaka Joe's*, 2F IM Excellence
Bldg, 1-11-20 Sonezakishinchi,
Kita-ku ☎ 344 0124, the stone crabs
are straight from Florida. For
Chinese food, *Peking*, 12F Osaka
Ekimae Daiichi Bldg, 1-3-1 Umeda,
Kita-ku ☎ 341 4071 and *Ching Ming*,
1-3-18 Dojimahama, Kita-ku
☎ 341 7001 are highly rated and
not exorbitant.

Bars

For early evening drinks, the bars of
the top hotels are the place. The
Royal's wood-panelled *Cellar Bar*,
reminiscent of a London gentlemen's
club, remains the classiest, though
the *Leach Bar*, with a fine collection
of pots by Bernard Leach, is also
popular. The *Library Bar* at the ANA-
Sheraton and the *Lipo* at the Hilton
are also well used, as is the Plaza's
Marco Polo. For views, the New
Otani's *Sky Lounge*, which looks onto
Osaka Castle, competes with the
Hilton's *Windows on the World* with
its panoramic views of Osaka by
night.

The best non-hotel bars are found
mainly in Kita and Minami. Kita's
drinking establishments tend to be
upmarket. *Fujita's*, 2F Hokoyu Bldg,
Kitashinchi, Kita-ku, for example, is
a cosy jazz bar where the landlord
plays the guitar and tenor sax and the
grand piano half fills the little room.
Samboa, 1-5-40 Dojima, Kita-ku, is
Osaka's oldest Western-style bar.

Minami has its share of sleek bars.
De-in, 26 Higashi-shimizucho,
Minami-ku, has a wonderfully stylish
all-white interior designed by
Sugimoto Takashi, with long cherry
wood counters and slick barmen who
serve any cocktail you care to ask for.
Scotch Bank, B1 Fukuhara Bldg, 2-8
Higashi Shinsaibashi, Minami-ku, is
high-tech in style and has an entire
wall lined with bottles of whisky, and
live piano music, while *Cellar Bar
Williams*, B1 Tamaki Bldg, 1-2
Shinsaibashi, Chuo-ku, sports beamed
ceilings and waiters in tuxedos.
France-ya, 1-9 Dotombori, Chuo-ku,
is also both sophisticated and
popular.

Those who yearn for the company
of expats may want to try the *Pig and
Whistle*, 2F IS Bldg, 2-1-32
Shinsaibashi-suji, Chuo-ku, or the
altogether more sedate *Sherlock
Holmes*, B1 Osaka Ekimae Daiichi
Bldg, 1-3 Umedacho, Kita-ku, which
feels like a British pub and,
surprisingly, is dominated by darts
enthusiasts.

Entertainment

Osaka is the home of Bunraku, the
puppet theatre, and also of the
pleasure quarters of Shin Sekai,
which Osakans like to boast are
famed throughout Japan. Most
entertainment is centred in the lively
Sennichimae area, in the south –
worth a stroll, particularly at night.
For current information see the
Mainichi Daily News, *Kansai Time
Out*, and *Discover Kinki*; the last is
available free in hotels. Make
reservations through your hotel or at
Play Guide ticket agencies in
department stores.
Theatre Bunraku is performed twice a
day during January, April, July and
October at the *National Bunraku
Theatre*, 1-12-10 Nipponbashi,
Chuo-ku. The *Kabuki* stars perform
in Osaka in May, at the *Shin
Kabukiza Theatre*, 4-3-25 Namba,
Minami-ku and at the *Nakaza
Theatre*, 1-7-9 Dotombori, Chuo-ku,
during the summer.

Cinema Several cinemas show English, American and Continental films – see local press.

Music Regular concerts of both traditional Japanese and Western music are held at the *Festival Hall* 2-3-18 Nakanoshima, Kita-ku, and the *Symphony Hall* 2-chome Oyodo Minami, Kita-ku.

Nightclubs Kita's nightclubs are smart and expensive; for a wild night out, Minami is the area to head for. Many hotels provide a complimentary "key" to enter the *Playboy Club*, 13F Sumitomo Nakanoshima Bldg, 3-2-18 Nakanoshima, Kita-ku ☎ 448 5271. For discos, the *Samba Club* in the Nikko Hotel is probably the smartest. At *Club Maiko*, B1 V.O. Bldg, Kitashinchi Hondori, Kita-ku ☎ 344 2913, you will be entertained by *maiko*, trainee geisha, as you dine.

Shopping

For high-quality goods, try Shinsaibashi – the classiest shopping area – or the shopping arcades of the major hotels; the Royal and the Plaza arcades are reputable but expensive. The Acty Osaka Building, above Osaka station, houses branches of well-known shops, and under Umeda and Namba are vast underground shopping complexes.

Department stores Osaka has nine major department stores, including the Osaka-based *Hankyu* and *Hanshin*. *Takashimaya* in Namba, *Daimaru* and *Sogo* in Shinsaibashi and *Mitsukoshi* in Koraibashi are considered to be the best.

Cameras There are plenty of bargain camera shops. One of *Doi Camera*'s seven branches is at 2-12-7 Sonezaki, Kita-ku. *Kawahara Camera*, 2-2-30 Umeda, Kita-ku is well established, and has an enormous stock.

Electrical goods Nipponbashi-suji, south of Nipponbashi station, is the area for electrical goods, with more than 300 shops. *Toa Denka*, 4-11-6 Nipponbashi, Naniwa-ku, specializes in tax-free goods.

Pearls Many Osaka shops specialize in pearls from the nearby Ise peninsula. The following shops offer international guarantees: *Mikimoto*, 1F Shin Hankyu Bldg, 1-12-39 Umeda, Kita-ku, and *Tasaki Shinju*, 1F Namba City Main Bldg, 5-1-60 Namba, Minami-ku.

Sightseeing

Osaka has a long history and the castle is worth seeing, although the original buildings have long since been destroyed and replaced by modern reconstructions.

Fujita Art Museum In a splendid setting in the railway tycoon Baron Fujita's former mansion, the Fujita Art Museum is his collection of Japanese and Chinese paintings, ceramics and calligraphy, and one of Japan's best private museums. *10-32 Amijimacho, Miyakojima-ku. Open Mar–Jun, Sep–Dec, Tue–Sun, 10–4.*

Museum of Oriental Ceramics Absolutely not to be missed, this houses the magnificent Ataka Collection. Designed specifically for viewing ceramics, with an exceptionally fine collection of Chinese and Korean ware. *1-1 Nakanoshima, Kita-ku, Open Tue–Sun, 9.30–5.*

National Museum of Ethnology A celebrated and lively new museum with exhibits and videos. *Expo Memorial Park, Suita. Open Thu–Tue, 10–5.*

Osaka Castle Hideyoshi's original castle, built in 1583, was a great fortified city, 11 kms/7 miles around; the present castle is a 1931 ferroconcrete reconstruction (inaccurate, according to the Japanese press), set in an attractive park. *Kyobashi, Higashi-ku. Open daily, 9–5; from mid-July to the end of August, the castle is lit up and open until 8.30pm.*

Shitennoji Temple Founded in 593, the temple is the oldest in Japan; the present temple is a modern reconstruction, but the abbot's chamber in the main sanctuary and

the stone *torii* (sacred gate) are the originals. *Tennoji-ku. Open 8.30–4.*
Sumiyoshi Shrine A faithful 1810 reconstruction of the shrine founded in 202 to the guardian deity of the sea, who protects the port of Osaka. *Sumiyoshi Koen. Open 6–5.*
Temmangu Shrine The site of Osaka's most spectacular annual festival (in July), Tenjin Matsuri, Temmangu was built in 949 to enshrine Sugawara Michizane, the great calligrapher who is now the god of scholars; students pray here for exam success. *Minami Morimachi. Open 9.30–5.*

Guided tours
There are five different half-day tours; commentary in Japanese only. Make reservations through: *Osaka Municipal Bus* ☎ 311 2995; *Tourist Information Office* ☎ 345 2189; or *JTB* ☎ 344 0022. There are industrial tours of, for example, a brewery, car factory, broadcasting centre, the Mint and the port, in March, April, July, August and October, for 10 days each month. Individual companies such as Matsushita Electric, Suntory and Asahi Breweries also arrange tours, sometimes with English-speaking guides. Book through your hotel, or the TIC.

Out of town
To the north of Osaka are the two old capitals, *Nara* and *Kyoto*, the latter less than 1hr away by train and top of every traveller's list. To the south, and easily accessible for a weekend trip, is an area of surprisingly remote and wild countryside. *Mount Yoshino*, less than 2hrs from Osaka on the Kansai line, is famous for its cherry blossoms and is crowded in April. It offers fine views, old temples and good hiking throughout the summer. *Mount Koya*, 3hrs by train from Namba, is the main centre of the Shingon Buddhist sect, the largest sect in Japan. The flat top of the mountain is covered with temples, and many famous people are buried in the mile-long avenue of

mausoleums. The train ride from Osaka is spectacular. If you stay in a temple, expect vegetarian fare, and a 5am call to prayers – given on a gong.

Spectator sports
Baseball Osaka has two major league teams, the Hanshin Tigers and the Kintetsu Buffaloes, backed by the Osaka-based railway/department store chains. The annual high school baseball tournaments, which the whole nation follows avidly, take place in July in the *Nissei Stadium*, 2-1-55 Morinomiya Chuo, Chuo-ku ☎ 941 5505.
Sumo Sumo comes to Osaka in March, and all of Osaka crowds to the *Prefectural Gymnasium*, 2 Shin Kawamachi, Naniwa-ku ☎ 631 0120.

Keeping fit
There are plenty of public keep-fit facilities in Osaka, but they tend to be very crowded; hotel facilities are more comfortable.
Cycling There are two cycle tracks in Osaka: *Kansai Cycle Sports Centre* is 3kms/2 miles long; *Sakai City Bicycle Road* is slightly shorter.
Fitness centres The Royal, New Otani, Hilton and Miyako hotels have health clubs, open to members and hotel guests, which include a fitness centre/gym with instructors and a pool. Several hotels have saunas. *New Japan Sauna*, B3 Toyo Hotel, 3-16-19 Toyosaki, Oyodo-ku ☎ 372 8181, is a famous sauna complex with a gym; for men only. The *Dotombori New Japan Sauna*, 2-3-8 Dotombori, Chuo-ku ☎ 211 0832, is open to men and women and includes pools, massage rooms and a beauty salon, as well as a sauna, but no gym. *The Prefectural Gymnasium*, 2 Shin Kawamachi, Naniwa-ku ☎ 631 0120, has facilities for basketball, volleyball and judo, as well as a gym.
Jogging Nakanoshima Park, in the business area, is full of joggers in the morning; a jogging map is available

from the ANA-Sheraton. The Nikko provides a jogging map for south Osaka.

Skiing During the short skiing season, special trains run from Osaka to the ski slopes of Mount Kannabe (Hyogo prefecture) and Mount Daisen (Tottori prefecture).

Swimming If you want to brave a public pool, go early in the morning. *Osaka Municipal Pool*, 1-1-21 Ogimachi, Kita-ku ☎ 312 8121.

Tennis There are courts at the Hilton, Miyako and New Otani hotels. Public courts are always booked up.

Local resources
Business services

The best business centre is at the New Otani. In general the hotel business centres (also in the Royal, ANA and Hilton) are better than commercial agencies. All hotels provide photocopying, telex and fax services and most will arrange secretaries, translators or interpreters as required. Companies providing a wide range of business services are *ISS (Royal Hotel)* ☎ *441 2090*, *Manpower Japan* ☎ *222 6300*, *Kao Co Ltd* ☎ *344 4520* and *Temporary Centre Corporation* ☎ *204 1431*. *Secretarial and translation* Kokusai Shinko IBP ☎ 266 1901, *Kansai Manpower* ☎ 538 0515.

Communications

It is easier to send an important document or package abroad than to another city in Japan; outside of Tokyo the domestic courier network is limited and unreliable.

Long distance deliveries Federal Express ☎ 942 9292, DHL *Japan Inc* ☎ 445 8151, *Overseas Courier Service* ☎ 473 2631, *World Courier Japan* ☎ 365 9670.

Post Office Osaka's main post office is at 3-2 Umeda, Kita-ku ☎ 347 8006

Telex and fax At most hotels. Otherwise, use the KDD at Shinhanshin Bldg, Umeda, Kita-ku ☎ 343 2571

Conference/exhibition centres

INTEX OSAKA, 1-1-12 Nanko-kita, Suminoe-ku 559 ☎ *612 3773*, was opened in 1985 as part of Osaka's 21st Century Plan; annual international trade fairs are held here, organized by the Osaka International Trade Fair Commission. Other centres include *Osaka Foreign Trade Institute*, Otemai Usami Bldg, 2-5 Hommachibashi, Chuo-ku ☎ 942 2251. *Osaka International Trade Centre*, 5-3-51 Nakanoshima, Kita-ku ☎ 441 9131. *Osaka Merchandise Mart*, 1-7 Kyobashi, Higashi-ku ☎ 943 2020.

Emergencies

Hospitals The following hospitals have English-speaking staff: *Yodogawa Christian Hospital*, 2-chome Higashi Yodogawa-ku ☎ 322 2250, *Osaka National Hospital* Hoenzakacho, Chuo-ku ☎ 942 1331. For dental treatment try the *Osaka University Dental Clinic*, Kita-ku ☎ 943 6521.

Pharmacies Drugs are available in hospitals. There are no 24hr pharmacies.

Police Osaka Prefectural Police Headquarters, 3 Otemae, Chuo-ku ☎ 943 1234. There are English-speaking staff at *Sonezaki Police Station* ☎ 315 1234.

Government offices

Osaka Municipal Centre for Business and Trade ☎ 262 3261. *Osaka Municipal Office*, 1-3-20 Nakanoshima, Kita-ku ☎ 208 8181.

Information sources

Business information American Chamber of Commerce in Japan (Kansai Chapter), c/o Searl, Nishi P.O. Box 47 ☎ 541 3333. *British Chamber of Commerce*, c/o Hongkong and Shanghai Banking Corp, 3-6-1 Awaji-machi, Chuo-ku ☎ 223 7004. *German Chamber of Commerce and Industry*, 23F Nakanoshima Centre Bldg, 6-2-27 Nakanoshima, Kita-ku ☎447 0021. There are also Indian and Korean Chambers of Commerce in Osaka. *Osaka Chamber of Commerce and Industry*, 2-8 Honmachibashi, Chuo-ku ☎ 944 6412, may be willing to help provide contacts. *JETRO*, 4F Bingomachi Miura Bldg, 218 Bingomachi, Chuo-ku ☎ 203 3601.

Local media The *Mainichi Daily News*, based in Osaka, covers Kansai as well as national news. *Kansai Time Out* is a monthly magazine produced in Kobe, with features on life in Kansai and listings of films, exhibitions, etc.

Tourist information Osaka Tourist Information Office, 3-1-1 Umeda (Osaka station, East Exit) ☎ 345 2189 and at Shin Osaka station, 3F ☎305 3311 (ask for Mrs Miki), has information on sightseeing, accommodation and transport. The Tourist Association has recently produced a glossy English-language guidebook to sightseeing, hotels and restaurants: the Osaka City Tourist Guidebook, available at TICs.

Thank-yous

The top department stores are the appropriate place to buy a gift, and they will arrange delivery: *Takashimaya* ☎ 631 1101; *Daimaru* ☎ 271 1231; *Mitsukoshi* ☎ 203 1331; *Sogo* ☎ 281 3111.

SAPPORO

City code ☎ 011

Sapporo is the capital of Hokkaido, Japan's "Last Frontier." A large island to the north of Honshu (the main island), Hokkaido was settled by the Japanese as late as 1869. With 22% of the country's total land area, it still has only 5% of the population, the majority pioneering Japanese, plus a few original inhabitants, the Ainu, Gilyak and Oroke. Hokkaido's spacious rolling pastures supply much of Japan's food. The main products include potatoes, sweet corn, wheat, beans and almost all of the country's dairy produce. Fishing and forestry are other key industries. More than 70% of the land is under timber, and the annual lumber production is a quarter of the nation's total. Sapporo is Hokkaido's main link with the outside world, and is the island's cultural, economic and political centre, and a focal point for winter sports.

Arriving

Although Sapporo is accessible by ferry or train (a gruelling 11hrs from Tokyo), most visitors arrive by plane. From Tokyo the journey takes 1hr 25mins and from Osaka 1hr 45mins. The overnight train from Tokyo to Sapporo, the Hokkutosei, takes 16hrs and has luxury sleeping cars with shower, audio system and a direct telephone link to the dining car; it also costs more than the plane.

Chitose airport

Chitose is a large, efficient, modern airport, handling one flight weekly from Honolulu and regular domestic flights. There are 24 flights a day from Tokyo, plus flights from major Japanese cities. Facilities include a good range of restaurants (open 7am–8pm) on landside, none on airside; a non-smoking VIP lounge; plenty of shops with limited local goods; a bank open Mon–Fri 9–3, Sat 9–noon. JAL Cargo Services ☎ (0123) 26 0111. Airport information ☎ (0123) 23 0111 or (0123) 41 2111. *Nearby hotels Nikko*, 4-4-4 Honcho, Chitoseshi, 066 ☎ (0123) 22 1121 ⊠ 949959 fax (0123) 22 1153. *Airport*, 6 Chiyodacho, Chitoseshi, 066 ☎ (0123) 26 1155 fax (0123) 22 4048. *Chitoseya*, 2-17 Nishikicho, Chitoseshi, 066 ☎ (0123) 23 2811 fax (0123) 27 1647.
City link The 45min taxi ride is the simplest way to get into the city, but there are alternatives.

Car rental If you plan to drive in Sapporo, it is sensible to rent a car at the airport. Budget, Nippon, Nissan, Toyota and Mitsubishi have branches at Chitose.
Bus JAL and ANA operate bus services which depart at about 15min intervals, but only during plane arrival times. The buses stop at major hotels, reaching Sapporo station 1hr 10mins after departure.
Train If you are staying near the station, or have little luggage, you might take the train. Departure times are shown in the airport, and the station is a few minutes' walk. Local trains take 50mins, and express trains 35mins.

Getting around

Sapporo is conveniently laid out in a regular grid. Above and below Odori Park the streets are respectively numbered north (*kita*) and south (*minami*). Either side of Soseigawa Canal they are numbered east (*higashi*) and west (*nishi*). Although it is easy to find your way around, it is less easy to locate a particular place from the address. For example, 4 Nishi, Kita-2 (West 4, North 2) refers to several blocks, and it is helpful to know the name of the building. The best way of getting around, apart from taxi, is a combination of walking and subway.
Driving If you want to try driving in Japan, Sapporo is the place to do it. The roads are wide, not too crowded,

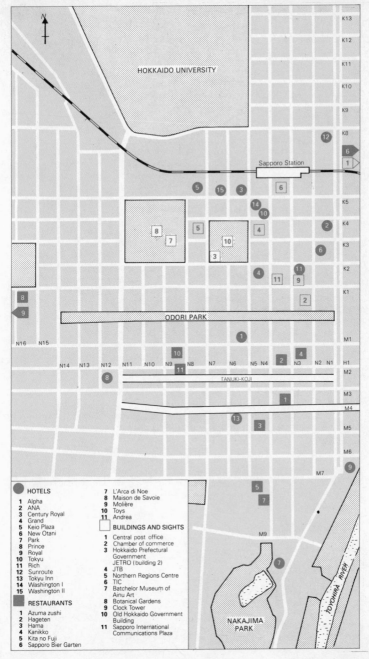

HOKKAIDO UNIVERSITY

Sapporo Station

ODORI PARK

TANUKI-KOJI

TOYOHIRA RIVER

NAKAJIMA PARK

HOTELS

1 Alpha
2 ANA
3 Century Royal
4 Grand
5 Keio Plaza
6 New Otani
7 Park
8 Prince
9 Royal
10 Tokyu
11 Rich
12 Sunroute
13 Tokyu Inn
14 Washington I
15 Washington II

RESTAURANTS

1 Azuma zushi
2 Hageten
3 Hama
4 Kanikko
5 Kita no Fuji
6 Sapporo Bier Garten
7 L'Arca di Noe
8 Maison de Savoie
9 Molière
10 Toys
11 Andrea

BUILDINGS AND SIGHTS

1 Central post office
2 Chamber of commerce
3 Hokkaido Prefectural
  Government
  JETRO (building 2)
4 JTB
5 Northern Regions Centre
6 TIC
7 Batchelor Museum of
  Ainu Art
8 Botanical Gardens
9 Clock Tower
10 Old Hokkaido Government
   Building
11 Sapporo International
   Communications Plaza

and the grid system makes navigation easy. Outside the city, on Hokkaido's broad highways, driving is the ideal way to travel. The main car rental firms have offices in the city.
Bus The extensive bus network is best avoided unless you are feeling adventurous.
Subway Sapporo's subway, which opened in 1972, runs smoothly and quietly on huge rubber tyres. There are three lines, which intersect at Odori. The north-south Nanboku Line passes through the railway station, Odori, Susukino and Nakajima Park; the east-west Tozai Line runs from the suburbs under Odori Park; and the new Toho line runs diagonally across the city, linking Susukino in the southwest with Sakaemachi in the northeast. Subway maps at stations and on ticket machines are in English and Japanese. Green ticket machines are for subway tickets only; tickets from yellow machines allow you to transfer onto the bus or streetcar. For more than five journeys, get a one-day pass (available at Sapporo JR station and Odori subway station), which may be used on subways, buses and streetcars.

Streetcar If you have time, the bumpy streetcar does a long loop around the south of the city, from Odori back to Susukino, and is useful for out-of-the-way places.
Train JR lines run out to the suburbs from Sapporo station.

Area by area
At the city's centre is *Odori Park*, a long, narrow expanse of lawns and fountains. The main business area extends from here north to the station: full of modern offices, hotels and banks, it is often called "Little Tokyo." The Prefectural Assembly and Sapporo's top hotel, the Grand, are here. North of the station are the grounds of Hokkaido University. The main shopping area stretches south of Odori Park, while under the park is a vast shopping arcade. Farther south is *Susukino*, with its many bars and restaurants and beyond that *Nakajima Park*.

The suburbs
The better residential areas are around Maruyama, in the hills west of the city. The most exclusive district is Miyanomori, farther to the west.

Hotels
The Grand, opened in 1934, is Sapporo's oldest and finest Western-style hotel. More recent competitors include the Park and the Royal, both built in 1964, and many newer hotels, some of them built for the 1972 Winter Olympics. High season in Sapporo is from May to October, at the New Year and during the February Snow Festival. Room rates drop by as much as 60% during the off-season.

Alpha ¥////
5 Nishi, Minami-1, Chuo-ku, 060
☎ 221 2333 TX 935345 fax 221 0819
• *Okura* • *AE DC MC V* • *145 rooms, 2 suites, 4 restaurants, 2 bars, 1 coffee shop/tea room*
A relatively small hotel right in the centre of the city, the Alpha is particularly popular with visiting foreign executives. It offers the fine service to be expected of an Okura hotel, with a distinct individual style.

The bedrooms are spacious, designed for living in, not just sleeping, with elegant rattan furniture. There is a cinema and the Sapporo branch of the Playboy Club, which doubles as a spaghetti house by day. La Couronne (see *Restaurants*) is highly rated and La Rouge (see *Bars*) is generally considered the best bar in town. Concierge, beauty salon, limited hotel parking • pool, sauna • 4 meeting rooms (capacity up to 250).

ANA 𝑌‖
1 Nishi, Kita-3, Chuo-ku, 060
☎ *221 4411* ⊤ˣ *934712 fax 222 7624*
• *AE DC V* • *458 rooms, 2 suites, 5
restaurants, 1 bar, 1 coffee shop*
This is not one of the better ANAs.
The lobby is small and cluttered, but
has a lounge (rare in Japan) with a
fireplace. The rooms are cramped but
acceptable, with a desk and views
over the city. The best rooms are
those on the 20th floor, which have
been recently renovated and are
altogether more luxurious. Shopping
arcade • men's sauna • 8 meeting
rooms (capacity up to 200).

Century Royal 𝑌‖
5 Nishi, Kita-5, Chuo-ku, 060
☎ *221 2121* ⊤ˣ *934439 fax 231 2538*
• *AE DC MC V* • *332 rooms, 2 suites,
3 restaurants, 2 bars, 1 coffee shop*
Near the station, this is a solid,
respectable hotel showing signs of
age. It is popular with Japanese
business travellers. The rooms are
vast and full of old-fashioned
furniture. The revolving restaurant
offers good views. Limited hotel
parking • 4 meeting rooms (capacity
up to 300).

Grand 𝑌‖
4 Nishi, Kita-1, Chuo-ku, 060
☎ *261 3311* ⊤ˣ *932613 fax 231 0388*
• *Nikko* • *AE DC MC V* • *577 rooms,
8 suites, 4 restaurants, 2 bars, 2 coffee
shops*
The Grand easily outclasses Sapporo's
other hotels. Redecorated in 1986, it
is a mini-city of four linked buildings,
which are extremely elegant
throughout. Most rooms have views
over the city or onto the Japanese
gardens. There is an Executive Floor,
with particularly spacious and
attractive rooms. The many fine
restaurants and bars include the
Grand Chef (see *Restaurants*) and the
Old Saloon 1934 (see *Bars*), where
executives gather in the evening.
Concierge, theatre and travel
booking, arcade of shops, beauty
salon • men's sauna • 21 meeting
rooms (capacity up to 1,000).

Keio Plaza 𝑌‖
7 Nishi, Kita-5, Chuo-ku, 060
☎ *271 0111* ⊤ˣ *933271 fax 221 5450*
• *AE DC MC V* • *523 rooms, 2 suites,
6 restaurants, 1 bar, 1 coffee shop*
The Keio Plaza was conceived on a
grand scale, with the visiting foreign
executive in mind, and offers many of
the amenities of an international
hotel. The lobby is an impressive
place to meet clients, and the rooms
are furnished for comfort. Concierge,
travel bookings, car rental, shops,
hairdresser, medical centre • gym,
sauna, massage room, pool • 11
meeting rooms (capacity up to 2,000).

New Otani 𝑌‖‖
1 Nishi, Kita-2, Chuo-ku, 060
☎ *222 1111* ⊤ˣ *933650 fax 222 5521*
• *AE DC MC V* • *340 rooms, 1 suite,
1 restaurant, 1 bar, 1 coffee shop*
In a developing area near the station,
the New Otani has a restrained but
classy air, and is one of the more
impressive places to stay. The lobby
is elegant and the rooms carefully
designed to make the most of the
limited space. The staff – especially
the concierge – are helpful and
friendly. Concierge, shops • 7
meeting rooms (capacity up to 400).

Park 𝑌‖‖
3 Nishi, Minami-10, Chuo-ku, 064
☎ *511 3131* ⊤ˣ *932264 fax 511 3451*
• *AE DC MC V* • *223 rooms, 4 suites, 3
restaurants, 1 bar, 2 coffee shops*
A subway ride from the city centre, the
Park is a large and gracious hotel,
overlooking Nakajima Park and its
lake. The lobby is impressive, the
rooms spacious and the staff courteous
and efficient. Ask for a room on the park
side. Concierge, shops, beauty salon •
secretarial services, 17 meeting rooms
(capacity up to 2,000).

Prince 𝑌‖‖
11 Nishi, Minami-2, Chuo-ku, 060
☎ *241 1111* ⊤ˣ *933949 fax 231 5994*
• *AE DC MC V* • *319 rooms, 3 suites, 5
restaurants, 1 bar, 1 coffee shop*
In the business district to the west of
town, close to the mountains, the

Prince is favoured by Japanese business travellers and sportsmen. Both lobby and rooms are rather idiosyncratic, with dark red carpets and ornate brocaded furniture. The staff are friendly and efficient, and the concierge very helpful. 24hr room service, concierge, small shop, hotel bus to winter ski slopes • 23 meeting rooms (capacity up to 1,000).

Royal [Y]//
1 Higashi, Minami-7, Chuo-ku, 060
☎ *511 2121* [TX] *932330 fax 511 2133*
• *AE DC MC V* • *82 rooms, 6 suites, 3 restaurants*
Within walking distance of Susukino, the Royal is a small and friendly hotel. The rooms, refurbished in 1989, are spacious and quiet. The helpful manager speaks good English and can provide business contacts and information. Concierge, travel bookings • 11 meeting rooms (capacity up to 300).

Tokyu [Y]//
1-4 Nishi, Kita-4, Chuo-ku, 060
☎ *231 5611* [TX] *934510 fax 251 3515*
• *AE DC MC V* • *261 rooms, 2 suites, 2 restaurants, 1 bar, 1 coffee shop*
A few minutes' walk from the station,

the Tokyu is not one of Sapporo's top addresses. The lobby is looking a little shabby, but the rooms, decorated in the usual Tokyu style, are homely and spacious. Shopping arcade, florist, • 6 meeting rooms (capacity up to 500).

OTHER HOTELS
Rich [Y]/ *3-3-10 Nishi, Kita-1, Chuo-ku, 060* ☎ *231 7891 fax 231 7913* • *AE DC MC V*. A business hotel 5min walk from the station.
Sunroute [Y] *1 Nishi, Kita-7, Kita-ku, 060* ☎ *737 8111* [TX] *932202 fax 717 8946* • *AE DC MC V*. A very pleasant budget hotel on the wrong side of the tracks, 3min walk from the station.
Tokyu Inn [Y]/ *1-5 Nishi, Minami-4, Chuo-ku, 064* ☎ *531 0109* [TX] *935301 fax 531 2387* • *AE DC MC V*. At the centre of the Susukino entertainment district.
Washington I [Y]/ *1-4 Nishi, Kita-4, Chuo-ku, 060* ☎ *251 3211 fax 241 8238* • *AE DC MC V*. A large hotel opposite the station.
Washington II [Y]// *6 Nishi, Kita-5, Chuo-ku, 060* ☎ *222 3311 fax 241 8901* • *AE DC MC V*. A 4min walk from the station.

Restaurants

Like everything else in Hokkaido, business dinners are more relaxed than in mainland Japan; far from nibbling at tiny morsels of *kaiseki*, you will find yourself confronted with gigantic feasts. You can dine on lamb or beef from Hokkaido's luxuriant pastures, or on hairy crab, huge salmon or scallops, fresh from its coasts. To wash it all down, there is plenty of Sapporo beer, said to be the best in Japan.

JAPANESE
Azuma zushi [Y]
3 Nishi, Minami-4, Chuo-ku
☎ *261 7161* • *closed 3rd Tue of month*
• *AE DC V*
Located in the heart of Susukino, Azuma zushi first opened as a small sushi shop in 1890. Now, run by the founder's great-great-grandson, it has expanded into a vast four-floor restaurant, serving the best and cheapest sushi in Sapporo. Lunchtime

and evenings, the pine counters and tatami rooms are packed with noisy groups of Japanese businessmen, often accompanied by Western colleagues. As well as sushi, Azuma zushi serves local seafood.

Hageten [Y]
B1 Kataoka Bldg, 3 Nishi, Minami-2, Chuo-ku ☎ *271 2018* • *closed Mon*
Hage means "bald" and *ten* is short for "tempura" – a reference both to

the menu and to the physical appearance of the founder and of his grandson and successor, Mr Yanno. Highly recommended by the top hotels, Hageten serves many kinds of Japanese food, but the speciality is, of course, tempura, freshly cooked before your eyes.

Hama *Y*////
3F No 8 Polestar Bldg, 4 Nishi, Minami-5, Chuo-ku ☎ *512 2541* ●
AE DC MC V
Much of Sapporo's top-level business entertaining goes on among the Roman statues and potted palms of Steak House Hama. Discreet tuxedoed waiters serve the distinguished clientele with best Kobe beef, cooked teppanyaki-style on steel plates at the table. The classical decor extends to the bar, where there is an enormous range of pre- and post-prandial liquors. This is a highly appropriate place to return hospitality.

Kanikko *Y*
B1 Togashi Bldg, 2 Nishi, Minami-2, Chuo-ku ☎ *231 4080* ● *AE DC MC V*
Enormous hairy crabs are caught between April and November around Shiretoko, in the farthest reaches of Hokkaido. At Kanikko you can eat them raw, baked, boiled, stuffed and fried, or minced and made into dumplings.

Kita no Fuji *Y*/
1F Keikyu Susukino Plaza, 4 Nishi, Minami-7, Chuo-ku ☎ *512 1339* ●
DC V
Kita no Fuji is the name of the sumo wrestler who owns this restaurant, and if you come here in August you can shake his enormous hand. Among the Japanese business community, this is a favourite place for celebrations and other formal dinners. To reach the dining rooms you walk around a full-size sumo ring. The restaurant serves *Chanko* – enormous casseroles heaped with giant prawns, crabs and scallops. This is the food that makes sumo wrestlers huge.

There is another branch of Kita no Fuji in Sambangai Bldg, 3 Nishi, Minami-2.

Sapporo Bier Garten *Y*
9 Higashi, Kita-6, Higashi-ku
☎ *742 1531* ● *AE DC*
This beautiful old red-brick 19thC brewery, with its towering chimney, is packed out daily with feasting Japanese businessmen; you will not be able to avoid being brought here for a meal. As well as beer, served in great mugfuls, the house speciality is Genghis Khan, heaps of Hokkaido lamb and vegetables grilled on a cast-iron plate at your table. For a few thousand yen, you eat and drink as much as you can for two hours.

NON-JAPANESE
L'Arca di Noe *Y*/
4 Nishi, Minami-8, Chuo-ku
☎ *521 3300* ● *AE DC MC V*
For students of design and of the architectural wonders to be found in Japan, L'Arca di Noe is not to be missed. This extravagant creation (brainchild of British designer Nigel Coates) represents Noah's Ark, in the process of being excavated from a cliff. Perversely, the cuisine on offer is Chinese, with the emphasis on seafood and fresh vegetables.

Maison de Savoie *Y*/
Odori Haim, 15 Nishi, Kita-1, Chuo-ku ☎ *643 5580* ● *closed Mon* ●
AE DC
It is worth a special trip to Sapporo for Takashi Ohara's cooking. Mr Ohara spent 10 years in France, studying mainly with Michel Guérard, and cooks *nouvelle* and traditional French cuisine, both superbly. There is an enormous and carefully chosen wine list, one of the best in Japan. The small, quiet dining room is extremely elegant, and there is a patio outside for warm days. The clientele includes French residents and professional people; your Japanese hosts will be flattered if you entertain them here. There is also an excellent value five-course set lunch.

OTHER NON-JAPANESE
RESTAURANTS
Of the hotel French restaurants, *La Couronne* at the Alpha and *Grand Chef* at the Grand are particularly highly rated. For business entertaining, these are probably the most appropriate. But if it is simply fine French food that you are after, Sapporo has plenty of excellent restaurants. *Molière*, 2-1-1 Miyagaoka, Chuo-ku ☎ 631 3155, is well used by the resident Western community and highly recommended, as is *Toys*, 1F Koroku Bldg, 8 Nishi, Minami-1 ☎ 261 7545. For top quality Italian food, the place to go is *Andrea*, 8 Nishi, Minami-2 ☎ 271 4479.

Bars
Any Japanese executive on a trip to Sapporo is likely to be teased that what he is really interested in is the pleasures of Susukino. With 3,700 bars, restaurants, cabarets, nightclubs and strip joints, Susukino is said to be the liveliest nightlife area north of Tokyo. The hotel bars offer a more civilized alternative to Susukino's backstreets.

The refined and classy *La Rouge*, at the Alpha, is where the city's top executives keep their bottles of whisky, chosen from 20 varieties available. Many high-powered discussions are concluded around the tables of the Grand's dignified and comfortable *Old Saloon 1934*. *Lorelei*, B1 Keiai Bldg, 4 Nishi, Minami-4, is altogether lighter. This is where local executives come to relax, over *rosti*, German potatoes and Sapporo beer, and the local German community is in evidence. As night draws on, a band with violins and accordions may strike up German folk songs.

Entertainment
In spite of its sizeable foreign population, Sapporo still feels a little like a frontier town. Visiting Japanese and overseas entertainers provide some culture but, apart from Susukino's colourful nightlife, local activities seem to be largely restricted

to sports and the ever-popular Snow Festival. For current information, check *The Monthly Hokkaido* or *What's on in Sapporo*, or enquire at TIC or your hotel.

Ticket agencies Reserve tickets through your hotel or at Play Guide ticket agencies in major stores.

Theatre, cinema and music Japanese and international theatre companies, orchestras and rock bands often perform in Sapporo. *Mitsukoshi Cinema*, in the Alpha hotel, shows English-language films.

Nightclubs To compensate for the lack of cultural activities, Sapporo has an enormous variety of nightlife. Before being dragged off to Susukino's more decadent establishments by your Japanese colleagues, you may wish to try the *Playboy Club* in the Alpha hotel, a smart gathering place for executives, both male and female. In Susukino, the vast and glittering *Emperor*, Aoki Bldg, 2 Nishi, Minami-4 ☎ 511 0458, claims to be Hokkaido's top cabaret and the playground of the rich and famous. It offers live entertainment, *karaoke* and English-speaking hostesses. As for discos, *Maharajah*, 4F Suzuran Bldg, 4 Nishi, Minami-4 ☎ 261 8866, used to be rated Sapporo's best, and is still very popular. The smart set flock to *Exing*, 8F Dai-san Green Bldg, 3 Nishi, Minami-4 ☎ 511 3434, to nibble sushi and dance among Art Nouveau sculptures.

Shopping
Sapporo is the island's capital, and the quality of its shops reflects this. Several of the best Tokyo stores, including *Mitsukoshi*, *Parco* and the excellent bookshops *Maruzen* and *Kinokuniya* have branches here. These and other high-class shops are clustered at the east end of Odori Park, around Odori subway station. Sprawling for several blocks under the park is an underground shopping arcade, essential during the long, snowbound winter. There is another vast underground mall in the station

area. *Tanuki-koji*, "Badger Alley," is a seven-block-long covered arcade parallel to Odori Park, a few blocks south. It is crammed with restaurants and shops, including antique, craft and tax-free shops. You can see the full range of Hokkaido crafts – especially wood carvings – at *Hokkaido Boeki Bussan Shinkokai*; *Seibansha*, 4 Nishi, Minami-7, has a particularly fine selection.

Sightseeing

Sapporo has few historic sights. Its main attractions are the fascinating relics of the Ainu culture and the wide open spaces of Hokkaido, which are nearby.

Batchelor Museum of Ainu Artifacts
Dr John Batchelor, an English clergyman who lived here in the late 19thC, collected 20,000 Ainu and Gilyak artifacts, ranging from embroidered costumes to canoes. The collection is in the old wooden house that was Batchelor's home. *Botanical Garden. For opening times see below.*

Botanical Garden Around the pleasant lawns of the spacious Botanical Garden, a favourite place for strolling, are planted more than 4,000 varieties of Hokkaido plants. *8 Nishi, Kita-3. Open May–Sep, Tue–Sun, 9–4; Oct, Tue–Sun, 9–3.30.*

Clock Tower The small white wooden Clock Tower was built in 1878 and now houses a museum of local history. *2 Nishi, Kita-1. Open Tue–Sun, 9–4.*

Hokkaido Museum of Modern Art
This dramatic modern building houses a collection of modern Japanese art and hosts visiting exhibitions. *17 Nishi, Kita-1. Open Tue–Sun, 10–5.*

Mount Moiwa Mount Moiwa is Sapporo's nearest mountain, with views over the city and, on a fine day, across to the centre of Hokkaido.

Nakajima Park Nakajima Park, a beautiful park to the south of the city, contains a landscaped Japanese garden, a tea house and a manor house which was once used by the Imperial family.

Old Hokkaido Government Building
Familiarly known as the Red Brick Building, this is a stately Victorian mansion surrounded by lawns. *6 Nishi, Kita-3. Open Mon–Fri, 8.30–5.30; Sat 8.30–1.30.*

Guided tours

There are seven half-day bus tours covering sights within the city, run by the *Municipal Bus Company* ☎ 221 8875. *Chuo Bus* ☎ 251 8141 and *JTB* ☎ 241 5851 have day trips to scenic areas. *Sapporo Beer Company* ☎ 741 9191 and *Snow Brand Dairy Products Museum* ☎ 748 2289 are open to visitors.

Out of town

Hokkaido's spectacular mountains, steaming hot springs, lakes and rolling plains are within easy reach. If you have only half a day to spare, *Shikotsu-Toya National Park*, 70kms/45 miles southwest of Sapporo, will give you a taste of Hokkaido's glories, although, as a popular tourist spot, it is fairly tame. Within the park are Lake Toya, a circular volcanic lake, mountains, forests and volcanoes. Of the park's hot springs, *Noboribetsu* is one of the most famous in Japan. Its "Hell Valley" is a cauldron of boiling streams and sulphorous fumes but you can bathe in comfort at the spa. If you have a weekend free, head for the wildernesses east of Sapporo. The ugly town of Asahigawa is just over 1hr on the express train from Sapporo: hire a car there or in Sapporo and head into *Daisetsuzan National Park*, Hokkaido's most spectacular, with five soaring mountains, ravines and spas, including the popular *Sounkyo*. Farther east, *Akan National Park* has volcanoes, forests and three magnificent lakes.

Spectator sports

Winter sports Sapporo made its name by staging the 1972 Winter Olympics. In 1986 it hosted the first Winter Asian Games, and there is an annual

International Ski Marathon in February. The *Teine Olympia Ski Ground*, Mount Teine ☎ 681 3191, is the main location for alpine, bobsled and toboggan events. Ski-jumping events take place at the 90 metre/295 ft *Okurayama Ski Jump*, Maruyama Park, and there is a summer jump tournament every August at the neighbouring 70 metre/230 ft *Miyanomori Ski Jump*, also in Maruyama Park.

Baseball June to August is the time for professional baseball; games take place in the *Maruyama Baseball Stadium*, Maruyama Park ☎ 641 3015.

Keeping fit

Many of Hokkaido's visitors come here specifically for the sporting opportunities, and locals, too, are great sport enthusiasts. In winter you can take advantage of being near Japan's best ski slopes; the closest are only a 30min drive away. Hokkaido's summers are pleasantly cool compared to the rest of Japan, and many Japanese come here for the hiking and mountain climbing.

Golf The rolling fields of Hokkaido are perfect for golf, and there are plenty of courses within easy reach of Sapporo – generally cheaper and less exclusive than on Honshu. As always, it is best to be introduced by your hotel or by colleagues. The 27-hole course at *Teine Olympia*, Mount Teine ☎ 681 3191 is especially popular. The sports-oriented Prince hotel ☎ 241 1111 has its own course, the 36-hole *Sapporo-Hiroshima*, open to non-hotel guests.

Fitness centres Of the hotels, the Keio Plaza has a health club with a gym and sauna, and the Grand, Alpha and ANA all have saunas. There is a large public sports centre with a pool in *Nakajima Park*. ESPO, 4-chome Plaza, 4 Nishi, Minami-1 ☎ 251 6111, is a 10-floor 24hr sauna with boutiques, hairdressers, dance classes and a snack bar. It is very much *the* place to go.

Hiking There is plenty of superb hiking around Sapporo. If time is short, stroll up *Hitsujigaoka* or *Mount Maruyama*. For more taxing hikes, head for the *national parks* (see *Sightseeing*).

Jogging You can jog around *Odori Park* if you watch out for traffic, but it is better to join the students in the vast grounds of *Hokkaido University*.

Mountain climbing Nearest to Sapporo is *Mount Moiwa*. For serious climbing, the *national parks* (see *Sightseeing*) are the place.

Skiing Japan's best slopes are in Hokkaido. Those nearest to Sapporo are *Maruyama Park*, *Mount Moiwa* and *Mount Arai*. A little farther afield, *Teine Olympia*, Mount Teine ☎ 681 3191, the site of the 1972 Winter Olympics, is the most famous and therefore very crowded. *Niseko* and *Furano* are slightly farther still, and also popular. The Prince chain has hotels in all the ski resorts, and there are direct buses from the Sapporo Prince. The skiing season is from late November to mid-April.

Swimming There are pools in the Alpha and Keio Plaza, and a public pool in *Nakajima Sports Centre*.

Tennis Sapporo's tennis courts are not crowded or expensive. There are many courts in *Toyohiragawa*; reserve through your hotel.

Local resources
Business services

At present none of the Sapporo hotels has a business service centre. The Park offers limited secretarial services. Nationwide companies providing business services are *Manpower Japan* ☎ 222 4881 and *Kao Co* ☎ 222 5661.

Photocopying and printing Arrange through your hotel or one of the business service companies. Some department stores, camera shops and stationers have photocopiers.

Secretarial Contact a business service company or *Career Staff* ☎ 221 0681, *Temporary Centre Corporation* ☎ 241 2171 or *Tempstaff* ☎ 222 5817.

Translation TS *International Co* ☎ 222 5817 provides interpreters;

Manpower Japan has both translators and interpreters.

Communications

International couriers Nippon Express Co, 3-1-7 Odori Chiazashi, Chuo-ku ☎ 241 4764.

Post office Central post office, 1 Higashi, Kita-6, is open Mon–Fri, 9–7; Sat, 9–5; Sun 9–12.30.

Telex and fax Major hotels offer both, as does KDD Telecom Sapporo, 5 Nishi, Kita-4 ☎ 241 6802.

Conference/exhibition centres

The main venues for conferences and exhibitions in Sapporo are the Alpha and Grand hotels and the *Northern Regions Centre*, 7 Nishi, Kita-3 ☎ 221 7840.

Emergencies

Bureaux de change Go to the major hotels, whose exchange offices open 7 days a week, from early until late.

Hospitals For an ambulance ☎ 119. The best hospitals in Sapporo are the *City General*, 9 Nishi, Kita-1 ☎ 261 2281, and the *Hokkaido University Hospital*, 5 Nishi, Kita-14 ☎ 716 1161. The *Emergency Dental Clinic*, 10 Nishi, Minami-7 ☎ 511 7774, is open in the evenings from 7–11.

Pharmacies Prescription drugs are supplied by hospitals.

Police In an emergency, dial 110 or go to the nearest *koban* (neighbourhood police box) or the city's main police station, 5 Nishi, Kita-1 ☎ 241 3201.

Government offices

For municipal inquiries contact *City Hall*, 2 Nishi, Kita-1 ☎ 211 2032; for prefectural matters, *Hokkaido Government*, 6 Nishi, Kita-3 ☎ 231 4111. *JETRO*, 6F Hokkaido Keizai Centre, 2 Nishi, Kita-1 ☎ 261 7434/ 231 1122 ext 263, is a good source of advice and statistics.

Information sources

Business information Junior Chamber Incorporated, Keizai Centre, 2 Nishi,

Kita-1 ☎ 231 1122.

Local media The *Mainichi Daily News* and *Japan Times* are the most useful of the Japanese English-language newspapers. For international news, foreign papers can be found in large bookshops and hotels.

Tourist information The *Tourist Information Centre* (TIC), B1 Sapporo station ☎ 251 0828, is a source of essential information, maps and pamphlets. The *JTB*, 4 Nishi, Kita-3 ☎ 241 6201, is also helpful. To call TIC direct, ☎ (0120) 222 800. For detailed information and statistics, contact *Tourism Department, City of Sapporo* ☎ 211 2376 or *Sapporo Tourist Association* ☎ 211 3341, both at City Hall, 2 Nishi, Kita-1. *Hokkaido Tourist Association*, Keizai Centre Bldg, 2 Nishi, Kita-1 ☎ 231 0941, is the place for information on the whole of Hokkaido. *The Monthly Hokkaido* and *What's on in Sapporo* are useful guides to current events.

Thank-yous

For gifts, go to the top department stores, *Mitsukoshi* ☎ 271 3311 and *Matsuzakaya* ☎ 531 1111.

YOKOHAMA

City code ☎ 045

For centuries a small fishing village, Yokohama rose to prominence as Japan's gateway to the West. After the centuries of isolation ended in the mid-19th century, it was through the port of Yokohama that foreign merchandise, technology and ideas poured into the country. Foreign traders, diplomats and businessmen were allowed to settle here and formed a large community. Today, Yokohama retains its international flavour. It is Japan's largest trading port and second largest city, with a population of over 3m. It is also a commercial and industrial metropolis, with shipbuilding, engineering, automobile and petrochemical plants in the factory zone along the shore, and offices of many major international corporations. The city is now engaged in a major land reclamation project, Minato Mirai 21 (MM21 – Future Port 21). By the 21st century a large area of the harbour will be reclaimed, and a vast convention centre, several hotels, a teleport, and business and cultural facilities will be built there.

Arriving

From Tokyo's Narita airport there is a half-hourly limousine bus service to Yokohama's air terminal, but it is probably as quick to make your way into Tokyo and take the train to Yokohama. The entire journey will take over 2hrs during rush hours. From Tokyo's Haneda airport a bus or a taxi to Yokohama take about 30mins. Buses to YCAT and Yokohama station depart every few mins. There is also a helicopter link between Yokohama and both Haneda and Narita: ☎ 221 5750.

Railway stations

Travellers arriving from Tokyo should avoid the Bullet Train and take the Yokosuka (the fastest), Tokkaido or Keihin Tohoku lines direct to Yokohama station. The Keihin Tohoku line will take you on to Kannai, the main business centre, and Ishikawacho. The private Toyoko line (cheaper and faster than the JR lines) connects Shibuya with Yokohama.
Shin Yokohama station, the Bullet Train station, is 8kms/5 miles from Yokohama. Travellers coming from Nagoya and points west will arrive here. Change to the subway or the Yokohama line for the 7min journey to Yokohama station.

Yokohama station This vast complex leads directly into Takashimaya. There are several excellent restaurants here. The station is the transport communications centre for the city, housing the bus terminal and subway line, as well as the JR, Toyoko and Sotetsu lines.

Getting around

Getting to Kannai, which is likely to be your centre of operations, is a quick train journey from other points in Yokohama. From the station, most destinations are a short walk or an easy taxi ride away. There are good maps available, and it is easy to find your way around.
Taxis Hailing a cab on the street is easy. In the middle of the day it may be quicker to walk.
Driving Driving through Yokohama's congested streets is not advisable. Nippon, Rentacar and Japaren have branches in the city.
Bus Even for old Yokohama hands, the buses are confusing.
Subway There is a subway line from Shin Yokohama to Totsuka passing through Yokohama, Sakuragicho and Kannai.
Train The Keihin Tohoku and Yokohama lines go to Sakuragicho, Kannai and Ishikawacho, and on west to Ofuna.

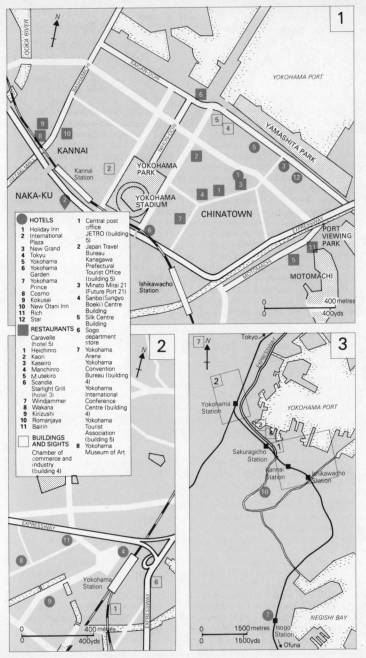

1

YOKOHAMA PORT

KANNAI

Kannai Station

NAKA-KU

YOKOHAMA PARK

YOKOHAMA STADIUM

CHINATOWN

YAMASHITA PARK

PORT VIEWING PARK

Ishikawacho Station

MOTOMACHI

0   400 metres
0   400yds

● HOTELS
1 Holiday Inn
2 International Plaza
3 New Grand
4 Tokyu
5 Yokohama
6 Yokohama Garden
7 Yokohama Prince
8 Cosmo
9 Kokusai
10 New Otani Inn
11 Rich
12 Star

■ RESTAURANTS
Caravelle (hotel 5)
1 Heichinro
2 Kaori
3 Kaseiro
4 Manchinro
5 Mutekiro
6 Scandia Starlight Grill (hotel 3)
7 Windjammer
8 Wakana
9 Kirizushi
10 Romanjaya
11 Bairin

□ BUILDINGS AND SIGHTS
Chamber of commerce and industry (building 4)

1 Central post office
   JETRO (building 5)
2 Japan Travel Bureau
   Kanagawa Prefectural Tourist Office (building 5)
3 Minato Mirai 21 (Future Port 21)
4 Sanbo (Sangyo Boeki) Centre Building
5 Silk Centre Building
6 Sogo department store
7 Yokohama Arena
   Yokohama Convention Bureau (building 4)
   Yokohama International Conference Centre (building 4)
   Yokohama Tourist Association (building 5)
8 Yokohama Museum of Art

2

EXPRESSWAY

Yokohama Station

EXPRESSWAY

0   400 metres
0   400yds

3

Tokyo

EXPRESSWAY

Yokohama Station

Sakuragicho Station

Kannai Station

Ishikawacho Station

YOKOHAMA PORT

NEGISHI BAY

Isogo Station

→ Ofuna

0   1500 metres
0   1500yds

227

Area by area

Yokohama's wilderness of factories, office blocks and housing complexes extends north to merge with Kawasaki and Tokyo. To the south it lightens gradually beyond Totsuka and Ofuna. The hub of all this is the Kannai area, with Yokohama station as a secondary focus. There are many new developments under way, including five high-tech industrial sites. Kohoku New Town, near Shin Yokohama, is already completed and is a business and research centre. Many foreign companies, including Du Pont, Kodak and Wang, have relocated here.

Yokohama station area Around Yokohama's smart new station complex is a glossy shopping and entertainment area, with arcades, both under and overground, cinemas, and department stores, including Takashimaya, Mitsukoshi and the vast Sogo.

Kannai means "within the barrier" and it was in this part of Naka-ku that foreigners were constrained to live. Foreign consulates are still located in this area, which has since become Yokohama's business centre. The square bounded by Kannai station, Bashamichi shopping centre, the harbour and Nihon Odori boulevard contains the City Hall, airline offices, banks, hotels and the head office of the prefectural newspaper, the *Kanagawa Shimbun*. Many major national and international companies have offices here, particularly shipping companies such as Nippon Yusen, Eastern Shipping and Swires. Along Nihon Odori, the wide boulevard stretching from Yokohama Park to the harbour, are the Bank of Japan, the law courts and the prefectural offices. Just east are Yokohama's famous and colourful Chinatown and the fashionable shops of Motomachi.

The suburbs

Yokohama itself serves as a vast suburb, a "bedtown" of Tokyo, with one in ten of its citizens commuting to Tokyo to work. Those who can afford it live in Kohoku, Midori and Hiyoshi or out beyond Yokohama's urban sprawl, among the hills of Kamakura.

Hotels

Yokohama's hotels have a lot of character. Some, particularly the still-prestigious New Grand, retain vestiges of the glamour that enticed foreign tourists by the boatload in the prewar years, though others can only be described as running colourfully to seed. For business travellers looking for a centrally located, modern luxury hotel, The Hotel Yokohama is the place to stay. There are plenty of new hotels in the planning and development stage. The Shin Yokohama Prince will open in 1991 and there will be several hotels on the MM21 site, including an extremely luxurious and futuristic InterContinental, also due to open in 1991.

Holiday Inn 🅈///
77 Yamashitacho, Naka-ku, 231
☎ 681 3311 ⓉⓍ 3822758 fax 681 5082
● *AE DC MC V* ● *186 rooms, 1 suite, 3 restaurants, 1 bar*
The Holiday Inn is located close to the business district, on the edge of Chinatown. While the ornate lobby feels distinctly Chinese, the bedrooms are decorated in standard Holiday Inn style and, apart from views of Chinese neon shop signs, could be anywhere in the world. Hairdresser ● pool ● 7 meeting rooms (capacity up to 500).

International Plaza 🅈///
2-3-3 Bandaicho, Naka-ku, 231
☎ 664 1133 ⓉⓍ 3823224 fax 664 0616
● *AE DC MC V* ● *159 rooms, 2 suites, 5 restaurants, 2 bars, 1 coffee shop*

The International Plaza is a glossy
new hotel, which opened in April
1989, right at Kannai station and very
convenient for the business area of
town. It is still gleaming and shiny,
from the lobby – acres of pale marble
– to the spacious, pleasantly furnished
bedrooms, with views over the city.
No room service, hairdresser, chemist
• pool • 3 meeting rooms (capacity
up to 370).

New Grand *Y*///
10 Yamashitacho, Naka-ku, 231
☎ *681 1841* TX *3823411 fax 681 1895*
• *AE DC MC V* • *187 rooms, 4 suites, 1
restaurant, 1 bar, 1 coffee shop*
The New Grand, dating from 1869, is
Yokohama's oldest hotel; the present
building – a monolithic pile sprawling
along the waterfront – was designed
in 1927 by Watanabe Gin. Before the
war, when Yokohama was the
premier port of call for international
travellers, the Grand was where they
stayed, and in 1945 General
MacArthur made it his headquarters.
Miraculously, it remains largely intact
– from the stone pillars in the lobby,
to the ornate headboards in the
bedrooms and the huge European
baths. The Starlight Grill and Sea
Guardian bar (see *Restaurants* and
Bars) are gathering places for
Yokohama's top executives. The new
300-room annex will be completed in
April 1990. Shops, florist, hairdresser
• 7 meeting rooms (capacity up to
500).

The Hotel Yokohama *Y*///
6-1 Yamashitacho, Naka-ku, 231
☎ *662 1321* TX *3822061 fax 662 3536*
• *AE DC MC V* • *Nikko* • *168 rooms,
2 suites, 2 restaurants, 1 bar, 2 coffee
shops*
Many foreign travellers choose this
modern luxury hotel. The American
Consulate used to stand here, and its
venerable chandelier hangs over the
bright marble lobby. The bedrooms
are a good size and well furnished; it
is worthwhile paying a little extra for
a room overlooking the sea. Caravelle
(see *Restaurants*) is one of

Yokohama's smartest French
restaurants. Florist, beauty salon • 5
meeting rooms (capacity up to 250).

Tokyu *Y*///
1-1-12 Minami-saiwai, Nishi-ku, 220
☎ *311 1682* TX *3822264 fax 311 1084*
• *AE DC MC V* • *209 rooms, 3 suites, 2
restaurants, 1 bar, 1 coffee shop*
The Tokyu is in a prime location,
right beside the station, and it is
always crowded. The rooms are
adequate but very small. Beauty salon
• 8 meeting rooms (capacity up to
250).

Yokohama Garden *Y*///
254 Yamashitacho, Naka-ku, 231
☎ *641 1311 fax 641 1395* • *AE DC
MC V* • *50 rooms, 2 restaurants, 1 bar,
1 coffee shop*
The Yokohama Garden looks onto the
park around the stadium and is close
to both Kannai and Chinatown. It is
a pleasant, very small hotel, with
unusually large rooms. International
calls through hotel operator • 6
meeting rooms (capacity up to 270).

Yokohama Prince *Y*///
3-13-1 Isogo, Isogo-ku, 235
☎ *751 1111* • *441 rooms*
Isogo is an industrial area 10mins by
train from central Yokohama, and the
Prince is where its many companies
house visitors. The hotel occupies the
beautiful grounds of a former prince's
palace. The old palace itself, with its
layers of curving roofs and pagoda-
like spire is perched on the very top
of the hill. The main hotel has been
completely rebuilt, and reopened in
February 1990.

OTHER HOTELS
Cosmo *Y*/// *2-9-1 Kita-saiwai,
Nishi-ku, 220* ☎ *314 3111*
TX *3823632* • *AE DC MC V*. A
Sunroute hotel, recently rebuilt, a
7min walk from Yokohama station.
Kokusai *Y* *2-16 Minami-saiwai,
Nishi-ku, 220* ☎ *311 1311*
TX *3822536 fax 313 3486* • *AE DC
V*. Superior business hotel near the
station.

New Otani Inn *Ɏ* 4-81
Sueyoshicho, Naka-ku, 231 ☎ *252*
1311 ☒ *3823651 fax 252 4884* • *AE*
DC MC V. Member of an excellent
chain, a few mins' subway ride from
Yokohama station, in the Isezaki
shopping area.
Rich *Ɏ⫼* *1-11-3 Kita-saiwai,*
Nishi-ku, 220 ☎ *312 2111*
☒ *3823761 fax 312 2143* • *AE DC*

MC V. Of the hotels in the station
area, the Rich is generally considered
to be the best.
Star *Ɏ* 11 *Yamashitacho,*
Naka-ku, 231 ☎ *651 3111*
☒ *3823578 fax 651 3119* • *AE DC*
MC V. One of Yokohama's newest
hotels, the Star is squeezed in next to
the New Grand, facing Yamashita
Park.

Restaurants

For an important dinner, many visiting businessmen, both Japanese and
Western, play safe and go to the grand old Tokyo establishments half an
hour away by train. However, Yokohama has many fine restaurants,
patronized by the local business community. Most are in Chinatown and
along the Bund (now Kaigan-dori), the old European area.

NON-JAPANESE
Caravelle *Ɏ⫼*
F13 The Hotel Yokohama, 6-1
Yamashitacho, Naka-ku ☎ *662 1321* •
AE DC MC V
Much expense-account dining goes on
at the Caravelle, with its spectacular
views over the harbour and live piano
music. The cuisine is French, and
fish and seafood are the specialities. A
good place to entertain Japanese
colleagues.

Heichinro *Ɏ*
149 Yamashitacho, Naka-ku
☎ *681 3001* • *AE DC MC V*
Chinatown's oldest and most
celebrated restaurant, Heichinro
celebrated its hundredth anniversary
by having a facelift. Its splendid
seven-floor building opened in April
1986 and makes a striking contrast to
the surrounding clutter of Chinese
restaurants, junk shops and cookie
stalls. The regular clientele seem to
like the elegant interiors with their
spotlights and tasteful Chinese motifs,
and the Cantonese cuisine remains
superlative.

Kaori *Ɏ*
70 Yamashitacho ☎ *681 4401* • *AE*
DC MC V
Kaori is the place where Yokohama's
potentates – the city governors,

representatives of the chamber of
commerce and top business figures –
entertain. The owner's father,
apparently, was a sailor, and the
restaurant has been providing the city
with good French food for over 50
years.

Kaseiro *Ɏ*
164 Yamashitacho, Naka-ku
☎ *661 0661* • *AE DC MC V*
Kaseiro's atmosphere is best
described as high-class Chinese. The
thick red carpets are top quality, and
the pale gold walls are adorned, not
with extravagant carvings, but with
tasteful framed black and white ink
paintings. The Peking cuisine is the
best in Chinatown, and the tatami
rooms upstairs are much used for
business entertaining.

Manchinro *Ɏ*
153 Yamashitacho, Naka-ku
☎ *681 4004* • *AE DC MC V*
Manchinro is a Chinatown institution,
with all the colour and flamboyance
of Hong Kong. Ladies in red and
gold silk *cheongsam* lead you past
screens carved with dragons to the
vast dining rooms full of ornate
wooden panelling and hung with red
paper lanterns. Here Western and
Japanese businessmen, as well as
Chinese families, crowd in for *yum*

cha at lunchtime or feast on Cantonese delights prepared by the 23 Chinese chefs, ranging from sautéed frogs to bear's paw.

Mutekiro *Y*/
2-96 Motomachi ☎ *681 2926* • *closed 1st and 3rd Mon of month* • *AE DC MC V*
At Mutekiro, while the cuisine is French, the service is Japanese. The main dining room of this vast Western-style house is like a ship's galley, with an enormous fish hanging on one wall and waiters dressed like ships' stewards in white jackets with gold braid on the shoulders; the speciality, appropriately, is fish. On the upper floors are tatami rooms where French cuisine is served on Arita china and you eat with chopsticks. The wine list includes some fine vintages.

Scandia *Y*/
1-1 Kaigan-dori, Naka-ku ☎ *201 2262* • *closed Sun L*
Japanese love the European atmosphere of Scandia, with its high ceilings, heavy draperies and wooden carvings. It is famous for its smorgasbord and serves French as well as Scandinavian dishes. The clientele is largely professional; this is a highly appropriate place to return hospitality.

Starlight Grill *Y*///
5F Hotel New Grand, 10 Yamashitacho, Naka-ku ☎ *681 1841* • *AE DC MC V*
In the days when fashionable and wealthy Europeans strolled the streets of Yokohama, they used to dine at the top of the New Grand, looking out over the harbour. Today the restaurant, with its tasselled gold draperies and courteous white-jacketed waiters, still preserves the atmosphere of Old World gentility, making this a very suitable place to entertain Japanese colleagues. The cuisine is still French, though the chef is now Japanese, and there is an extensive wine list.

Windjammer *Y*/
215 Yamashitacho, Naka-ku ☎ *661 0462* • *closed L* • *AE DC MC V*
American Jim Stockwell started Windjammer around 1970. It has since changed from a San Francisco-style dinner restaurant to French, serving traditional and *nouvelle* cuisine, but continues to be one of the most popular gathering places for Westerners, both resident and visiting. Many of the regular Japanese clientele came here first as guests of Western colleagues. The interior is designed like the inside of a ship, and the atmosphere is quiet and congenial. (See also *Bars*.)

JAPANESE
Many people come to Yokohama just to eat in Chinatown; but there are plenty of fine Japanese restaurants too. For lovers of eel, prepared Japanese-style, grilled over charcoal and brushed with a sweet thick sauce, *Wakana*, 5-20 Minatocho, Naka-ku ☎ 681 1404, is said to serve some of the best in Japan. You can dine on the fine sushi at *Kirizushi*, 1F No. 6 Suga Bldg, 5-72 Tokiwacho, Naka-ku ☎ 662 4150, either informally at the sushi bar or in one of the tatami rooms upstairs. *Romanjaya*, B1 Shin Kannai Bldg, 4-45 Sumiyoshicho, Naka-ku ☎ 681 2727, is a branch of Tokyo's Seryna (see Tokyo *restaurants*) and provides the local Kannai business community with reliably fine shabu shabu. *Bairin*, 1-69 Motomachi ☎ 662 2215, is a grand old restaurant which serves a variety of Japanese dishes not watered down to suit Western taste, including some which make raw fish look very tame.

Bars
Yokohama has little nightlife of its own to compete with the bright lights of Tokyo, 30mins up the line. The main bar area stretches from Sakuragicho to Kannai, but it caters mainly to foreign sailors. More civilized drinking can be found in Yamashitacho.

For a sophisticated drink, the place to go is a hotel bar. Once the haunt of fashionable young men-about-town, the New Grand's *Sea Guardian* bar is now the gathering place of the city's top executives. They are also to be found at The Hotel Yokohama's *Red Shoes*, which has a magnificent view across the harbour. The bar at Windjammer (see *Restaurants*) is where the local Western community comes to relax. Like the restaurant upstairs, it is designed like the inside of a ship, with closely packed tables and plenty of atmosphere. Jim Stockwell's latest venture, *Cable Car*, 200 Yamashitacho, on the other hand, looks like the inside of a San Francisco cable car. Both are excellent places to visit, either with Japanese colleagus, who enjoy the American atmosphere, or alone.

Entertainment

With Tokyo just up the road, Yokohama's cultural facilities are inevitably limited, though with the opening of the vast Yokohama Arena, 3-10 Shin Yokohama, Kita-ku (just in front of Shin Yokohama station), more and more cultural and sporting events are being held here. The arena holds 17,000 people and is Japan's largest stadium.

Theatre, cinema and music Visiting international and Japanese performers frequently make their way down to Yokohama. The main venues are in the Kannai area and around Yokohama station. Several cinemas show English-language films.

Nightclubs Yokohama's most popular nightspot is *Cowbell*, 12F Yokohama Centre Bldg, 3-33 Masagocho, Naka-ku; you can dine and dance until 4am. The *Bayside Club*, 3-7 Shin Yamashita, is also popular.

Shopping

Most of Yokohama's glossiest shops are clustered in the arcades around and under the station. At the west exit are the prestigious department stores *Mitsukoshi* and *Takashimaya*, along with the popular *Joinus*, several

shops selling high fashion, and a branch of the bargain camera chain, *Yodobashi Camera*. The shopping area east of the station is a more recent development, and includes a vast new *Sogo*, one of the largest department stores in the world. Yokohama's other major department store is *Matsuzakaya*, in the Isezakicho shopping mall. Isezaki is the area to look for souvenirs and tax-free goods. Motomachi is where the foreigners used to shop. It is now full of boutiques and antique shops.

Sightseeing

Chinatown is worth exploring and there are panoramic views of the port from the Port Viewing Park up on the Bluffs. The monuments, shrines and museums of Kamakura are only 30mins away.

Sankeien Garden Sankeien is a beautiful Japanese garden, laid out by Tomitaro Hara, a millionaire silk merchant, at the turn of the century. Dotted around the grounds are some fine old buildings brought from all over Japan, including a shogun's villa, a 17thC tea house and an old thatched farmhouse. *293 Honmoku-sannotani, Naka-ku. Open 9–4.*

Silk Centre Silk was the main export of the port of Yokohama, and the fascinating museum in the Silk Centre records the history of silk in Japan. The Centre also houses the Tourist Information Centre and the offices of many of the major shipping companies. *1 Yamashitacho, Naka-ku.*

Yokohama Art Museum The first building completed on the MM21 site, the museum opened March 1989. The emphasis is on contemporary art, including an excellent collection of photographs. *Open 9.30–5.30.*

Spectator sports

Baseball is the most popular sport. The Taiyo Whales, the city's team, play at *Yokohama stadium*, Yokohama Park, Naka-ku ☎ 641 1421. Many sporting events are also held at the *Yokohama arena* (see *Entertainment*).

Keeping fit

The first facilities were built by foreign residents – mainly the British. The Yokohama Country and Athletic Club (YCAC), which opened in 1870, provided a cricket pitch and continues to thrive.

Fitness centres The *YCAC*, 11-1 Yaguchidai, Naka-ku ☎ 623 8121; *Yokohama Cultural and Athletic Hall*, 2-7 Hurocho, Naka-ku ☎ 641 5741.

Jogging In the morning you can jog in *Yamashita* or *Yokohama Parks*.

Swimming Motomachi Park Pool, 15 Nihon Odori, Naka-ku ☎ 661 0691. If you prefer a beach, head for the *Miura Peninsula*.

Local resources

Business services

At present none of the hotels provides business services, though the InterContinental, when it opens in 1991, will be well equipped. The *Yokohama Convention Bureau*, 6F Sangyo Boeki Centre Bldg, 2 Yamashitacho, Naka-ku ☎ 221 2111, sponsored by the City of Yokohama, primarily organizes conferences and conventions, but it can also provide back-up services for foreign businessmen. Commercial companies providing business services include *Manpower Japan* ☎ 314 1222, *Kao Co* ☎ 319 8635 and *Temporary Centre Corporation* ☎ 681 0781.

Photocopying and printing All hotels provide photocopying services and will arrange printing for you.

Translation JES ☎ 313 3721; *TS International Co* ☎ 314 6608.

Communications

International couriers DHL ☎ 201 1022.

Post offices Main office: Yokohama station east exit ☎ 461 1385.

Telex and fax At major hotels; *KDD Yokohama* ☎ 671 8051.

Conference/exhibition centres

When the *Pacifico Yokohama Convention Centre* on the MM21 site is completed in 1991, it will be the city's main venue. Until then conventions are held at the *Yokohama International Conference Centre*, administered by *Yokohama Association for International Communications and Exchanges*, 3F Sangyo Boeki Centre Bldg, 2 Yamashitacho, Naka-ku ☎ 671 7128/7151. Conventions are also held at the *Yokohama Arena*.

Emergencies

Hospitals Saiseikai Kanagawa-ken Hospital, 6-6 Tomiyacho, Kanagawa-ku ☎ 432 1111, has a 24hr casualty department, as does *Washinzaka Hospital*, 169 Yamatecho, Naka-ku ☎ 623 7688. There are also several English and German-speaking doctors in Yokohama; ask at your hotel. No dentists offer 24hr emergency treatment, but several speak English or German. Ambulance ☎ 119.

Pharmacies Prescription drugs are supplied by hospitals.

Police ☎ 623 0110 (ask for the Foreign Affairs Department).

Government offices

International Relations Division, the City of Yokohama ☎ 671 2079.

Information sources

Business information The *Yokohama Chamber of Commerce*, 2 Yamashitacho, Naka-ku ☎ 671 7411; *JETRO*, Silk Centre Bldg, 1 Yamashitacho, Naka-ku ☎ 641 4990.

Local media The *Mainichi English Weekly* offers an English telephone service for an update on current news ☎ 322 1819. *JCTV* can be received in Yokohama.

Tourist information The *Yokohama Municipal Tourist Association*, Silk Centre, 1 Yamashitacho, Naka-ku ☎ 641 5824; *Yokohama Association for International Communications and Exchanges (YOKE)*, 3F Sangyo Boeki Centre Bldg, 2 Yamashitacho, Naka-ku ☎ 671 7128.

Thank-yous

A gift-wrapped item from a major department store (see *Shopping*).

Florist Misugi Florist ☎ 641 1187 or *Florist Sakata* ☎ 453 1120.

Planning and Reference

Entry details

The following requirements and regulations apply to visitors regardless of port of entry.

Documentation

Passports Required by all visitors and it must be carried at all times.

Visas Japan has mutual agreements with over 40 states. For example, citizens of the USA, most Western European countries, and South American countries may stay for up to three months without a visa. But it is always sensible to check the requirements. Short-stay permits can be extended at an immigration office in Japan.

Health regulations Certificates of vaccination are needed only if entering from an area where typhoid and cholera are endemic. Those travelling via Southeast Asia with stopovers en route should check the inoculation requirements of the countries concerned.

Driving licence If you intend to drive in Japan you will need an international driving licence.

Customs regulations

Personal effects and portable professional equipment not intended for sale are free from duty. Items, such as samples, can be sent separately by mail but a customs declaration form from your post office should be shown to customs officials on your arrival and to the Japanese post office upon collection. Parcels without a customs declaration are subject to duty.

Things you cannot bring in freely include pornography (defined as illustrations showing pubic hair, ie most men's magazines); some drugs; firearms and explosives; and some fresh foods, particularly fruit and vegetables from tropical countries. If travelling with prescribed drugs, carry a copy of the prescription or a doctor's certificate.

Customs allowances The duty-free allowances are: three 76cl bottles of alcoholic beverages; 400 cigarettes *or* 100 cigars *or* 500g of tobacco, *or* any combination with a combined weight of 500g; 57g/2 fl oz of perfume; gifts and souvenirs with a total market price of Y200,000 or its equivalent. If you have unaccompanied baggage arriving by a later flight, you *must* declare it to customs, on the form provided, when you arrive, otherwise it will not be allowed duty-free entry.

Climate

Japan is a long, thin, mountainous archipelago and climate varies considerably, depending on latitude, topography and ocean currents. There are four main climatic regions.

The Pacific Coast region comprises Shikoku, northern Kyushu and eastern Honshu, including Tokyo, Nagoya, Kyoto, Osaka and Kobe. Summers are hot and humid, with temperatures consistently over 27°C/80°F. Summer officially lasts from June 1 to September 1 but the warm weather often continues to the end of October; wear light clothing and take extra shirts or blouses – it may be necessary to shower several times a day. Winter temperatures in Tokyo can be very cold, similar to those in New York. It often freezes, but heavy snowfalls are uncommon. Annual rainfall is around 150cm/60in. Spring and autumn are wettest but there is also a short rainy season, *tsuyu*, beginning in mid-June and continuing into July. Winter is the driest season.

The Japan Sea region, to the west of Honshu, is characterized by severe winter snowfalls. Snow can reach depths of over 3 metres/10ft in places.

Hokkaido, in the north, has bitterly cold winters, short, late springs and early autumns. It escapes the June rainy season and summer temperatures are 21–24°C/70–75°F.

Southern Kyushu is sub-tropical; with cool winters, hot, humid summers and an early spring and autumn. The rainy season begins at the end of May and continues through June. September is the season of typhoons.

Holidays

There are three periods to avoid in planning a business trip to Japan; the New Year (Dec 28–Jan 5), Golden Week (Apr 29–May 5) and Obon (a week in mid-August) when families visit the graves of their ancestors. At these times, hotels and trains are filled to capacity and most businesses and many restaurants and shops are closed. During the other national public holidays listed below shops, restaurants and so on usually remain open but it is not normally possible to arrange business meetings on these days. Where a public holiday falls on a Sunday, the Monday is taken as a holiday.

Jan 1 *Gantan* (New Year's Day)
Jan 15 *Seijin-no-Hi* (Adults' Day)
Feb 11 *Kenkoku kinen-bi* (National Foundation Day)
Mar 20 or 21 *Shunbun-no-Hi* (Spring Equinox)
Apr 29 *Midori-no-hi* (Greenery Day)
May 3 *Kempo kinen-bi* (Constitution Memorial Day)
May 4 Holiday
May 5 *Kodomo-no-Hi* (Children's Day)
Sep 15 *Keiro-no-Hi* (Respect for the Aged Day)
Sep 23 *Shubun-no-Hi* (Autumn Equinox)
Oct 10 *Taiiku-no-Hi* (Health and Sports Day)
Nov 3 *Bunka-no-Hi* (Culture Day)
Nov 23 *Kinro kansha-no-Hi* (Labour Thanksgiving Day)
Dec 23 *Tenno Tanjobi* (Emperor's birthday)

Information sources

In your own country

Business information In capital cities your government agencies are good sources of information. The *Japanese*

Embassy will provide background information and addresses for other organizations. The *Japanese Chamber of Commerce and Industry* and the *Japan External Trade Organization* (*JETRO*) have information on the economy, business and market entry.
Tourist information The *Japan National Tourist Organization* (*JNTO*) has offices around the world giving information on travel, accommodation, culture and sightseeing. Other contact points are *Japan Airlines* (*JAL*), *All Nippon Airways* (*ANA*) and the *Japan Travel Bureau* (*JTB*), a private agency specializing in travel to and accommodation in Japan.

Money

Japan has traditionally been very much a cash economy. Personal cheques are still rare but major credit cards are increasingly accepted. If you need to pay by card, always check before making a firm hotel or restaurant reservation, or purchase.

Local currency

Japan's unit of currency is the yen (Y). Coins used are 1, 5, 10, 50, 100 and 500 yen. Banknotes are issued in denominations of 1,000, 5,000 and 10,000 yen. Only yen may legally be spent in Japan; unlike the rest of Asia, US dollars are not accepted in cash transactions.
Acceptable currencies The currencies of most European countries and those of the USA, Canada, Australia and Hong Kong can be exchanged. The currencies of Taiwan and Korea will not be exchanged in Japan.

You can convert yen into foreign currency before leaving, but only US dollars are readily available. There is no limit on the amount of yen which can be taken out of Japan.
Traveller's cheques are the safest way to carry your money, although in Japan this should be weighed against the low incidence of crime and the time it can take to cash the cheques. Yen cheques are more convenient than those denominated in other

currencies as they can be cashed at major hotels and at big city stores that have a large foreign clientele. Outside the cities, only yen traveller's cheques will be readily changed by a bank.

Credit and charge cards American Express (AE), Diners Club (DC), MasterCard/Access (MC) and Visa (V) are accepted in the major hotels and Western restaurants and in high-quality shops. Cards cannot be relied on to the exclusion of cash. Outside the main cities credit cards are often not acceptable, even by hotels, and you should check this when making reservations.

Changing money

On presentation of your passport, currency and traveller's cheques can be exchanged during office hours at the international airports, at banks that have a foreign exchange desk and at most major hotels, whose facilities are usually quicker and open longer. Banks offer the best exchange rate.

Banks

Most banks have a separate foreign exchange department. Show your passport and you will be given a number and asked to wait in line. A number of foreign banks have one or more branches in Tokyo. Banking hours are Mon–Fri, 9–3; Sat, 9–12; all banks close on the 2nd and 4th Sat of the month.

Tipping

Tipping is neither customary nor expected. Indeed, proffering a tip may well cause offence. If you wish to reward for exceptional personal service, a small token from your home country would be warmly received, though not expected; a sincere "thank you" (*domo arigato*) is all that is really required. Most hotel, bar and restaurant bills include a service charge. At airports and major stations, there is a fixed charge for baggage handling (between Y100 and Y300 per piece). Tariffs are always clearly displayed.

Getting there

Japan is well served by international flights. From Europe it is a long haul, although the introduction of direct flights has cut the journey time from London, for example, to 11 hrs. Direct flights from New York take around 15 hrs. Departing passengers must pay an airport tax of Y2,000.

Gateway airports

Most scheduled flights land at Tokyo's Narita airport. The Kansai international airport will be functioning by the mid-1990s, to relieve the pressure on Narita, and a new international airport, near Nagoya, is also planned.

Narita This busy international airport, 60kms/40 miles northeast of Tokyo, is served by most international carriers. Allow 2hrs plus to get from Narita to central Tokyo or to transfer to Tokyo's Haneda airport for a domestic flight.

Haneda China Airlines is the only international airline which lands here. Situated to the southwest of Tokyo, Haneda is now the main domestic air terminal.

Osaka Regular flights arrive from Los Angeles, Hong Kong, Singapore, Bangkok and other Asian cities. The airport is convenient for Kyoto.

Nagoya Direct flights arrive from Hong Kong, Seoul, Manila, Singapore, Vancouver and Sydney, Australia, and more direct connections are planned.

Others Kagoshima on Kyushu has direct flights from Hong Kong, Singapore and several other Asian cities. Kumamoto (also on Kyushu) receives flights from Korea. A limited number of flights arrive at Niigata on Honshu, Fukuoka on Kyushu and Naha on Okinawa.

Getting around

For inter-city journeys executives travel either by train or by air. Flying, though slightly more expensive, is the best option on longer trips, such as that from Tokyo to Fukuoka, or to cities not served by the Bullet Train. Driving is rarely a viable option.

Within cities, taxis are most convenient, although in the rush hour the subway may be quicker.

Air

There is a well-developed internal air network. The major carriers are Japan Airlines (JAL), All Nippon Airways (ANA) and Toa Domestic Airlines (TDA). Most major cities have an airport, although for Kyoto you have to fly to Osaka. Tickets can be purchased at all major travel agents in Japan. There are no discount tickets for internal routes, nor is there any type of air pass.

Train

The Japanese Railway (JR) runs one of the most efficient and comprehensive railway networks in the world. Trains are frequent, punctual and clean, and are categorized on the basis of speed. Fastest of all is the *Shinkansen* or Bullet Train, covering the 1,177kms/730 miles between Tokyo and Fukuoka in only 6 hrs. Other trains include limited express (*tokkyu*), express (*kyuko*), rapid (*kaisoku*) and local (*futsu*). Private railway companies run slightly cheaper suburban services from major cities.

Fares are calculated according to distance, with surcharges on all journeys except on rapid and local trains.

Seat reservations are advised on long distance trains, particularly at weekends and on national holidays. Reservations cannot be made more than one month prior to the date of travel.

Tickets for short rides are sold from vending machines. If in doubt about the correct fare, buy the cheapest ticket and pay the difference at the fare adjustment office at your destination. For longer journeys, ordinary and Green Car (first class) tickets can be purchased from the travel service centres at stations or from travel agents. There is a range of discount tickets; fares depend on the day of travel, distance and length of stay.

Rail pass Foreign visitors can buy a Japan Rail pass for ordinary or first class travel, which offers unlimited journeys at substantial savings for periods of 7, 14 or 21 days. The pass can be purchased only *outside Japan*, through a JAL office (if you fly with JAL) or authorized travel agency such as JTB. They will issue a voucher to be exchanged for a pass in Japan.

Facilities Long-distance trains have dining or buffet cars with a reasonable range of fare. *Ekiben* – lunch boxes of Japanese food – and a good selection of snacks and drinks are available on most long-distance trains and on station platforms. Smoking is prohibited on commuter trains. Other trains have cars or seats allocated for smokers. *Shinkansen* trains are equipped with telephone card-operated telephones.

Information The Japan National Tourist Organization (JNTO) produces a condensed railway timetable summarizing all JR's services and fares. The travel information and service centres at major stations will reserve tickets and supply information.

Taxi

Taxis are plentiful in the day, less easy to find at night. They are also clean and air-conditioned. Few drivers speak English and most have only a patchy knowledge of their city. Ask your hotel porter to brief the driver and to write down your destination in Japanese. For the return journey, carry matches or headed paper from the hotel to show to the driver. Allow plenty of time for your journey.

Hailing a cab Use your outstretched arm, fingers pointing slightly down; never whistle. When it's raining, or at night, you will see people hailing cabs with two, three or four fingers raised, indicating that they will pay that number of times the normal fare.

Cabs show a red light when free, yellow when answering a radio or telephone call (20% surcharge) and green when the night surcharge is payable (20% surcharge between 11pm and 5am). Fares are on a meter that measures time and distance; expressway tolls are added. Drivers operate the passenger door by automatic control; stand clear as it opens and do not try to close it yourself.

Subway

Tokyo, Osaka, Nagoya, Yokohama, Fukuoka and Sapporo have extensive subway systems which are relatively easy for foreigners to use. Tickets are sold from vending machines at the stations. If you are unsure of the fare buy a minimum fare ticket and pay the balance to the guard on the ticket barrier at your destination. There is no smoking on stations or trains.

Driving

Car rental is rarely worthwhile because of the poor road system, traffic congestion and parking problems. However, if you plan an extended stay and have friends to help with the directions, there are branches of the larger car rental chains in all major cities. The car itself, rather than the driver, will usually already be insured, but check this. Drinking and driving is illegal, and the law is strictly enforced. **Roads** Traffic jams are common during rush hours, weekends and holidays. The Japanese drive on the left and use conventional international road signs. The speed limit on expressways is 100kmph/62mph, on highways 60kmph/37mph, on most other roads 40kmph/25mph and in the cities 30kmph/19mph.

The *Japan Automobile Federation* (JAF) has reciprocal agreements with most automobile associations throughout the world; it produces a booklet giving details about Japanese traffic laws. Contact JAF at 3-5-4, Shiba Koen, Minato-ku, Tokyo ☎ (03) 436 2811.

Bus

City buses are frequent but often follow tortuous routes and display destinations only in Japanese. They offer a leisurely method of sightseeing and orientation.

Hotels

The 1980s saw an ambitious programme of hotel building. The number of hotels with business service facilities is increasing rapidly, and many hotels which do not yet have executive floors are planning them. Many hotels, particularly new ones, now have a gym and fitness centre. Traditionally, the most prestigious and expensive hotel in town has been the oldest, but this is less true today. Choice of hotel is crucial to the impression you create in Japan, and money spent on high-priced accommodation should be seen as a worthwhile investment. Outside Tokyo, more and more hotels of an international standard are being built. Many, however, still cater to the needs of Japanese rather than Western business travellers; service is excellent but rooms may be cramped.

Styles and standards

Western-style Most business travellers (including Japanese) stay in Western-style hotels. Service is always impeccable, and at the top end of the scale standards are very high.
Japanese-style Every hotel has a few Japanese rooms, largely unfurnished except for the beautiful straw tatami mats on the floor on which your bedding is laid out at night, and a deep Japanese bath. A *ryokan*, or Japanese-style inn, offers a relaxing and highly aesthetic experience. Your tatami-matted room, complete with television, will probably overlook a Japanese garden of stones and moss. The price of the room includes meals, served in your room by your personal maid; there is no restaurant or bar. A *ryokan* is ideal for a weekend off but is not suitable for working in.
Business and budget hotels The traveller on a tight budget can follow

the lead of many Japanese businessmen and use a business hotel. These are designed for sleeping, not working, and do not offer the facilities of a full-scale hotel. The majority of the rooms are singles and are extremely small.

The accommodation

Public areas Lobbies are vast and often extravagantly splendid. There is usually no lounge as such, but there will be at least one coffee shop or tea lounge suitable for an informal discussion. Hotel restaurants are often the most highly-rated places to eat in town, while the hotel bar is a favoured meeting place for local businessmen. Most hotels have shops or a shopping arcade, sometimes with branches of major department and luxury stores.

Bedrooms The standard hotel bedroom could charitably be described as compact; only those in the top hotels are big enough to work in comfortably. Most business travellers prefer a twin or double room for single occupation. From a few hotels you may have to make international calls via the front desk.

Prices

In a luxury Tokyo hotel, you can expect to pay more than Y20,000 a night for a twin or double room at single occupancy rates (exclusive of meals), and in the best hotels you will be paying as much as Y30,000. Prices are considerably lower outside Tokyo; budget for Y15,000 for a twin in a top hotel. A single room in a business hotel will cost Y10–12,000 in Tokyo, Y6–8,000 elsewhere. A 6% tax and 10% service charge will be added to your total bill (including meals and drinks at the hotel). *Ryokans* vary widely in price, but are generally more expensive than other hotels; the average cost is Y30,000 per head, inclusive of dinner and breakfast.

Few hotels offer corporate rates but many offer special executive packages, at an inclusive price which covers extras such as breakfast.

Making reservations

You should make reservations at least a week in advance. During the busy holiday periods – New Year, Golden Week in May and the first two weeks of August – hotels are fully booked weeks, if not months, beforehand. Reservations can be made directly by telephone, telex or fax, or, for the larger chains, through booking offices in the USA and Europe.

Major hotel chains

Most hotels in Japan belong to chains, which have fairly distinct characters and characteristics. Most hotel chains are Japanese owned and managed, are frequently part of a large conglomerate and linked to other business interests such as department stores and railway lines. The major airlines, for example, ANA and JAL, own enormous luxury hotels in many cities; and recently some of Japan's grandest old hotels, such as the Okura, have produced offshoots. In recent years international chains have begun to take a keen interest in Japan. There are several fine Hiltons here, for example, even in Nagoya, a city famed for its insularity; and chains such as Ramada are opening hotels here. Now that the InterContinental chain is Japanese owned and managed (by the extraordinarily vigorous Seibu Saisons group), the most interesting new development is likely to be the opening of InterContinentals in major Japanese cities, beginning with the luxurious Yokohama InterContinental, in 1991.

ANA 25 Mori Bldg, 1-4-30 Roppongi, Minato-ku, Tokyo 106 ☎ (03) 505 1181 ⊤ₓ *2223848 fax 505 1180. USA ☎ New York (212) 582-0700 fax (212) 582-3789. UK ☎ London (01) 493 4856 fax (01) 493 5577.* ANA (All Nippon Airways) opened several deluxe hotels in 1989 and 1990, bringing their total of non-resort Japanese hotels to 15. These hotels are built on the American scale, with abundant luxury and offer many services, including business service centres and foreign staff.

Hilton *6-6-2 Nishi Shinjuku, Shinjuku-ku, Tokyo 160* ☎ *(03) 344 5111/213 4053.* USA (toll-free) ☎ *(800) 358-1133.* UK ☎ *London (01) 631 1767.*

Hilton has hotels in Tokyo, Osaka, Nagoya and Tokyo Bay. All are well up to Hilton standards and particularly appropriate for the international traveller, with luxurious and well-equipped executive floors and comprehensive business service centres. The EBS (Executive Business Service) programme ensures preferential reservations, express check-out, and use of special business facilities.

Miyako *(Kintetsu chain) 1-1-50 Shiroganedai, Minato-ku, Tokyo 108* ☎ *(03) 447 3111.*

The 15 Miyako hotels, mostly in the Osaka/Kyoto area, vary widely in standard, from Kyoto's finest hotel to rather run-of-the-mill first class hotels. One can, however, expect excellent service and a certain quiet dignity from any Miyako hotel.

New Otani *4-1 Kioicho, Chiyoda-ku, Tokyo 100* ☎ *(03) 265 1111.* USA (toll-free) ☎ *(800) 421-8795.* UK ☎ *London (01) 731 4231/3.*

Any New Otani can be confidently assumed to be one of the best hotels in town, unfailingly elegant in decor, with efficient and pleasant staff. It will often be the first choice of visiting foreign executives. In addition to Tokyo's enormous New Otani, there are 18 others, including some budget New Otani Inns. The New Otani Club offers preferential reservations and discounts.

Nikko *9F Jowa Yaesu Bldg, 2-4-1 Yaesu, Chuo-ku, Tokyo 104* ☎ *(03) 281 4321.* USA ☎ *New York (212) 247-0330.* UK ☎ *London (01) 412 4288.*

Japan Airlines has built only a few Nikko hotels as yet, of a style and standard similar to the ANA hotels; but many of the best hotels in Japan come under the umbrella of Nikko Hotels International, bookable through JAL.

Okura *2-10-4 Toranomon, Minato-ku, Tokyo 105.* ☎ *582 0111, ext 3280.* USA ☎ *New York (212) 755 0733.* UK ☎ *London (01) 995 8211.*

With the opening of the magnificent new Okura in Kobe, the Okura chain now has 4 non-resort hotels in Japan. All are outstanding and all offer the same fine service and dignified environment as the first and most famous Okura, grande dame of Tokyo hotels.

Prince *8F Prince Promenade PePe, 1-30-1 Kabukicho, Shinjuku-ku, Tokyo 160* ☎ *(03) 209 8686.* USA (toll-free) ☎ *(800) 542-8686.*

Prince hotels are all different, and include some spectacular modern architecture. Standards vary widely; the Tokyo, Akasaka and Takanawa Prince hotels are among the best in Tokyo, but others are definitely second rate. There are preferential rates and privileges for members of the Prince Club International.

Tokyu *6-6 Kojimachi, Chiyoda-ku, Tokyo 102* ☎ *(03) 264 4436.* USA (toll-free) ☎ *(800) 822-0016.* UK ☎ *London (01) 493 2585.*

Every major city has a Tokyu hotel, built to a pattern several years ago and looking a little the worse for wear, but with a comfortably familiar decor and good service at a reasonable price. Apart from the Capitol Tokyu – considered by some to be the best hotel in Tokyo – and the wonderfully extravagant Nagoya Tokyu, the largest yet – the 18 Tokyu hotels are first class rather than deluxe.

Business hotel chains

The following chains have a good reputation among Japanese businessmen and offer cheap, good quality accommodation throughout Japan, at a consistent standard.

Dajichi ☎ *(03) 501 5161.* Top business hotels, usually very well situated near the business and entertainment areas of major cities.

JR Hotel Group ☎ *(03) 216 0489.* Major cities have a terminal or a station hotel. Usually the main attraction is the location, though

some – such as the Hiroshima Terminal – are pleasant and comfortable as well as well located.
Mitsui Urban ☎ *(03) 279 5711.* Has one of the best reputations among business hotel chains.
Sunroute ☎ *(03) 375 3211.* An extremely economical chain with about 50 small, friendly hotels, including four in Tokyo; the rooms, though small, are pleasant.
Tokyu Inn ☎ *(03) 462 0109.* Very pleasant business hotels, to be found in every major city.

Our recommended hotels

The hotels that we have selected are of a consistently high standard, conveniently located for the major business areas of each city, and particularly suitable for travelling foreign executives. We have included hotels ranging in style and price from the top hotels of each city, including some of the world's best, down to cheaper but reliable hotels designed specifically for the business traveller.

Standard facilities

Almost all hotels have at least one restaurant and a bar. Unless otherwise stated, the following facilities are standard at all hotels given full entries.
Credit cards Major credit cards are accepted. Check when booking.
Facilities Central heating and air conditioning (most Japanese hotel rooms are hermetically sealed, and an opening window is a rarity); Western bed and furniture, including desk; adjoining bathroom with a bath and/or a shower, toothbrush, toothpaste, razor, etc. and a Western toilet; television; radio; direct dial telephone; refrigerator; tea-making facilities; cotton dressing gown and slippers.
Services Room service (24hr service is unusual); laundry service.
Shops Several shops, including a gift shop.

Additional facilities

Good hotels will have an English-speaking concierge to make travel, restaurant and entertainment bookings. Massages are often available, conducted in your room. Many bedrooms have a minibar. Hotel parking, however, can be very limited.
Sports facilities Many top hotels have indoor or outdoor pools and a sauna. More and more have health clubs with gyms, whose facilities are available to hotel guests at special rates.

Business facilities

As yet few Japanese hotels have full business service centres. Unless otherwise stated, all hotels given full entries offer telex, fax and photocopying at the front desk. Other facilities – often open to non-hotel guests – are as follows.
Secretarial services This usually means a desk operated by a secretarial firm. They generally provide typing, translation and interpreting. Word processing, typewriter rental and business card printing may be available. All services are at Japanese commercial rates.
Business service centre with limited facilities A small centre provided by the hotel for the use of hotel guests. Facilities similar to those offered by secretarial firms are usually complimentary or offered at discounted rates.
Business service centre with extensive facilities A centre based in a sizeable lounge, equipped with a library of business reference books and a variety of facilities, likely to include a photocopier, a Kyodo News Service printer, typewriters and word processors. There will be high calibre secretarial assistance, which will include introductions to business contacts and business consultancy, as well as normal secretarial services. Meeting rooms with audio visual and simultaneous translation facilities are usually available.
Meeting rooms Most hotels have facilities for holding receptions, conferences and meetings, but

reservations should be made well in advance. Always remember that the prestige of the venue reflects the prestige of the host company.

Other hotels

Most hotels under this heading are economy hotels which are members of business hotel chains (see earlier). They are usually located near the station and business areas. Rooms, all with small private bathroom, will be cramped but pleasant and spotlessly clean. There is usually no room service and international calls must be made via the hotel switchboard. Shops are limited and rooms will not have a refrigerated minibar.

Price band system

The price symbols used in the *City by city* section have the following meanings for a standard twin or double room, at single occupancy rate, including service and tax:

Y/ up to Y10,000
Y/// Y10,000–15,000
Y//// Y15,000–20,000
Y///// Y20,000–Y25,000
Y////// Y25,000–30,000
Y/////// over Y30,000

Restaurants

Eating out plays a pivotal role in cementing a Japanese business relationship. If you are invited out by your Japanese countacts, make every effort to accept. The meal may begin rather formally with short speeches of welcome and toasts (be prepared to respond), and will usually end with the coffee or (if it is a Japanese meal) green tea.

The range of restaurants

In selecting a restaurant, matters such as status and expense come well before the quality of the cuisine; it would not do to take an important guest to a restaurant that offered superb cuisine at a moderate price. Many of the most expensive restaurants are in hotels, and this is where much business entertaining takes place. *Ryotei* (where geisha

entertain the guests) are the classiest Japanese restaurants, and are extremely exclusive and expensive. Entertaining in *ryotei* is best left to your Japanese hosts, who know the etiquette and can afford the prices (at company expense). If you want to entertain Japanese-style, the hotel restaurants are the safest bet.

In Tokyo, with its 77,000 restaurants, you can probably dine better than anywhere else in the world, on any cuisine you fancy. Outside Tokyo, you are likely to be eating Japanese (including the local specialities), Chinese and hotel French, although fine French restaurants are springing up in the most unlikely places.

For status and cost, French cuisine still holds sway, and is the safest bet for entertaining your hosts. The Japanese frequently entertain in Chinese restaurants, which have small private rooms with revolving tables and are particularly suitable for parties. Foreign cuisines are usually adapted to Japanese tastes, and can be disappointingly bland, especially in hotels. For a working lunch, it is worthwhile remembering that a Japanese meal takes less than an hour to serve and eat.

Prices An excellent meal at a small local restaurant will cost Y2,5000–3,000, whereas business entertaining can cost Y10–40,000 a head. All restaurants offer a set lunch which is extremely good value, often at a fraction of the cost of the same meal in the evening. A service charge and tax (totally about 13%) will be added to your bill in larger restaurants and hotel restaurants.

Opening hours Meals are taken early; lunch is from 12–2pm, and dinner around 6 or 7pm. Outside Tokyo, most restaurants are closed by 9pm.

Japanese cuisine

You may be faced with a plate of raw crab's brain or a dish of large prawns, very much alive, and your Japanese hosts will be impressed if you can down them without flinching. But generally Japanese food does not make such demands.

Traditional Japanese cuisine is the inspiration for *nouvelle cuisine*, designed to delight, and only incidentally to fill the stomach. The chef composes each dish like a picture, and you are expected to pause and admire before eating. Simple, natural flavours are preferred, and ingredients of the highest quality, particularly fish, are often served raw. The meal usually ends with rice, pickled vegetables and miso soup made from soya bean paste.

The following are the main Japanese cuisines and dishes.

Kaiseki-ryori is the cuisine of the *ryotei*, although also served, less expensively, in more accessible establishments. It is Japan's *haute cuisine*. A *kaiseki* meal is a succession of miniscule works of gastronomic art, including portions of raw and charcoal-grilled fish, a delicately flavoured soup and fresh vegetables.

Sashimi is the choicest parts of the best quality fish, sliced just before eating and served with soy sauce mixed with a little stingingly hot *wasabi* (a form of horseradish). It appears in most Japanese meals. Sometimes the fish's head, tail and skeleton are decoratively served with its finely sliced flesh.

Sukiyaki, shabu shabu Until the end of the last century, meat-eating was taboo in Japan, and both sukiyaki (the finest beef, sliced paper-thin, sautéed at table with a rich sauce) and shabu shabu (slices of beef swished in boiling broth) are recent inventions.

Sushi The best sushi is made from the finest rice, lightly flavoured with vinegar, topped with a slice of fresh raw fish. Sushi is a meal in itself, served in sushi bars. Hold the sushi with your fingers, with the fish underneath, and dip lightly in soy sauce before eating. There are delicious alternatives such as *hamachi* (young yellowtail), *katsuo* (bonito), *hotategai* (scallop), *ama-ebi* (raw shrimp), *uni* (sea urchin roe) and *anago* (grilled conger eel).

Tempura is seafood and vegetables deep-fried in a light, crisp batter. It should be freshly made before your eyes and eaten immediately, dipped in a light sauce.

Teppanyaki A teppanyaki restaurant is a Japanese steak house. Customers sit around a large counter topped with a gleaming steel plate, on which the chefs fry prime steaks and vegetables to your taste.

Unagi Freshwater eel, grilled over charcoal and brushed with a sweet sauce, is a rich and succulent dish, served in summer for its purported energy-giving and aphrodisiac properties.

Yakitori is a favourite snack of the Japanese businessman on his way home. It is chunks of chicken (including the gizzard, liver and tongue) grilled on skewers over charcoal and basted with a rich sauce.

Fugu is blowfish, whose liver contains a poison which causes instant death. It can only be prepared by licensed chefs. It is considered one of the great delicacies and is commensurately expensive. Fugu restaurants serve fugu sashimi – transparently thin slices of fugu spread out like a flower – and fugu simmered with vegetables. The season is November to March.

Our recommended restaurants
The restaurants selected for each city have been chosen with the needs of the business traveller in mind. They offer a variety of cuisines for different occasions. They include top restaurants which you are unlikely to visit independently but to which you may be invited; restaurants oriented towards business entertaining, where you can confidently take your Japanese colleagues; and restaurants to be visited for their cuisine and ambience. Among our restaurants are those generally agreed to be the best in town, as well as the more idiosyncratic favourites of Western executives. All have an excellent reputation for both their cuisine and service. They are convenient for the

major hotels and business areas, and it is usually possible to communicate without speaking Japanese.

Many restaurants accept major credit cards (see listings). You will usually find a public telephone, although it is seldom quiet or private. Some restaurants are closed on Mondays, and Friday nights are often busy. Most restaurants close over New Year (Dec 31–Jan 3). It is always best to reserve.

Price band system
The price symbols used in the *City by city* section have the following meanings for a typical mid-range evening meal, including drinks, tax and service charge:

¥/   up to Y5,000
¥//   Y5,000–10,000
¥///   Y10,000–15,000
¥////   Y15,000–20,000
¥/////   over Y20,000

Bars
Alcohol plays a major part in offsetting the stresses of the executive lifestyle. A survey of Japanese drinking habits has shown that two-thirds of Japanese men get drunk at least once a week and one in eight does so daily. The Japanese are very tolerant of even extreme drunkenness. The most common toast in Japanese bars is *"Kampai."*

Solo drinkers should head for their hotel bars, away from compulsory sing-alongs, hidden extras and students practising their English.

Women will feel most comfortable in hotel, *nomiya* and *karaoke* bars. Beer halls and hostess clubs tend to be all-male preserves. In recent years there has been a dramatic increase in the number of women drinking. All-female groups are not uncommon.

Opening hours Bars open from midday to the early hours. Alcohol is on unrestricted sale from restaurants, shops and vending machines.

Five types of bar
Hostess clubs are expensive. The services of the hostess who pours

Understanding sake
Sake, pronounced "sah-kay", is the national drink. It is a potent rice wine that is served in bars and restaurants, either hot or cold, in thimble-sized cups called *sakazuki* and poured from a small clay vessel known as a *tokkuri*. It can seem deceptively innocuous.

Sake has no vintage years; it is best drunk young, within three months of being bottled, or at the longest within the year. The purest sake is *junmaishu*; *honjoshu* is also fine sake. *Sanbaizoshu* is the lowest quality. In a restaurant you will be served *amakuchi*, sweet sake; connoisseurs demand *karakuchi*, dry sake.

Reading a sake label Most sake bottles have a small oval label on the neck. At the top is the grade: *nikyu* (second grade), *ikkyu* (first grade) or *tokkyu* (special). This is not a sure guide to quality, since sharp brewers may label their special as second grade to avoid tax. In the middle of the label is the alcohol content, and at the bottom the ingredients: the shorter the list, the better the quality.

Regional sakes The best of the country's 2,500 breweries are reckoned to be in the west and north, although most people swear by their local sake. Sake from the ancient port of Nada is said to be "masculine", clean and vigorous to the palate. Fushimi, to the south of Kyoto, produces a delicately "feminine" sake. Akita in the north and Hiroshima also produce excellent sake.

Recommended sakes The best brands are Tamano-hikari, Taruhei and Uragasumi. For the connoisseur, the following are excellent (regions in brackets). Dry: Madonoume (Saga). Sweet: Goshun (Osaka). Complex: Shikizakura (Tochigi), Kikuhime (Ishikawa), Hira Izumi (Akita).

your drink will go on the bill. Characterized by low lighting, soft music and pleasant decor, hostess bars are frequented by those in the upper echelons of business. Because they can be very expensive, it is inadvisable to visit any hostess bar you have not been taken to before.

Hotel bars in the older prestigious hotels have great charm and atmosphere, while those in the modern hotels tend to be more functional. Tariffs are usually displayed in English.

Nomiya (or *Aka-chochin*) are cheaper bars. Lively, noisy and popular with the young, they are easily recognized by the red lantern hanging outside. Their decor is simple and the drinks are limited mainly to sake and beer. Snacks are also available. Most display tariffs in Japanese only.

Karaoke bars can be either Western or Japanese in style. Customers are invited to take the microphone (you usually have little choice) and sing a favourite song accompanied by a backing tape. It is useful to have a Frank Sinatra or Beatles standard in your repertoire.

Beer halls are popular for company outings and are frequently overrun with inebriated businessmen. Many department stores turn their roofs into beer gardens in summer.

Popular drinks

Locally brewed lager beers account for 70% of the alcohol consumed in Japan. Imported wines are expensive and are rarely available in bars.

Mizuwari (whisky diluted 1:6 with water and ice) is popular in business circles, especially where there are foreigners to impress. Great snobbery attaches to different grades of imported whisky (Chivas Regal is reckoned the top brand). Show appreciation.

Shochu is a potent spirit, usually distilled from rice or sweet potatoes. The best *shochu* is said to come from the warmer regions of Japan and is known as *awamori*.

Shopping

An enormous range of products are on sale in Japan, from antique kimonos to the latest in high-technology. But it is not the place to look for bargains. If you can find what you want at home, it is probably as cheap as in Tokyo. Tax-free centres offer goods to foreign shoppers; show your passport for discounts of 10–20%. The same, or greater, reductions can often be found in the discount shops, which also offer a wider choice.

The brand-name stores in hotel arcades are invariably expensive. For leisure shopping use the department and ordinary stores, as the Japanese do. Shops stay open 10–6 (some stay open later) and close one day a week. Most are open on a Sunday.

Department stores

Not just places to shop, department stores include restaurants, travel agencies and even art galleries. When buying a gift, remember that the wrapping and the name on the paper often say more than the gift. Many Tokyo stores now have a foreigners' liaison office to provide for the needs of foreign customers.

Daimaru A popular chain selling high quality goods at sensible prices.

Hankyu Based in Osaka, Hankyu is expanding. A fairly down-market range of goods.

Matsuzakaya has a staid, rather unexciting image.

Mitsukoshi Despite recent scandals, still the most prestigious store; the only place to buy an important gift.

Seibu The most innovative of the chains with a wide range of goods. Seibu has a youthful, exciting image and is rapidly overtaking the older, staider stores.

Sogo A well-established but unexciting chain, Sogo has modernized its image with the largest department store in the world, in Yokohama.

Takashiyama Mitsukoshi's only rival so far as prestige is concerned, and with many more branches.

Local information

The first person to try is the concierge in your hotel. Some are famous for their endless funds of up-to-date information. They provide good maps and give directions, as well as recommending the best restaurants in town.

Tourist Information Centres (TIC) run by the JNTO (Japan National Tourist Organization) in Tokyo and Kyoto have well-informed, multilingual staff. They produce free maps and monthly publications on entertainment, sightseeing and festivals. In other cities the TIC may be less useful, although staff will speak some languages and supply an English map of the city. TIC are closed on Sundays.

Japan Travel Phone For toll-free information and assistance in English ☎ 0210-222-800 in eastern Japan, and 0120-444-800 in western Japan. In Tokyo ☎ 502 1461, and in Kyoto ☎ 371 5649. The service is available 9–5 throughout the year.

Japan Travel Bureau JTB has branches throughout the country. A useful source of information, and invaluable for making reservations and purchasing tickets.

Hotels Many hotels have travel agents' offices in their shopping arcades.

Public lavatories

There are toilets in hotels, restaurants, department stores and (best avoided) stations, usually clearly indicated by a symbol of a man or woman. They may be Western-style or designed for squatting, Japanese-style. If there are several cubicles, there will be a separate queue for each. Knock on a closed door – an answering knock indicates that it is occupied. Toilet paper may not be provided, so carry tissues. From time to time – in restaurants, for example – you may come across mixed toilets.

Crime

Japan's crime rate is low and its detection rate high. Both men and women can feel safe almost everywhere, even at night (but avoid dock areas and sleazier night-life districts). Hotel staff, taxi drivers and even complete strangers go to extraordinary lengths to trace owners of mislaid cameras and umbrellas.

The police Standards are high in police recruitment, training, discipline and morale. Police expect and get widespread public co-operation and know their "beat" to a degree some Westerners would find intrusive. They are more concerned with order than law and can and do exercise considerable personal discretion when deciding whether or not to invoke the law. Police boxes (*koban*) can be found every kilometre or so in urban areas and, subject to limitations of language, visitors can generally be confident of courteous assistance.

Hotel staff are very trustworthy but it is wise, nevertheless, to consign valuables to the hotel safe.

If you are arrested

Japanese law requires that an arrested person be charged or released "as soon as possible" and, in any case, within 24 hours. An arrested person will usually wish to contact his embassy or consulate and Japanese authorities are likely to co-operate as consular presence will probably make their task easier. The authorities may well be content with a stern warning if the matter is a minor one or where some practical restitution can be made. When dealing with the authorities, contrition is more effective than bluster or aggression. If discussing restitution, take care not to look as though you are trying to buy your way out or offer a bribe. If a serious crime is involved an accused person may at least be comforted to know that several leading British and US law firms have close links with Japanese counterparts (see *The law*).

Embassies

All the embassies listed below are in Tokyo (city code 03).

Australia 1-1-12 Shiba Koen,
Minato-ku, 108 ☎ 453 0971
Austria 1-1-20, Moto Azabu,
Minato-ku, 106 ☎ 451 8281/3
Belgium 5 Nibancho, Chiyoda-ku, 102
☎ 262 0191/5
Canada 7-3-38 Akasaka, Minato-ku,
107 ☎ 408 2101/8
Denmark 29-6 Sarugakucho,
Shibuya-ku, 150 ☎ 496 3001
Finland 3-5-39 Minami Azabu,
Minato-ku, 106 ☎ 442 2231
France 4-11-44 Minami Azabu,
Minato-ku, 106 ☎ 473 0171
Germany, West 4-5-10 Minami Azabu,
Minato-ku, 106 ☎ 473 0151
Greece 3-16-30 Nishi Azabu,
Minato-ku, 106 ☎ 403 0871
Ireland No. 25 Kowa Bldg, 8-7
Sanbancho, Chiyoda-ku, 102
☎ 263 0695
Italy 2-5-4 Mita, Minato-ku, 108
☎ 453 5291/6
Netherlands 3-6-3 Shiba Koen,
Minato-ku, 105 ☎ 431 5126/9
New Zealand 20-40 Kamiyamacho,
Shibuya-ku, 150 ☎ 467 2271
Norway 5-12-2 Minami Azabu,
Minato-ku, 106 ☎ 440 2611
Portugal Olympia Annex 304, 305,
306, 6-31-21 Jingumae, Shibuya-ku,
150 ☎ 400 7907
Spain 1-3-29 Roppongi, Minato-ku,
106 ☎ 583 8531/2
Sweden Mori Bldg 25, 1-4-30
Roppongi, Minato-ku, 106
☎ 582 6984/9
Switzerland 5-9-12 Minami Azabu,
Minato-ku, 106 ☎ 473 0121
United Kingdom 1 Ichibancho,
Chiyoda-ku, 102 ☎ 265 5511
United States 1-10-5 Akasaka,
Minato-ku, 107 ☎ 224 5000
Yugoslavia 4-7-24 Kita Shinagawa,
Shinagawa-ku, 140 ☎ 447 3571/3

Health care

Japan offers health care of a very high
standard. Most Japanese citizens are
under the national health insurance
scheme introduced in 1961. Visitors
to Japan should always take out
comprehensive medical and dental
insurance to avoid the high fees
charged for treatment.

Western medicine is the most
common form of treatment, although
alternatives such as Chinese medicine
(*kampo yaku*), acupuncture and
Japanese acupressure massage
(*shiatsu*) are available. Mineral baths
(*onsen*) are also thought to have
curative properties.

If you fall ill

Your first recourse should be to the
hotel doctor or to one of the
reputable English-speaking clinics
that provide emergency cover with a
doctor on call (see *City by city*). Help
can also be obtained by calling Tokyo
English Life Line (TELL) ☎ (03) 264
4347. TELL will make emergency
arrangements or be able to refer the
caller to a reputable doctor.
Pharmacies Most pharmacies sell
medicines produced and packaged in
Japan with names and instructions in
Japanese. Western brand-name drugs
are available only from specialist
pharmacies (see *City by city* for
details). Many large hotels have a
pharmacy selling Western drugs.
Doctors Most ailments and injuries
are dealt with by hospital doctors.
You can visit a hospital clinic (*byoin*)
as an out-patient but it is unwise to
do so unless you are with a Japanese-
speaker or have been referred by an
English-speaking doctor. Hospitals
vary markedly in atmosphere and
decor; nursing standards are low
compared to the West, and
administrative staff are often less than
helpful. Long queues are the norm.
    Private specialist clinics, however,
are of a high standard and equipped
with up-to-date medical technology.
    Some big-city hospitals have
English-speaking staff (see *City by city*
for details). Apart from these
hospitals, most doctors can speak
some English. *The Tourist's Handbook*
– free from JNTO or the TIC – has a
bilingual section on emergencies and
illnesses which may be helpful.
    If you fall ill at your hotel, they
will usually make the necessary
arrangements and add the cost of
treatment to your bill. Otherwise you

may need to pay doctors in cash, reclaiming the money from your insurers.

Dentists are very expensive and are highly qualified. Western-style surgeries have ultra-modern equipment. For a complete list of dentists, including those who speak English, contact the nearest TIC.

Emergencies If you need urgent treatment, go to a doctor in the out-patient department of your nearest hospital. If it is a dire emergency and you are not at your hotel or with Japanese colleagues, find a Japanese speaker. Emergency calls are answered in Japanese and it is unusual to find anyone who speaks English. To call an ambulance dial 119 and state which service you require; better still, call TELL.

Communications

Telex and fax services are widely available and the telephone and postal systems are of a high standard, but not cheap. Two useful information sources are the *Japan Yellow Pages* ☎ (03) 239 3501 and the *Japan Times Directory* ☎ (03) 453 5311.

Telephones

Phones are operated by Nippon Telegraph and Telephone Company (NTT). Local calls (Y10 for 3mins) may be made on pink, red or blue ones. For long distance and international calls use yellow or green ones. Green ones take telephone cards.

Making a call Insert coins (Y10 for local calls, otherwise Y100). The dial tone is a continuous hum. "Beep" means you are running out of money. Engaged is a "bao-bao" noise. Unused coins (but not fractions of Y100) are returned at the end of the call. The Japanese answer calls with "Moshi-moshi", but "Hai, X desu," ("Yes, this is X,") is also common.

Cutting costs Long distance calls (over 60kms/37 miles) cost 40% less from 7pm to 8am and from 6am to 9pm on Sundays and holidays. From 9pm to 6am calls over 320kms/200 miles are 50% cheaper.

International calls are handled by Kokusai Denshin Denwa (KDD). Calls can be made from KDD offices in major cities, as well as from other phones (see *International dialling codes*). KDD operators use American English, so say "collect", not "reverse charges", and "zero", not "nought". Most countries can be dialled direct.

Emergency calls Police is 110 and Fire and Ambulance 119, but these services operate in Japanese only. Use Tokyo English Life Line ☎ (03) 264 4347.

Telegrams can be written in Roman script and handed in at post offices and railway stations. International telegrams can be sent from KDD offices, some post offices and larger hotels and always from the Central Post Office in front of Tokyo station. After midnight use KDD offices in Tokyo, Kyoto and Osaka or ☎ (03) 344 5151.

Telex and fax

Both services are widespread in hotels and offices; larger places will have both domestic and international facilities. KDD offices (see *City by city*) provide public facilities.

Mail

Post offices (*yubin kyoku*) are indicated by the symbol of a red capital T with a bar over it, which is also used in addresses to denote a postal district (written in the right-hand corner of the envelope). All post offices open Mon–Fri 9–5 and Sat 9–12.30 but close on the 2nd and 4th Sat of each month. There are 24hr post offices in Tokyo, Kyoto and Osaka and post offices in some other cities open late (see *City by city*). Hotels usually sell stamps and air letters.

Mail boxes are red and free-standing. In Tokyo they often have two slots: the right-hand one is for city mail.

Couriers There are excellent internal and external courier services. Much of Japan's traffic in packets is handled by private carriers, such as Yamato, who offer guaranteed delivery times.

International dialling codes

Operator-connected calls

You can make station-to-station, person-to-person, collect, credit card or conference calls. There are no discount rates on operator-connected calls.

Operator ☏ 0056
Directory inquiries ☏ 0056

Direct dialling is cheapest. Discount rates apply at the following Japanese times: 5am–8am, 7pm–11pm 20% cheaper; 11pm–5am 40% cheaper. On Sundays all calls are at discount rates: 5am–11pm 20% cheaper; 11pm–5am 40% cheaper. Before dialling the country's code, dial 001.

Areas	Country Code	Time differences
Alaska	1	$(-18 \sim -19)$
Algeria	213	(-8)
Argentina	54	(-12)
Australia	61	$(-1 \sim +1)$
Austria	43	(-8)
Bahrain	973	(-6)
Belgium	32	(-8)
Bolivia	591	(-13)
Brazil	55	$(-12 \sim -14)$
Burma	95	(-2.30)
Canada	1	$(-12.30 \sim -18)$
Canary Islands	34	(-9)
Chile	56	(-13)
Colombia	57	(-14)
Costa Rica	506	(-15)
Cyprus (Rep. of)	357	(-7)
Czechoslovakia	42	(-8)
Denmark	45	(-8)
Ecuador	593	(-14)
Egypt	20	(-7)
El Salvador	503	(-15)
Fiji	679	$(+3)$
Finland	358	(-7)
France	33	(-8)
Germany (Dem. Rep.)	37	(-8)
Germany (Fed. Rep.)	49	(-8)
Gibraltar	350	(-8)
Greece	30	(-7)
Guatemala	502	(-15)
Guyana	592	(-12)
Hawaii	1	(-19)
Honduras	504	(-15)
Hong Kong	852	(-1)
Iceland	354	(-9)
India	91	(-3.30)
Indonesia	62	$(-2 \sim \pm 0)$
Iran	98	(-5.30)
Iraq	964	(-6)
Ireland	353	(-9)
Israel	972	(-7)
Italy	39	(-8)
Ivory Coast	225	(-9)
Jordan	962	(-7)
Kenya	254	(-6)
Korea (Rep. of)	82	(± 0)
Kuwait	965	(-6)
Lesotho	266	(-7)
Liechtenstein	41	(-8)
Luxembourg	352	(-8)
Macao	853	(-1)
Madagascar	261	(-6)
Madeira	351	(-9)
Malawi	265	(-7)
Malaysia	60	(-1)
Malta	356	(-8)
Mexico	52	$(-15 \sim -17)$
Monaco	33	(-8)
Morocco	212	(-9)
Mozambique	258	(-7)
Namibia	264	(-7)
Netherlands	31	(-8)
New Zealand	64	$(+3)$
Nicaragua	505	(-15)
Nigeria	234	(-8)
Niger	227	(-8)
Norway	47	(-8)
Oman	968	(-5)
Pakistan	92	(-4)
Panama	507	(-14)
Papua New Guinea	675	$(+1)$
Paraguay	595	(-13)
Philippines	63	(-1)
Poland	48	(-8)
Portugal	351	(-9)
Qatar	974	(-6)
Romania	40	(-7)
San Marino	39	(-8)
Saudi Arabia	966	(-6)
Singapore	65	(-1)
South Africa	27	(-7)
Spain	34	(-8)
Sri Lanka	94	(-3.30)
Sweden	46	(-8)
Switzerland	41	(-8)
Taiwan	886	(-1)
Tanzania	255	(-6)
Thailand	66	(-2)
Tunisia	216	(-8)
Turkey	90	(-7)
Uganda	256	(-6)
United Arab Emirates	971	(-5)
United Kingdom	44	(-9)
Uruguay	598	(-12)
USA (Mainland)	1	$(-14 \sim -17)$
USSR	7	$(-6 \sim +4)$
Vatican	39	(-8)
Venezuela	58	(-13)
Yemen	967	(-6)
Yugoslavia	38	(-8)
Zambia	260	(-7)

Conversion charts

Japan has embraced the metric system almost totally (dual imperial/metric markings on packaging are generally not acceptable). Currency, distances, lengths, weights, liquid capacity, temperature and large measurements of area (hectares) are all metric. However, S.I. units are not widely understood, sizes for shoes and clothing differ from those used in the West, and years are sometimes enumerated from the start of the Emperor's reign.

The main traditional measurements still commonly in use are those for floor area. The tatami is based on the straw floor mat of that name, and is used for domestic room measurements. The tsubo is used for office areas or whole apartments.

1 tatami = 1.8×0.9 metres = 1.62 square metres.

1 tsubo = 3.3 square metres.

Temperature

Length

centimetres (cm)	cm or in	inches (in)
2.54	1	0.394
5.08	2	0.787
7.62	3	1.181
10.16	4	1.575
12.70	5	1.969
15.24	6	2.362
17.78	7	2.756
20.32	8	3.150
22.86	9	3.543
25.40	10	3.937
50.80	20	7.874
76.20	30	11.811
101.60	40	15.748
127.00	50	19.685

Mass (weight)

kilograms (kg)	kg or lb	pounds (lb)
0.454	1	2.205
0.907	2	4.409
1.361	3	6.614
1.814	4	8.819
2.268	5	11.023
2.722	6	13.228
3.175	7	15.432
3.629	8	17.637
4.082	9	19.842
4.536	10	22.046
9.072	20	44.092
13.608	30	66.139
18.144	40	88.185
22.680	50	110.231

Distance

kilometres (km)	km or miles	miles
1.609	1	0.621
3.219	2	1.243
4.828	3	1.864
6.437	4	2.485
8.047	5	3.107
9.656	6	3.728
11.265	7	4.350
12.875	8	4.971
14.484	9	5.592
16.093	10	6.214
32.187	20	12.427
48.280	30	18.641
64.374	40	24.855
80.467	50	31.069

Volume

litres	litres or UK galls	UK galls
4.546	1	0.220
9.092	2	0.440
13.638	3	0.660
18.184	4	0.880
22.730	5	1.100
27.276	6	1.320
31.822	7	1.540
36.368	8	1.760
40.914	9	1.980
45.460	10	2.200
90.919	20	4.399
136.379	30	6.599
181.839	40	8.799
227.298	50	10.998

Background reading

General Surveys

The Sun at Noon Dick Wilson (Hamish Hamilton, 1986).
The Japanese E.O. Reischauer (Harvard University Press, 1979).
Japan As Number One: Lessons for America Ezra Vogel (HUP, 1979).

The Economic Scene

Inside Japan: Wealth, Work and Power Peter Tasker (Sidgwick & Jackson, 1987).
The Japanese Financial System Yoshio Suzuki (ed) (Clarendon Press, 1988).

The Industrial Scene

Management and Worker: The Japanese Solution James C. Abegglen (Kodansha, 1976).
Industrial Organization in Japan R. Caves and M. Uekusa (Brookings Institution, 1976).
Japan's Multinational Enterprises M.Y. Yoshino (HUP, 1976).
British Factory-Japanese Factory Ronald Dore (George Allen & Unwin, 1973).

The Political Scene

The Japanese Way of Politics Gerald L. Curtis (Columbia UP, 1988).
Politics in Modern Japan: Development and Organization Koichi Kishimoto (Japan Echo, 1978).
Policymaking in Contemporary Japan T.J. Pempel (ed) (Cornell University Press, 1977).
Political Change in Japan T. Tsurutani (Longman, 1977).

The Business Scene

Kaisha; The Japanese Corporation James C. Abegglen and George Stalk Jr (Harper & Row, 1986).
The Japanese Company Rodney Clark (Yale University Press, 1979).
Japan's Public Policy Companies Chalmers Johnson (American Enterprise Institute, 1978).
Sogo Shosha: The Vanguard of the Japanese Economy Yoshihara Kunio (OUP, 1982).
Marketing Opportunities in Japan Dentsu Inc (McGraw-Hill, 1978).

Current Legal Aspects of Doing Business in Japan and East Asia John O. Haley (ed) (American Bar Association, 1978).

Business Awareness

Corporate Strategies in Japan K. Odaka, R. Grondine, S. Mizushima (Longman, 1985).
Not For Bread Alone Konosuke Matsushita (PHP Institute, 1984).
The Strategy of Japanese Business James C. Abegglen (A. Ballinger, 1985).
Dealing with Japanese Mark Zimmerman (George Allen Unwin, 1985).
The Art of Japanese Management R. Pascale and A. Athos (Penguin, 1981).

Cultural Awareness

History Japan vs Europe: A History of Misunderstanding Endymion Wilkinson (Penguin, 1983).
The Development of Japanese Business 1600–1973 J. Hirchmeier and T. Yui (George Allen & Unwin, 1979).
East Asia: Tradition and Transformation J.K. Fairbank, E.O. Reischauer, A.M. Craig (Houghton Mifflin, 1973).
Culture A Japanese Mirror: Heroes and Villains of Japanese Culture Ian Buruma (Penguin, 1984).
Japan: A Comparative View A.M. Craig (Princeton University Press, 1979).
Understanding Japanese Society Joy Hendry (Croom Helm, 1987).
Japanese Society Chie Nakane (Penguin, 1973).
Manners and customs Simple Etiquette in Japan Helmut Morsbach (Paul Norbury Publications, 1984).
Land of the Rising Yen George Mikes (Penguin, 1972).
Japan Unmasked Ichiro Kawasaki (Tuttle, 1969).
Language Hugo's Japanese (Hugo's Language Books, 1986).
Survival Characters (Institute of Linguists, 1986).
Japanese Business Glossary Mitsubishi Corporation (Oriental Economist, 1983).

Index